ACTA UNIVERSITATIS UPSALIENSIS
Studia Historica Upsaliensia

Utgivna av
Historiska Institutionen vid Uppsala Universitet
genom Rolf Torstendahl,
Torkel Jansson och Jan Lindegren
180

Tsegaye Tegenu

The Evolution of Ethiopian Absolutism

The Genesis and the Making of the Fiscal Military State, 1696–1913

UPPSALA 1996

Dissertation for the Degree of Doctor of Philosophy in History presented at Uppsala University in 1996

ABSTRACT

Tsegaye Tegenu (1996). The Evolution of Ethiopian Absolutism. The Genesis and the Making of the Fiscal Military State, 1696–1913. Acta Universitatis Upsaliensis. *Studia Historica Upsaliensia* 180. 286 pp. ISBN 91-554-3856-3.

The central purpose of this study is to identify and explain the resource base of the Ethiopian state during its process of organizing into a centralized power in the period 1696 to 1913.

In the period under discussion, military campaigns were the major means for extracting and distributing social surplus. Particularly after the sixteenth century, there was a change in the mode of military organization and in techniques of warfare which depended heavily on extensive use of manpower and land. However, the needs and demands of continuous campaigns could not be met by the old resource allocation system which was characterized by communal ownership rights in land, territorial assessment and collection of taxes, and by private methods of revenue administration. By the beginning of the 18th century in central regions of the country, a new type of resource acquisition and use appeared that was more in harmony with the size, frequency and mode of organizing military campaigns. The new type of resource acquisition and use was characterized by the principles of private ownership rights in land, individualized registration and payment of taxes, tenancy arrangements, the conducting of land surveys, and consolidated and centralized methods of revenue administration. These principles spread and developed country-wide when the capitalist world economy and an international state system was formed on the Horn of Africa during the second half of the nineteenth century.

The new challenges and opportunities compelled Kings Tewodros, Yohannes and Menelik to introduce major fiscal reforms both at the institutional level (administration of taxes) and in the structure of the taxes (tax-technical measures). The other reforms they introduced were in: the system of transportation and communication, finance, the security and promotion of trade, the encouragment of manufacturing and mining sectors, and the securing of land ownership rights. The major objective of the reforms was to increase government revenue and logistic capacity of the state, and not the productive capacity of the economy and the creation of new relations of production. Government expenditure gave priority to the building of a standing field force that had a superior number of soldiers, high quality of weapons and an improved provisioning system. The aristocracy benefited from the reforms through the acquisition of government office, titles, and taking advantage of new business opportunities. However, the aristocracy did not reinvest its wealth in agriculture and could not strengthen its economy through direct management of property. The aristocracy was more interested in the tradition of keeping military power through increasing recruitment of soldiers and the holding of regular banquets. Aristocratic capital, development of towns and expansion of trade did not thus promote economic development. The contemporary intelligentsia blamed this lack of development on the aristocratic economic behaviour and criticised the Kings' reforms as insufficient. The intelligentsia promulgated a development strategy aimed at creating a prosperous peasant class whose demand and exchange would promote domestic industralization.

Key words: absolutism, resource system, logistic system, land ownership rights, tax structure, revenue and expenditure, fiscal policy, aristocratic patrimony, structural economic problems and reforms.

Tsegaye Tegenu, Department of History, Uppsala University, S:t Larsgatan 2, 753 10 Uppsala, Sweden

ISSN 0081-6531
ISBN 91-554-3856-3

Typesetting: Editorial Office, Uppsala University
Printed in Sweden by Gotab, Stockholm 1996
Distributor: Almqvist & Wiksell International, Stockholm, Sweden

To Nighisty, Alexander, Simon, Joel
and in memory of
my Mother

Contents

Part IV: The Use of Existing Resources, 1855–1913

Part V: Structural Problems of Economic Development and Government Economic Policy, 1855–1913

Part VI: Conclusion

Maps

List of Tables

Note on Transliteration

There is no standardized transliteration from the Ethiopic alphabet into Latin script. For the purpose of simplification, and following some conventional practices, authors have followed various spellings of names, persons and places when transliterating Ethiopic character into Roman. In the present work, the problem of inconsistencies in transliteration also arise, especially for readers who are seeking for correct pronunciations.

Established spellings of geographical and personal names are used in the present work as written down in the documents and literature. The seven sounds of the Ethiopic alphabet are represented by the following table:

Ethiopic Forms	1st	2nd	3rd	4th	5th	6th	7th
European vowel	ä	u	i	a	é	e	o

Glottalized vowels are not represented in the present transliteration in order to facilitate printing. Palatalized consonant sounds are represented as follows:

sh for ሽ, *ch* for ች, *gn* for ኝ, *z* for ዘ, *zh* for ዥ, and *j* for ጅ. Of the glottalized consonant sounds, those shown as ቀ represented by *q*, *ts* standing for ፀ, and *ch´* standing for ጨ.

List of Abbreviations

AAU	Addis Ababa University
BL.Or.	British Library, Orient
E.C.	Ethiopian Calendar
FO	Foreign Office, Public Record Office
HSIU	Haile Selassie I University
IES	Institute of Ethiopian Studies
MT$	Maria Theresia Thaler, Menelik's Thaler

Preface

My generation has witnessed swift, incredibly dramatic and profound changes in Ethiopia, the country to which the Bible's description of heaven was said to refer. It had turned into a nightmare in a span of two decades. The myth of Ethiopia as the breadbasket of the Horn of Africa was shattered by hunger and starvation taking its toll of millions of lives. The "Sun King", Haile Selassie I, was dethroned by a middle-class revolution and labelled the "prominent reactionary". A country whose culture was said to be based on the philosophy of human love and dignity turned into a place of terror, torture and horrifying scenes of dead corpses on the streets. The tradition of appreciating the merits of bravery and kindness was replaced by judging people on their ethnic affiliation, a changed criterion used to redefine the collective identity and the reorganization of state and society. Almost a million people died as the result of brutal civil war and within a short period of time over a million Ethiopians left the country they loved, dispersed as refugees over all parts of the world.

What went wrong? How could all the shocking scenarios and traumas be explained? Even though some of the events had their own immediate explanation, studying the background was a challenge to a student of Ethiopian history. When, for the first time, I came to the Department of History, Uppsala University, I had a vague idea of what to look for. My background as a student and lecturer in Ethiopian history gave me a professional instinct to consider the second half of the nineteenth century as a turning point that would trace and explain aspects of the current problems facing Ethiopia. I believed that something new had emerged in both state and society since that period, but I really did not know the essence of the particular historical process and its consequences. I would like to thank the Department of History, Uppsala University, for giving me and my fellow countrymen the chance to know *what it was* and *what it means*.

The Department of History is an archive of knowledge, and acquiring the knowledge I needed would have been difficult without the guidance and support of my advisors Professor Torkel Jansson and assistant Professor Thomas Lindkvist. Foremost my deepest thanks goes to Professor Torkel Jansson for his constant support, care about my work, and constructive criticisms. This work could not have taken its present shape without his confidence in me, the respect he has shown my ideas, and freedom of thinking, his appreciation of my ambitions, his understanding and prompt reply to all my requests. The questions he posed often led me to attain further similarity between European and Ethiopian absolutism. My second advisor, assistant Professor Thomas Lindkvist has understood my ideas from the beginning and aided me to sharpen my points of discussion. The ongoing debate I had with him helped me to appreciate the Ethiopian "*sonderweg*" (exceptional route) to absolutism.

Professor Rolf Torstendahl and Professor Jan Lindegren have read the final manuscript and I thank them for their comments and reflections. Thanks also to Professor Donald Crummey for valuable comments, some of which I was able to incorporate. My colleague Dr. Tekeste Negash has read an earlier draft and proposed to me suggestions. He provided me with some Italian materials and books from his collection. I thank him very much for his help, criticism and friendly advice. Dr. Nighisty Ghezae has also been immensely involved in the progress of this work. She has helped me in the translation of the Italian sources and commented in detail upon conceptual problems of economic theories and ideas discussed in the book.

I would also like to thank Professor Torkel Jansson's seminar group who, in spite of a barrage of *geez/amharic* terms, read portions of my work and came up with helpful suggestions. The list of names is too long to mention, but to all of them I owe a debt of gratitude. I am grateful to Shiferaw Bekele, Alemseged Asefa, Dr. Tekalgn Wolde Mariam, Mekonnen Lemma and Dr. Tadesse Zerihun for reading and commenting on some of the draft chapters. *Ato* Zena Markos Endalew has helped in the translation of *geez* texts, and Professor Florence Christoplos edited my English language. I acknowledge the assistance given by *ato* Kassela Markos in drawing the jacket illustration.

My archival research in Addis Ababa was aided by staff members of the Institute of Ethiopian Studies, who supplied me with all available material and allowed me to get microfilm copy of some manuscripts. The National Library, Ministry of Culture and Sports, and the Patriarch's Office of the Ethiopian Orthodox Church, Addis Ababa, provided me with the assistance I requested. In Mäkälé, capital of Tigray, I had permission from the regional Patriarch's Office to read documents kept by some of the *däbr* churches in Tigray. My informants, *ato* Gäsäsä Bezabh, *fitawrari* Iyasu Asbäha, and *mälakä gänät* Serse Dingel Arefe Ayne gave freely of their time for a lengthy discussion.

My travel to Addis Ababa and Mäkälé was funded by a grant from the Historical-Philosophical Division of the Faculty of Arts, Uppsala University, and from the Scandinavian Institute of African Studies, Uppsala. Without their support it would have been difficult to carry out a project such as this. The Department for Research Coperation (SAREC), SIDA, accorded me grants to cover part of the publication costs, and I am grateful for the kind consideration bestowed on me.

At various times I have received friendly and family support from Sara Indrias, Kibrom Gebremariam and Amleset Kahassay. I am very grateful for their help and readiness to look after our children when I needed it most. I express my appreciation to Alula, Ruth, Lulit and Haben for their love and warmest friendship to our children.

Finally my deepest thanks and indebtedness go to my family who above anyone else bore the demands and responsibility for the realization of this work. Beyond professional assistance, my wife and my colleague, Dr. Nighisty Ghezae, gives warmth to our family as a mother and a wife. Our children, Alexander, Simon and Joel devoted part of their prime life time to the curiosity of their father. My hopes of carrying this work through to fulfillment were nurtured by my family's understanding and constant love.

Over this work stands the presence of my mother, Amarech Mergia. She was the first to take me by the hand and register me at school. With indomitable love, she more than anyone stood as the backbone of my educational life at school and university.

Uppsala, September 1996
Tsegaye Tegenu

Part I
Introduction

Introduction

1. Objectives of the Study

The central purpose of this study is to identify and explain the resource base of the Ethiopian state during its process of organizing into a centralized power in the period 1696 to 1913.

In the period under discussion, military campaigns were the major means for extracting and distributing social surplus. Particularly after the sixteenth century, there was a change in the mode of military organization and in techniques of warfare which depended heavily on extensive use of manpower and land. However, the needs and demands of continuous campaigns could not be met by the old resource allocation system which was characterized by communal and collective ownership rights in land, territorial assessment and collection of taxes, and by private methods of revenue administration. By the beginning of the 18th century in central regions of the country, a new type of resource acquisition and use appeared that was more in harmony with the size, frequency and mode of organizing military campaigns. The new type of resource acquisition and use was characterized by the principles of private ownership rights in land, individualized registration and payment of taxes, tenancy arrangements, the conducting of land surveys, and consolidated and centralized methods of revenue administration. These principles spread and developed country-wide when the capitalist world economy and an international state system was formed on the Horn of Africa during the second half of the nineteenth century.

This study has two interrelated tasks to accomplish. The first is to explain the reasons behind the emergence of the necessary preconditions for the rise of a centralized state power. The sustainability of the old resource allocation system was severely strained by the changes in scale, frequency and organization of military campaigns. The present study explains the new demands on the resource system and the conditions which favoured the development of a centralized regional power. The second task is to explain why and how the new type of resource system developed country wide and came to serve as the economic base of a centralized state during the second half of the nineteenth century.

The mechanisms of the economic life of the society, and the social, institutional and economic basis of the state, are identified through an analysis of a collection of hitherto only tangentially and partially approached socio-economic phenomena such as: the system of taxation (tax assessment and distribution, tax collection and administration, preferences for tax introduction), and property relationships (manner and conditions of land ownership). These elements are here analysed from both synchronic and diachronic perspectives as they hinder or facilitate the logistic needs and demands of the state. Under logistic needs are included recruitment of manpower and means of remuneration, methods of provisioning, transportation system, and the supply of war materials and equipment. This study attempts to explain the functional and structural relationships between the fiscal imperatives (the revenue) of the government and its war endeavours (patterns of expenditure).

This study emphasizes what is called the 'system of acquisition, distribution and use of social surplus'. No systematic focus has been placed on the legal and ideological aspects of the system which transfer social surplus. The development of the state organization and institutions is explained primarily in terms of the structural changes and continuity in the fiscal and military functions of the state. In this study, therefore, institutions, ideologies and legal relations are discussed only when necessary for the analysis of the resources and objectives of the state.

The selection of the time period for this study was not arbitrary. It corresponded to a distinct problem of periodization in Ethiopian history and the appearance of a new historical process. 1696 is a year that traces the genesis of the fiscal military state. In this year, King Iyasu I (1682–1706) came to the region of Shewa, reconciled the local notables, and appointed a governor called Nägasi Kiristos who founded the Shewa aristocratic dynasty. From this time onwards the Shewan aristocrats began to build the new mode of military organization on a different type of resource allocation system that favoured development of a centralized power. The qualities and properties of this enclavistic regional development spread, becoming standardized and uniform country-wide in the second half of the nineteenth century. During this time a new phenomenon appeared, qualitatively divergent from the past, namely, the formation of a capitalist world economy and an international state system on the Horn of Africa. As a result of the new opportunities and pressure, Kings Tewodros (1855–1868), Yohannes (1872–1889), and Menelik (1889–1913) undertook a number of reforms to create the material basis of the state and the centralization of power. The reign of Menelik II was the pinnacle of the full development of the fiscal military state, and the end of his reign in 1913 marked a transition to an enlightened absolutist state.

2. The Theory of Absolutism and the Model of an Absolutist State

2.1. Interpretation of Absolutism and the Absolutist State

A study of social change and transformation requires a theoretical hypothesis. Empirical facts are not the same as knowledge. They are products of ideological/theoretical practices conducted under specific conditions. To validate or refute facts requires theoretical analysis and argument. Besides, investigation into the 'unity of an epoch' or structures of society over centuries, requires an imposition of hierarchical concepts for the purpose of establishing coherence and identification of the essential elements of the historical situation.

Constructing a theory of social change requires basically two distinctive stages. The first stage is an identification of the transition itself, i.e., classification of either the change or the transformation in order to understand the "laws" governing the evolutionary dynamics of the historical period. In this study this stage is conceived and analyzed by the general theory of absolutism. The second stage explains that particular historical event and action, and this is accomplished here by constructing a resource system model of an absolutist state. The general theory of absolutism and the models of the absolutist state are used as the methodological framework for analysis and interpretation.

As can be concluded from a great number of studies, there is an agreement to consider absolutism as a historical phenomenon lying between the medieval monarchy on the one hand and the post-revolutionary constitutionalism on the other.[1] After reading the massive literature on absolutism, one still wonders if there is any coherent theoretical knowledge (laws of state and social development) that can explain this ephemeral historical phenomenon? In the present work, it is assumed that the theory of absolutism is constructed in such a way as to explain the links among the three *necessary conditions*, namely the feudal mode of production, the international state system and merchant capitalism. Methodologically, the structural and functional relationships among the *necessary conditions* can be explained by way of constructing models of the political and economic system of the transition. The models represent orderly state forms or distinctive phases of absolutism called here the *fiscal military state* and the *enlightened absolutist state*.

In varying respects, the premises, approach and interpretation of absolutism discussed in this work differ from previous studies. A review of the literature to illustrate how and why they differ is of relevance. Scholars who represent the

[1] Periodization of absolutism is problematic. The discussion is marked by national interest, but often the changes in view are related to the historiography of absolutism itself. Yet there seems to be a consensus among historians to consider the period between the beginning of sixteenth up to the end of the 18th century as the "epoch" of absolutism. For an insight see Kunisch, J. (1986), *Absolutismus*. Göttingen. pp. 179ff.

"old research" fix the premises of discussion focusing on the term absolutism. They claim absolute as the most characteristic quality, and interpret absolutism as personal rule, which was the result of the conscious effort of kings. These researchers view contemporary ideologies of monarchs as examples of the theory of absolutism.[2] Researchers of the last few decades, particularly those who emerged since the second world war, began to view absolutism from below and underline the limits of absolutism in practice. They assessed the effectiveness and limitations of the royal power. Though there is a consensus on what absolutism is not, there is no agreement on what it is. Depending on the field of specialization (e.g., institutional historians, economic historians, constitutional historians, etc.) absolutism is defined and explained from different perspectives.

There are those who maintain that the right to legislate is a cornerstone of monarchical power. They emphasize the legislative power exercised by the sovereigns' command; "absolutism was the belief that the king had absolute ability to make positive law".[3] This interpretation is based and fixed on etymological meaning of absolutism. It tries to define the state by looking at the relations of domination (manner of control) and not by studying the economic basis of the state. There are researchers who see absolutism as an organized system of government with a chain of command and the delegation of rights and authority radiating from the centre. Cabinet government, the sale of office and bureaucratic tendency are part of this conception.[4] This approach discusses the growth and effects of the state rather than the causes and the essence of the process which made possible those changes.

Other researchers consider war as a stimulus to the establishment of absolutism, and success in war as an indicator of the strength of a monarch. The increasing scale of warfare, tactical changes and the new concepts of strategy demanded central leadership and a concentration of power in the hands of the monarch. The term "military revolution" was coined to describe these military

[2] For a discussion of the political ideas of the period see Mousnier, R. (1970), "The Exponents and Critics of Absolutism" in Cooper, J. (ed.), *The New Cambridge Modern History, IV*. Cambridge. Others who still focus on the meaning of the term, deny the existence of absolutism. Henshall, N. denies absolutism, since he finds no meaning of it in practice. For him absolutism is a "myth"; the alternative is monarchy, despotism or republicanism. see Henshall, N. (1992), *The Myth of Absolutism. Change and Continuity in Early Modern Europe*. London, particularly, the introduction part and chapter six.

[3] Collins, J.B. (1994), *Classes, Estates and Order in Early Modern Brittany*. Cambridge. p. 14; For a critique on this view, see Mettam, R. (1990), "France", in Miller, J. (ed.), *Absolutism in Seventeenth Century Europe*. London.

[4] See Lublinskaya, A.D. (1980), "The Contemporary Bourgeios Conception of Absolute Monarchy", in *Economy and Society, 1: 1*. For a critic on the view see Oestreich, G. (1969), *Neostoicism and Early Modern State*. Cambridge; Ranum, O.A. (1963), *Richelieu and the Councillors of Louis XIII. A Study of the Secretaries of State and Superintendents of Finance in the Ministry of Richelieu 1635–1642*. Oxford; and Kettering, S. (1986), *Patrons, Brokers and Clients in Seventeenth-Century France*. Oxford.

changes.[5] This approach laid emphasis on the art of conducting war (issues of strategies and tactics) rather than on the supply side of the war. The research focused on the study of weaponry innovation, its role in battle, and analysis of battle strategies and tactics. An emphasize on the art of warfare neglects the study of the logistics aspect of military endeavour. One consequence of this approach is the continuous debate on the nature and periodization of the military changes.[6] The solution to this debate could be found if one studies the needs and demands of military changes in relation to the resource potential and capacity of the state, possibly differentiating what was structural from what was specific to place and time.

Besides, there can be no strategy and tactic without an effective logistic system. Limited resources, both in manpower and supply system, dictate a given plan of limited objectives in war: short, quick and decisive battles. It is thus important to find the cause and strength of the absolutist state in the logistic aspects of military campaigns.[7]

Absolutism is defined by some researchers in terms of its capacity to create financial resources for the state. The ability to tax and spend at will was viewed as a key attribute of the absolutist state.[8] Financing wars led to rises in taxation, a system of borrowing, and thus growth in state revenue. The fiscal imperatives of war led to changes in financial administration at the center, and prompt collection and distribution of taxes.[9] The study on fiscal system laid emphasis

[5] See, among others, Roberts, M. (1956), *The Military Revolution*. Parker, G. (1988), *The Military Revolution. Military Innovation and the Rise of the West, 1500–1800*. Cambridge.

[6] See Parker, G. (1988). For a critique on periodization of the major changes see Black, J. (1991), *A Military Revolution? Military Change and European Society 1550–1800.* London. For an alternative thesis to that of Roberts and Parker, see Eltis, D. (1995), *The Military Revolution in Sixteenth-Century Europe*. London.

[7] There are studies which attempted to analyze war and the resource base of the state. Among others, see Pickl, Othmar (ed.) (1980), *Krieg, Militärausgaben und wirtschaftlicher Wandel. Proceedings of the Seventh International Economic History Congress*, Edinburgh, 1978; Lindegren, J. (1992), *Maktstatens resurser*. Unpublished manuscript. Department of History, Uppsala University; Ladewig Petersen, E. (1983), "War, Finance and Growth of Absolutism: Some Aspects of the European Integration of Seventeenth Century Denmark", in Rystad, G. (ed.), *Europe and Scandinavia: Aspects of the Process of Integration in the 17th Century*. Lund; Finkel, C. (1988), *The Administration of Warfare: the Ottoman Military Campaigns in Hungary, 1593–1606*. Wien; Collins, J. (1988); Dickson, P.G.M., (1987), *Finance and Government under Maria Theresia, 1740–1780. V.II.* Oxford; Redlich, F. (1964), *The German Military Enterpriser and His Work Force, 2 vols.* Wiesbaden; LeDonne, J. (1984), *Ruling Russia: Politics and Administration in the Age of Absolutism, 1762–1796.* Princeton. Part IV; Kennedy, P. (1988), *The Rise and Fall of the Great Powers: Economic Change and Military Conflict from 1500 to 2000*. London. pp. 89–111. In some of these studies the ideas and/or models used to explain the resource base of the state are not problematized with the theory of absolutism, a structurally defined social transformation.

[8] Collins, J. (1988), *Fiscal Limits of Absolutism. Direct Taxation in Early Seventeenth Century France.* Berkeley; For a discussion on the struggle over taxation between the monarch and provinces, see Hickey, D. (1986), *The Coming of French Absolutism: The Struggle for Tax Reforms in the Province of Dauphine, 1540–1640.* Toronto.

[9] For further review articles and summary of discusssion points see Bonney, R. (1987), "Absolutism: What's in a Name", in *French History, 1: 1*, pp. 109–112.

on the burden of taxation under absolutism and on the social groups which supported and/or opposed tax reforms. There was less argument on the relationships between the financial needs of the state on one hand and the demands created by structural changes of the logistic system on the other.

Another major issue in defining absolutism was the debate about the social nature of the absolutist state, i.e., the position of the nobility and the bourgeoisie vis a vis the role of the state. There were controversies as to whether the state was allied with the bourgeoisie or with the nobility. The argument followed the classical Marxist approach which viewed absolutism as the product of the class equilibrium between the old feudal nobility and the new urban bourgeoisie. Some researchers made cases for the "progressiveness" of absolutism stressing the state's aid to the rising bourgeoisie.[10] However, the empirical analysis was not based on critical examination of the absolutist state's policies as they affected the bourgeoisie.[11] Others saw absolutism as beleaguered defender of the feudal class rejecting the equilibrium approach between bourgeoisie and nobility.[12]

Absolutism was also investigated through a series of biographical studies of monarchs, regents and ministers. These studies were written to illustrate the effectiveness of monarchical power in practice. Biographical studies emphasized personal rule, and emperors were seen as driving forces behind innovations of the system. Biographies created good images of kings and either divorced absolute monarchy from society or subordinated all groups to the crown.[13] Some scholars discussed absolutism as a political system at a country level[14], often in isolation, stressing particularities and avoiding comparative structural approaches. There were also scholars who used a comparative method to study the origin of the modern European state from a liberal point of view. They viewed the period of absolutism as a state building process, emphasising conscious human action in the process of territorial consolidation, centralization of government and differentiation of functions.[15] These scholars discussed "activities necessary for the making of strong states". But activities and changes are not structured, and it is thus difficult to understand the nature and orientation of the dynamics. These authors have agreed to ignore theoretical constructs for fear of "losing" sight.

[10] Lublinskaya, A.D. (1968), *French Absolutism: The Crucial Phase, 1620–1629.* Cambridge.

[11] For a critism of Lublinskaya view see Parker, D. (1971), "The Foundation of French Absolutism 1610–1630" in *Past and Present, n.53*, pp. 67–89.

[12] For a critic of "equilibrium approach", see Anderson, P. (1974), *Lineages of the Absolutist State*. London, pp. 15ff.

[13] For a review of literature see Bonney, R. (1987).

[14] see Parker, D. (1983), *The Making of French Absolutism*. London. LeDonne, J. (1991), *Absolutism and Ruling Class. The Formation of the Russian Political Order 1700–1825.* New York; for a further list on countries see Henshall, N. (1992), pp. 225f.

[15] See the collected articles in Tilly, C (ed.) 1975, *The Formation of National States in Western Europe*. Princeton.

There is indeed a massive body of literature on absolutism and the absolutist state, but it is not as unmanageable as it may appear to be. Using the criteria of philosophical and methodological considerations, the literature may be divided into two categories, that which studies events/action, and that which studies structures. In the first category the object of inquiry and the line of emphasis is primarily individual and group behaviour. Scholars belonging to various disciplines and with varying capacities have approached the subject of absolutism emphasising different aspects. In this category absolutism was studied either from above or below perspectives, and in such cases the same aspect could be interpreted differently. In the second category, in the study of structural analysis, the aim is not to understand the meaning of each individual aspect and cause for a particular event. The approach is holistic which permits to view different aspects as if they existed as whole entities or subsystems interacting with one another. The primary strategy of emphasis is on the structures that produce, organize and determine movements of actions and events, either towards reproducing themselves or transforming themselves to a different scale.

The present study adopts a holistic view and a structural approach. Elements and argument lines of its theory have analogy to the works of Perry Anderson, who conducted a comprehensive empirical investigation of the general theory at a European level. In his work, absolutism is linked to the concept of the feudal mode of production, "towns" and state systems (war).[16] He approached absolutism structurally, and defined it "as a historical category" and a "new form of feudal state" determined by socio-economic change.[17] Absolutism is thereby considered a necessary step for transition from feudalism to capitalism.

The work of Anderson underlines at least three *necessary conditions* for the rise and development of absolutism. First, the existence of a "threatened" nobility and aristocracy with its own independent traditional basis, which collided and colluded with the monarch. This power structure is summed up as "parcellized sovereignty". Secondly, the formation of a system of European states (absolutism as the first international state system). Thirdly, the existence of merchant capitalism and its link with absolutism.

In the work of Anderson, none of these *necessary conditions* are treated independently and their mode of links is not explained. There is a brief reference made to each of them on a few pages. In the case of feudalism, he emphasised only the politics of "parcellized sovereignty", without problematizing the

[16] Anderson, P. (1974). Perry Anderson interpreted absolutism from a Marxist point of view (from a historical material point of view), which upholds class conflict (particularly ownership structure and appropriation of surplus) as the motor for economic and social change.

[17] Anderson, P. (1974), pp. 6, 18.

sphere and role of production or the forms of surplus appropriation.[18] Particularly, the interrelationships among categories of property ownership rights, system of taxation and economic base of the aristocracy were relevant themes of discussion that should not have been ignored[19].

His thesis that "warfare was not the sports of kings, it was their fate", did not serve as a base for the interpretation of war among countries. No satisfactory empirical explanation was made for why war became a necessity for the acquisition and distribution of societal surplus[20]. One expects an explanation of the complexity that existed between the needs and demands of war vis a vis the resource capacity of the state.

Even though Anderson mentioned the role of towns as a necessary condition, he did not discuss, as he himself stated, the phenomenon of merchant capitalism; he deferred explaining that task to another volume.[21] Hobsbawm also commented that Anderson neglected to clearly demonstrate the effect of a world economy on the structural features of absolutism, and the economic policy of the latter as regards the rising bourgeoisie.[22]

2.2. Towards an Explanation of the Absolutist State

What made Anderson's work different from that of others who studied absolutism was mainly his structural approach[23] and his association of absolutism with the transition from feudal to capitalist mode of production. In his work, the main concern was to account for political change, and the state is the centre of his study.[24] At the general level, he put the state in the perspective of the feudal mode of production and the concept of the transition from feudalism to

[18] Lüdtke, Alf (1980), "Genesis und Durchsetzung des "modernen Staates". Zur Analyse von Herrschaft und Verwaltung", in *Archiv für Sozialgeschichte. B. XX.* p. 476.

[19] On summary of the problem see Pryor, J.H. (1985), "The Historical Foundation of a Feudal Mode of Production", in Leach, E., Mukherjee and Ward, J. (eds.) *Feudalsim: Comparative Studies.* Sydney. As an example for the components and management of aristocratic patrimony see Astarita, T. (1992), *The Continuity of Feudal Power. The Caracciolo di Brienza in Spanish Naples.* Cambridge.

[20] For a general discussion see Lindegren, J. (1993), "Two thousand years of warfare", in *The Roots of Western Civilization. Two Thousand Years of Warfare*. Hilversum; Anderson, M.S. (1988), *War and Society in Europe of the Old Regime, 1618–1789.* Leicester. pp. 13–135.

[21] Anderson, P. (1974), p. 10. For different views on merchant capitalism see Kriedte, P. (1980), *Peasants, Landlords and Merchant Capitalist. Europe and the World Economy, 1500–1800.* Leamington; Zanden, J.L. (1993), *The Rise and Decline of Hollands Economy. Merchant Capitalsim and the Labour Market.* Manchester. At the international level see Wallerstein, I. (1974), *The Modern World-System. Capitalist Agriculture and the Origins of the European World-Economy in the Sixteenth Century*. London.

[22] Hobsbawm, E. and Bourn, D. (1976), "Feudalism, Capitalism and the Absolutist State", in *Communist Review, pamphlet 66*, summer 1976.

[23] Anderson, P. (1974), p. 7f.

[24] See Anderson, P. (1974), p. 11.

capitalism. At the empirical level, he tried to explain the state through a combination of various methods: by reference to its needs[25], by describing the features of the state[26], and by a comparative method.[27]

He attempted to explain an absolutist state in reference to its instrumentality for the ruling class. In the west, the dissolution of serfdom and the growth of commodity relations threatened the position of the feudal lords, thus causing "displacement of politico-legal coercion upwards towards a centralized, militarized summit—the Absolutist State".[28] In the east, Anderson saw Swedish aggression as a major stimulus to the emergence of absolutism in Russia, Prussia and Austria.[29] In both west and east, the nobility and aristocracy were threatened. The difference was "the structure of the absolutist state in the West was over determined by the rise of an urban bourgeoisie".[30] The conclusion was that a threatened nobility needed a centralized and militarized state to continue its domination.

Logical and empirical problems arise when one ponders Anderson's methods of explanation. In the first place, the need for a centralized state is not necessarily the same thing as having one. The ruling class may need an absolutist state, but it is another question if they might have one. Secondly, if one considers the case of Poland, the absolutist state was not the only alternative for a "threatened" nobility.

Again, one faces the problem of chronological phases vis a vis the method used to explain the state by way of discussing its distinguishing features, namely, a standing army, a national bureaucracy, a national system of taxation, a codified law and diplomacy. Clarification is needed as to which features result from the process, and which are effects of the events (consequences) at a point in time. It appears obvious that all the features of the whole historical period, starting from Renaissance[31] up to 1789, cannot be ascribed to the state at one and the same time. For instance, distinguishing features such as bureaucracy and a unified market belonged, both structurally and functionally, to a later stage of absolutism starting from the beginning of the 18th century.[32] Moreover, it was possible that at a given stage of development, these two features could be consequences of an ongoing-process, and not necessarily explained by the essence of the process. For instance one finds bureaucracy in the Italian states where there were no sufficient conditions and causes for the

[25] Ibid, pp. 17–24, 197–202.

[26] Ibid., see page 29–42

[27] Ibid, the rest of the chapters deal with the countries of western and eastern Europe and the Notes section is on Japanese feudalism and the "Asiatic Mode of Production".

[28] Anderson, P. (1974), p. 19.

[29] Ibid., pp. 198–202.

[30] Ibid., p. 22.

[31] Anderson, (1974), pp. 48f.

[32] See enlightened absolutism section 2.4. below.

rise of an absolutist state.[33] Descriptions of features of the state may not necessarily explain the essence of an actual process marked with change and continuity. Specific structures are required for the exercise of specific functions at a given stage of development.

The third method which Anderson heavily depended on to explain the absolutist state was the comparative method. He discussed west and east European absolutism, and compared European with Japanese feudalism and Asiatic modes of production. The lesson drawn from any comparison depends on the purpose which they intended to serve. Anderson's motive and point of departure was clear. He sought to explain why industrial capitalism developed endogenously in western parts of Europe. Since the endpoint of this process is known, changes had to be linked in an expected sequence that could lead to the success of industrial capitalist development in western parts of Europe. Such a framework of explanation does not provide room to hypothesize various other possible combinations of conditions which could lead to the success or failure of the process. For the purpose of explaining an expected sequence, empirical facts were narrated without giving any special explanation.[34] As a result, conditions, differences, and explanations could be ignored for the sake of commitment to an expected sequence and purpose.[35]

One faces inconsistency and unexplained questions in the methods used to explain the absolutist state. Anderson only identified the necessary conditions from which one could expect the rise of an absolutist state. It seems that he did not find it necessary to prove and problematize those conditions. But the presence of sufficient conditions alone does not suffice to ensure the occurrence of an absolutist state. Prevalence of necessary conditions tells why an absolutist state is expected to occur, not how it actually occurred. One has to answer not only *why* but also *how* that form of state came into being.

Even though the present study interprets absolutism structurally as did Perry Anderson, there is a methodological difference. The present study takes the position of the *how possible?* type of explanation[36], adapting an intentional and consequence mode of explanation to the understanding and inter-

[33] See Litchfield, B. (1986), *Emergence of a Bureaucracy. The Florentine Patricians 1530–1790*. Princeton. Bureaucracy should not be confused with officialdom. The latter, meaning officers and their function can exist without the former. Bureaucracy is a technique of organization which needs the existence of permanent staff and permanent budget as a prerequisite, and this condition had to be created first by and in the process of making the fiscal military state.

[34] Runciman, W.G. (1980), "Comparative Sociology or Narrative History? A Note on the Methodology of Perry Anderson", in *Archives Européennes de Sociologie, tome xxi, n.1*. p. 171f.

[35] A good example is the case of discussing "English absolutism", for it was immediately dropped out by his definition of features of an absolutist state. Had he considered the evolution as open-ended, he could not ignore differences that could have resulted as part of the various attempts to respond to pressures imposed by the environment.

[36] For the logical status see, Wright, G.H. (1971), *Explanation and Understanding*. London. pp. 13f, 57,58, 83f, 135ff, 141.

pretation of an absolutist state. This mode of explanation refers to the different phases of human purpose and action; and in the case of the absolutist state, it is a question of describing and explaining the declared and undeclared objectives and the consistent activities of the state. In other words, in the present study an absolutist state is defined from a perspective of resource system.

2.3. Resource System Model of the Fiscal Military State

The actual mechanism at work to attain the existence of an absolutist state can be specified and investigated through construction of a resource system model, which is here intended to synthesize the links among the *necessary conditions*, namely the feudal mode of production, world economy and an international state system. In the broader sense, a resource system refers to the size, the forms of acquisition, the manner of distribution and the use of societal surplus by the state and the ruling class. Before embarking upon the discussion of the various parametres and postulates of the resource system model of the first type of absolutist state, it is important to clarify the use of some terms. There are two points that need to be clarified. The first deals with the context in which the term fiscal is used, and the second point refers to the assumption behind the link between the terms fiscal and military.

The term fiscal is problematic and it raises a number of conceptual problems. The term was derived from the Roman central treasury called *fiscus*, and in line with this origin, researchers of the mercantilist period used the term to refer to the state's endeavours to increase government revenues; "fiscalism is concerned only with the revenue of the public treasury and has nothing definite to say about its expenditure".[37] In this study, however, the revenue of the state is not separated from the objectives of the government and its items of spending.

In the study of capitalist economy, particularly in the field of public finance, the term and concept of fiscal (or fiscal policy) is used to refer to the study of the influence of the financing of the government on the economy (on production, employment, and national income). Fiscal policy is one of the two main tools of a capitalist state for influencing the general level of economic activity—the other being monetary policy. For an economist, therefore, the term fiscal suggests a wide range of policy issues such as system of taxation, government expenditure, budget, and public debt and its influence over the level and activity of the economy.

[37] Klaveren, J. (1969) "Fiscalism, Mercantlism and Corruption" in Coleman, D. C. (ed.), *Revisions in Mercantlism*. London. p. 140.

In the present study, however, the term fiscal is used in a different historical and socio-economic setting; it is used to refer to the manner in which the government spends its funds and finances its spendings; it deals with the creation of resources in a way that is profitable to the objectives and functions of the state regardless of local interests and economic consequences.

This gives rise to the question What is the state? In this work the state is primarily the King, his military, judicial and financial officials and other categories of authorities who exercise power in the name of the King.[38] The state is thus the dynasty, its functionaries, and members of the ruling class (aristocracy, nobility and urban business class) who benefited from the growth and expansion of the state. The state is a form of monarchical government, fiscally and militarily centralized. It has the function of mobilizing manpower and finances for the purpose of assuring its well being and safety.

Proceeding on from the definition of terms, the discussion now turns to the two major classess of elements included in the resource model of the fiscal military state. On one side there is a system of property and forms of distribution (i.e., land ownership rights, volume of production, principles of tax assessment and collection, and forms for arranging of revenue administration), which are referred to here as fiscal systems, or ways of creating revenue for the state. On the other side there are elements of the logistic system, namely, recruitment of manpower, methods of provisioning, transportation systems and the supply of weapons, all of which point to how the revenues were used by the state. There are causal and structural relationships between the fiscal imperatives (the revenue) of the government and its war endeavours (patterns of expenditure).

In reality, this link was expressed quantitatively and qualitatively in the reform policy of the state. Quantitatively, the largest size of state expenditure was allocated for the military and the payment of war debt. Qualitatively, the preference for tax reform was made to enhance the logistic capacity of the state and the sources of aristocratic patrimony (e.g., tax exemption of the military nobility, the creation of a standing army on the basis of allotment, etc.), and not to influence economic growth. The economic objectives of the government were designed to increase revenue and the group interest of the military nobility, and not primarily private traders, international capitalists and peasants. An illustrative example is the royal and aristocratic privileges and

[38] The ruling class does not reproduce itself through the state only. There are other institutions such as religious establishments, corporations, local associations and non-governmental organizations which regulate the mutual relationship between social groups in various spheres of activities. By definition, these institutions and establishments are omitted from the discussion, unless they are related to the means and objective of the state. Even though, there exist such institutions as provincial estates, representative bodies, and churches, etc., the core of the political organization of the society is the state.

the monopolization of trade through share holding companies, credit and financing of trade.[39]

The set of statements mentioned above concerning the interrelationship between the fiscal and military aspects provide a set of postulates. The principal line of argument is that the logistic system of an absolutist state could be successfully formed in a resource system where the principles of property rights and forms of distribution allowed technical and administrative measures aimed to maximize revenue and expenditure of the state. An absolutist state which succeeded in creating a harmony between the logistic needs and fiscal system, has the capacity to use new economic opportunities and expand a limited economic potential. A resource system, which because of its type of property ownership rights, its methods of acquisition, and principles of distribution, promoted a local and individualized economic privileges, created a permanent imbalance between the fiscal imperatives and war endeavours of the state. Consequently, there was constant instability and violence in society. For instance, the varied demands and permanent logistic needs of a feudal state could not be successfully fulfilled in a resource system which was based entirely on the principle of communal or collective ownership rights in land, territorial forms of tax assessment, and privatized methods of revenue administration. The resource system of an absolutist state was based on regulated private property rights, regularized and individualized payment of taxes, and centrally controlled methods of revenue administration; principles staunchly followed for the "safety and growth" of the state. For purposes of analysis and presentation, this set of postulates on the link between logistic needs and the fiscal system are further represented by two major categories, namely, the creation of "new" resources and the use of existing resources.

2.3.1. Creation of New Resources

2.3.1.1. Ways and Means

To highlight the significance of revenue to the state, the sixteenth century political theorist Jean Bodin wrote that "financial means are the nerves of the state". In another version, Colbert, the first minister of France in the 1660s, said "money is the vital nerve of war". These often-repeated dictums illustrate the need and significance of finance in the early development of the state. There were, however, limitations including an absence of economic develop-

[39] It was probably for reasons of such an interrelationship btween warfare and fiscal system that many famous writers of the time say "warfare is the moving motor for the whole development of public finance" and the treatment of public finance as "essentially a science of war and not of peace". Qoted in Braun, R. (1975), "Taxation, Sociopolitical Structure, and State-building: Great Britain and Brandenburg-Prussia", in Tilly, C. (ed.), *The Formation of National States in Western Europe*. Princeton. p. 310.

ment, lack of technical capacity and problems concerning the structure of power. If governments wanted to have more finance then they had to either enrich their economy and/or they had to learn to tap society's assets more effectively. Governments used various ways and means, depending on circumstances. Which way and method used at a point in time is an interesting aspect of this study. Hypothetically speaking, there were four major types of ways and means, categorized on the basis of their revenue yielding capacity and techniques.

i) Increasing Tax Rate: This is a discretionary or legal method used to increase taxes. Reforms were attained by discretionary measures without taking into consideration the paying capacity and the welfare of peasants and merchants. Rates could be increased by tax-technical measures, such as fixing the rate of tax payment, standardizing of tax payment, individual registration of tax payment, merging of different tax payment obligations, and introducing new tax payments. Taxes could also be increased by legislation and through parliamentary means. It is assumed here that taxes are no longer "an expedient" collected in times of emergency. They constitute permanent regular revenue for the state. In cases where taxes were alienated, the state could reclaim.

ii) Increasing Tax Base: In this case revenue base was enlarged by increasing national wealth following various economic policies. In the case of agriculture, it could increase if and when the taxable units were known in census and on that basis if the government updated its property assessment register. Mercantilist policy could encourage commerce and thus could expand consumption tax. Commerce could be encouraged through the development of infrastructure and financial institutions, and the guaranteeing of the merchant class. Joint-stock companies were a legal device by which the state shared profit from lucrative luxury trade by sharing risk with private capital.

iii)Reducing the Costs of Revenue Collection: This deals with the efficiency of tax collection. Administrative reforms may reduce costs of revenue collection, for example, if the state employed salary paid officials. As individuals have devised ingenious methods for evading taxes and siphoning off tax receipts for personal use, governments have tried to counteract the loss of revenue by multiplying the number of state collectors. Emperors may have found ways of controlling tax payment and collection through the creation of a network of separate organizations outside the control of the nobility and peasant community, and that depended on central headquarters. This change could have been effected both at central and regional/local levels.

iv) Tax-Farming: To avoid problems in costs of revenue collection and/or to secure badly needed short term funds, governments often contracted with private entrepreneurs to collect some or all of their taxes.

v) Borrowing: When revenues were inadequate and/or slow to reach the centre, states obtained advances on anticipated taxes by borrowing at high interest rates from selected private lenders; bankers, financiers, and tax farmers.[40]

Revenue could also be increased through confiscation. For instance, during the Reformation, Protestant states seized property and income from the Catholic church. The Reformation also abolished clerical exemption from taxes. In subsistence economies, rulers increased revenue sources through conquest. Yet wars often cost more than they brought in. Both conquest and confiscation were expedient measures which caused rebellion.

By and large, there are different ways of creating revenue for the state depending on the conditions of each country: as regards economic opportunity (productivity, expansion, number of population), as regards power (the ability to tax, privileges in tax exemption of the ruling class), etc. The dynamic part of the financial system of the state is the revenue aspect, as it shifts with circumstance, and as it changes with increasing expenditure. The scarcity or limit of resources and consequently the endeavour to create means for the state was the most creative part of the financial system of the fiscal military state. How to obtain resources was more important than its forms of acquisition (in kind or cash).

2.3.1.2. The Structure and Level of Government Revenue

Describing the ways and means of government revenue indicates nothing about the types and amounts of government revenue. The latter is related to what the major sources, structure and size of government revenue were. The structure of the government revenue is related to the study of the major objects of taxation, their time of introduction, their share in the total revenue, and their capacity to increase. Furthermore, one has to quantify and show the importance of each of the elements of the tax system over time. The size of the revenue depended on how much money the system collected, who paid and how much, how much was supposed to be levied and how much was really paid.

In an economy still close to the natural subsistence level and, in some cases, short of cash and credit, the number of taxable commodities capable of producing a respectable and expanding yield was very small. As a result, the greater part of the revenue came from heavy personal taxes collected from the peasantry. During the period of enlightened absolutist state, however, indirect tax constituted the greater share of government revenues.

[40] See Webber, C. and Wildavsky, A. (1986), *A History of Taxation and Expenditure in the Western World.* New York, pp. 250–260.

2.3.2. Use of Existing Resources: Government Expenditure

2.3.2.1. The Structure and Level of Government Expenditure

The structure and level of government expenditure deals with the forces served by budgetary decision, and it shows the main purpose of each budgetary item, and how much was allocated for each item of spending. The creation of the standing army, ensuring of adequate provision, war equipment, and the building of a transport system were the objectives of the fiscal military states. Redressing past military barriers were major priorities. There were internal and external pressures which compelled governments to embark on reforms. Internally the desire to centralize power led to exertion of force to suppress independent, parcellized authority. Internationally, there was commercial rivalry, religious wars, possession of geopolitical territories, etc. which led and increased the scale of warfare.[41]

In this situation what counted in decision making was the military needs of the state, not economic and social objectives (welfare of the society in terms of health and education). Recruitment of manpower (ways of remuneration), methods of provisioning, the transportation system and the supply of war materials and equipment were items of expenditure which in a way were the non-discretionary parts of the government budget. On them rested the pillars of the state.

What were the levels and items of spending? This is difficult to know as there was no clear line between war and peace and consequently between wartime and peacetime expenditure. War was a normal feature of the early modern period, and it was a cause and effect of the economic basis of the state. The frequency of troop movements and the number of conflicts were so numerous that war became pervasive, forcing states to maintain troops on a permanent basis. This means that analysis of military expenditures of state should not be limited to "financing of a war" or considered as "extraordinary costs". If war was a normal feature of society, then all "peace time" activities were by implication also military expenditures. But, for the purpose of analysis, one can assume that there could be "peace time" and "war time" (campaign) activity; the former could be regarded as ordinary military expenditure and the latter as extraordinary expenditure.

Permanent expenditure (or "peace time military" expenditure), included payment of wages to regular soldiers, officers and bureaucrats of the army, and in some cases payment to mercenary troops. It also included remuneration and support of the cavalry; maintaining of garrison troops; and annual salary payment made to some principal provincial officials. Administrative costs, re-

[41] "In early modern Europe everyone regarded war as a normal, perhaps even a necessary part of human life" Anderson, M.S. (1987), *Europe in the Eighteenth Century, 1713–1783*. Third Edition. London, p. 13.

wards (cash payments and valuable materials), and supply of war materials and equipment (guns, mortar, firearms, ammunitions, swords, spears, etc.) belonged to the category of permanent military expenditure. Payment of wartime debt was also an independent element of the expenditure.

Extraordinary expenditures consisted of expenses for prolonged and intensive military campaigns, and these particularly included provisioning and transport, and auxiliary troops which accompany the main troops. Payments made to allied troops and military transportation (such as building of military roads and procurement and feeding of transportation animals) were classified as extraordinary expenses.

To what extent were the components of the logistic system ranked to bring about a desired effect? In other words were they planned? These questions are answered empirically. No matter which way they are ranked, the needs must be met for a successful military outcome to occur. Here it is presumed that growth in military activity was influenced more by resource creation than resource allocation to parts. "Peaceful" military needs were known and remained constant in the sense that obligations were fixed and were already prioritized. On the other hand, the proportion of available resources for military ends were not constant.

2.3.2.2. Forms of Revenue Administration and Allocation

Forms of revenue administration and allocation is a question of who collects revenue and who uses it; who finances what types of expenditures; and is revenue collection and disbursements done by separated or fused administration.

First, who collected the revenue and why? Was it collected by central treasury through salaried officials, or by each government department, or by provincial governors, or by private contractors? Was there a "tax code" to guide local governors? Were some taxes and fees collected without legal authorization, and were others cancelled?

The second question is, who finances what types of expenditure? Who financed fixed expenditures? Extraordinary expenditures? Was it the central treasury, the provincial governor, creditors, or all? Broadly speaking, these are questions related to the manner in which the state defined its revenue and expenditure. The approach is first to lay down the structure of expenditure, and then proceed to inquire whose expenses each of the items of spending were: central, regional, local or private? This again led to the investigation of how items of spending were traditionally administered or prepared. Was it prepared functionally (e.g., army, navy, etc.) or institutionally (court, church, etc.) or a combination of both?

Revenue administration methods were basically decentralized and might have had varieties of combinations depending on the form of the economy, tradition and the power structure. In most cases one found market methods and sharing principles, each containing a number of variations. In the process there was a transition from one variety to another, probably something that required different (separate) administration of collection and disbursement. What was important, however, was which methods embodied built-in mechanisms of central control.

Market administration included venal office and tax farmers. The sharing system was more complex. There were different kinds: tax-base sharing, tax-grant sharing, and revenue-sharing systems. There was a difference between tax-base sharing and the tax-grant. Tax-sharing meant a share in some proportion of the collected tax between the central and local governments from a fixed tax base, e.g., tithe payment. The amount each level of government received depended on the amount raised. But in the case of tax-grant, the amount that the local government received depended on the size of the expenditure, often determined by the central government.

In the tax-grant system, the size of the grant allowed by the government depended on the nature of the expenditure. The form of the grant was often arranged or fixed, for instance, at the time of land survey and registration.[42] In the tax-sharing system the governor general could raise as many troops as possible depending on the limit of the share. This could be achieved either by efficient administration or through promotion since the share one got depended on military rank. In a revenue share system, one level of government collected the revenues (direct and/or indirect taxes) and the other level was entitled to receive a given proportion of the revenue on the basis of the criteria mutually agreed upon.

In both the market and the sharing principle systems there were independent administrators who had jurisdiction over each fund. Each of the agencies were supposed to fund themselves. Since revenue was not consolidated, those who dealt with government financing comprehended neither the scale of spending nor the deficits, nor did they exert much influence over the disposition of state assets. Besides, association of each type of revenue collection with different agencies created a kind of rigid dependence on specific items of expenditure from a definite source of revenue. This situation created problems of either surplus or permanent deficit which had to be covered from other sources. Moreover, funds collected by each of the agencies might not have

[42] In case of Ethiopia, it was revealed that one *gasha* land for the local *balabat*, three *gasha* land for the local land tax administrator, one *gasha* land for clergy, and one *gasha* land for a soldier was customarily given. This whole phenomenon was called *yä-mängets wäg* (state custom). As such, the cases mentioned in these categories were not arbitrary but followed government policy. The governor-general had no jurisdiction to decide on the number and size of grants mentioned, even though he was commander of the regional troops. Jurisdiction over such allocation meant the right to make land tax exemptions, a right which was in the province of the central government. For further discussion see section 6.3. below.

reached the centre. From these complex possibilities it is not difficult to see problems of control. Government did not know how much was collected and spent.

2.3.2.3. Methods of Control

During the period under discussion, in order to improve its financial situation the government tried improving financial control rather than plan spending. This was attempted at two levels: at an organizational level (creation of a central receiver or consolidation of funds) and at a technical level (a central accounting system).

The fiscal military state made an effort to create a single central treasury into which all funds would flow. In some cases, it created a central budget office responsible for the preparation of the annual budget. A single treasury was a means not only of keeping track of all government revenue and expenditures, but also of relating one to the other to attain a rough balance between the government's resources and its commitments.

Fragmentation of jurisdiction over spending into special funds inhibited accounting of the total amount spent. The desire to control expenditure, to consider it together with revenue, required a comprehensive account of receipts or of spending. To avoid the practice of ad-hoc expedients in taxing to cover emerging spending, expenditures should be allocated within the total. This required clearly establishing how much was in the various accounts or precisely how much was being spent for what.

Technically, a central treasury must be facilitated by double-entry book keeping, the conceptualization of a uniform system of accounts, and other devices for keeping track of revenues and expenditure. Regular keeping of accounts showed anticipated revenue and actual receipts. Lack of technical capacity, lack of opportunities offered by techniques, and social circumstances might have limited the implementation of such reforms. Even if applied, in some cases the reform could be partial and accounting became difficult. Separate revenue funds existed for each of the many taxes collected by government; current fund balances could never have been estimated nor future balances predicted; and government audits of tax collectors stood years in arears.

The model of the fiscal military state could be one of the computing models used to interpret and explain the absolutist state. Though absolutism is a concrete historical development, it is conceptualized and interpreted by various models: tax state (*Steuerstaat*)[43], finance state (*Finanzstaat*)[44], dynastic state[45],

[43] Schumpeter, J. (1951), *Die Krise des Steuerstaates*. Wiesbaden.

[44] See Ladewig Petersen, E. (1975), "From Domain State to Tax State. Synthesis and Interpretation", in *The Scandinavian Economic History Review, XXIII: 2.*

[45] See Bonney, R. (1991), *The European Dynastic States, 1494–1660*. Oxford.

organized feudalism[46], military state[47], "state feudalism"[48], and "power state"[49]. There are structural differences among these models in the interpretation of absolutism. It is beyond the scope of this study to comment on each model, but the differences in approach and premises, which affect and shape the final result of any study on absolutism are important.

The resource system model of the fiscal military state contains its own demise: it is based on a thesis that qualitative and quantitative changes in the objectives and means of the state would bring about a new set of relations and attributes essentially belonging to another phase. For instance, in the fiscal and military state, components of the logistic system were the base line of the budget, and any attack on them marked a new change. Any sequential and simultaneous orders for changes in the fiscal and military aspects led to another period. During the second half of the eighteenth century, rulers of most European countries carried out wide range reforms aimed at improving educational opportunities, social conditions and the economic life of the subjects. These reforms, together with the ways and means of the government, brought change in the fundamental priorities of the state, i.e., who is taxed how much and for what purpose. During this period taxes began to have educational, social and economic functions.

The resource system model of the fiscal military state, therefore, shows the nature and time of change over the long period of absolutism. According to the postulate of this model, the period of absolutism has two political system phases which had their respective institutional features and functional characteristics and dynamics belonging to itself. In the first stage, absolutism manifested itself in the form of the fiscal military state. Centralization occurred first in the area of the fiscal and military aspects of the state, and both aspects were functionally and structurally related, giving a defining form and feature to the

[46] See Dahlgren, S., Lindkvist, T. and Stadin, K. (1993), "Skattesystem i förändring—en kommentar", in *Historisk tidskrift, 1*. pp. 131–139.

[47] Oestreich, G. (1969), *Geist und Gestalt des Frühmodernen Staats*. Berlin; Nilsson, S. A. (1990), *De stora krigens tid. Om Sverige som militärstat och bondesamhälle*. Uppsala; Lindegren, J. (1984), "The Swedish 'Military State', 1560–1720", in *Scandinavian Journal of History, X: 4.*

[48] This term is used in the Soviet literature, see Jansson, T. (1988), "Rättsuppfattningar och sockenrätt. Tsarer mot baroner och baroner mot bönder i strid om lokaladministrationen i estlandssvenska områden vid 1800-talets mitt", in *Scandia*, 54, 1, note 6, p. 48.

[49] Lindegren, J. (1992). The author considered power state partly as a resource system and partly as a control system. His subject of investigation was the resource system consisting of the following elements: the size of societal surplus, the forms of acquisition (use- and exchange values), the recruitment of soldiers and the demographic consequences of the wars. The basic idea of the model was based on the thesis that there was a contradiction between the production character and the financial demands and exchange value needs of the feudal ruling class. The model was used to analyse the Scandinavian reality. However, the model was not problematized with the theory of absolutism, even though it implicitly discussed the links among the necessary conditions that allowed for the emergence of centralized power. In the absence of theoretical argument, it is difficult to know the criteria used to select the constituting elements of the model and the justification used to uphold the principal postulate and the argument lines.

state. This stage lasted from the late sixteenth century up to the early decades of the eighteenth century. Functionally this form of state is linked to dynastic interest and well-being and safety of the state. The second stage is the period of the "Enlightened Absolutism", a continuation period characterized by the state's activism in the economic life of the period, extending up to the end of the eighteenth century.

2.4. Enlightened Absolutist State, 1720s–1789

Using the term enlightenment to characterize the period and the form of state entails a conceptual and chronological problem. Traditionally, this term is associated with the ideas and thinkers of the 18th century. The classical studies of this period asserted that the domestic policies of the states were influenced and even dictated by the ideas of the Enlightenment. Later, researchers and critics found that the reforms were undertaken for reasons other than Enlightenment ideas; military and fiscal considerations, peasant rebellion, concepts of cameralism and mercantilism, middle class rise to state power, etc. For various reasons, both the critics and opponents of the enlightened absolutism agreed that there were reforms.[50] In this work the term enlightened is used not to indicate ideas and their influence, but rather to indicate the nature and content of government reforms which is assumed to have social and economic objectives.

The new changes are labelled as "enlightened" because of the new awareness by the state that its strength lies in the welfare of society. One observes state activism affecting the economy and the awareness that a state's prosperity ultimately depended on its subjects (cameralist thinking). New awareness developed based on the interrelation between the state and its guaranteeing needs on the one hand, and the economy's ability to support those needs on the other.[51] The state also began to use capitalist institutions and means to promote its interest. The interest of the enlightened absolutist state emanated from the idea that economic power would achieve political ends, not vice versa.

Even though the revenue-raising capacity of the state increased during the phase of the fiscal military state, kings could not count on regular income of revenue because the revenue base was founded on direct taxation. Because income depended mainly on agricultural output, fortunes of rulers and individual cultivators alike were dominated by the uncertainties that have plagued agricultural output since time immemorial. It seemed that during the period of enlightened absolutism, governments turned their interest to market taxes. Indirect tax (market tax) increased along with economic expansion, and by the

[50] For a review of the state of research and period of enlightened absolutism, see Scott, H.M. ed., (1990), *Enlightened Absolutism. London*; Anderson, M.S. (1987).

[51] See Vries, Jan De (1976), *The Economy of Europe in an Age of Crisis, 1600–1750*. Cambridge. 242.

late eighteenth century consumption provided the greater part of the state revenue. Of all sources of government revenue, consumption tax had a revenue raising capacity. It was this structural part of the tax that was capable of producing a respectable and an expanding yield in the age of growing commerce.

Productive revenue-expenditure systems began to emerge during the period of the enlightened absolutism. Financial institutions became more diversified and developed during this period: institutionalization of insurance and credit systems, creation of central state banks, administrative consolidation and simplification of accounts, etc.[52] With these institutions came a stable market and a great potential for state borrowing. Governments learned how to borrow from the public, how to fund debt in an orderly fashion, and were beginning to learn how to control state expenditure.

The enlightened absolutist state heralded the beginning of a causal relationship between the growth of state and the development of capitalism both at the national and international level. First in its regulative functions, and later in its spending and programmes, the state began to function increasingly for the interest of capitalism. In its regulative function, it gave guarantees in securing property. Thus, there was the development of absolute ownership rights in property, the initiation of socially oriented functions and reforms, the establishment of order that could create stability and facilitate the accumulation of capital. This was not the function of the fiscal military state.

Bureaucracy, diplomacy, sovereignty, judiciary system etc. were characteristics belonging to the enlightened state and were products of the reforms themselves. In the fiscal military state, taxes were designed and allocated to support the new military system. The military organization and administration, in turn, enforced payment of these taxes and eventually collected and administered the revenues with its own administrative apparatus. In the period of the enlightened absolutist state, the military apparatus was separated from the administration of revenue, and was replaced by a civil bureaucracy. The emergence of bureaucracy also separated the royal court from the state, i.e., the public. The royal court developed its own independent bureaucracy which administered the king's "own" treasury, and that of its domains and prerogatives.

Centralized capacity to plan and control spending was attributed to governments of the nineteenth century.[53] But it can be said that this capacity started with the second phase of absolutism, namely, the period of the enlightened absolutist state. "Each age had its own patterns of taxing, spending and borrowing constant with its political system and technical opportunities".[54] But there is a difference in techniques of accounting. Devicing procedures and mechanisms to combine taxing, spending and borrowing for making political

[52] See, Kennedy, P. (1988), 98f.
[53] Webber, C. and Wildavsky, A. (1986), p. 29.
[54] Ibid., p. 18.

choices, i.e., formal budget, can be attributed to the period of the enlightened absolutist state.

It is beyond the scope of this book to build a model of enlightened absolutism, but it is necessary to mention some points of consideration which help to identify its features and to account for its functions. Since this state was functionally and structurally related to the development of capitalism, both at the national and international levels, emphasis will be placed on elements of the model that should include the following points: character of production, the form of the economy (exchange values), international spheres of trade and capital circulation, the state and the urban business class, the role of the state in the regulation (institutionalization) of property rules vs. network strategy of the merchants, items of state expenditure, rise of absolute private property, primitive capital accumulation, etc. Instead of state regulations, economic laws began to drive the economy and this was accompanied by a liberalization policy and separation of the private from the public. During this phase, the state was separated from the court and dynasty, and the state became public.[55]

To sum up, in the present study absolutism is used to refer to a structurally defined social transformation belonging to the last stage of feudalism. Absolutism is interpreted and put to use not as an empirical category, but as a theoretical model of a transtional period. The theory of absolutism pertains to the complex links existing among three necessary conditions, namely the feudal mode of production, the international state system (war) and merchant capitalism. These conditions constituted the structural elements of absolutism and they were articulated to give a particular form at the level of the state and the economy. The process of power centralization was the essence and dynamics of the transitional period and it was expressed primarily in the fiscal and military basis of the state.

Generally, the states of absolutism were alluded to as absolutist states and they are defined here from the perspective of a resource system. An absolutist state was a type of feudal state in which the systems of resource acquisition and distribution were centralized. It was created under conditions in which war presented itself as a necessity for internal exploitation and distribution of societal surplus among nobles and aristocrats. Military capacity and needs were essential factors for the coming into being of an absolutist state.[56] But wher-

[55] For the various meanings of the term public, for the emergence and transformation of the public sphere see Habermas, J. (1991), *The Structural Transformation of the Public Sphere. An Inquiry into a Category of Bourgeois Society*. Cambridge.

[56] The Polish gentry and aristocracy did not need to develop a military apparatus as a means for internal exploitation and distribution of societal surplus. The absence of a military bureaucratic apparatus led to the partition of the country and the extinction of the state during the formation of the European states system. See Downing, B.M. (1992), *The Military Revolution and Political Change. Origins of Democracy and Autocracy in Early Modern Europe*. Princeton. Chapter Six.

ever there was war or military capacity, there was not necessarily an absolutist state. Centralization of power was possible in a system of private property rights and fiscal arrangement forms which had the tendency to maximize revenues of the military state and diversify sources of aristocratic patrimony.

Any sequential and simultaneous changes in the means and objectives of the state brought about qualitatively different functions and structures belonging to another form. The transitional period was marked by two types of state forms that had their respective institutional features and functional characteristics and dynamics belonging to itself. These states, which in the literature were ascribed to the absolutist state, have been distinguished here as the fiscal military state and the enlightened absolutist state. They represented necessary and orderly forms that manifested the distinctive phases of absolutism.

The present study aims to examine and explain the genesis and the making of the fiscal military state, adopting the resource system model extensively treated in the sections above. Before proceeding to the main objective of the study, it is relevant first to raise a general question of whether there was a period of absolutism in Ethiopian history. When did it exist? Why? and How was it understood and interpreted?

3. Ethiopian Absolutism: Problems of Periodization and Interpretation

3.1. Periodization of Ethiopian Absolutism

In the Ethiopian historiography there is a unanimous consensus among historians to mark 1855, the coronation of king Tewodros, as the beginning of a new period. The 1974 middle-calss revolution is also considered the turning point to mark the end of the *ancien régime*. Although authors accept the validity of these landmarks, there is no interpretative framework for the period 1855–1974. Often the whole period is referred to as modern[57], and this term does not refer to its essence and social organization. Those who use the term add other concepts such as semi-feudalism and semi-capitalism, to further expand its character. In the absence of general agreement, it became possible to discuss certain periods in between as particular historical phases. For instance, the period after the Italian occupation of 1935–41, up to the revolution of 1974, is referred to as absolutism.[58] In this case, Haile Selassie's process of power centralization was taken as a fundamental criteria for identifying a turning point. But power

[57] Note the title of a book by Bahru Zewde (1991), *A History of Modern Ethiopia, 1855–1974*. London.

[58] Bahru Zewde (1984), "Economic Origins of the Absolutist State of Ethiopia (1916–1935)" in *Journal of Ethiopian Studies, 17*; Bahru Zewde (1991), pp. 135ff.

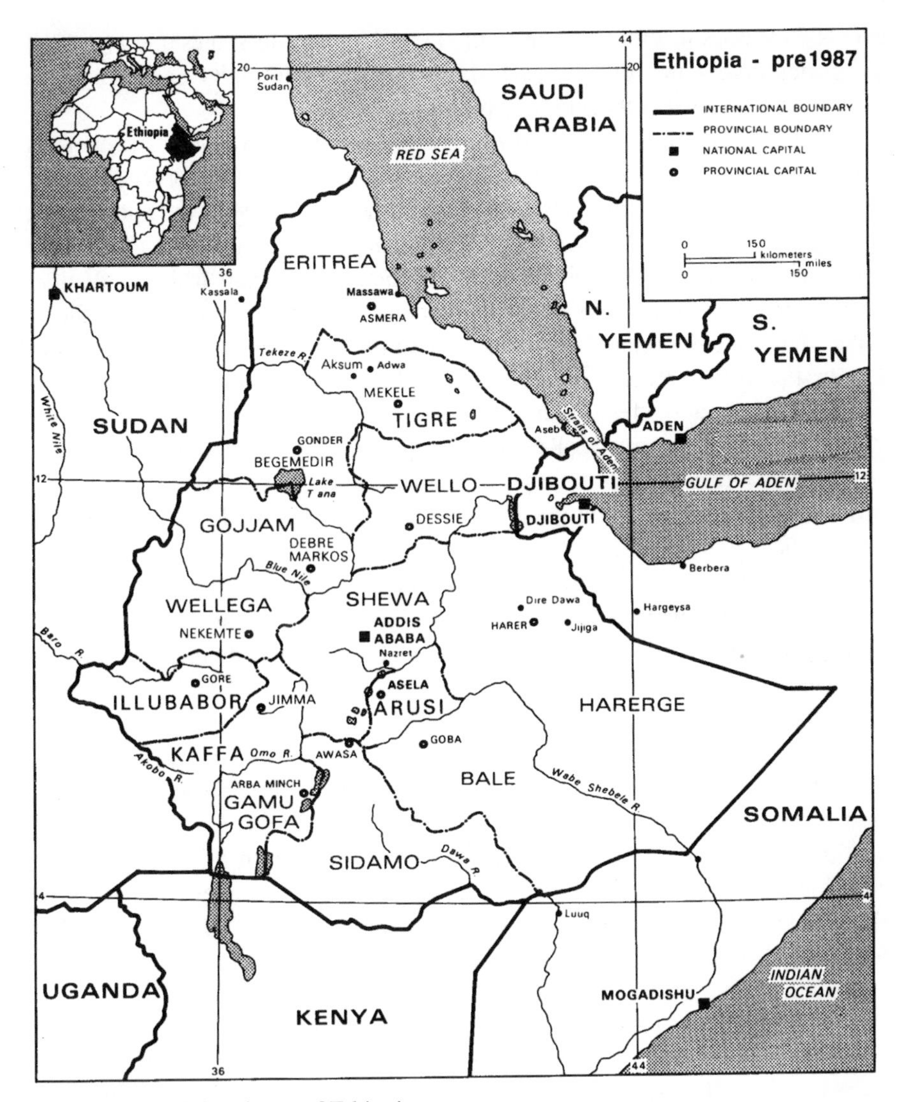

Map 1. Pre 1987 Provinces of Ethiopia.
Source: Gebru Tareke (1991), *Ethiopia: Power and Protest.*

centralization had been a continuous process since 1855, and if there was any difference it was mainly in the means and degree of centralization.

Periodization of the historical process between 1855 and 1974 requires a principle discussion. What is the criterion on which an interpretation of the historical change is based and periodization is motivated? Is it a political event or a change in the material and social base of the state and society? What does the whole period 1855–1974 constitute? Does it refer to a 'sequence of events'? Or does it refer to 'time settings', i.e., particular stages and historical categories divergent from the past? If so how can continuity and change be explained, and what is their logical relationship?

In the present study, 'time setting' is considered the criterion and there is both theoretical and empirical justifications for doing so. The preceding section on the general theory of absolutism identified the 'unity of the epoch', i.e., the period 1855–1974 as Ethiopian absolutism. According to the theory and resource system model construction, Ethiopian absolutism had two distinct phases representing two types of socio-economic systems singular by themselves, but logically related and belonging to the same transformation process. The first phase stretched from 1855 to 1913 and covered the period of Tewodros, Yohannes, and Menelik, and this phase is here called the fiscal military state. The second phase is called the period of an enlightened absolutist state (1916–1974), constituting mainly the reign of Haile Selassie I.

There were certain conditions and processes which made the period after 1855 radically different from its preceding one. In terms of environments that conditioned qualitative reforms, mention can be made of Ethiopia's integration with the capitalist world economy and debut into an international state system. These peculiar and new historical phenomena became permanent features of Ethiopian society ever since the scramble for colonization of Africa. These two conditions presented a challenge and an opportunity for the unfolding of internal developments.[59] The present study examines in detail the qualitative reforms that underpin structural change belonging to the first phase. The discussion on the second phase, namely the period of enlightened absolutism, is outside the purpose of this study. However, for the sake of a complete understanding of Ethiopian absolutism, it seemed relevant to review the period of Haile Selassie I sufficiently to show change and continuity of the epoch. The following discourse is limited to the level of the political process.[60]

Actually some of the "enlightened" reforms had begun during the short period of *lij* Iyasu in 1916 and these included, among others, the security of property and lifting the burden of *asrat* tax (tithe) collection.[61] It was during the reign of Haile Selassie I, starting from the formative period, that enlightenment reforms were introduced from above. As before, centralization of power continued, but there was a difference in the degree and means of cen-

[59] For a synopsis of the reforms see Tsegaye Tegenu, (1994), "A Revolution from Above? Change in the Fiscal and Military Organization of the Ethiopian State, 1855–1913", in Marcus, H. (ed.), *New Trends in Ethiopian Studies. Papers of the 12th International Conference of Ethiopian Studies, I*. pp. 1005–1029.

[60] For an analysis of the various socio-economic reforms during the period of Haile Selassie, readers are advised to read the collective articles written by specialists of various fields in Shiferaw Bekele, ed., (1992), *An Economic History of Ethiopia. The Imperial Era, 1941–1974. V. I.* Draft Manuscript. Department of History, Addis Ababa University.

[61] See Gebre-Igziabihr Elyas (1994), *Prowess, Piety and Politics. The Chronicle of Abeto Iyasu and Empress Zewditu of Ethiopia (1090–1930)*. Köln, pp. 328–331, 342f.

tralization. His centralization process was attained by attacking privileges and by removing the power of the military nobility and traditional territorial aristocracy; and the means of attaining royal power was qualitatively different from the past. The process of demilitarization of society can be explained in terms of the reorganization of the army, the central government, regional administration, and through analysis of the socio-economic reforms undertaken by the King.

The first step was the creation of a centrally controlled loyal army. Haile Selassie I began this process in the late 1920s when he was given the title of *ras.* His reorganization of the army had two aspects and stages. First he reorganized the central troops known as *mähal säfari.*[62] This force was no more to be led by military nobility who belonged to the traditional ruling class, but by army cadets who graduated from military schools. In 1928, some sections of the central troops were renamed the Imperial Body Guard; in the same year students were sent to Europe for military training.[63] In 1934 a military school was opened at Holeta, called the Haile Selassie I Military Training School, with an objective to train officers for the Ethiopian army. This process eliminated the military nobility from their traditional position. The section of the central troops soldiers were recruited anew to strengthen the newly formed Imperial Body Guard.[64] Soldiers first began to receive modern training (drilling and weapon handling) from European military officers and after the European model. A manual was prepared for both the soldiers and officers.[65] The consequence of this reform was that the size of the previous central force was reduced greatly. Menelik had commanded 90,000 central troops, but Haile Selassie I commanded about 5,000 Imperial Body Guards on the eve of the Italian occupation in 1935.

After the end of the Italian occupation of 1935–1941, the King began the process of reorganizing the provincial troops, the second aspect and phase of reorganization of the army. During the time of Menelik, the provincial troops consisted of different sections and were commanded by governor generals,

[62] On the discussion of *mähal säfari* troops see section 5.1.1.

[63] For an account on the development of the Imperial Body Guard of Haile Selassie, see Tekeste Melake (1990), "The Genesis and Growth of the Imperial Body Guard of Ethiopia up to 1960", in *Proceedings of the Fifth Seminar of the Department of History. Addis Ababa University*.

[64] See Mahteme Selassie Wolde Maskel (1962 E.C.), *Zekrä Nägär*. Addis Ababa. p. 110f, (here afterwards abbreviated as Mahteme Selassie (1962 EC).

[65] See *yä Tor Särawit Dänb*, 1927 E.C. Addis Ababa. Deposited at IES Amharic Collection. Haile Selassie's reorganization of the army on 'modern' line should not be confused or interpreted as the creation of a standing army. Often, the creation of a standing army is wrongly understood to mean parades, disciplined fighting, uniforms, use of modern weapons. This view emphasizes only techniques, and does not refer to the nature of the service base of the troops (paid, unpaid, ad hoc or permanent), nor to its size and structure. The structure of a standing army had already been created: a system of permanent military command and combat hierarchy had been developed by Tewodros; a permanent budget for the military was created by Menelik (see chapters three and six below).

centrally appointed officers, and traditional rulers.[66] Haile Selassie I began to form a centralized command by the system of *endärasé* (meaning "like myself") appointed directly by him.[67] The newly organized provincial troop was called *näch´ läbash*, and it was later renamed the Imperial Territorial Army.[68] The formation of this force was to reduce the power of the traditional military nobility and of the governor generals of Menelik. Their power was further undermined by the creation of a regular police force in the provinces.[69] Haile Selassie I not only reorganized the army under a loyal central command staffed by military cadets, but also issued an edict which declared a state monopolization on the import of weapons[70] (in contrast to the time of Menelik, when provincial governors had purchased their own weapons, including private imports from Europe).

Haile Selassie's reforms were not limited to the army; he also reorganized the central government and regional administration. Compared to his predecessors, Haile Selassie I followed a different principle in the form of the organization of central government and regional administration. At the level of central government, the King used a written constitution issued in 1931 and revised in 1955.[71] The 1931 constitution set the formal pattern for a three branch government, namely the executive, the legislative and the judiciary. It was a new form of division and organization of central government carried out on the basis of functional principles. It introduced a bicameral parliament composed of Senate and Chamber of Deputies. Members of the Senate came from the aristocracy (*mäsafint*) elected by the king himself. Members of the Chamber of deputies were elected from and by the class of the *mäkwanent* and the royal military nobility. The parliament's duty was discussion of law submitted to it by the king, and could be dissolved by the king as he pleased. The provision governing the judiciary prescribed that judges shall be elected by the king.[72] The 1931 constitution confirmed and formalized the supremacy of the King in

[66] See section 5.1.2. below.

[67] For the responsibility of the *endärasé*, see *Chärchär Dänb*, manuscript no. 734, IES, Addis Ababa; and *yä-Luel Ras Kassa Hailu Astädadär Dänb: Sgawi ena Mänfäsawi*, manuscript no 1190. IES. Addis Ababa. pp. 12–16.

[68] For the process and formation of this type of force in the region of Wello, see Fekadu Begna (1990), The Wello Territorial Army, 1943–1974", in *Proceedings of the Fifth Seminar of the Department of History*. Addis Ababa University.

[69] see Ibid.

[70] See the decree on the *yä Tor Mäsariya Dänb* issued on May 1924 E.C. deposited at IES, Amharic collection.

[71] For an entire document and introduction to the 1931 constitution, see Mahteme Selassie (1962 E.C.), pp. 756–814. For a further discussion on the 1931 and 1955 constitution see also Markaksi, John and Asmelash Beyene (1967), "Representative Institutions in Ethiopia", in *Journal of Modern African Studies, II.*

[72] For a discussion on the judiciary system see Worku Tafara (1977), "Judicial Administration in Ethiopia: A Reform Oriented Analysis". Thesis on Law, Northwestern University, School of Law, Chicago.

all state affairs. Though the constitution was ratified by 24 members who belonged to the aristocracy and military nobility, it was envisaged as eliminating the threat from traditional aristocrats.[73]

This process was synchronized with the expansion and institution of ministerial departments in the provinces. With the formation of a ministerial system in 1907, government functions became specialized, with an independent institutional representation at the centre.[74] However, with few exceptions, most ministries did not have their own local agencies during the reign of Menelik. In the provinces, government functions were concentrated in the governor-general who received all orders and requests from the king's secretary, a co-ordinating organ of the central government. The governor general had administrative, fiscal, and military power, and often presented a threat to the central government if the governor belonged to the traditional ruling class. Haile Selassie I gradually abolished the office of governor general by establishing local agents of the ministries with specialized jurisdiction in the given area.[75] At first the activities of these local agencies were co-ordinated by a director appointed by the King himself.[76] During the time of Haile Selassie I there was thus a complete change in the principle of regional administration.

Haile Selassie's initial reforms had the intent of eroding the power of the military nobility and bringing an end to "f*eyudal agäzaz*" (feudal rule), to borrow his words.[77] His reorganization of the army and administration of government attacked the fundamental principle of the *gezat* system, a fiscal military territorial unit consolidated at the time of Menelik.[78] By the separation of civil and military functions and the creation of civil servants, Haile Selassie's reforms had demilitarized the society, i.e., the fiscal military system.

From the empirical evidence form the period 1917–1935, Haile Selassie's reforms focused on the economy and social conditions[79] such as codification of the civil and criminal laws (aimed at avoiding arbitrary judgement and pun-

[73] On the power of the aristocracy conferred by the constitution see articles 34–46, in Mahteme Selassie (1962 E.C.), pp. 782–784; For a debate between the emperor and the aristocracy on the drafting of the constitution, see Haile Selassie (1965), *Heywäté ena yä Ityopiya Ermega, vol. I*, Addis Ababa. p. 148f.

[74] For a general discussion see Tzadua, Paulos (1974), "Organization of the Central Administration in Ethiopia", in *Studies in Ethiopian Government and Administration*, Mimeographed, compiled by Asmelash Beyene, HSIU. Addis Ababa.

[75] See his view on the system described in Haile Selassie 1965. p. 45

[76] For a model of regional administration, see *yä Chärchär Dänb*, manuscript no. 734. IES. For regulations promulgated to reform *atbiya dagna* (local judge), custom offices, and others see the collection of decrees in the various chapters of the book by Mahteme Selassie (1962 E.C.)

[77] Haile Selassie 1965. p. 54.

[78] In some European countries the enlightened absolutist state is marked by renewal of crown-noble co-operation. In the Ethiopian case it marked by systematic undermining of the power of aristocracy and military nobility both in the provinces and at the center.

[79] For an analysis of the reforms of the major sectors of the economy, see the collected essays in Shiferaw Bekele, ed. (1992).

ishment by governors); the printing press (which facilitated and encouraged publications); regulations of the credit system (that abolished higher interest); establishment of a central bank (Bank of Ethiopia); expansion of infrastructure (such as roads, and import of airplanes and cars) for transport; establishment of hospitals, schools and construction of plants for electricity; secularization through the formation of an independent central administration of the Ethiopian Church (the Office of *bétä kehnät* at Addis Ababa), thus separating the church from the state; abolishment of corvee labour (free exploitation of peasant labour for cultivation of governors' lands, fencing his house, grinding his corn, etc.)[80]; etc. In the post 1941 period, commercial and economic development was encouraged, and the Haile Selassie I University and many secondary and primary education facilities were established.

Haile Selassie's reforms at the central level, in regional administration, and in the army, required a bureaucratic technical form of organization. The permanent budget for this form of organization had been laid down since the time of Menelik. But the staff of the bureaucratic organization had to be created by the promotion of education. During the time of Haile Selassie I, formal education had expanded and this is one area where all supporters and critics agree. Before Haile Selassie I, the purpose of introducing formal education was for translation.[81]

The principles which Haile Selassie I followed to reorganize the army and to administer the country and other central organs of the state, led to qualitative changes and quantitative expansion. The effect of these reforms was the rise of a middle class which demanded an expansion of exchange value production, (i.e., commodity) and the liberalization of society. This was the contradiction whereby the social and economic base of an enlightened absolutist state was not suited to the character of an absolute rule. Haile Selassie's effort to maintain absolute power based on the growing needs and interests of the middle class led to the revolution of 1974, which ousted him from power.

Seen from the perspective of periodization, the state of Haile Selassie I (1930–1974) is different from the preceding ones, both in its fundamental objective priorities as well as its means. The principles on which he based his policy to organize central power (such as a constitution, the office of prime minister, etc.), and to administer the country (the functional principle of territorial administration), his encouragement of the expansion of the middle class,

[80] Haile Selassie had listed his achievements in his autobiography: Haile Selassie (1965), chap. 12 and passim. It is not clear whether some of his achievements are a continuation of *lij* Iyasu or new policies of his own. Compare the list with that of Iyasu in Gebre-Igziabiher Elyas (1994), chap. 13, pp. 328f translation.

[81] See Mersehe Hazen Wold Qirqos (1935 E.C.), *bä-Dagmawi Menelik Zämän Kayähutna Käsämahut*. Manuscript no. 267. IES. Addis Ababa. pp. 30–32. For Haile Selassie's contacts with Sweden in reorganizing the army, see Halldin Norberg, V. (1977), *Swedes in Haile Selassie's Ethiopia 1924–1952*.

(the preference for an educated elite rather than a military nobility), reforms in the economic base of the state (attack on the privileges of the military nobility, and emphasis on indirect tax), etc. sharply distinguished his period from what had gone before, and the principles and reforms could be called enlightened. Going backwards from the period of enlightened absolutist state, the discourse now turns to review literature pertaining the first phase of Ethiopian absolutism, namely the fiscal military state and society.

3.2. Conceptualization and Interpretation of the First Phase, 1855–1913

In the absence of a theoretical debate on periodization, it was natural to find conflicting and divergent views in characterizing the first phase and in conceptualizing the historical process. This section is a review of the dominant views used to interpret and conceptualize the first phase of Ethiopian absolutism which is here called the fiscal military system. There are four classes of interpretation of the historical situation, whose authors differ in their approach and conceptualization depending on their field of specialization and ideology. There are those who emphasised and interpreted the period as centralization-unification. There are others who discussed empirical facts based on the concepts (or information) of feudal relations, 'modernization', and dependency theory. There are also those who viewed the process in terms of ethnic domination.

The Unification-Centralization View

The unification-centralization view emphasized the untiring campaigns conducted by kings to eliminate regional powers and withstand external aggression.[82] This view stressed the end of the *Zämänä Mäsafint* (Era of Princes) and the coming of the colonial challenge, first by Egypt (1870s), followed by Italy (1880s) and Britain and France (1890s). The period of Tewodros, Yohannes and Menelik was described as the period of unification and the beginning of centralization. The process was understood and explained in the context of consciousness and identity symbolised in the success of battles fought against internal and external forces.

But what was it in terms of unification and centralization? Recounting of battles and campigns may not lead to an understanding of the purpose of the continuous wars and the 'secrete' of Ethiopian independence. Qualitative and quantitative needs, and demands of the logistic system and power structure of

[82] Among others, see Tekle Tsadik Mekuria 1981 E.C. *Asé Tewodros ena yä-Ityopya Andenät*. Addis Ababa. *idem*. 1982 E.C. *Asé Yohannes ena yä Ityopya Andenät.* Addis Ababa. *idem*., 1983 E.C. *Asé Menelik ena Yä-Ityopya Andenät*. Addis Ababa; Rubenson, S. (1976), *The Survival of Ethiopian Independence*. London; *idem*, (1969), *King of Kings Tewodros of Ethiopia*. Addis Ababa; Zewde Gebre-Sellassie (1975), *Yohannes IV of Ethiopia: A Political Biography*. Oxford. For a list of troop movements and conflicts see Appendix B.

society, should have been studied to understand the purpose of those battles. Political and diplomatic history explained mainly appearances. In essence, war was a process of mobilization of resources in a conflicting and threatening environment. War was not only a way of spending but also a redistribution of resources within the ruling class. The collection and use of resources demanded increasing capability in administrative and organizational areas. Reforms were geared to standardization and uniformity of institutional functions for the purpose of centralization of resources. What was centralized through various means was a resource system, and what was unified was the power (decision-making process) to redistribute the resources thus centralized.

The 'Modernization' View

Others understood the period as the beginning of "modernization".[83] The term "modern" was used with reference to time (late nineteenth century) and for the purpose of evoking reforms such as the introduction of some "European" system of institutions and learning (such as formation of a ministerial system, and establishment of schools), and expansion of foreign trade and diplomacy with Europe. The 'modernization' view studied changes, but what kind of changes? According to those who first coined the term, "modernization is a social process of which development is the economic component". The concept of modernization was used essentially to study "economic growth, a shift from agriculture to manufacturing and service, urbanization, educational expansion, and differentiated individuals".[84] In the Ethiopian context, one cannot strictly apply the concept of 'modernization' to explain the social and economic developments of the second half of the nineteenth century for the simple reason that there was no development of capitalist relations.[85]

The internal reforms, which the 'modernization' view attempted to recount were not explained by the essence of the process. Again it was only the appearances of the reforms which were described. The objectives of reforms were not explained in relation to changes in power structure, interest of the state and system of production. For instance there was no analysis as to who had benefited from the reforms. The present work specifies and explains the nature of the internal changes.

Feudalism, Semi-feudal and Semi-capitalist Views

Another understanding of the social system was based on the terms feudalism, semi-feudalism and semi-capitalism. There was a conceptual difference and

[83] See Marcus, H.G. (1975), *The Life and Times of Menelik II: Ethiopia.* Oxford; Darkwah, R.H.K. (1975), *Shewa, Menelik and the Ethiopian Empire, 1813–1889*. London. Rubenson, S. (1969); Pankhurst, R. (1990), *A Social History of Ethiopia.* Addis Ababa.

[84] See Tilly, Charles (1984), *Big Structures, Large Processes, Huge Comparisons.* New York.

[85] See Part IV below.

empirical problem among those scholars who use the feudalism category. A group of scholars saw feudalism as a lord-vassal relationship, and from this perspective they characterized society as a disintegrated polity.[86] This definition emphasized the political and personal aspects of the kings.

Others reduced the definition of feudalism to rent-ownership and defined it as 'private' ownership of land by the nobility. This view not only ignored the aspect of non-economic coercion in the system, but also based its claim on a merely semantic discussion.[87] The empirical ground of this view has been critically examined by Donald Crummey and his colleagues who documented land holdings registered in monasteries in the regions of Bägémder, Gojjam, Wollo and northern Shewa. Although not yet conclusive, important research results as regards the land holdings of the nobility and the transgenerational continuity of the class have been brought to light.[88]

Still others defined feudalism in terms of social status, and on this ground they rejected characterization of Ethiopia as a feudal society since they saw no material and cultural difference between the nobility and the peasantry.[89] In the first place status cannot be taken as a crucial factor to define and characterize a feudal society. Secondly, material development or underdevelopment can be explained by different approaches and by different conceptual categories[90], and there is no logical ground for using it to define feudalism. A society with a developed material culture is not necessarily feudal, and feudalism is a type of social formation, not an economic theory such as the theory of economic growth.

[86] Based on the definition of feudalism as a lord-vassal relationship, Shiferaw Bekele wrote an essay reinterpreting the state of the *Zämänä Mäsafint* and extended this interpretation to analyze the career of Emperor Tewodros (1855–68) and Emperor Yohannes (1878–89). See, Shiferaw Bekele (1990a), "Reflections on the Power Elite of the Wärä Séh Mäsafint (1786–1853)", in *Annales d'Ethiopie, XV*; see also Taddese Beyene, Pankhurst, R. and Siferaw Bekele, eds., (1990), *Kasa and Kasa. Papers on the Lives, Times and Images of Téwodros II and Yohannes IV (1855–1889).* Addis Ababa.

[87] See Donham, D. (1986), "Old Abyssinia and the new Ethiopian empire: themes in social history", in Donham, D. and James, W. (eds.), *The Southern Marches of Imperial Ethiopia*. Cambridge, pp. 8–17.

[88] See among others, Crummey, Donald (1983), "Family and Property amongst the Amhara Nobility" in *Journal of African History, XXIV, no.2*, pp. 207–20; *idem.* (1989), "Three Amharic Documents of Marriage and Inheritance from the Eighteenth and Nineteenth Centuries" in Taddase Beyene (ed.) *Proceedings of the Eighth International Confrence of Ethiopian Studies, vol 1*, Addis Ababa, pp. 315–327; *idem.* (1988), "Theology and Political Conflicts During the Zämänä Mäsafint: the case of Esté in Begemder" in *Proceedings of the Ninth International Congress of Ethiopian Studies, Moscow*; Crummey, D. and Shummet Sishange (1988), "The Lands of the Church of Däbrä S`ähay Qwusqwam, Gonder" in *Proceedings of the Tenth International Confrence of Ethiopian Studies*. Paris; Crummey, D., Shumet and Daniel (1991), "A Gondariane Land Grant in Gojjam: The Case of Qäranyo Mädhane Aläm" in *Proceedings of the XIth International Confrence of Ethiopian Studies*, Addis Ababa. Crummey, D. and Shumet Sishagne (1991), "Land Tenure and the Social Accumulation of Wealth in Eighteenth-Century Ethiopia: Evidence from the Qwesqwam Land Register" in *International Journal of African Studies, 24: 2.*

[89] See Merid W. Aregay (1984), "Society and Technology in Ethiopia, 1500–1800" in *Proceedings of the Seminar of the Departmnent of History, vol. I.* Addis Ababa University. p. 166.

[90] See for instance the treatment of economic problem in Chapter Seven below.

There is thus a conceptual and empirical problem in the use and definition of feudalism. Not very far from this problem was the use of the term semi-feudal and semi-capitalist.[91] This approach tried to "synthesize" aspects of feudalism and "modernization", and to this end it attempted to give empirical substance to the social context of power and emergence of a "market economy". Though the insights of these authors were understandable, their interpretation lacked exhaustive empirical data and, above all, an elaborated theoretical framework to grasp the essence of the period and understand its dynamics. Certain aspects (reforms or developments) such as foreign trade were picked up and discussed to understand their individual meaning and if possible the cause of their introduction. But the kind of change which they discussed is not structured, so much so that certain factors were overemphasised and described as the determing influence on everything else. In their works, changes were not discussed within the context of structural constraints, objectives of the state and class interests of the military nobility.

There are still others who adopted dependency theory to characterize developments of the period as "enclavistic capitalism".[92] Interpretation of the period using dependency theory is not applicable for various reasons. By dependency it was meant that Ethiopia's economy was compelled to reflect the development and expansion of another economy which subordinated it. As we shall see it was not the whole economy, but only the import and export sector which was relatively integrated into the capitalist economy, and that too was on the conditions and terms of the Ethiopian state. The whole economy was serving the interest and well being of the fiscal military state and its social basis, the military nobility. The dependency view emphasized only external factors and their influences, and ignored internal changes as related to structural problems. For instance, the production processes were not addressed; nor were the property relationships and the fiscal system and its effect on productivity.

Ethnic and Regional Domination View

This category includes a wide range of views. From this perspective, motives and mechanisms of internal reforms were seen as a means of regional domination and ethnic subjugation. Most of the studies belonged to the centre-periph-

[91] This type of characterization is used by Addis Hiwot, (1975), *Ethiopia: From Autocracy to Revolution*. London. Review of African Political Economy; Bahru Zewde (1984); Lapiso G. Delebo (1983 E.C). *Yä-Ityopya Yä-Gäbar Serä`at ena Jimer Kapitalizm 1900–1966*. Addis Ababa.

[92] See Schaefer, Charles G.H. (1990), "Enclavistic Capitalism in Ethiopia, 1906–1936. A Study of Currency, Banking, and Informal Credit Networks". Vols. I & II. Dissertation in History, Illinois, University of Chicago. His conclusion is drawn from his analysis of banking institutions. Presumably he understood banking as representing a higher form of exchange, which is capitalism. But capitalism involves not merely monetary exchange but also the domination of production processes by capital.

ery perspective of anthropologists.[93] Some Master theses written on internal/ regional history[94] also entertained such perspectives. Recently there emerged views which interpret the process of centralization as a form of ethnic domination, in particular as an Amhara ethnic domination.[95] This view is trying to shape itself as some intellectuals began to "discover the ethnic past" for the purpose of creating ethnic consciousness. In this view, there is no difference between cultural domination and system oppression, a difference which is crucial in seeking solutions to the problem under discussion.

The ethnic perspective interpreted internal migration and settlement as colonialism. National conflicts were not characteristic of preindustrial states and societies. National conflicts belonged to the era of 'national capitalism', and Ethiopia was a preindustrial society. But the internal history of the country was marked by interregional population migrations and settlements. Some migrations were spontaneous and others were impelled by conquest and reconquest.[96]

The motive behind Tewodros' campaigns in north and central Ethiopia, and Menelik's power expansion to southern Ethiopia, were not to extend an ethnic domination. The campaigns were launched for the purpose of centralizing the distribution and use of resource systems. When looked at from the traditional agricultural policy of the Ethiopian state, the phenomenon was not unique to the period. For instance, throughout its history, the state had encouraged settlement and cultivation of new areas (called *hagär maqnat*) since any one who cultivated land had the obligation to pay tax. Increase in revenue depended on the given size of available land and the labour force. This interest and agricultural reforms of the Ethiopian state continued during the times of Tewodros, Yohannes and Menelik.[97]

What gave the period its particular characteristic was the concerted effort of the kings to take responsibility for the remuneration of troops and to secure an

[93] See collection of essays in Donham, Donald and James, W. (ed.) 1986; see also Triulzi, A. (1981), *Salt, Gold and Legitmacy. Prelude to the History of a No-Man's Land Belä Shangul, Wallagga, Ethiopia (ca. 1800–1898)*. Napoli; McClellan, C. W. (1988), *State Transformation and National Integration: Gedo and the Ethiopian Empire, 1895–1935*.

[94] See Tesema Ta`a (1980), "The Oromo of Wallaga: A Historical Survey to 1910". M.A. Thesis in History, A.A.U; Tecle Haimanot Gebre Selassie (1984), "The Wayto of Lake Tana: An Ethno-history". M.A. Thesis, Department of History, Addis Ababa University.

[95] A serious attempt, at least in its methodology, which aspires to write history from an ethnic perspective is the one written by Mohammed Hassen (1990), *The Oromo of Ethiopia. A History 1570–1860*. Cambridge.

[96] This phenomenon existed throughout history: since the Semitic movement to the south in the 330s, Agews during Gudit in the tenth century, central Amhara during Amde Sion, Gurage in Shewa, Ahmed Gran of Hara, Oromo settlements up to Eritrea highlands, Tigrean settlements on Afar regions during Yohannes, Shewan settlements in the south during Menelik. See among others, Aläqa Tayye Gabra Mariam, (1922), *Yä Ityopia Hezb Tarik* ("History of the People of Ethiopia"). Hudson, G. and Tekeste Negash, translators. Uppsala.

[97] See Chapters Three and Five below.

independent provisioning system for the army. They wanted the logistic basis to be under the expense of the state. This required increasing the fiscal capacity of the state. In an agrarian economy this could be nothing other than controlling the system of direct taxation. Change in the system of taxation was effected by all possible means. Kings introduced major reforms both at the institutional level (administration of tax) and in the structure of the direct taxes themselves (tax-technical measures) to enhance the financing capacity of the state. Among the different tax-technical measures, are found such devices as fixing the rate of land tax payment, standardizing land tax payment, individual registration of land tax payment, merging of land tax payment obligations, introducing tithe as regular and universal payment and/or base-broadening as done during the time of Menelik. Standardization and uniformity introduced in the system of taxation and military organization are wrongly conceived as colonization by the proponents of the ethnic domination view.

Centralization was an attack on political and economic particularization and was effected through standardization and uniformity. Politically, centralization broke the military power of the princes by way of creating a centrally controlled standing army; economically, by changing the systems of direct and indirect taxation. Centralization, defined as standardization and uniformity of a system, is mistakenly understood to mean colonization of an ethnic group. However, this does not mean that there was no cultural domination which one may expect in a feudal society.

Colonialism as a motive and a method is used mainly in connection with the phenomenon of monopoly capitalism which subjugated Asian, Latin American and African countries when seeking raw materials, markets and labour forces. It is a concept used in reference to the stages of and changes in the structure of the capitalist economic system. Unless one is tempted to define settlement as colonialism, the use of the term in the Ethiopian context is irrelevant not only on the grounds of historical definition of the term, but also on its basic political and economic assumptions about the Ethiopian reality. The present work explains the political and economic reality of the period, based on the model of a resource system.

The various views and conceptualizations of the historical phenomena during the second half of the nineteenth century have been thus summarized. In spite of their differences in ideology and conceptual tools of analysis, all the four views have one similarity. In their methodology, they emphasized particular events and focused on understanding the motives and meanings of individual actions and events. In such studies the object of inquiry was to explain individual Kings, namely Tewodros (1855–1868), Yohannes IV (1872–1889), and Menelik II (1889–1913), and their motivations for action.

This methodology encountered problems when it came to an explanation of a historical process. First some historians use eclectical methods to explain historical events, which created difficulty in understanding changes in a social system. The most dominant form of eclectical interpretation was the combination of class and ethnic domination[98], which some authors turned to one mode or the other when their constructs failed to explain a process. Secondly, these authors and readers alike engaged in emotionally charged debate to give meaning to the actions and thoughts of each King, but not to the structural peculiarities.[99]

Analysis of the period by studying individual Kings and their motivations for action set a methodological limit to identifying the qualitative elements that marked 1855 as a turning point. Controversies often pleaded for revision and further research; consequently, there was no consensus on delineating qualitative aspects attributed to the second half of the nineteenth century.

There is another approach which this present work suggests and analyses, namely, the study of ensemble rules, relations and meanings that are not reducible to individual Kings. In this approach, the study of events and actions are methodologically tied to the study of structure. The actions of the kings are produced, motivated, channelled and organized by the structures.

Structure here means the spatial distribution of integral parts and the mode of their linkage. Structure refers to the properties of distinguishable parts of an entity and the rules that specify their relative arrangements with respect to each other. Structural analysis reveals what the parts are in a structure and how they are related to each other. *Change* comes in the lack of linkage on the interdependent parts of the structure. *Process* is an attribute of a structure; it is structure in function. In this study process is not conceived as different from and external to structure. In historical study, structural study refers to an inquiry on the ensemblance of rules, roles, and relations that produce and reproduce human thought and action. By *system* is meant a collection of parts that are interrelated in such a way that there is some sense in regarding them as a coherent entity. Structure is a methodological issue related to the process of

[98] Among others see, Markakis, J. (1974), *Ethiopia: Anatomy of a Traditional Polity*. Oxford; McClellan, C. W. (1988).

[99] On Tewodros see the collected articles in Taddese Beyene, Pankhurst, R. and Shiferaw Bekele (eds.), 1990; Zänäb, (1902), *yä Tewodros Tarik* : (*"The Chronicle of King Theodore of Abyssinia")*. Litman, E. (ed.). Leipzig, passim; See also Täklä Iyasus, *yä Negus Täklä Haimanot Tarik*, manuscript no. 254, IES, pp. 68, 72, 73, 74, 75; Rassam, H. (1869), *Narrative of the British Mission to Theodore. vol. 2*. London 1869. p. 18. On Yohannes see Caulk, R.A. (1972), "Religion and the State in Nineteenth Century Ethiopia", in *Journal of Ethiopian Studies, X, 1*. Crummey, D. (1978), "Orthodoxy and Imperial Reconstruction in Ethiopia, 1854–1878", in *Journal of Theological Studies, XXIX, 2*. Zewde Gebre Selassie (1975). On Haile Selassie see among others Bahru Zewde (1992), "Haile Selassie: from Progressive to Reactionary" in *Preproceedings of the Sixth Michigan State University Conference on Northeast Africa*. Compiled by Hinnant, J. and Finne, B. Michigan. pp. 29–43. For motivation and leadership of Haile Selassie see Marcus, H. (1994), "Haile Selassie's Leadership", in *New Trends in Ethiopian Studies. Papers of the 12th International Conference of Ethiopian Studies. Vol.I.*, pp. 840–845.

cognition, while system is a method which describes technical problems in approaching detailed empirical research. However, method is not separated from cognition itself; both form a framework for interpretation and explanation.

A structural approach and system analysis as a methodology for social cognition, provide a holistic mind-frame which will permit one to view different aspects as if they existed as whole entities or sub-systems interacting with one another. This approach offers a diversity of methodology to investigate the dynamic interrelationships in campaigns, independence and modernization. In the present work, this task is accomplished by the theory of absolutism which is holistic (depicts structural elements of a system), and by a resource system model (which explains human purpose).

4. Source Material, Method and Disposition

Source materials for this study came from the manuscript section and the library of the Institute of Ethiopian Studies, Addis Ababa University; from documents in the main archive, library and some departments of the Patriarch's Office in the Ethiopian Orthodox Church, at Addis Ababa; materials from the manuscript section of the national library at the Ministry of Culture and Sports, Addis Ababa; documents from the Medahni Alem *däbr*-church of Mäkälé, and the Chäläqot *däbr*-Church, both located in the region of Tigray; reports from the Public Record Office, London; and manuscripts from the British Museum Library, London and Paris.

A wide range of narrative sources and documentary materials were used for explanation and analysis. These source materials included chronicles, fiscal sources such as tax documents and land surveys, legislative sources like edicts, administrative sources such as rules and codes of governance and correspondences, church records, private sources in the forms of wills, newspapers, traveller accounts, and other miscellaneous sources. These sources, even if they are considered as primary source materials, are not descriptive testimonies. They are products of organizational objectives and polices and they require theories for their understanding before yielding reliable information. The selection and use of source materials is not separated from the hypothesis and method adopted by the research.

The purpose of this study is to synthesize the development of Ethiopian state and society at a particular historical stage as constructed in the theoretical model. The social system was characterized by the essence of the state (the fiscal military system). It was a specific socio-economic system belonging to the last stage of feudalism. Conceptually, for the purpose of analysis, the system could be divided into subsystems. The breakdown consisted of the fiscal subsystem and the military subsystem. Again the fiscal subsystem was broken down into sub-subsystems such as private land ownership, tax and revenue structures. The military subsystem was composed of sub-subsystems such as forms and principles of revenue allocation, items and priorities of spending and structure of the army. Each particular sub-and subsystem had its own interrelated parts and conceptual argument lines as outlined in the parameters of the model. But all the subsystems were causally and structurally interrelated into a higher and complex whole: the fiscal military system. This system again interacted with the larger environment, namely the capitalist world economy and the international state system. Based on such systematic methods sources were selected and used in this work.

In dealing with a broad, complex topic and hypothetical model such as in this work, in the best of circumstances, authors often rely heavily on synthesis and research results prepared by other scholars. This work did basic studies in areas of land ownership, systems of taxation, government revenue and expenditure as well as structural organization of the army. There was an obvious need for collecting and using primary and contemporary source materials that were left behind. Source criticism, which involved deciphering texts, interpreting their contents, and confirming authenticity and reliability, is assumed self-evident to readers. Discussing every source material by following each process of source criticism would have made this work too cumbersome and could make readers lose sight of essential meanings.

The effort in this work was not intended to impress readers with a large collection of *new* source materials which, following the empirical tradition, is considered as an end in itself. As a work of interpretation, the study is compelled to offer a coherent and qualitative meaning to available and accessible source materials hitherto used by researchers. For instance, in the case of land ownership, scholars have collected documents[100] which they believe throw light on the system of land tenure. Before the second world war, Conti Rossini collected land charters of northern Ethiopia and translated them into French.[101] He never used these documents for studying the system of land tenure.[102] Huntingford translated these documents into English and used them to study the land tenure system of the middle ages along with their type of administration.[103] Pankhurst used the sources to write his book on state and land.[104] Following the descriptive manner of Huntingford and Pankhurst, Haddis Gebre-

[100] The documents are called *Däbdäbé*, which literally means letter. The *Däbdäba* deal with grants, wills, sales, gifts and records of judicial decisions. They are recorded in the blank folios and margins of holy books of the churches. They are thus also known as Marginalia.

[101] Conti Rossini (1954), "Documenta ad Illustrandam Historiam: I. Libre Axumae", in *Corpus Scriptorium Christianorum Orienalium, Vol. 54 text, Vol. 58, French version.*

[102] Huntingford, G.W.B. (1965), *The Land Charters of Northern Ethiopia*. Addis Ababa, p. XI.

[103] Ibid. pp. 8–14.

[104] Pankhurst, R. ((1966), *State and Land in Ethiopian History*. Addis Ababa.

Meskel completed a Ph.D. manuscript.[105] All of these authors discussed the source documents following the normative aspect: division and discussion of documents as Church lands, private lands, crown lands, land sale and land dispute. The documents had never been used for the study of aristocratic patrimony and the economic base of the state. In the present study, the documents collected by those authors, supplemented by new ones procured from archival works[106], are analysed to discuss types of historical land ownership rights. The principles and rights of ownership are explained based on available codified laws which register, among other things, the earlier custom, usage and rules as regards land ownership.

A systematic study of land ownership based on the concept of property ownership, facilitated a separate study of taxation as an independent historical subject. The intricate relationship between ownership and taxation has been systematically differentiated, and sources which once have been difficult to comprehend, and which lend themselves to limited use, have now been set into context to give them wider meaning. A case in point are the documents and details contained in the book of *Zekrä Nägär.*[107] In this major work of documentation and account, undifferentiated categories of taxes are mentioned intricately along with ownership right, principles of assessment, rates of taxation, forms of payments, forms of revenue allocation, described together with local and time variations. Sometimes, all these explanations were found in a paragraph, with all their obscure and complex forms as they existed in reality and so there was the problem of how to differentiate them from each other. Based on a systems approach, the various component parts of taxation were sorted out and studied as they interrelated with and affected the state and the economy[108]. With this approach it became possible to use the documents contained in *Zekrä Nägär* and land charter documents mentioned above.

The study of taxation as an independent subject presented an opportunity to analyse the revenue of the state. In earlier works, tax documents were not analysed for sources of government revenue at a given point in history. The focus was mainly on translation, and in some cases the translated work was

[105] Haddis Gebre-meskel (June 1992), "A Survey of Representative Land Charters of the Ethiopian Empire (1314–1868) and Related Marginal Notes in Manuscripts in the British Library, The Royal Library and the University Libraries of Cambridge and Manchester". Ph.D. Thesis submitted to School of Oriental and African Studies, University of London.

[106] The new documents are referred to as *Mäzgäb* which is a land register document of a church. It gives a detailed list of the number and size of individual holders of church lands found in different districts. These documents, which are microfilmed by Crummey and his colleagues, are deposited at the Center for African Studies at the University of Illinois (USA) and at the Institute of Ethiopian Studies at Addis Ababa University. Their project however covers only a number of churches in Gondar, Gojjam, Shäwa and Wällo. One might find documents of such a nature in the *Ethiopian Manuscript Microfilm Library*. Addis Ababa/Collegeville, Minnesota. (EMML), catalogued by Getachew Haile.

[107] Mahteme Selassie (1962. E.C.).

[108] For further comments see the first three pages in Chapter Three below.

accompanied by a general comment on government revenue.[109] In the present study available tax documents are analysed for the study of government revenue. The approach used to study the documents facilitated the understanding of the historical meaning, use, and significance of certain document such as *seratä gebr*[110] and *seratä mängest*[111], which hitherto received only translation and limited general comments.

The study of government revenue and expenditure helped to clarify the structure and size of the army. It also helped to synthesise the fragmented accounts on provision and campaigns stated in chronicles; it also made it possible to comment on the size of the army.[112] Increase or decrease in revenue clarified structural change in the army and because of this, the intention and meanings of various reforms expressed separately and in disconnected form also became clear.

Research results and information stated in secondary source materials were also used as supplementary sources. In fact, some of them were rich in details and yielded reliable facts, thanks to the empiricist tradition dominating Ethiopian historical studies. In the present study, the data quoted or referred to from these sources have been given qualitative meanings because they were used in a qualitatively different hypothetical context, and in a complex milieu which was necessary to the understanding of their full meaning and expression. Even then, secondary source materials were subjected to close examination; the purposes for which they were written, and the levels and field of expertise mattered very much. Accounts of contemporary travellers[113] and interviews held with knowledgeable and authoritative persons[114] imparted broad views and

[109] For further comments and literature review see Chapter Four below.

[110] As to the list of documents and for partial translation of *Serä`atä Gebr* see Kropp, M. (1989a), "The Seràtä *Gebr*: A mirror view of daily life at the Ethiopian Royal court in the Middle ages" in Taddese Beyene (ed.) *Proceedings of the 8th International Conference of Ethiopian Studies, I.* Addis Ababa, p. 219.

[111] Literally, *Säräte Mängest* means the Laws and Order of the State. On the list where one finds the documents of *Seräte Mängest* see Huntingford, G.W.B. (1990), *The Historical Geography of Ethiopia. From the First Century AD to 1704.* Oxford, pp. 8–9. For translation of the document see Bairu Tafla and Scholler, H. (1976), "Sera`ata Mangest. An Early Ethiopian Constitution", in *Verfassung und Recht in Übersee. A Quarterly on Law and Modernization, Vol. 9, No. 4.* pp. 487–499. The text is translated into German by Varenbergh, Joseph (1915/1916), "Studien zur Abessinischen Reichsordnung", in *Zeitschrift fur Assyriologie, band XXX.*

[112] For further comment see section 5.2.

[113] For a list of bibliography and brief comments on travellers account see Pankhurst, Rita and Pankhurst, Richard (1978), "A Select Annotated Bibliography of Travel Books on Ethiopia, Part One and Pat Two", in *African Journal, IX, 2*, and 3 respectively.

[114] Among others, interviews were held with *Ato* Gäsäsä Bezabh, age 78, who was a former judge of the High Court of Tigray region, and a relation to Emperor Tewedros through the descendants of his father and Emperor Yohannes IV through the descendants of his mother; Fitawrari Eyasu Asbäha, age 75, former provincial governor in the region of Tigray; and Malaka Genet Serse Dingel Arefe Ayne, Head of the Däbrä Gänät Medahini Alem Church, age 67. He had served at the church in different capacities since the age of 28. All of my informants are residents of Mäkälé, capital town of Tigray region. The interviews were held in August 1993, two times each.

gave clarity of understanding to the mechanisms involved, and in this way showed how the system functioned.

Initially, the project was conceived with curiosity and investigative questions rather than with the available sources in clear sight. The subsequent search and work on primary sources proved to be time consuming. Though approached systematically, the analyses herein rested on heterogeneous, and widely dispersed collections of materials, and it was difficult to treat all questions with equal thoroughness.

The present study is divided into six parts consisting of eight chapters, in addition to the appendix. Part I is an introduction which deals with the theoretical and methodological framework and source materials of the study. A resource system model is constructed whose parametres and properties are believed to catch the essence of the process and development of the fiscal military state and society. In Part II, the background and genesis of the fiscal military system are explained. In Chapter One, the changes made in the mode of military organization and techniques of warfare as consequences of the crisis of the sixteenth century are probed, as well as the limited economic opportunites and potentials that put constraints on military capacity. In this chapter, the conflict between military needs (principles of revenue allocation) and aristocratic and local lords' interests (principle of revenue distribution and administration) are stressed. In Chapter Two some of the favourable conditions for the emergence of the fiscal military state are deliberated, and the types of land ownership rights and the structure of taxation to facilitate the collection and allocation of revenue for military purposes are dealt with.

In Part III the ways and means of creating revenue for military ends is investigated. In Chapter Three, the major reforms and changes in the structure of taxes, and in the area of tax administration, both at the central and local level are examined. Chapter Four treats the structure and size of government revenue, and attempts to answer two central points: the question of how much the system collected, and who was paying and how much.

In Part IV, priorities and items of government spending are explored with the objective of determining how the planned nature of the logistic system was used to solve earlier military barriers. This task is mainly accomplished in Chapter Six, which handles on recruitment, methods and levels of remuneration, nature of payment, and on ways of supplying and distributing provisions to the army. To facilitate discussion on items of government expenditure and structured changes, the various components of the army are analysed, and this is the task of Chapter Five. In this chapter types of army organization, systems of command, military administration and number of troops mobilised for campaigns and engagements are elucidated.

Part V of the book deals further with the objectives of revenue and expenditure distribution clarified in Parts III & IV. Government economic policy as related to structural problems of economic development are analyzed. Attempts are made to see reforms as they affect and influence the development of the private economy, and to identify those who benefited from the system as well as the economic dynamics of the period. To facilitate the discourse, hypotheses on structural economic problems are argued in Chapter Seven. In this context, there is an exposition of the objective of the state *vis à vis* the immediate and practical socio-economic problems of the period. In Chapter Eight, the major areas of change brought about by the motives and interests of the state are accounted and the driving force of economic change is scanned.

In Part VI, the study's premises, approach and major findings are given. The findings are highlighted through a contrast with the historical development in other African countries and with European absolutism.

Part II
The Genesis of the Fiscal Military State

Introduction

In Part II, one of the necessary preconditions for the rise of an absolutist state is explained. The economic and military power base and the class transformation of the aristocracy in relation to the changes that occurred in the fiscal and military organization of the feudal state from 1563–1855 are analyzed. The purpose of the analysis was to look for answers to the question of why the fiscal military state came into being.[1]

The Ethiopian state had experienced a long history of continuity and change emanating from a central core. The feudal state was influenced by the Aksumite Empire (131 BC–940 AD) which was dissolved as a result of unfavourable internal and external conditions.[2] Upon the fall of the Aksumite empire, different principalities emerged to form a loose confederation under the Zagwe dynasty (1150–1270). This dynasty was replaced by the "restored Solomonic dynasty" whose rulers launched successive military campaigns to subdue and absorb regional and local rulers.[3] By the second half of the 15th century, the rulers succeeded in establishing a centralized state in which Kings had absolute control over the affairs of state and church. From 1540s onwards this autocratic state began to decline as the result of three major historical events.

The continuous war between the Solomonic Christian Kings and the Moslem aristocrats of Adal in the years 1527–1541[4] was one of the factors contributing to the crisis. The intermittent and often swift migration and wars of the large Oromo ethnic groups, commencing in 1522 and escalating more at the turn of the century[5], was the second factor. The third factor was external, related to the Turkish occupation of Massawa and their encroachment into the interior[6] as well as the coming of the Portuguese and Jusuit missionaries[7]. It is

[1] The attempt to present an analysis of Ethiopian feudalism has made this work bulky thick with facts. In order not to derail readers from the purpose of the present work, it was advised to cut out a substantial portion of the work intended to deal with aristocratic patrimony and system of taxation in the period before the rise of the fiscal military state. Instead, readers are advised to refer to, among others, the works of Donald Crummey, particularly his forthcoming work tentatively titled as "*Property and Polity. Land and Society in Christian Kingdom of Ethiopia 1300–1900*".

[2] See Sergew Hable Sellassie (1972), *Ancient and Medieval Ethiopian History to 1270*. Addis Ababa.

[3] For details see Taddesse Tamirat (1972), *Church and State in Ethiopia*, 1270–1527. Oxford.

[4] Ibid.

[5] Among others see Mohammed Hassen (1990).

[6] See Dombrowski, F.A. (1985), *Ethiopia's Acess to the Red Sea*. Koln. pp. 21ff.

[7] For the endeavour of Jusuits missionaries to spread the Catholic religion at the royal court and for the concomitant religious controversy see Bartricki, A. and Mantel-Niecko, J. (1971), "The Role and Significance of the Religious Conflicts and Peoples Movement in the Political Life of Ethiopia in the Seventeenth and Eighteenth Centuries", in *Rassegna di Studi Etiopici, XXIV*. 1969–1970. Roma.

beyond the purpose and scope of this work to present a detailed discussion about the immediate effects of the sixteenth century crisis.[8]

The long term effects and consequences of the crisis can be traced in two major interrelated trends and developments. On the one hand there was a dramatic change in both the mode of the military organization and the institutional organization of the state power which required a consolidated and centralized system of revenue acquisition and distribution; on the other hand there was a rigid type of land ownership rights, structure of taxation, and administration of revenue that had a limited capacity for continuance vis-a-vis the new military changes and organization of the aristocracy. The following two chapters attempt to explain the the long-term structural effects of the sixteenth century crisis and the internal contradictions and dynamics which led to the genesis of a new fiscal military system.

[8] The work of Mered Welde Aregay is described as the best on this period, but it is not available for a detailed review. The full title reads Merid W. Aregay (1971), "Southern Ethiopia and the Christian Kingdom, 1508–1708, with Special Reference to the Galla Migrations and their Consequences". Ph.D. Thesis, University of London. See also Abir, M. (1980), *Ethiopia and the Red Sea: the rise and decline of the Solomonic dynasty and Muslim-European rivalry in the region.* London.

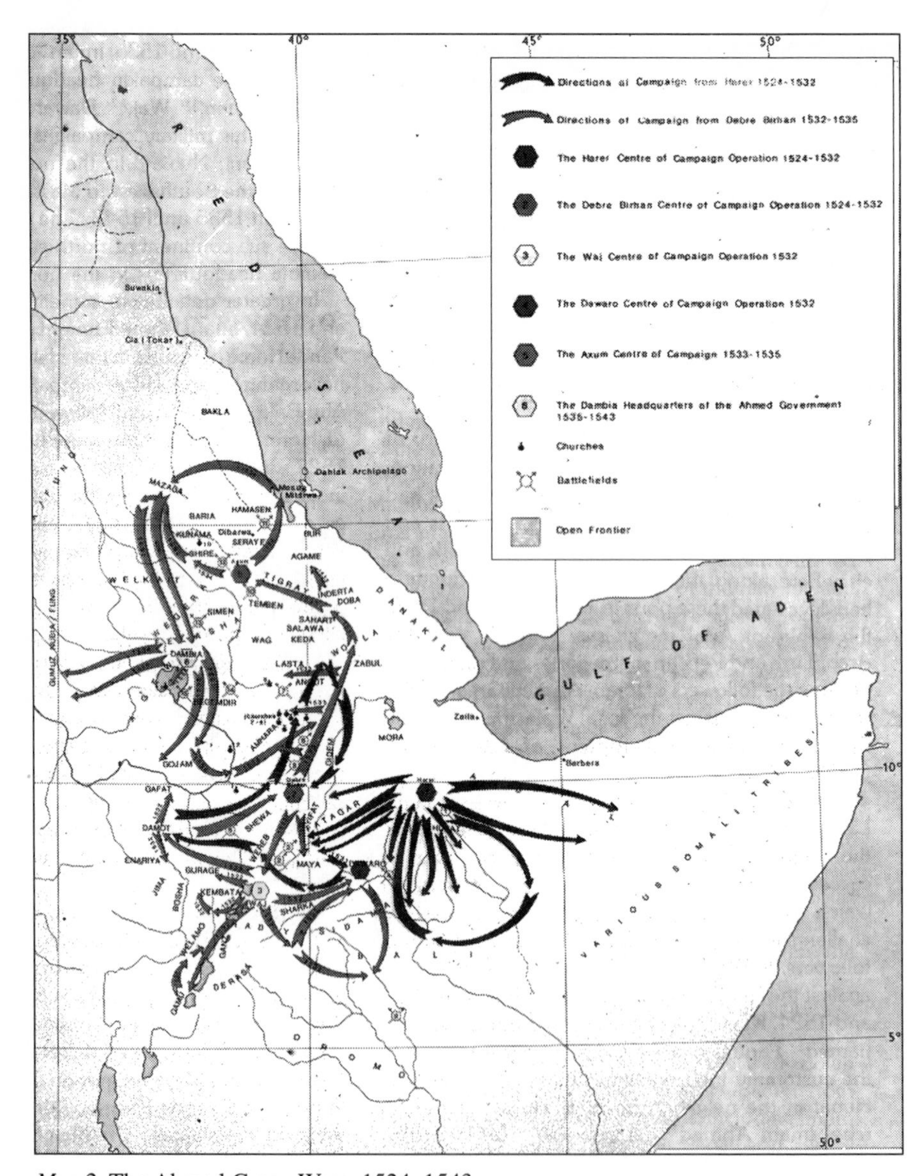

Map 2. The Ahmed Gragn Wars, 1524–1543.
Source: *Ethiopia: a Cradle of History* (1989), Addis Ababa.

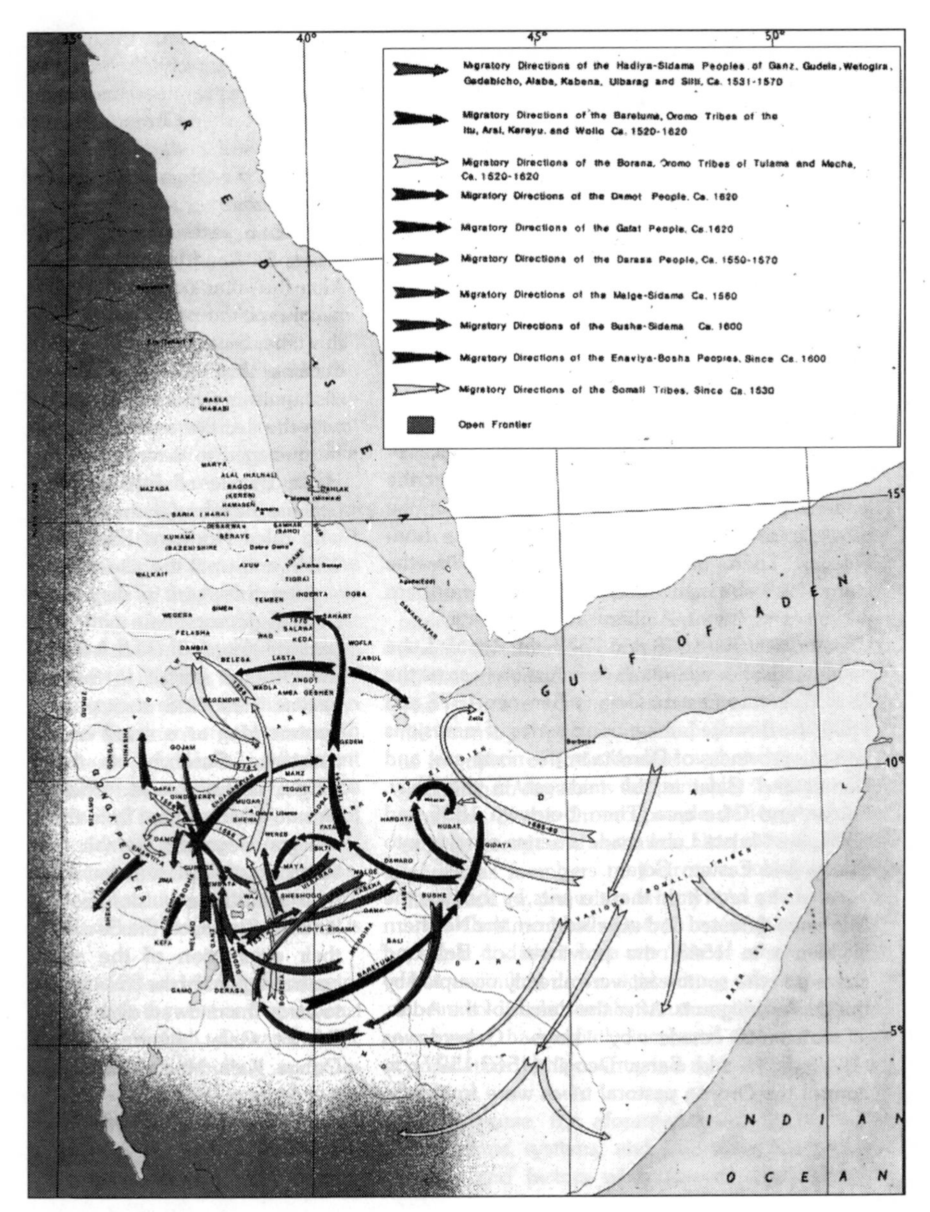

Map 3. The Great Ethnic Migrations, 1520–1660.
Source: *Ethiopia: a Cradle of History* (1989), Addis Ababa.

CHAPTER ONE

Organization of the Aristocracy and Logistic Base of the Power Struggle, 1563–1855

The purpose of this chapter is to discuss the changes made in the mode of military organization and techniques of warfare resulting from the crisis of the sixteenth century. The chapter deals with the organization and power base of the territorial aristocracy who were the agents and bearers of the system. It also deals with methods of troop remuneration with the aim of measuring the performance of fiscal systems against military developments and incessant warfare.

1.1. Militarization of the Court and Provincial Governorship, 1563–1632

After the crisis of the sixteenth century, institutional changes occurred at the court and in the provinces. The royal court of the princes was being organized entirely along regimental lines, called *shaläqa*, (commander of a thousand soldiers). Formerly, court troops were organized along a functional line (*kitab*) or identified by their functional assignment such as *bét-ayet*. In this system the function was given to a region, not specifically to a regiment. This system was later replaced by the title of *shaläqa*, which inaugurated the establishment of a permanent regimental unit under a permanent command at a rank of major (*shaläqa*). This form of regimental organisation probably appeared late during the reign of Susenyos (1563–97).[9] Since then, the title and the kind of functional organisation attached to it, became very important in the order of ranks.[10] During the Era of Princes (1755–1855), the term *shaläqa* came to

[9] Berry, L.V.B. (1976), "The Solomonic Monarchy at Gonder, 1630–1755: An Institutional Analysis of Kingship in the Christian Kingdom of Ethiopia". Ph.D. Thesis. Boston University, pp. 256f.

[10] See the 1690 list of precedence document in Huntingford, G.W.B. (1965), pp. 109–110.

refer to all regiments that performed various functions at the King's or prince's palace.[11]

Another important change which indicated militarization of the court was the disappearance of the office of the *gera bitwädäd*, who was responsible for civil administration. According to the new arrangement (as stated in the document of *seratä mängest*), the chief court military administrator (*blaten-géta*) began to assume the power of administrating justice (control over the *azazh* and *wämbär*) in the court.[12]

In the provinces, a relatively new military governorship office developed resulting from decentralization of the command and organization of the army for the purpose of fostering effective regional defence. Formerly, troops were under central command fed by the court and by the regional tax secretariat, the *ras mareqé*.[13] In the new system, governors were delegated to use the tax from their regions for organizing the royal army. In the areas where the old administration survived, Kings began to assign new governorship titles with fiscal and military power. In the middle of the crisis, some four decades after its commencement, and for the first time, one sees the introduction of new military governorship titles in the feudal hierarchy. It all began with the emergence of the *däjazmach* title, literally meaning one responsible for campaigns into hostile or rebellious territories; in other words he should not only be able to protect the province but also to conduct an offensive campaign. This title emerged during the time of King Serse Dengel (1563–1597) who awarded it to governors of provinces troubled by and adjacent to the new Oromo settlers in the south and to the provincial governor of *bahrä-nägash* in the north whose territory was encroached on by the Turks.[14] What was left of the royal regiments was integrated with the *ch´ifra* (retainers and soldiers) of the *däjazmach*-governors. Provincial rulers of Gojjam and Damot were exempted from taxation to enable them to increase their defence against the Oromo.[15] The *ch´ifra* of *dä-*

[11] For instance, the court of *dägazmach* Wube, a prince who governed Seimen and Tigray (1831–1855) had the following parts: *Shieläka Zufan Bét, Elfin Shaläqa, Eqa Bét Säläqa, Säyfä Jagré Saläqa, Segga Säläqa*, see Parkyns, Mansfield (1855), *Life in Abyssinia*. London, pp. 220–223. For Shawa See, Ege, Svein (1978), "Chiefs and Peasants: The Socio-Political Structure of the Kingdom of Shawa in about 1840". M.A. Thesis. Bergen. For Gojam See D' Abbadie, Arnauld (1980), *Douze ans de séjour dans la Haute-Éthiopie (Abyssinie)*, Vaticano, chap. VIII, pp. 327–379; Fantahun Brihun (1973), "Gojjam 1800–1855". B.A. Thesis submitted to Department of History, AAU. For Wollo see Asefa Balcha (1984), "The Court of Negus Mikael: An Analysis of its Structure and a Description of the Role of "Ayteyefe" Hall. B. A. Thesis in History, Addis Ababa University. That civil functions were carried out by military commanders and (*ch´ifra*) soldiers shows the extent of militarization of prince's courts.

[12] See the document of *seratä mängest*. On the list where one finds the documents of *seratä mängest* see Huntingford, G.W.B. (1990), pp. 8–9.

[13] See section 1.3.1 below.

[14] See Conti Rossine, C. (1907), *Historia Regis Sarsa Dingel (Malak Sagad)*. Lonvain. pp. 48–49, 56.

[15] See Almeida (1632), "The History of High Ethiopia or Abyssinia", in Beckingham, C.F. and Huntingford, G.W.B. (eds.), 1954. p. 86.

jazmach thus began to replace the status and function of the provincial royal regiments of *ch'äwa*.[16]

At first the *däjazmach* was a provincial campaign commander, but later the title holder assumed control over the judicial and fiscal administration of the provinces, functions that had once been carried out by the 'civil' court officials of the Kings.[17] At least by the second half of the seventeenth century the title of *däjazmach* gradually replaced higher titles in the hierarchical structure of the King's court. In the title of precedence we see the disappearance of the King's provincial tax, and of cattle and grain collectors.[18] Gradually *däjazmach* became a full prerogative title of certain provincial and local hereditary ruling families called *nägädä balabat*. This group belonged to certain aristocratic houses in different regions.

One other factor which played a part in the process of militarization of territorial administration was the appointment of court military officials as governors who assumed the title of *bitwädäd*. Court military commanders with the title of *ras*, heads of the various *ch'ifra* of the court who defended the various gates of the royal camp, came to receive provinces ostensibly for the organization of royal troops. For instance, *ras* Wold Kristos was given the province of Bägémder to govern.[19] The provincial governor combined all functions just as the *däjazmach* did.

1.2. Consolidation of the Regional Aristocracy

After the crisis of the sixteenth century, there was also a process of consolidation of regional nobility and aristocracy. The class of nobility included those who held titles usually associated with court office and territorial administration, e.g., the higher ecclesiastical magnates (bishops, abbots of monasteries), military commanders, and the gentry and local office holders (local administrators and parish clergy). The minority members of higher nobility who effectively exercised court and administrative power are here referred to as aristocracy.[20] The power of the aristocracy emanated from its institutional and

[16] See Berry, L.V.B. (1976), pp. 255f.

[17] The civil court officals included the *mäkonnen* (royal provincial judges), *jan hasen* and *jan maseré* (administrators, judges and tax surveyors), *tsehafélam* (cattle tax collectors), *nägasi* (grain tax collector), *käntiba* (town administrator and custom tax collector). For these titles see Huntingford, G.W.B. (1965), appendix, and TaddesseTamrat (1972), passim.

[18] For comparison see the document in Bairu Tafla and Scholler, H. (1976), pp. 490f; and for traditional titles see Huntingford, G.W.B. (1965), pp. 102–109.

[19] See Bairu Tafla and Scholler, H. (1976), p. 495.

[20] An insight into the class structure of the nobility at the end of the sixteenth century can be inferred from the account of Bahrey (1522), "History of the Galla", in Beckingham, C.F. and Huntingford, G.W.B. eds., 1954. Another source material for the understanding of classes during this period come from the first part of *seratä gebr*, the list of documents where one finds *serä`atä gebr* see Kropp, M. (1989a), p. 219. Also, the document of *seratä mängest* described the ranks and duties of the different royal court officials and territorial governors.

legal rights[21] and from the ownership of ecclesiastical and military offices/titles[22].

In the seventeenth and eighteenth century, regional aristocratic houses became the basis for a military territorial administrative unit called *nägarit*. Literally, *nägarit* is a special war-drum used as an insignia of power by the sovereign and governors. *Nägarit* now meant judicially independent regional centres of power responsible for the government and administration of a territory.[23] *Nägarit* became hereditary with the title of *däjazmach*. Judicial, military and administrative functions were fused or combined in one and the same person, family or office at the local, regional or central levels.[24]

The core of the *nägarit* administration was the aristocratic house which formed an *alga* (regional throne) a term which refers to the regional ruling house which had the traditional right of governorship. The wealth, power and status of the *alga* was acquired by traditional right of descent (*nägädä balabat*)—a right that had existed independent of the King—and by a mechanism of successive war and of patrimonial forms of relationships such as marriage and kinship. The *alga* served as the core for a pyramid of structural authority and relationships established at the regional level. The *gult* holders found at the provincial and district levels formed a patron-client relationship with the territorial prince (*mäsfin*). Together with the prince's court officials, they constituted the advisory council of the *alga*. By virtue of private administration of revenue, they had an obligation to fulfil.[25] In a way, the *alga* had served as a corporative body or board representing the collective interest of the regional aristocracy and nobility (*mäsafint*, *mäkwanent* and *balabat*) as opposed to the King or other regional powers (princes). Regionalism represented a territorial interest fostered as a result of fear of others.

In the region of Tigray the consolidation of territorial aristocracy was asso-

[21] See the constitutional arrangements drawn in the document of *Seratä Mängest*.

[22] See the documents discussed by Crummey, Donald (1983), pp. 207–20; idem (1989), pp. 315–327; Pankhurst, R. (1979), "An Eighteenth Century Ethiopian Dynastic Marriage Contract Between Empress Mentwab of Gonder and Ras Mikael Sehul of Tigre", in *Bulletin of the School of Oriental and African Studies, XIII, 3*, and B.L. Or.776, 271r.

[23] There is a difference between a province and *nägarit*. The former refers to a region which constituted natural communities based on ancestral traditions, sets of customs and privileges. For a list of the names of provinces in the 16th century see Merid W. Aregay, 1974. "Political Geography of Ethiopia at the Sixteenth Century" in *IV Congresso Internazionale di Studie Etiopici, 10–15 April. Tomo I.* Roma; see also Huntingford, G.W.B., (1990). Provinces might not be coterminous with *nägarit*, which was a military territorial administrative unit related to status and wealth (fiscal capacity) of the territory.

[24] On the number of *nägarit* in the land north of the Märäb river comprising Hammasen, Säräye and Akalä Guzay, see Pankhurst, (1983–4), "Ethiopian Taxation Prior to the Time of Menelik: A Collection and Analysis of Estimates, Part I", in *Northeast African Studies, 5, 3* pp. 63f; Bruce, J. (1790), *Travels to Discover the Sources of the Nile in the Years 1768–1773. V* , Edinburgh. pp. 248f.

[25] See Plowden, W. (1868), *Travels in Abyssinia and the Galla Country, with an Account of a Mission to Ras Ali in 1848.* London, chapters 3 and 4.

ciated with the time of the powerful noble known as *blatta* Michael Sehul who proclaimed himself ruler of Tigray after he fought against and executed his master *ras* Anda Haimanot in 1759. In the region of Yejju, prince's family was founded by *ras* Ali Gwangwil, known as Ali the Great, who was followed by six members of his family as *ras*. From 1770 up to the coronation of King Tewodros in 1855, the guardianship of the King was in the hands of this family. In the name of the King they controlled all higher appointments, conducted foreign policy and gave leadership to the regional aristocracy.[26] In the southern parts there was an important development with the rise of the Shewa dynasty. The founder of this dynasty was called Nägasi Kristos (ruled between 1696-1703). He and his successors conducted a successful war against rival local noble families and brought many districts under their control.[27] In Gojjam a royal house was established by *ras* Hailu (the great) who died in 1794. Unlike the new self-made aristocratic families of Shewa and Yejju-Amhara, the ruling aristocrats of Gojjam were descendants of the royal family since the time of King Iyasu II (1730-55). *Ras* Hailu (the great) was succeeded by *ras* Maerd (d.1821) *däjazmach* Gwalu (d.1826) and *däjazmach* Goshu (d.1853.).[28] By the last quarter of the 18th century, the different parts of Wollo came under the hegemony of the Muslim ruling family of Warra Himano founded by Mohammed Ali (popularly referred to as *abba jib*). The power of this family was at its height under his son Kollase Amade and his successor Liban Amade in the 1790s and during the first quarter of the 19th century. The leaders assumed the politico-religious title of *imam*.[29]

The formation of princely rule in southern Ethiopia was a theme not as exhaustively studied as it was in the northern regions. The princes of the southern regions were not royal aristocracy but were self-made aristocracy (as was the case with some of the territorial aristocrats in the northern regions). The formation of princely rule in the south was a synthesis of migration and existing political culture and social organization. Before the migration of the Oromo ethnic groups, the wide area between Awash, Muger, Gibe, Abay, Didesa and Baro was known in the literature as belonging to the Peoples of Gonga.[30] The most important ones were the kingdoms of Damot, Enariya and Kafa. By coming in touch with these principalities (through war and assimilation politics "*gudifecha*") the ethnic confederation of the Oromo people began

[26] For detail discussion see Shiferaw Bekele (1990a). For a discussion on the family of Wärä Séh see Molla Tikuye (1994), "The Rise and Fall of the Yajju Dynasty (1784–1980)", in Bahru Zewde, Pankhurst, and Taddese Beyene (eds.), *Proceedings of the Eleventh International Conference of Ethiopian Studies, vol. I.*, Addis Ababa. pp. 197–216.

[27] For details see Ege, S. (1978).

[28] For details see Fantahun Berihun (1973).

[29] See Asnake Ali (1983), "Aspects of the Political History of Wallo: 1872–1917". M.A. Thesis in History, A.A.U. chap. 1

[30] See Lange, W.J. (1982), *History of the Southern Gonga (Southwestern Ethiopia)*. Studien zur Kulturkunde, 61. Wiesbaden. pp. 1–18.

to disintegrate and formed what was called the *Gibe States*.[31] In western parts of Wellega and in other regions, new centres of power were also formed as land and office began to be given to individual families.[32]

By the beginning of the 19th century, the territorial aristocrats were too strong to be absorbed by the King. The latter was a puppet in the hands of the territorial princes. For instance, King Tekle Giorgis was dethroned six times in eleven years (1779-84, 1794-95, 1795-96, 1797-99, 1800). Later he was exiled to the region of Tigray until his death in 1817. The territorial princes, though they were powerful, did not assume the title of *negusä nägäst* (King of Kings) or take over the imperial throne. This could be attributed to a number of factors. In the first place, there were contractual norms and habits of interaction among the princes as laid down in the document of *seratä mängest* and *Fetha Nägäst* (Laws of the Kings).[33] *Seratä mängest* and *Fetha Nägäst* were written laws which laid down the fundamental principles of government through the kingship institution and the exercise of royal power. In practice the law prevented the formation of an independent kingship by regional aristocrats. The Solomonic line was enshrined in the traditional laws of *Kebrä Nägäst* (glory of Kings), which was written in the early 14th century to provide the documentary and Biblical supports for the Solomonic dynasty. The church was the centre of this ideology and, above all, it was the institution which gave actual legitimacy to an emperor.

The necessity and fundamental importance of kingship was not only based on ideological, traditional and legal grounds. There were practical reasons to consider Kings as the ultimate source and the legal authority for the titles. Regionally speaking, *nägarit* were very much interdependent, for any expansion and contraction of an *alga* (regional throne, power) was at the expense of the neighbouring *alga*. Kings had to intervene to restrain and check conflicts among the nobility. The King could also intervene directly in the acquisition of more surplus in the interest of the *mäkwanent* and *mäsafint* (princes and nobles). The King was the only legitimate force for confiscation of communal land and distribution of office and titles. Kings could follow a policy of re-

[31] See Mohammed Hassen (1990), chapter three.

[32] There is literature dealing with southern princes. For Wellega See Tesema Ta`a (1980). For the political organization and rule of Keffa princes, see Cecchi, A. (1886), *Käfa ena Tarikua, 1390–1897,* (an abbrivated Amharic translation. Original title reads Cecchi, A. (1886), *Da Zeila alle Frontiere del Caffa, 3 vols*. Roma.). For the region of Harar, See Waldron, Sydney, (1984), "The Political Economy of Harri-Oromo relationship, 1559–1874", in *North East African Studies., nos. 1–2*. The difference in the *Zämänä Mäsafint* in the North and South was related to the very factors that shaped their process and organizational make up. In the south, there was no need and capacity to exploit the abundant resources. In the north, scarcity of resources and incessant conflicts led to developments in the art of organizing a military force, mobilization of human and material resources for the accomplishment of military ends.

[33] The law deals with personal and property matters and consisted in part with ecclesiastical law (chapter 1-22) and another part on secular subjects (chapter 23–51) and an appendix part on sucession. See Tzadua, P. (1968), *The Fetha Nagast. The Law of the Kings.* Addis Ababa.

straining both peasants and nobles (for instance, through land edicts). The choice of these alternatives in any historical conjuncture depended, among other things, on the constellation of forces and in this respect there were very rich historical instances, specifically during the *Zämänä Mäsafint* (Era of Princes).[34]

All said, the underlying reason why princes did not claim the throne was because they themselves had limited resources to maintain a strong army that supported the state. The process of militarization of provincial governorship posed the need to increase recruitment of standing troops, provisioning, organization of transport corps and animals, recruitment of cavalry, and meeting the daily needs of household consumption and expense. The next section explains the qualitative developments in the modes of military organization and the consequent needs and demands imposed on the material basis of the aristocracy.

1.3. Changes in the Mode of Military Organization and Methods of Troop Remuneration, 1563–1855

1.3.1. Organization and Remuneration of Court Troops of the Princes

Militarism, though a profound element in the history of Ethiopian state organization, assumed qualitatively different modes of organization and characteristics during the emergence and development of the triangular fiscal system[35] from the seventeenth century onwards. One area of change was in the methods of troop recruitment and remuneration. At the court of kings and regional princes, one finds basically two categories of troops which differed in the methods of being remunerated, command hierarchy, and function. The first category consisted of body guard troops who were assigned purely military functions. They were in charge of the personal security of the prince and power of the *alga* (throne or "seat of government").[36] The second category of court troops consisted of commanders and troops assigned to the court departments established for "civil" or "peace time" functions (referred to here as *ch´ifra*). Often they performed household services and administrative functions.[37] The

[34] Blundell, W. (1922), *The Royal Chronicle of Abyssinia, 1769–1840*. Cambridge.

[35] For an explanation of the term see section 2.4. below.

[36] For a discussion on the various sections of body guard troops see Fantahun Berihun (1973), p. 49; for the court of Ras Ali, see Plowden, W.C. (1868), pp. 48–9; Parkyns, M. (1855), pp. 221–222.

[37] The civil and military functions were difficult to distinguish. It was civil in the sense that some of the departments had function of civil nature, for instance, administration of finance as in the case of the *bäjirond* and *azazh*. During war time they served as an auxiliary force for provisioning and transport. That civil functions were carried out by military commanders and (*ch´ifra*) soldiers shows the extent of militarization of prince courts.

size of the regiment depended on its status and the type of function assigned to it. Components of the *ch'ifra* troops corresponded to the number of court departments.[38]

From the organizational point of view (command hierarchy), body guard troops and *ch'ifra*/department troops could be called court troops as they were commanded by court military officers called *mäkonnen*. But there was a slight difference in the forms of remuneration. Body guard troops were partly paid in "cash". In addition to *qäläb*-ration payment, they received annual salaries in Maria Theresia Thalers (MT$), salt and *shäma*-cloth.[39] Before the crisis of the sixteenth century, taxes were paid in kind such as in cereals, honey, horses, cloth and wheat, depending on the produce of the region and availability of resources.[40] With the advance of militarization of court and provincial govornorships, there was a change in money payment in the form of MT$[41], gold[42] and salt-bar[43]. Travellers reported the amount of gold received by Kings as ordinary land tax from different provinces.[44] The greater quantity of the gold payment was received from the provinces along the trade routes to the coast.[45]

[38] See among others, Fantahun Berihun (1973), pp. 33–36; Plowden, W.C. (1868), pp. 47–48; Parkyns, M. (1855), p. 220.

[39] See Fantahun Berihun (1973), pp. 48, 49; On *qäläb*-ration and *shäma*-cloth payment see Pankhurst, R. (1968c), *Economic History of Ethiopia, 1800–1935*. Addis Ababa. p. 552.

[40] For instance, in a document belonging to the reign of Yeshaq (1412–1427), there is a list of 46 names of regions with corresponding taxes payable by each region. In many cases the taxes were paid in the forms of cotton cloth, goats, cattle, horses, and gold. For the list of these regions, see the document of *Säratä Gebr* catalogued as Bodl. Bruce 88, pp. 41–45; see also Huntingford, G.W.B. (1990), pp 92–95. The regions which paid cotton were located between Abbay and Didesa river, payment in cattle was from the pastoral regions of the Oromo, gold came from regions where there were alluvial deposits. According to Bruce, Emperor Zara Yaqob (1434–1468) divided his kingdoms into "separate governments, assigning to each the tax it should pay, at what time and in what manner, according to the situation and capacity of each province". See, Bruce, James (1790), *Travels to Discover the Sources of the Nile*. II. Edinburgh. p. 72, see also Pankhurst, R. (1961), *An Introduction to the Economic History of Ethiopia, from early times to 1800*. London.p. 180.

[41] For 18th century evidences see the land sale documents in Crummey, D. (1978), "Gondarine *Rim* Land Sales: An Introductory Description and Analysis", in Hess, R. (ed.), *Proceedings of the Fifth International Conference on Ethiopian Studies*. Session B. pp. 469–479. For 19th century account see Pankhurst, R. (1979/80), "The Advent of the Maria Theresia dollar in Ethiopia. Its Effect on Taxation, and Wealth Accumulation, and other Economic, Political, and Cultural Implications", in *Northeast African Studies,I:3;*

[42] See *Wärq zä-wängél* of *däbrä* Selassie Chäläqot, Tigray Region (Table 2 below); see also the document in Guidi (1905), "Il racconto di Näraga" in *Rendiconti della Reale Accademia dei Lincei*. Roma, Serie V, XIV. p. 264.

[43] See Mahteme Selassie (1962 E.C.), p. 152; See also Asfaw Tesema Werke (1969 E.C.), *yäRas Gugsa Wäle Tarik*, IES, manuscript no. 998. p. 25; On Salt as curency see Pankhurst (1961), pp. 261–265.

[44] For the analysis of the data see Pankhurst, R. (1983–84), pp 61ff.

[45] *Ibid*., p. 63. It seemed that in the eighteenth century *wäqet*-gold was used as curency. In documents dealing with land sale we see reference to the fractions of *wäqet*, i.e. *alad* (gold weighing half an ounce), *drim* (a tenth of an ounce), *aqämät* (one-tweentieth of an ounce). See Haddis Gebre-Meskel (1992), p. 39; Crummey, D. (1978).

But there was a problem of money supply, and gold was extracted in limited regions far beyond the kings' and princes' control. It was not, therefore, possible to pay all body guard troops in cash.

Body guard and departmental troops were maintained largely by a sytem of *gult*[46] (a jurisdictional and beneficial right to ordinary land tax). The origin of *gult* appears to be associated with the introduction of Christianity in Ethiopia in the second quarter of the fourth century.[47] Until the beginning of the 16th century the grant of *gult* land was made mainly to the church[48] and (royal) military establishments. After the crisis of the sixteenth century, the *gult* arrangement was also extended to militarized provincial governors referred to by different names such as *yä-nägarit* in Tigray, *gult-bét* in Gojjam, *yä-shaläqa hagär* in Bägémder, *yä-ras qämäs* in Dämbiya and again in Bägémder, *wusti gult* in Hammasen. *Gult* were also granted to royal and aristocratic families as hereditary estates.[49] Consequently, *gult* became the private property of aristocratic families either by *de facto* ownership after a long period of administrative possession, or by royal grant. The process of privatization of *gult* had affected the remuneration of court troops. The continued transfer and privatization of *gult* had reduced central government revenue[50] and Kings and princes became dependent on *gult* holders for their military needs.

To improve their finances and facilitate payment to court troops, Kings and princes resorted to an imposition of extraordinary land tax. One such type of extraordinary land tax was called *fäsäs.* In the document one finds it mentioned during the time of King Gigar (1821), and when *ras* Gugsa (1800) was the *rise mäkwanent* (head of the military nobility).[51] *Ras* Ali, the grand son of *ras* Gugsa tried to impose this tax on regions in central Ethiopia.[52] In Gojjam, *däjazmach* Tadla Gwalu attempted to introduce a *fäsäs* tax but was strongly opposed by the peasants.[53] It seemed that *fäsäs* tax became permanent in central regions where there was constant movement of troops owing to conflicts.[54]

[46] See D'Abbadie, Arnauld d' (1868), pp. 327–379.

[47] For instance, see the land charter document of king Ezana in Huntingford, G.W.B. (1965), pp. 29f.

[48] Huntingford, G.W.B. (1965), pp. 23–24.

[49] See Huntingford, G.W.B. (1965), p. 17, and pp. 101–102 for the list of land grants made to individuals; for royal gults see the document in Haddis Gebre-Meskel (1992), p. 208; Bairu Tafla (1987), *Asma Giyorgis and His Work: History of the Galla and the Kingdom of Shäwa.* Stuttgart. p. 287.

[50] Symptoms of financial problems partly as a result of land alienation and "waste" have been mentioned in chronicles. Pankhurst, R. (1985a), "Ethiopian Taxation Prior to the Time of Menelik: A Collection and Analysis of Estimates, Part II," in *Northeast African Studies, VI: 1*: pp. 23, 24.

[51] See a document in Conti Rossini (1954), p. 55.

[52] See, *Yä Tewodros Tärik*, manuscript no. 91. IES. p. 5.

[53] Täklä Iyasus, *Yä Ngus Täklä Haymanot Tarik*. Mans. n. 254, p. 63.

[54] On the importance of these regions see Crummey, D. (1975), "Cächaho and the Politics of the northern Wällo-Begemder Border", in *Journal of Ethiopian Studies, XIII: 1.*

Nonetheless, *fäsäs* tax was introduced only in limited regions, and even in that case it became an extra burden to the peasant community.

1.3.2. Recruitment of Campaign Troops, 1780s–1855

Another area of the change in the structure of the army as a consequence of the sixteenth century crisis was the new phenomenon in the organization and recruitment of territorial troops which is here identified by a new status called *campaign troops*, different from mobile and garrison troops. The former *ch'äwa* troops belonging to the autocratic state (1150–1540) were dislodged by the incessant wars of Ahmed Gragn and by continous engagement with the Oromo warriors. Formerly, the *ch'äwa* troops were garrisoned in provinces and remunerated by the *gult* system.[55] After the crisis of the sixteenth century, *ch'äwa* troops were replaced by campaign troops which had different functions and methods of remuneration.

There were various ways of recruiting campaign troops depending on the type of historical land ownership rights. In northern and parts of central Ethiopia, land was owned communally by descent. Access to land was acquired by right of descent and inheritance, and the land thus acquired was called *rist*.[56] In the *rist* areas, campaign troops were recruited by exempting peasants from the payment of an ordinary annual land tax in return for their participation in campaigns. These peasant soldiers were called *balä rist zämach*, because of their possession of the land they cultivated by right of descent. However, when they ceased to participate in campaigns they paid all types of taxes without being evicted from their lands. In the province of Tigray, for instance, this form of recruitment was introduced during the governorship of Shum Agame (1814) and by his son and successor *däjazmach* Sebegadis (1823–1831).[57] In Gojjam it was called Tigray and Wollo *zämach*, named after the places of campaign.[58] In Wollo there was *zämach* land where tax-obligation was to par-

[55] For the purpose of maintaining themselves and covering the expense of the court, military officials and their detachments were allocated provinces (Shewa, Bägémder, Gojjam, etc.) known as *mäzäkr bétä gebr*, and *ahgurat*, see d`Abbadie 118, fol 43. p. 31 cl2–3; p. 36- cl2–3; p. 38 cl 1; during the reign of King Naod (1478–1508), the different contingents of the central army (i.e., soldiers that were attached to the royal court), numbering sixteen, were allocated estates (*ahgurat*) numbering 124; ibid., pp. 38–39. Contrast this document with B.L. Or 821, fol. 133 c2.

[56] The principles and working mechanism of the *rist* system is described in detail by many of the field studies, see, among others, Perini, R. (1905), *Di Qua dal Mareb. Florence*; Pollera, A. (1913), *Il Regime delle Proprietà Terreria in Etiopia e nella Colonia Eritrea*. Roma; Nadel, S.F. (1946), "Land Tenure on the Eritrean Plateau", in *Africa, 21, 1*; Hoben, A. (1973), *Land Tenure among the Amhara of Ethiopia: The Dynamics of Cognatic Descent*. Chicago; Stitz, V. (1974), *Studien zur Kulturgeographie Zentraläthiopiens*. Bonn.

[57] Gebre Wold Ingida Worq (1948 E.C), *Yä-Ityopia Märetna Gber Sem*. Addis Ababa, p. 53. *idem*., (1962), "Ethiopia's Traditional System of Land Tenure and Taxation", in *Ethiopia Observer*, V, 4, p. 318.

[58] *idem*., (1948 E.C)., p. 61.

ticipate in campaigns.[59] In Yejju the *balä rist zämach* was exempted from a type of tax called *mägäzo*, which was allocated to the *mälkägna* who gave military service.[60]

The *balä rist zämach* had a number of problems. When he was exempted, it was not an individual peasant household that was exempted but the kinship land, and by definition all descendants would be free from payment of tax. In principle the collective compact money imposed on the locality was paid by the descent group.[61] The amount supposed to be paid by each peasant household depended on the number of the descendants.[62] However, if there were a great number of incidences of tax exemption, the amount of payment was high. Tax exemption would not reduce land tax income for the state, since the amount of tax paid by the descent community was fixed. The burden lay on those who shared the tax exemption given to campaign soldiers.[63]

Another problem of *zämach* land was the proxy system which made military service irregular; "either all the owners of that land did it in turns, or they would pay a given sum (usually one-fifth) of their produce to a soldier or a senior member of the descent group, who was called *aläqa*; he would do the service in return for which he would have a larger share of the land and other privileges".[64] The peasant descent community could thus decisively influence the kind of service and the size (increase or decrease) of campaign troops.

Partly to solve their military problems, Kings had begun to confiscate communally owned lands on the pretext of peasant rebellion[65] and the founding of churches. The actual process began during the time of King Iyasu I (1682–1706), who was said to have begun measurement of land in Bägémder.[66] In principle, two thirds of the confiscated communal farm lands were distributed equally to soldiers (one-third) and to the clergy (one-third). However, it appears that most confiscated lands were transferred for the maintainance of the

[59] *Ibid..*, p. 47. *idem.*, 1962, p. 316.

[60] *Ibid..*, p. 50; *idem.*, 1962, p. 317. Mahtame Selassie Wolde Meskel (1962 E.C), p. 153.

[61] For a discussion of tax documents from the end of the tenth century up to 1540, see Crummey, D. (1993), "Medieval Ethiopian Land Grants, 1200–1540" A paper presented to the symposium on "State, Land and Society in the History of Sudanic Africa", Center for African Studies, University of Illinois, Urbana, April 22–24, pp. 25–29. See also the document in Haddis Gebre-Meskel (1992), p. 40. For assessment of taxes see Tekeste Negash (1986), "Land Tenure and the Organization of Surplus Appropriation on the Eve of the Colonial Period", in *No Medicine for the Bite of a White Snake: Notes on Nationalism and Resistance in Eritrea, 1890–1940*. Uppsala.

[62] On the distribution of the land tax payment among descent members see Perini, R. (1905), p. 58.

[63] For the region of Wag, see Mahteme Selassie (1962 E.C.), p. 160.

[64] Quoted in Shiferaw, B. (1992), "The Land Question in the Ancien Regime" in *An Economic History of Ethiopia. The Imperial Era, 1941–1974.* Draft Manuscript. Department of History. A.A.U. p 92.

[65] Quoted in Pankhurst, R. (1966), p. 56.

[66] See next page.

church service and functions in the name of *däbtära* (cantors)[67], *mäswat* (Holy Sacrifice), *qurban* (Eucharist)[68], *qedasé* (Mass service)[69], *zker* (Commemoration)[70], and *eqa* (Sancritsan Possession)[71]. These forms of beneficial titles allocated to the church were commonly known as *rim*, and they constituted the larger part of the aristocratic patrimony.

Confiscated land allocated for campaign soldiers was called *amisho gasha*. In its literal meaning *gasha* means shield, and it was used to refer to the collection and use of fixed land tax in return for military service. One *gasha* of land consisted of about eight farm lands (*medr*).[72] It is important to note that a peasant might have had about ten farm lands and these fields might be scattered in different places.

A soldier who was given *gasha* land (eight pieces of land) collected *amisho* (one-fifth) from the produce of each farm land allocated to him as his *qäläb*. During harvest time the soldier went around and fixed the amounts; if they disagreed, then he took one-fifth of the produce.[73] There were various problems in the collection of *amisho-qäläb*. The size of the *qäläb*-ration was paid in kind (grain) and, as it taxed production itself, the quantity was not fixed but rather depended on the amount of the harvest. The *amisho* soldier received less if there was a bad harvest due to drought, locust damage or spoilage by excess rain. Besides, the soldier got his one-fifth *qäläb* only from cultivated farm lands and was not entitled to claim any compensation for farm lands left fal-

[66] Gebre Wolde Ingda Werq (1948 E.C.), p. 57. What had been started in Begémder, began to be spread into other regions, particularly during the Era of Princes. In the region of Gojjam, state confiscation of communal land was first introduced for military purposes by *ras* Hailu in 1730/31. See Täklä Iyasus, *Yä Ngus Tälä Haymanot Tarik*. Manuscript Number 254, IES. pp. 48, 50. Emperor Iyasu I (1688–1706), might have distributed land to the clergy in the region of Märäb Mälash, particularly in province of Hammasen. Kolmodin, J., (1915). *Traditions de Tsazzega et Hazzega*. Uppsala. trans. p. 97–98. In the region of Tigray *ras* Mikael had quartered *däbtära*-cantors of the Mikael church at Adwa, referring to the Qusqwam tradition. *wärq zä wängél* of the Adwa Mikael. (This document is copied and coded by Crummey, D. as 92.I.16.19); for a later period see also Huntingford (1965), p. 74.

[67] For the grant of *däbtära* land see the documents in Huntingford, G.W.B. (1965), p. 62–63; B.L. Or. 659, p. 239; B.L.Or 813, pp. 188, 189, and Crummey and Shumet (1991), pp. 247ff.

[68] For evidences see B.L. Or.518ff, 15v; and Crummey and Shumet (1988), p. 3.

[69] See the Amharic note written above on the left corner of the Qusquwam charter, B.L. Or. 636. There is a copy of this document both in Pankhurst (1966), p. 66, and Crummey and Shumet (1988); see also B.L. Or. 777, 4v; B.L. Or. 604, 2v; Haddis Gebre-Meskel (June 1992), pp 209–210; B.L. Or. 776, 269r; B.L. Or. 518,15v; B.L. Or. 828*, 47r.

[70] See the land charters in Huntingford (1965), nos. 7, 13, 14, 15, 19, 20, 22, 23, 27, 30, 31, 50, 53, 71, 80, 89, 93 and 94. See aslo Guidi, I. (1905a), pp. 255, 256 text; Euringer, S. (1933/34), Die Geschichte von Närga. Ein Kapitel aus der abessinischen Kulturgeschichte des 18. Jarhunderts" in *Zeitschrift fur Semitistik und verwandte Gebiete, Band 9, Band 10* , 1935, p. 105,107 trans.

[71] See B.L. Or.659, p. 239v.

[72] In one document it was stated that 33 *bäläbret* (riflemen) were quartered on 264 *medr* lands, which makes one *gasha* land equal to 8 farm lands, see B:L: Or. 829*, 51r. Crummey and Shumet found out that in the land register of Qwsquam church the *gasha* land was standardized at about 8 fields, see Crummey, D. and Shumet Sishangne (1991), p. 247.

[73] See Gebre Wold Engda Worq (1948 E.C.), p. 61.

low.[74] The fallow system would obviously decrease income of the *gasha* soldier, and it was possible that peasants could use this as an excuse if they were not on good terms with the assigned soldier.

In a somewhat similar manner to *rim* lands, *amisho gasha* lands were controlled by the aristocracy, and the office was transmitted by a system of inheritance called *aläqnät*.[75] In the descent areas, *zämach* campaign soldiers were commanded by *gultägna*. Here, as well, the office of the *gult* was hereditary, belonging to the local ruling kinship family. The *gultägna* had to mobilize and command armed (campaign) soldiers under his jurisdiction.[76]

Amisho gasha lands and *zämach* lands, were transferred as *gults* for the collective or private foundation of churches. The problem with *Balä rist zämach* was that once the land was transferred to the church, the governor lost his army because the peasants then paid the ordinary land tax to the church.[77] There was a similar problem with the *amisho gasha* land, the difference being that the *amisho gasha* soldiers were sometimes compensated by land grant to continue collecting farm tax revenue in other districts.[78] *Amisho gasha* lands were obtained by confiscation of peasant lands or changing the status of the land. In most cases these led to peasant rebellions. Since the beginning of the seventeenth century, there were peasant revolts: in Semien in 1608, in Shire in 1617, in Agäw and Fälasha in 1616-1626/27. Other provinces such as Bägémder, Shewa and Lasta had rebelled in 1619, 1620 and 1622 respectively.[79] The most illustrious example came from Lasta and Fälasha.[80] The recruitment of campaign troops was therefore at the expense of the peasant community.

[74] *Report submitted by a Committee established to investigate and to make recomendations on solving the continues litigation problem arising between Amisho (one-fifth) paying peasants and Amisho (one-fifth) receivers*. July 2, 1954 E.C. pp. 1–3. This document is in the hands of Ato Gäsäsä Bezabeh, who was a member of the committee and judge of the Supreme Court of Tigray Province.

[75] See Crummey, D. and Shummet Sishange (1988), p. 318.

[76] See Pollera, A. (1913), p. 17.

[77] See the dispute mentioned by Pearce, N. (1830). *The Life and Adventures of Nathaniel Pearce Written by himself during a Residence in Abyssinia from the Years 1810 to 1819; together with Mr. Coffin's Account of his Visit to Gonder*. J.J. Halls, ed., I. London, p. 220.

[78] See the land grants of Iyasu II (1730–1755) in Pankhurst, R. (1966a), p. 66; see also the chronicle of Annale Iyasu II et Iyoas, in *Corpus Scriptorium Christianorum Orienalium*, (CSCO) *vol.61*, p. 102; Huntingford, G.W. (1965), p. 15f.

[79] See Bartricki, A. and Mantel-Niecko, J. (1971).

[80] On the continuous rebellion of the Wag peasants, see Pankhurst, R. (1984), "Wag and Lasta: An Essay in the Regional History of Ethiopia from the 14th Century to 1800", in Rubenson, S. (ed.), *Proceedings of the Seventh International Conference of Ethiopian Studies*. On Fäläsha see Taddesse Tamirat (1986) "Process of Ethnic Interaction and Integration in Ethiopia History: the case of Agew", in *Journal of African History, 29*.

1.3.3. Recruitment of Cavalry and Auxiliary Troops

Yet another consequence of the crisis of the sixteenth century was the effect on techniques of warfare. The Wars of Ahmed Gragn and the Oromo ethnic groups underlined the significance of cavalry and use of musketeers in the conduct of war.[81] Since muskets were not available for purchase and use, the lesson drawn in the use of cavalry became even more significant in the continued wars among regional princes. Nonetheless, princes could not, by themselves, organize a standing household cavalry. The cavalry was drawn entirely from the provinces, and the main specialized corps was the one recruited from the *gultägna*, or by system of *gult*.[82]

Theoretically cavalry was different from auxiliary troops who performed different functions such as transporting war materials and provisions necessary for campaigns. In the period under discussion, there was no specialized body of auxiliary troops, which accompanied the main force and performed specific tasks such as the preparation and supply of grain, meat, drinks, fodder, etc. At the prince's court, these functions were performed by departments such as the *azazh* and the *bäjironde*. Courts of Kings and princes had selected lands which were allocated for organizing the transport system and/or for raising war horses. In the Era of Princes, there were *färäs* (horse) and *bazra* (mare) lands that were held by peasants who were obliged to breed and tend horses and mules.[83] However, the transport troops organized through reservation of land were not sufficient in view of the scale and recurrent nature of campaigns. Hence, the task of transportation was shared collectively by peasant communities. For instance, in Gojjam, during the period of *däjazmach* Goshu (1840s), the district of Mächakil was responsible for carrying and pitching tents.[84] In spite of differences in functions and remuneration base, there was no marked difference between auxiliary troops and main troops during battle engagements. During campaigns, troops recruited from the peasants served as field forces and transport corps.

In the system of remuneration, there was no difference between payment and provision. Campaign troops were expected to bring with them their *qäläb*-provision. When they finish their *senq*, they were billeted on the lands of peasants living in the direction of the march. Billeting was the common method of provisioning, particularly in the first half of the nineteenth century. If there was any form of requisitioning made on the spot, it was often without compensation to peasants. Many foreign observers noted that in the first part of the nineteenth century, looting was a common occurrence.

[81] See Merid Welde Aregay (1980), "A Reappraisal of the Impact of Firearms in the History of Warfare in Ethiopia (c.1500–1800)", in *Journal of Ethiopian Studies, XIV*.

[82] See among others, Plowden, W.C. (1868), p. 49; Fantahun Berihun (1973), pp. 48–49.

[83] Crummey, D. (1988); Kropp, M. (1989b), *Die Äthiopischen Königschroniken in der Sammlung des Däggazmc Haylu*. Frankfurt am Main.pp. 85, 278 no.3,

[84] Fantahun Berihun (1973).

1.4. Conclusion

One of the major consequences of the crisis of the sixteenth century was the militarization of society. Royal courts began to organize entirely along regimental lines. In the provinces, a new military governorship office developed with control over the military command and the judicial and fiscal administration of provinces. The militarization of regional and court governorships created a class of military aristocracy who came to form an independent power base in their respective provinces. Concomitantly, there was the creation of campaign troops who replaced the former *ch´äwa* troops, field and garrison troops, who belonged to the autocratic state (1150–1540). Campaign troops were recruited from the peasants by tax exemption and could serve as field forces or in the transport and provision corps. The cavalry also came to acquire importance after the crisis and it required more grain production and extensive grass land. Military campaigns also required auxiliary troops which performed special tasks necessary to accomplish the expedition.

There was not only an increase in military capacity. During the period under discussion, there were frequent campaigns which became a means of survival both in defence of territorial interest and in the extraction of surplus from the peasantry. If conducted successfully, their immediate advantage was rewards in the form of booty. If used to install long term interest, they had to be sustained until the type of system accommodated the interest of the victor and the vanquished. Campaign as a regular means of acquisition, and the consequent warfare and rivalry, required a continuous improvement in organizational efficiency and an increase in production. This had many implications both for the local lord and the peasantry.

Princes were dependent on the peasant community to recruit campaign troops for their provisioning and means of transport. In the *rist* areas, land was owned by the community and the state had no right to make a land survey to increase tax.[85] Land tax assessment and distribution was in the hands of the peasant community, and the princes did not know who was paying or who was exempted at the local level and were thus unable to increase tax. Logistic expenses were largely the responsibility and the expense of the peasant community. The presence or absence of *zämach* soldiers, who were exempted from payment of land tax, could increase the burden of tax payment on other members of the community. Peasants and their community could thus directly affect the size and effectiveness of the service in question.

Taxes could increase if there was an effective way of collection and admin-

[85] However, there were various ways by which kings acquired communal lands. One method was confiscation of land as a consequence of rebellion or treason. Land belonging to an extinct kinship family was also considered as state land. Land which was abandoned as a result of voluntary migration was counted as state land. In the region of Märäb Mälash these lands were called *medri negus*. See Pollera, A. (1913), p. 24.

istration. But there was lack of intermediary royal officers between the King and the peasants. Revenue allocated for soldiers was collected by the *gultägna*, who were not salaried crown officials. Kings could not attack the privilege of the local *gultägna* to increase their income. In the system, the *gultägna* served as cavalry (*mazazo*), as commander (*aläqa*) of *zämach* and as *amisho* soldiers.

Incessant campaigns and increased militarization of provincial governorship meant increasing recruitment of standing troops, preparation of *senq*-provisioning, organization of transport corps and animals, and recruitment of cavalry. The form of revenue allocation of the *gult* system which emphasized the institutional and private line (court, church) was not suitable for the purposes of the many specialized and varied services created by the change in the mode of military organization. The arrangement form of allocation, i.e., *gult* as a compact territory probably extending to cover a district, could not be divided into portions for meeting various functional needs.[86] The whole revenue jurisdiction, including decisions on the form of payment, rate of taxation, and exemption, was given to the *gult* holder. Any breakdown would have been in violation of a delegated authority. Thus no flexibility of allocation was made on the basis of military functional lines. Princes could not transfer resources from one part of the logistic system to the other as the war situation demanded.

Neither could the demands of continuous campaigns be matched by increasing production. The peasantry had reached the height of its dynamism by adopting the efficient land use system. There was no further investment in the promotion of agricultural production nor in expansion in land to increase production.[87] Rather, the system of food production was further exacerbated by periodic natural catastrophes.

Kings and princes could not change methods of assessment of taxes (by census and/or land survey). Also, they could not make changes in the administration of taxes (replacing *gultägna* with a salaried officer) and stop transfer of government revenue to private ends (which means against aristocracy). Consequently, they introduced extraordinary taxes such as *fäsäs* and *täsäri* (billeting) which became a burden to peasants and caused rebellion in some areas. They had also introduced changes in the forms of land tax payment. Money payment in MT$ was introduced in some parts for the purchase of weapons and payment of court troops. But there was a problem of money supply, and gold was extracted in limited regions far beyond the King's control.

In a situation where there was a constant agricultural output, and a precarious peasant class, the demand for continuous campaigns could be met only at the expense of the other partner. The growing power of regional princes at the expense of disposing *gult* rights and titles and offices led to rebellion of the

[86] See for instance, Villari, G. (1938), "I'gulti della Regione di Axum" in *Rassegna Economici dell' Africa Italiana. XVI.*

[87] See the argument in section 7.1.1. below.

aristocracy and the local military nobility. In central and northern Ethiopia there was s*hifta* "outlawry" since the first decade of the nineteenth century.[88]

On the other hand, the ruling class itself was open and susceptible to upward mobility owing to its demography (death rate), and system of succession (type of legitimacy). The right to an office by virtue of aristocratic descent created ambitious warriors and rebels, causing internal instability. Devices such as *aläqnät* could not contain upstart and ambitious men and stifled internal rivalry. Ennoblement through the acquisition of title and office from the crown further complicated the class structure.[89]

The aristocracy was in a situation where it could not detach itself from violence and internal instability and nor could it make itself independent of the class of local lords and the peasantry for its military needs. Measures undertaken to redress the problem or ward off danger were ironically the ones that exacerbated the problems. Kings confiscated communal land at the cost of peasant rebellion. The need for confiscation of land increased with *shum shir* (appointment and dismissal) campaigns. But the land was shared by the church because the Abun could excommunicate those who violated land charters made by the King. State land was held as *de facto* private property through the acquisition of ecclesiastical offices and tiltles. Confiscated lands nurtured aristocratic patrimony; they were not used for creating an independent military power of Kings.

In northern Ethiopia there was thus a contradiction between the acquisition of resources[90] and distribution of resources[91] on the one hand, and the mode of military organization and technique of warfare which came as a result of the crisis of the sixteenth century on the other hand. Military needs and military means caused incessant campaigns, plunder, rebellion, etc. as reported by travellers and accounted in the chronicles. The creation of a fiscal system that suited the nature and demand of campaigns, and that decided the means and survival of the aristocracy, could only be conceived in areas where the class struggle was weak for various reasons. Here lay the genesis of the fiscal military state and system.

[88] The term *Shifta* defined as "one who stirs up trouble while taking to the forest or the bush, departing from the king, the government rule (*Gizat*), instituted order (*Serat*) and the law". On Shifta see Crummey, D. (1984), "Banditry and Resistance: Noble and Peasant in Nineteenth Century Ethiopia", in Rubenson, S. (ed.), *Proceedings of the Seventh International Conference of Ethiopian Studies*. Uppsala.

[89] Gonderian kings were recruiting support from the new upstarts coming from Agew and the Oromo to counter-balance the traditional aristocracy.

[90] Particularly, the volume of production, assessment and collection of taxes.

[91] Privatization of taxes, tax exemptions, lack of administration and technical capacity to transfer surplus resource from one to another.

CHAPTER TWO

Conditions for the Emergence of the Fiscal Military State

In the preceding chapter changes and developments in the system of military organization and techniques of warfare as a consequence of the crisis of the sixteenth century were explained. Courts of kings and princes were organized along regimental lines; provincial governorships were militarized, fusing judicial, fiscal and military functions; there were partly cash paid permanent court troops armed with muskets; there was recruitment of a large number of campaign troops; use of cavalry became predominant; there were frequent campaigns which required provisioning and transport. Apparently, there was an increase in military capacity which needed an extensive use of land and manpower. However, there was a limited economic potential and opportunity owing primarily to the type of communal and collective land ownership rights and private methods of revenue administration which promoted localized interests not suitable for centrally led and institutionalized military functions.

The fiscal military state and system emerged during the beginning of the eighteenth century when the Gonderian mode of military organization merged with the landlord-tenant and owner-cultivator types of land ownership commonly used in southern Ethiopia. The system developed first in Shewa which was strongly affected by the crisis of the sixteenth century.[1] The system was the outcome of local and provincial arrangements made by the territorial lords of the area; in a word, it was a system that developed from below, not by royal decree or initiative of Gonderain kings. In the central and southern regions, there were favourable class conditions (both in the system of property and forms of distribution) that suited the military needs and demands for change. There were factors such as private land ownership rights, individual registration and payment of land tax, administration of revenue independent of local traditional forces, and a revenue sharing system defined by central aims. Not only the existence of these peculiar elements was important, but also the qualities and principles needed to resolve structural military barriers and increase the logistic capacity of the regional powers.

[1] Compared to other regions, Shewa and the southern parts of present day Wello were affected considerably by the war of Ahmed Gragn and Oromo settlements. Study the details described in the chronicles and literature. See among others, Dombrowski, F.A. (1983). *Tänäsee 106: Eine Chronik der Herrscher Äthiopiens*, B. II. Wiesbaden.

2.1. Private Land Ownership Right

By private ownership is meant here individual ownership and exercise of exclusive property rights based on the legal and cultural principles governing the ownership and transfer of property among members of society.

The emergence and development of private ownership of land in the Ethiopian context is a subject not yet explored. Though there are limitations, the state of research recognizes the existence of private ownership of land in southern Ethiopia at least as an immediate consequence of the crisis of the sixteenth century. With the disintegration of older provinces and the emergence of territorial aristocratic power in the Gibe region, in Wellega and probably in Kafa, there developed a new type relations of production. In these regions there was landlord-tenant *Moti Biya* (father of the land)-*Qubsisa* (tenant) and owner-cultivator (*gabbaro*) types of ownership. The *gabbaro* were probably the original settlers who after the conquest of the Oromo were left with holding their land on a freehold basis.[2] They cultivated a variety of grains, lentils and fruits. There was a favourable climate and rich soil for agricultural activity and the whole area was surrounded by the great rivers of Awash, Muger, Gibe, Abbay, Diddesa, Gojebe and Baro.

One consequence of the permanent settlement of the Oromo ethnic groups in the Gibe region was the emergence of a land tenure system which favoured private accumulation of land. The practice of *Qabiye* (claim over land on the basis of order of arrival) and a primogeniture inheritance system created a land owning group (formation of class of *sorésa*) and a dependent landless group.[3] A similar land holding system occurred in the region of Wellega.[4] In the Kingdom of Kafa, the predominant form was a landlord-tenant relationship. The King and his councillors (*mekroch*) had enserfed the peasantry by disposing of their land.[5]

In the literature cited, there was no detailed discussion of the definition and allocation of private land ownership rights and its legal enforcement, an important criterion for examining logistic influence. Since the process commenced as local arrangements (not by royal decree and initiative of Gonderain kings),

[2] The term *gabbaro* or *gabero* refers to owner cultivator, See Lange, J.W. (1982), p. 7; and Mohhamed Hassen used the term to refer to the original settlers who were assimilated by the Oromo ethnic groups at the time of conquest. See Mohammed Hassen (1990) p. 119. See also the anthropological study in western Wellega prior to its integration into the imperial fiscal system, Hultin, Jan (1977), "Man and Land in Wallaga, Ethiopia", in *Working Papers of the Department of Anthropology, no. 10.* University of Gothenburg.

[3] See Takalign W. Mariam (1986), "Land, Trade and Political Power Among the Oromo of the Gibe Region, A Hypothesis" in *Proceedings of the Third Annual Seminar of the Department of History*. AAU. p. 154; Mohammed Hassen (1990), chapt. Four.

[4] Hultin, Jan (1977); It is extensively quoted in Mohammed Hassen (1990) p. 119,

[5] Cecchi, A. (1886), an abbreviated Amharic translation, p. 9; See also Lagne, W.J. (1982), pp. 260f

it is difficult to trace documents and discuss the terms and conditions of ownership rights for the initial period. Based on documents pertaining to the Menelik period, what follows is the explanation and definition of the allocation of private land ownership rights.

The most frequent forms of private ownership were freehold (peasant) including leasehold (of *balabat*) and state holdings (state as owner with full right to exclude all others). Actual owners of the land were the *balabat* (landlord-tenant), *gäbar* (owner-cultivator) and the state (*madäriya*-tenants). During the practice of confiscation and distribution of lands, or in the practice of land survey, these three parts were always mentioned.[6] Literally *balabat* means notable. Originally the title belonged to south and south west Ethiopia in the Oromo and Sidama areas and referred to local notables.[7] In these areas the *balabat* might have been the class of *sorésa* who were rich in land, slaves and other properties.[8] In eastern Ethiopia, the *balabat* were similar to *dämina* and *gärada*, first settlers.[9] When land was distributed during confiscation or measurement, the state allocated land to the local *balabat*-chiefs.

The second category included the *gäbar* and *gendäbäl* peasants.[10] *Gäbar* was a free and exclusive owner of farm land with the obligation to pay government land tax in kind and in labour. The land holding of the system was identified by the name of the individual, and land tax was paid on a calculation of the size and fertility of the holding. When individuals were identified by their possession of property, including land, and when they paid their share on such a basis directly to the treasury of the state, this form of ownership and share of tax burden (*serit*) was called *gäbar*. *Gäbar* could be an individual household or an extended family land holding with full right to exclude all others. The holder had tax payment obligations by virtue of his ownership of the land. The tax was paid in kind and in service. There were various names given to the service[11], and the tax paid from the land could be allocated for various purposes[12].

[6] See the land distribution made by Negasi (1670s–1703) in Shewa, mentioned in Bairu Tafla (1987), p. 503; See also the report on land measurement in Shewa during the time of Menelik, discussed by Haile Zalaka (n.d.) *Yä däjazmach Girmame Hiwet Tarik*; See also Mahteme Selassie (1962 EC), p. 108; See also *bä-Itiyopia Tintawi yäferd mäzgeb yätägägnä fttabher hegawi dreget, 1945. Manuscript, Addis Ababa (*hereafter abbreviated as *Codified Laws),* art. no.357, p. 97.

[7] Guidi, I. (1901), *Vocabolario Amarico-Italiano*. Rome, p. 90.

[8] Takalign W. Mariam (1986), p. 154.

[9] Mahtama Selassie (1962 E.C.), p. 161; Gebre Wold Engda Worq (1962), "Ethiopia's Traditional System of Land Tenuer and Taxation", in *Ethiopia Observer*, V, 4. p. 314.

[10] In this part of the work *gäbar* is not defined in its fiscal/legal meaning. According to such a definition *gäbar* and *gendäbäl* were different, corresponding to the kind of obligation attached to the land. But both forms operate under similar terms and conditions belonging to a private land ownership regime (hereafter both legal types are referred to as *gäbar*, in the sense of owner-cultivator).

[11] See section 2.2 below

[12] See section 2.3 below

There were conditions attached to the ownership of land. The owner had an obligation to cultivate the land. "The *bälä-rist* could plough any portion of the land he wished, and could leave the rest fallow or lease it. Unless there is a special decree, the *mälkägna* (government official) had no right to give it to another person and no other peasant was allowed to cultivate the land".[13] But if the owner-cultivator left the land because he was unable to pay tax or moved out to another area, and if the government gave the land to the one who could pay all due tax, and that one continued to pay the tax, the former owner had no claim over the land.[14] The new cultivator was given the status of ownership if he paid continuously for three years.[15] So to keep the land as *rist,* any owner-cultivator had to find a representative[16] or proxy who could continue to pay the land tax.[17]

In addition to the right to give representation, the owner had the right to transfer his resources to others by way of inheritance and sale[18], or parcellization[19]. If the owner had no child to inherit the land he could give the land to whomever he liked, or to those who had served him.[20] The owner could give the land to his servant as *rim* but could claim it back.[21] The land owner could lease the land to a tenant, and the tenant could leave the land if the owner wished him to do so.[22]

Another category of owner was the state, and state land was called *madäriya.* This category of ownership developed when the Gonderian military organization was synthesised with the private ownership of southern Ethiopia from the period of Nägasi Kristos. Before that, only the landlord-tenant (*bala-bat*) and *gäbar* (owner-cultivator) were categories of ownership. With the emergence of the fiscal military system, there appeared a third category, the state as individual owner, with similar rights as found in the landlord-tenant and owner-cultivator categories. The beginning of the state as owner of private land in the same capacity as an individual, did not change the essence of private ownership rights that prevailed in the preceding decades.

State land refered to as *madäriya* had different forms used for different purposes. The first one was called *hudad*, and this land was either deducted from the land belonging to each cultivator owner, or if extra land existed, it

[13] See *Codified Laws*, art.n. 3373, p. 877.
[14] Ibid., arti. N. 3362, p. 875.
[15] Gebre Wold Engda Worq (1948 E.C.), p. 11.
[16] *Codified Laws*, art. no. 3281.
[17] This type of conditional ownership was diferent from the communal ownership in which the peasant had always been given acess to the land and was eligible to acquire land by descent right, even after many years of absence.
[18] See *Codified Laws*, art. n. 423, p. 113f; right to sale, art. n. 381.
[19] Ibid., art. 427, p. 114.
[20] Ibid., art. 3278, p. 853.
[21] Ibid., art. 3279, p. 853
[22] Ibid., see art. nos. 3284, 3286, 3287, 3288, 3296, 3304, 3418, among others.

was reserved from that part belonging to the state. *Hudad* lands were cultivated by peasants of the surrounding area, by tenants or by salaried paid government servants. *Hudad* lands were given as salary to the local land tax collector called *gätär mälkägna*, as well as provincial governors who were assigned to the palace in order to collect supplies for their banquet expenditure. The other type of state land was called *mätäkiya mänqäya* and was reserved for soldiers who were supposed to stay in the region temporarily. When they moved to another place, or when they were deprived of the land because of crime, the land was given to another soldier. The land was thus called 'uprooting and transplanting'. Land was also reserved for officials and this land was called *shum shir* land (land for appointment and dismissal).[23] In some instances there were unused reserved lands belonging to the state, and these lands were under the control of the governor general. State land was used for remuneration of officers and soldiers. Generally it was referred to by the name "*mängest*" (state), but depending on the purpose of allocation, the land was also referred to by different names.[24]

State land was not exchanged or sold without government permission and was given to those who served the government.[25] The holder of government land had no right to sell the land without government permission.[26] It was possible to transfer the land or sell part of it, but the transaction could not be recognized by a new state land holder.[27] A state land holder could be accused if he leased the land to a tenant to have him pay land tax.[28] He was not allowed to give the land as *rist* (heritable land) to another person even if that person was ready to pay land tax.[29]

A state land holder could pass the land to his heirs, but a new governor had the right not to recognize the inheritance.[30] If the government did not accept the transfer, the heirs could be dispossessed.[31] Women were not allowed to inherit state land unless the central government confirmed it, normaly the land passed from a father to a son.[32] A daughter could hold the land if she continued to give her father service through her husband or her servant.[33]

State lands, no matter how long one paid land tax (honey) or kept the lands, could not be considered as one's own.[34] Government land could be considered

[23] Read the articles written in the *Codified Laws*.
[24] See Gebre Wold Engda Worq (1948 E.C.), p. 34.
[25] For definition see *Codified Laws* p. 123.
[26] Ibid. art. no. 475.
[27] Ibid, art. no. 504
[28] Ibid, art. no. 544
[29] Ibid., art. no. 547.
[30] Ibid., art. no. 479.
[31] Ibid., art. no. 529.
[32] Ibid., art. 494.
[33] Ibid., art. no. 499.
[34] Ibid., art. nos. 462, 472, 489, 528.

as one's own only when the government agreed.[35] If a governor gave *rist* right over state land to an individual, the right was not recognized unless the central government confirmed the grant.[36]

If the holder of government land had debts, it was his other properties, not the government land, which was liable for confiscation.[37] If the *madäriya* holder was forced to leave the land, he had no right to ask compensation for the building and the plants on the land but he could destroy them and leave the land.[38] If a state land holder commited a crime against a government official, the central government could dispossess him from the land.[39] If a state land holder could not participate in a campaign, he could be uprooted from the land unless the court found his case satisfactory, or unless the government forgave his deeds or the governor general changed his punishment to another form.[40] The state land holder could be dispossessed by the *mälkägna* if the land was found to be useful to the state because it contained minerals or hot springs.[41] An individual could not claim government land by right of descent.[42] Forests belonged to the government and were not allowed to be cleared by any one.[43] A governor had no right to grant market land or *ch´ifra*-troops land to another person as a *rist* or to build a house.[44]

The relations among the three agents of land owners and the conditions and terms of access to land changed depending on the balance of power. The King who had a claim of reversionary right over land by right of imposing tax obligation, tended to assert those rights strongly when he needed more land. On the other hand the aristocracy enriched its patrimony through the accumulation of office and land when the King's authority showed signs of political weakness.[45] The shift in the configuration of political power and the needs of the state brought about changes in the distribution and terms of access to land. The terms of access were subject to re-negotiation and redefinition depending on the balance of power.

The private ownership rights that developed in central and southern Ethiopia had a considerable potential and flexibility to meet the logistic needs developed over centuries. Private ownership clearly defined property rights among the

[35] Ibid., art. nos. 463.
[36] Ibid., art. nos. 466, 497.
[37] Ibid., artcles nos. 461, 478.
[38] Ibid., articles nos. 542,543.
[39] Ibid., articles nos. 498, 527.
[40] Ibid., articles nos. 513, 545.
[41] Ibid., art. nos. 518.
[42] Ibid., art. no. 465.
[43] Ibid., art. no. 501.
[44] Ibid., art. no. 511.
[45] See Tekalign W. Mariam (1995), "Land Tenure, Urban Supply and Regional History: A Political Economic Approach to the History of Shoa and the Provisioning of Addis Ababa", Ph.D. Thesis, Department of History, Boston University. pp. 100–103, 109–112.

state (King and his officials), regional aristocrats and local *balabat*. Though it seemed unfair, there was division of land on a one-third principle. The state had *madäriya* land and the *balabat* had their own pieces of land. Neither of them interferred with each other's possessions; they exercised their rights independently. *Gäbar* peasants (owner-cultivator) who held the land were also secure in their position. A neighbouring community could not come and request a redistribution of land. Their position was customarily and legally defined and recognized. The clarity of definition and allocation of property rights had the potential to resolve possible conflicts over the distribution of surplus.

The private ownership right provided the freedom to make contracts (tenancy arrangements). Both *madäriya* land (state-land) and *balabat* could make tenancy arrangements. This was impossible by the *rist* type of land ownership which gave access to land by right of descent and thus tied the labour to the land.[46] Besides, the private land ownership system provided the opportunity for the state to make land surveys (for various purposes), and use the labour force (in this case by tenancy arrangement) for military purposes. Available lands and labour facilitated troop recruitment on a permanent basis. Campaign troops were recruited from the peasants not by the method of partial tax exemption, but through the grant of state land, which ensured their loyalty to the regional prince. Also, the cavalry was not recruited by the system of tax exemption. Cavalry needed large amounts of land (volume of production, at least an annual expense of ten *dawula* of grain, and grass land) to feed mules or horses.[47] Availabilty of *madäriya*-state land facilitated recruitment of a dependable cavalry consisting of the *siso balabat* (local lord with large tracts of land) and government *mälkägna* (*balä madäriya* with *gasha* land). Under such a system, kings and princes were not dependent on the peasant community and local lords for recruitment of troops.

2.2. Tax Payment on the Size of Land Holding

Payment of ordinary land tax belonging to the fiscal military system had three stages of development. The first stage covered the period of Nägasi Kristos

[46] In the *rist* areas there was scarcity of land and labour mainly as the result of the type of land ownership right and principles of tax assessment. Labour obligation was, therefore, given as a privilege only to local tax collectors. See Gebre Wold Engda Worq (1948 E.C.), p. 59. In these areas kings and governors used slave labour (termed as *bariya gäbar*) to cultivate their land. See, Beckingham, C.F. and Huntingford, G.W.B. (eds.), (1961), *The Prester John of the Indies, I*. Cambridge. p. 248. See the document in Haddis Gebre-Meskel (1992), p. 208; see also Täklä Iyasus, *Yä Ngus Tälä Haymanot Tarik*. Mans. n. 254. p. 50; Gabrä Selassie Walda Aregay (1959 E.C.), *Dagmawi Menelik Neguse Nägäst zä-Etyopia*, Addis Ababa, p. 116; Pankhurst (1979), p. 463; and Crummey (1989), p. 326 text, p. 315 tran.

[47] See Mahteme Selassie (1957), "The Land System of Ethiopia", in *Ethiopia Observer, I*, p. 219.

(1696–1703) extending to the end of the reign of Amha Yesus (1743–1774). At this stage the system was expanding mainly by means of conquest and the aim was allocation of state land to provincial campaign troops and *hudad* land for the court. At this stage, payment of ordinary land tax was in the form of *hudad*: a corvee labour obligation of *gäbar* (owner-cultivators) for cultivation of reserved lands for the court, and probably for the *mälkägna*, local government tax administrator. The second stage began with the reign of Asfa Wasen (1774–1808), whose reign saw the introduction of a proper payment of ordinary land tax (through the imposition of the honey payment) and changes in territorial administration.[48] During this stage the system expanded from northern Shewa into the regions of Yejju and Wollo.

In 1696, during the fourteenth year of his reign, King Iyasu I (1682–1706) came to Shewa, reconciled the local notables, and appointed a govornor called Nägasi Kristos (1670s–1703) who founded the Shewa aristocratic dynasty. This governor and his successors followed a polciy of expansion and they distributed state lands to the provincial campaign troops and reserved *hudad* land for the court.[49] Owner-cultivators of the surrounding areas near to the *hudad*-reserved land had the obligation to cultivate the land. The labour obligations of the peasant covered the whole labour process until the grain was stored in *gotära*: ploughing, weeding, harvesting, threshing, and storage. Peasants of the surrounding area cultivated the land based on different arrangements. In some places the peasants worked two days on their field and one day on the *hudad* of the governors[50], and this type of arrangement was called *siso arash*. If peasants wanted to work continuously on their own fields, and would like to work on the *hudad* land after they had finished their own, then they divided the *hudad* land, and this was called *eta* (lot). Under whatever kind of arrangement, peasants had labour obligations, and this type of labour obligation was called *siso arash*. It included the labour for cultivating, weeding, harvesting, threshing, loading and transporting to the granary.[51]

The obligation of owner cultivators was at first cultivation of reserved *hudad* land, but during the time of Asfa Wasan (1774–1808), an additional obligation was the payment of ordinary land tax. During this time, the *Gäbar Madäriya* system had extended over a relatively larger area in central Shewa.[52] This ruler introduced payment of land tax in honey, and this payment was proof of pos-

[48] On changes in territorial administration see Darkwah, R.H.K. (1975), p. 13f.

[49] See Bairu Tafla (1987), pp. 503–4; See also Marse Hazan Walda Kirqos (1948 E.C.), *Yä Amarigna Säwasäw*. Addis Ababa. p. 37; see also Ege, S. (1978), pp. 23f, 129f, 168, 169, 170; Stitz, V. (1974), pp. 99–104.

[50] See Gebre Wold Engda Worq (1962), p. 306.

[51] The corvee obligation (cultivation of *hudad* land) should not be confused with other types of labour obligations of the peasants, which probably came late during the reign of Menelik. Peasants pounded cereals, erected fence, and constructed houses for governors, and this labour was not part of land tax; it was an additional imposition. See sections 3.3., 5.1.4., and 6.2.2 below.

[52] See Darkwah, R.H.K. (1975), pp. 14f.

session of a field.[53] The ruler also decreed a law which "forbade the subjects from the manufacture or drink of hydromel (*täj*), reserving the privilege only for the rulers".[54] Honey was important to make the luxurious wine drink called *täj*, and the nobles would like to have control over this production. This might have been the background to the introduction of land tax payment in honey. The ruler also introduced payment in grain, farmstock, and cotton cloth.[55] Probably the introduction of grain payment was introduced to ease the problem around *hudad* cultivation. As the size of the army increased and campaigns intensified, presumably more *hudad* and state land was needed, but allocation of *hudad* land depended on the availability of land and labour. Probably to overcome this constraint, the ruler had introduced grain payment in areas where there was no *hudad* cultivation.

Whatever the background, during the time of Asfa Wasen land tax began to be paid in honey and *hudad* cultivation. Payment of ordinary land tax thus had two aspects: cultivation of *hudad* land and payment of honey. The labour part of the land tax payment obligation was fixed and defined, but its distribution among households depended on the size of reserved land and availability of labour in the neighbourhood. On the other hand the amount of honey payment is not known. No information was available for its assessment. It was probably assessed by the size of the land holding measured by an eye estimation.[56] The point is, however, that both the labour part and the honey part appeared to have had no similar basis or unit of assessment.[57]

In the fiscal military system, land tax was fixed in such a way as to fulfil the needs of a campaign soldier. An ordinary soldier was given *gasha* land.[58] As can be inferred from a later document (from the 19th century), a peasant who cultivated *gasha* land (unit of land measurement) had to pay annually one gundo of honey (ca. 19 kgs.) and three *dawula* (ca 300 kgs.) of grain to a soldier assigned to use the tax as salary. In lieu of the payment of grain, the

[53] See Ege, S. (1978), p. 171, and reference note 200.

[54] For the sources, see Darkwah, R.H.K. (1975), p. 15, n.38.

[55] See the source in Ege, S. (1978), footnote 201.

[56] Mahteme Selassie (1962 E.C.), p. 132.

[57] The labour and the honey part of the land tax merged and acquired the same basis of assessment, i.e., unit of measurement, when land was surveyed on the basis of *qälad*. This type of assessment started with the period of Menelik. See section 3.1.1.

[58] Both in the *Amisho Rim* system and in the *Gäbar Madäriya* system, the term *gasha* was used. In both cases the use of the term was correct so long as it refered to allocation of land tax to a campaign soldier. However there was a diference. In the *Amisho Rim* system of the Gonder period *gasha* land was a tax unit measured in the number of farmlands called *medr* cultivated by peasants who had use right. The level of the tax was fixed at one-fifth of the produce of the land, and a peasant paid from those farm lands he cultivated. In the *Gäbar Madäriya* system *gasha* was a land tax allocated to a soldier, but its level was determined not by proportion but by considering the basic needs of a campaign soldier. In other words it included not only grain payment but also the labour of the peasant. In the *Gäbar Madäriya* system it refered to a measured unit of land (ca 42 hectores).

peasant was forced to provide one *quna* of ground *teff*-grain, one *quna* of ground beans, and three *quna* of cereals. In other words the peasant had the obligation to fulfil the food and drinking needs of a soldier, in addition to an obligation to cut wood and provide grass to war horses. These quantified needs (ideal needs) of an ordinary fighting (field or campaign) soldier served as a basis to fix the level of land tax. The distribution of the land tax (amount paid by the individual) depended on the size of his holding and was calculated based on the knowledge of land size possessed by the household. The importance of this type of tax assessment was, thus, its security as an assured amount of income for a soldier, i.e., for permanently putting a soldier in the field and meeting his needs. The payment of land tax in kind was in harmony with the form of the economy and actual current logistic needs. The level of tax payment was not affected by price, circulation of money, etc. The disadvantage was that, since needs were not met by a market method, it was physically difficult to transport the large amount of grain and other materials needed for war.

2.3. Consolidated Forms of Revenue Administration

The evidence available on the earlier forms of revenue allocation of the system is meager. For the region of Shewa, Nägasi (1670s–1703) who founded the Shewa aristocratic dynasty, distributed land as follows: "a *gasha* is allotted to each of *samongna* (clergy), one *gasha* for *gendäbäl*; *gendäbäl* is a campaigner, and it is called *ch´äwa* in Gonder; one *gasha* is for the *gäbar* that is, *mad bét*. A *mälkägna* would be appointed above them".[59] The aim of Nägasi could have been the creation of *madäriya* land for campaign soldiers and *hudad*-reserved land for the revenue purpose of his court. In other words it had a military aim to secure remuneration for campaign soldiers and court *ch´ifra* troops. A similar type of military organization and distribution of land occurred in the region of Yejju during the time of *ras* Ali Guangul who defeated an imperial troop which was sent on expedition to Shewa in 1784. After he deposed the King, *ras* Ali introduced a fiscal arrangement similar to the one in Shewa, commonly known as Ali *gäbar* and Ali *zämach*.[60] A similar process took place in the region of Wollo proper. The system was introduced by Kollase Amäde of the Mommadoch family in 1799 after his return from the campaign to Gonder.[61]

[59] See Bairu Tafla (1987), p. 503; In another source it was stated that Negasi carried out a land survey (in the conquested areas) and allocated the land to *gäbar* farmers, *gendäbäl*-soldiers, and to the clergy *qes awädash*. See Marse Hazan Walda Kirqos (1948 E.C.), p. 37.

[60] See Fekadu Begna, (1990), "Land and the Peasantry in Northern Wallo 1941–1974: Yajju and Raya and Qobbo Awrajas". M.A. Thesis in History. A.A.U., p. 72; Gebre Wold Engda Werq (1948 E.C.), p. 51, Mahteme Selassie (1962 E.C.), pp. 156, 157.

[61] See Gebre Wold Engda Worq, (1948 E.C.), p. 47; Mahteme Selassie, (1962 E.C.), p. 153.

One may infer from the document of Nägasi that both state lands for campaign soldiers and *hudad* lands for the court were under the administration of the *mälkägna*.[62] This local official also came under the supervision of higher governors. An *abägaz*, governor of frontier districts and a campaign leader of garrisoned troops could be supervisor of *mälkägna* in his area of administration. In the 1840s there were about 50 *abägaz* in Shewa as reported by the European traveller Harris.[63] An *abägaz* was responsible for the administration of frontier territories and was also in charge of recruiting and leading campaign soldiers remunerated by *madäriya* lands.[64]

As the system expanded and as proper land tax was imposed (such as the honey part of the land tax), the administration of the revenue began to be separate. There was a separation of revenue administration of the governor and garrison troops. Particularly, what belonged to the court and to the governor general began to be administered by *mesläné*, which means "like myself". Generally the *mesläné* is used to refer to an official who represented the ruler, but it was mostly used to refer to the administration of *mad bét* lands and market dues belonging to the court.[65] Governor generals had also developed their own *mesläné* administration similar to the royal court. On the other hand revenue for garrison troops and auxiliary forces were administered by *mälkägna*, who was still under the supervision of the governor general.

Madäriya-state land continued to be administered by the local *mälkägna* official under the supervision of the governor general. The soldier held *madäriya* land as long as he gave military service or as long as the court wished. The size of the land they received depended on rank and title. *Madäriya* lands were centrally controlled and administered by the court. At the initial stage, troops recruited by the system were not given the right to collect and use ordinary land tax. The collection, custody and disbursement of ordinary land tax was under the control of the ruler, either through the court or through the district governor. Soldiers were given *madäriya* land and officers were given *hudad* land which they used directly. They were not apportioned

[62] *Mälkägna* was at first administrator of *madäriya* lands and *hudad* lands belonging to the government. In the discussion of Svein Ege there is a confusion of the function of *mälkägna* with state ownership of land in the capacity of a private person. He considered the *mälkägna* as local land lord, see Ege, S. (1978), p. 62f. *Mälkägna* was, however, a state official responsible, among other things, for the administration of state land, often cultivated by tenants who had contractual agreements with holders of the state land. The land belonged to the state, not to the *mälkägna*. Local land lords were the *balabat* group.

[63] See Harris, W.C. (1844), *The Highlands of Aethiopia. vol. III*, London. p. 30; see also Ege, S. (1978), chapter seven, footnote 80.

[64] See Tsehai Berhane Selassie 1980. "The Political and Military Traditions of the Ethiopian Peasantry." Ph.D. Dissertation, University of Oxford, Faculty of Anthropology and Geography. p. 191 and footnote 18. The military function and its responsibility in the administration of *madäriya* lands was not stressed by Ege in his discussion of Shewan administration, see Ege, S. (1978), pp. 147f.

[65] See Ege, S. (1978), pp. 144–145.

gult as in the case of the *rist* system. The separation of revenue administration for the King's and governor's court on one side, and for the field (garrison) troops on the other, was an important development.

In the emergent fiscal military system, though revenue allocation was decentralized, it was not localized like the *rist gult* system. The system was not administered by traditional local rulers and private methods. The King had his own officials to collect and administer land tax and manage reserved lands. The same was true for the governor. Territorial soldiers had their own source of revenue administrated by the provincial governor as chief supervisor. Governors were fiscal agents of the central government, and had no jurisdiction to decide on the form of payment, rate of taxation, and exemption. They had to follow centrally laid down principles and guidelines.

The emergent fiscal military system had principles of allocation of revenue that were favourable for the kind of military needs and organization developed by the Gonderian kings. As land tax was paid individually, it was possible for the state to control each owner-cultivator. Because the state had control over land tax (through its officials) and had state land, it was not difficult to transfer extra land when the need arose. There were no intermediary hindrances like the *gultägna* and the descent communities.

2.4. Conclusion

The study of the background and emergence of the fiscal military state in Ethiopia leads to a number of conclusions. One observation is that feudalism is not a single and a homogeneous system. Depending on the interest and motives of social forces, a feudal society can have different fiscal systems at one and the same time. In addition to the existing one, it can develop a new type of fiscal system in response to the shift in power. The dynamics of feudalism lied in its different forms of organization; there is no linear development from the feudal to the capitalist mode of production. The study of feudalism should not be dominated primarily by a search for the sources of the development of capitalist society, such as the study of issues of primitive accumulation of wealth, expansion of trade and growth of towns, merchants and a money economy, agrarian change and class differentiation, etc. In fact, it was the type of logistic system, and the needs and demands of continuous war which brought changes in the social and economic conditions of the feudal societies.

In the context of Ethiopian history, there were three different types of fiscal subsystems which had their own respective properties and principles since the beginning of the eighteenth century. These fiscal systems coexisted and operated concurrently as alternative economic bases for aristocratic power, and they are thus here called the triangular fiscal systems. These were the *Rist Gult* system (from 1150), the *Amisho Rim* system (from 1563) and the *Gäbar Madäriya* system (from 1696). In the literature, the *Rist Gult* system of this period is referred to as the Christian Kingdom.[66] The *Amisho Rim* system is referred to by the regional/geographical name as Gonderian period (1630s–1755).[67] The *Gäbar Madäriya* system is identified by a regional name as Shewa state, and the growth and expansion of this system is referred to as Shewa's reconquest and conquest of southern regions.[68] In the present study, however, the different subsystems are identified by their properties that differentiate each as a system as shown in the table 1.

Before the coming of the triangular fiscal subsystems, there was only the *Rist Gult* system. It was the fiscal system of the autocratic state (1150–1540) at a period when state and church were under the absolute control of a King. This fiscal system decentralised with the decline of the state in the sixteenth century. After the crisis of the sixteenth century, the *Amisho Rim* and the *Gäbar Madäriya* fiscal systems appeared at different times and in different regions.

The *Amisho Rim* system began with the quartering of the clergy during the last decade of the sixteenth century. Quartering of the clergy was a long process, starting with Serse Dingel (1563–97), followed by Fassillodus (1632–64), and later by Iyasu I (1684–1707).[69] Initially it was related to the development of a new form of financing the needs and functions of the church. The system expanded so long as the Gonderian kings were able to confiscate land and could impose imperial authority.

The *Gäbar Madäriya* system emerged in Shewa during the beginning of the eighteenth century and spread north to the region of Wollo. This system came to constitute the economic base of the fiscal military state during the second half of the nineteenth century. The structure of direct taxes belonging to the *Gäbar Madäriya* system favoured the development of a centralized power. These properties included the ability to impose a corvee labour obligation to cultivate reserved government land, the ability to fix the level of ordinary land tax payment to the ideal needs of a permanent soldier, individualized registration and payment of land tax, assessment of land tax payment based on the size of the land holdings, changes in the forms of land tax payment, and the emergence of extraordinary land tax payment—qualities that harmonize logistic needs with the acquisition and use of resources.

[66] See Taddesse Tamirat (1972).

[67] Among others, see Berry, L.V.B. (1976).

[68] Among others, see Abir, M. (1968), *Ethiopia: the Era of Princes. The Challenge of Islam and the Reunification of the Christian Empire, 1769–1855*. London, chapter eight; Levine, D. (1974), *Greater Ethiopia: The Evolution of a Multiethnic Society*. Chicago; Darkwah, R.H. K. (1975); Ege, S. (1978), chapter two note one.

[69] See the document in Tarekegn Yibab (1988), "The History of Mahdara Maryam ca. 1596–1939". B.A. Thesis in History, AAU. p. 8, and Appendix A , p. 89. For King Fasiledes see Haddis Gebre-Meskel (1992), pp. 93f; for King Iyasu (1682–1706), see Huntingford, G.W.B. (1965), pp. 62–63; B.L.Or. 813, p. 190. For King Bakaffa (1721–1730) see B.L. Or. 799.

Table 1. *Summary Table Showing the Properties of the Subsystems of the Triangular Fiscal System, 1563–1855*

Issues Related to Land Ownership Rights and Fiscal Organization of the State	Principles of the Subsystems		
	The *Rist Gult* System, from 1150	The *Amisho-Rim* System, from 1563–	The *Gäbar Madäriya* System, from 1696
Land ownership right:	communal-descent.	communal and state/collective.	private: local gentry, peasant freehold and state.
Labour Obligation:	only to privileged groups.	only to privileged groups.	universal to all gov't officials, an integral part of land tax payment.
Forms of land tax payment:	in kind, produce of the region.	in kind, church needs.	in kind, military needs.
Size and distribution of land tax payment:	descent principle, amount based on the number of descendants.	proportional, one-fifth, amount based on the number of farm lands.	individual possession of property, amount depended on the size and/or fertility of land.
Tax administrators and levels of collection:	*gultägna*, *adi* and Parish, private since crisis of 16th Cent.	*gultägna*, at the level of *ch'iqa*, parish, private administration.	crown officials *mälkägna* & *färäsägna*.
Method of Remuneration, Campaign soldier, transport & provisioning:	grain-salary payment, land tax exemption, community financed.	grain-salary payment, right to land tax collection, proportional; confiscated lands.	grain-salary payment, grain payment, right to land tax collection, and land grant; state expense.
Priorities in revenue allocation:	mainly court and clergy.	clergy and aiding aristocracy wealth accumulation.	military: efficient provision and transport system; regular troops.
Revenue administration:	institutions with an independent jurisdiction.	localized and private method.	state controlled, based on centralized principle.
Budgetary concepts:	*gult*.	*rim*.	*mad bét* and *gezat*.
Manner of rev. allocation:	institutional line.	functional line.	institutional and functional line.
Regions (predominant forms):	Märäb Mälash (present day Eritrea), Tigray, Parts of Bägémder, and Gojjam.	Märäb Mälash (present day Eritrea), Tigray, Parts of Bägémder, and Gojjam.	Wollo and Shewa.

Unlike the *Rist Gult* system, the *Gäbar Madäriya* system was more flexible and assured imperial control. In the first place the principles of tax assessment and payment and of administration of land tax revenue enabled the state to have more control over land and labour, and could, if the need arose, increase its revenue as needed, and could determine the size and nature of expenditure. Moreover, the state could allocate the land tax to meet varying logistic needs, without a concern for collection. It did not take centuries for the Gonderian military organization culture to find its sudden and expressive development in the regions of Yejju and Shewa. It was on the eve of the reform that the Were Seh assumed central power and ruled from the 1780s to1855. The Shewan aristocracy also played a significant role in the centre of power.[70] The *Gäbar Madäriya* system illustrated the capacity to serve as a fiscal base of a functionally highly differentiated and centralized mode of military organization. It was the properties of this regional enclavistic development which became universal and standard in the period 1855–1913. Why and how it spread and developed country wide is the theme of the next chapters in parts III and IV.

[70] In the literature, different reasons are given for the success of the Were Sehu and the consolidation and expansion of Shewan dynasty. In the case of the former, often their proficiency in cavalry and aristocratic marriage arrangements were cited as factors that contributed to success. The relative tranquillity in the region of Shewa was often attributed to Shewa isolation from Gonder. However, the basis of the Shewa tranquillity and the success of Were Seh family was a harmonious development between the survival need and mode of military organization of the aristocracy and the type of fiscal system.

Part III
The Creation of New Resources: Ways and Means, 1855–1913

Introduction

The background section dealt with military barriers particularly of the *Rist Gult* system, in the north and parts of central Ethiopia. Under this system, kings and princes depended on the peasant community and *gultägna* for their logistic needs. On the other hand, a centralized regional power evolved based on a new type of fiscal system. During the second half of the nineteenth century, while the various fiscal systems were influencing and remoulding each other, new and threatening external conditions appeared. First Egypt became ambitious to control the water sources of the Nile and the coasts of the Red Sea. This was followed by Italian, British and French colonialism on the Horn of Africa.[1] Probably for the first time, kings and princes were afraid of losing territory to outside powers. From 1855 onwards, kings introduced major reforms both at the institutional level (administration of tax) and in the structure of the taxes themselves (tax-technical measures) to enhance the financing capacity of the state. Part III deals with the new pressures and opportunities, and the consequent administrative measures and policies taken to ensure availability of sufficient funds for military pursuits. Chapter three deals with the major reforms and changes in the structure and administration of taxes; chapter four deals with revenue.

Concerning the presentation of the research results, it should be pointed out that at first each chapter presents detailed empirical data in order to explain to the reader the structure and functions of the system under discussion. To this end, each chapter begins by introducing basic questions derived from the purpose of the study. The last section and/or the conclusion of each chapter reviews the analytical part of the discussion and describes the changes made in the system.

[1] For a detailed account of the events see, among others, Rubenson, S. (1976).

CHAPTER THREE

The Making of a National and Standardized System of Direct Taxation, 1855–1913

This chapter deals with government tax policy and the consequent changes made in the structure of the tax system. Taxes are here differentiated as direct tax and indirect tax. Taxes levied on the basis and measure of agrarian property (land, cattle, crop, oxen) and agrarian production, which were related to the legal rights, social status, role and power of the individual or corporation in society made up direct taxation. Direct taxes were divided into different categories depending on the nature of the tax objects and regularity of payments. The first element was the ordinary regular land tax (*gebr*) based on ownership and/or use rights. There were extraordinary land taxes (*fäsäs* and *täsäri*), some of which were at times paid irregularly depending on the needs of the hour. There was a difference between ordinary and extraordinary land tax. An ordinary land tax was a tax based on land property and use, and had traditional legitimacy, and was automatically paid from year to year unless basic changes were made; in other words it was fixed and permanent. Extraordinary taxes were taxes levied either as a consequence of the inadequacy of the ordinary taxes or unexpected or unforeseen expenses. There were various types of surtaxes which were additional taxes imposed not on the basis of agricultural wealth and income but for the celebration of certain occasions (such as New Year's Day, Christmas, and Easter), payment of additional fees to government officials (such as appointment fees), and payments made in return for the administration of justice. Finally there was livestock tax. These categories (ordinary land tax, extraordinary land tax, surtaxes, and livestock tax) made up the structural elements of direct taxation. Structure did not mean only objects of taxation (different categories of taxes) but included as well the size/level of each tax and the forms of payment and principles of assessment and collection. Taxes were imposed indirectly on transactions regardless of the nature of property ownership involved. Indirect taxes were government taxes on certain goods manufactured by craftsmen, goods sold by merchants and goods bought in market places. It also included customs tolls and salt production.

Before proceeding to the subject matter of this chapter, it is of prime importance to comment on the state of the historical research on taxation during the period under discussion. The research pioneers were Mahteme Selassie and

Gebre Weld Engda Worq, who had high positions at the royal court and served as Ministers of Agriculture at different times.[2] Both authors focused on the concept of *serit*, a term which is used to express the kind of obligation attached to the use and possession of land by the state and private persons.[3] In the works of both authors, taxation was discussed by region, lumping together all of the following aspects: ownership rights (communal, state and private); the principle of assessment (using forms such as descent, proportion, size/fertility of land); rate of taxation (how much and why); forms of payments (salt, honey, grain, MT$, etc.); aims and forms of revenue allocation (*gäbar*, *gendäbäl*, *samon*, *madäriya*, etc.); categories of taxes (such as ordinary land tax, extraordinary land tax, surtaxes); and local and time variations. At times one finds all these explanations in one paragraph, in obscure and complex forms as they existed in reality, with technical terms from the little known and remote past. In their works, it is difficult to differentiate which was which and what was what.

The concept of *serit* fused many aspects of the system of taxation, namely forms of payment, principles of assessment, methods of collection and its juridical structure. Taxation in the literature was discussed intrinsically with politics and institutions. What is even more bothersome is that details and regional variations of types of taxes were discussed without diachronic perspective. The whole approach ignored the type of fiscal organization of the state that existed at a definite point in time. The discussion on taxes was not related to the structure and administration of government revenue and expenditure. Nonetheless, in spite problems with method of presentation and analysis, the information and data given by the authors were authentic and basic.

The economic historian Pankhurst presented a systematic discussion of the tax system. However, his discussion picked up only the subjects of taxation (peasants, hunters, handicraft workers and traders).[4] Based on this, he discussed the forms of taxation with a focus on the kind of payment (grain, honey, cloth, livestock, ivory, gold, and MT$). When it came to the presentation of the information by region, he simply followed the works of Mahteme Selassie and Gebre Weld Engda Worq, falling into the same traps as both those authors.

[2] See Mahteme Selassie (1962 E.C.); *idem.*, (1957); Gebre Wold Engda Worq (1948 E.C.); *idem.*, (1962). To avoid some of the distortion made in the area of translation, this work used mostly the Amharic versions of the texts.

[3] It appears that the term *serit* came into use with the coming of the *Amisho Rim* system at the end of the sixteenth century. It was a time when a large number of clergymen were quartered in confiscated lands.

[4] See Pankhurst, R. (1967), "Tribute, Taxation and Government Revenues in Nineteenth and early Twentieth Century Ethiopia, Part I", in *Journal of Ethiopian Studies, V, 2*, pp. 37–87; *idem.* (1968a), "Tribute, Taxation and Government Revenues in Nineteenth and early Twentieth Century Ethiopia, Part II", in *Journal of Ethiopian Studies, 6, 1*. pp. 21–72. idem (1968b), "Tribute, Taxation and Government Revenues in Nineteenth and early Twentieth Century Ethiopia, Part III", in *Journal of Ethiopian Studies, 6, 2*, pp. 93–118; *idem.* (1966a).

Apart from the lack of clarity created by inconsistency, his major problem in discussing taxation by subject led to the consequent difficulty created in trying to understand the structural relationship among tax object categories (say direct and indirect tax). More so, in his works there was no identification of an ordinary land tax, its principle of assessment, and differences in time and region. With the kind of method and discussion used by these authors, it is particularly difficult to study sources of government revenue and items of expenditure.[5] Consequently, it is difficult to analyse the implications and effects of the system of taxation on the socio-economic situation.[6]

In the present work, successive stages are followed to avoid confusion and to get a clear understanding of the system of taxation and its economic implications. First, it is necessary to separate the system of taxation from the discussion of land ownership and principles of revenue allocation. This would have better been followed by a study of objects of taxation (such as land, livestock, goods, etc.), instead of subjects of taxation; thus facilitating the understanding of the structure of taxes by focusing on respective forms of payment, principles of assessment and methods of collection. Studying the structure of taxes within a time perspective helped to understand the correlation among sources of government revenue. Finally, it became possible to analyse the implications of fiscal policy for the function and development of the economy.

3.1. Ordinary Land Tax Payment

King Tewodros (1855–1868) made no changes in the structure of direct taxes.[7] The evidence came through comparison of tax documents of King Tewodros and the *gult* land charter document granted by *ras* Wolde Selassie, territorial prince of Tigray. There is a difference of some six decades between the two documents, the Chäläqot document being written in 1794/95. Comparison of the same regions revealed that ordinary land taxes, surtaxes and indirect taxes had similar composition in both documents.[8]

It appears that it was difficult to introduce a new tax and a new principle of tax assessment and collection within the *Rist Gult* system. Instead, Tewodros attempted to increase the amount and forms of tax payment. In other words, he

[5] See further comments made at the beginnings of chapters four and six.

[6] See further comment in Part V.

[7] For a broader outline and attempt to systematically present taxation during the reign of Tewodros, see Tsegaye Tegenu (1994), "The Taxation System of Ethiopia, 1855–1868", in Bahru Zewde, Pankhurst, R. and Taddese Beyene (eds.), *Proceedings of the Eleventh International Conference of Ethiopian Studies*. vol. I. Addis Ababa. pp. 351–372.

[8] For Tewodros see the tax documents in Pankhurst, R. and Germa Selassie Asfaw, eds., (1979), *Tax Records and Inventories of King Tewodros of Ethiopia (1855–1868)*. London.

Table 2. *Gult lands Given to däbrä Selassie Chäläqot by däjazmach Wolde Selassie in 1794/5*

Regions	Regular Land Tax		Surtaxes			Indirect Tax
The seven *adi* Däqi Sandud	23 *wäqét*	44 *mäzoriya*	3 *frida*	*madga mar*	12 Birr per *däbr* for *liqä kahnat*; Kfla *mar*, goats per village to the *liqä diyaqon*[i]	
Habas	12 *wäqét*	12 *ch´an*	6 *frida*; 30 sheep	*nefk mar*	800 salt for the *diaqon*; 3 sheep and 70 salt for *liqä kahnat*	*mäshomiya* laden *mar*;
Däbr	10 *wäqét*	4 *ch´an mäba*	4 *frida*	4 *quna mar*	200 for *liqä kahnat*, goats per village[ii]	400 salt *mäshomiya*
Qorqora	3 *wäqét*	2 *ch´an mäba*; 2 *ch´an*	2 *frida*	3 *madga mar*	160 salt for *liqä diyaqon*[iii]	200 slat *mäshomiya*
As Gäbta	700 salt	*ch´an* Teff	1 *frida*	2 *quna mar*	2 *madga* & *nefk mar*; 100 salt for *liqä diaqon*[iv]	100 *mäshomiya*
Astha	600 salt[V]	*ch´an mäba*	1 *frida*	2 *quna mar*	100 salt & " *quna mar* for *liqä diaqon*	100 *mäshomiya*
adi Solest	1,000 salt	10 *ch´an*	3 *frida*		2 *birr* for *liqä diaqon*	4 *birr mäshomiya*

Source: *Wärq zä-wängél* of *däbrä* Selassie Chäläqot, Tigray Region.
Notes:
[i] custom tolls of the *gult* were given to the *mahber* (association) of the *däbr*. One of the seven villages, *adi* Maklo, paid 200 salt.
[ii] the *gult däbr* had four *got´* (villages), namely, Däbr, Tselam, Hagara Maryam and Kurtan. The document made distinction in payments by each of the *got´*. What is written in the table is only for Däbr. Of the other villages, Tselam paid *amisho* (one-fith) of the payment made by Däbr; Hagarä Mayam paid 200 salt, Kuntram 200 salt, *quna mar* and *kiflo mar* for the *liqä diakon*.
[iii] a village, *adi* Qusr, pays *quna mar* and *nefk mar* for the *liqä diaqon*. Income from the custom toll of *entalo* is given for the *mahber* of the *däbr*.
[iv] Quna *mar* and custom tools is for the *mahbär*; the custom tolls of Sänafe paid one-third (*siso*) (of the collected revenue).
[v] another village Makarm pays 200 salt
In addition to the above taxes, the document finally stated that the right of appointing *liqä kahnat* was given to the *likä kahnat* of Chäläqot. Appointments in the *gult* (*yä gultoch shumät*) were given to the *mahbär*. Collector of the Arho paid the Chäläqot church "*gäbila lebd*" from the Wäsama (toll).

followed a discretionary policy for increasing the rate of tax payment; and this policy was implemented in the regions of Yejju and Bägémder.[9]

Tewodros also wanted to increase the number of people who should pay

[9] See, Dimotheos, S. (1871), *Deux Ans de Sejour en Abyssine, ou vie Morale, Politique et Religieuse des Abyssines, V.I.* Jerusalem. p. 114, and Feqadu Begna, (1990), p. 73.

taxes. He turned to the church, which had employed a relatively abundant number of clergy who, by virtue of their profession and traditional privileges, were exempted from payment of tax to the state. In this manner, the King reduced the number of clergy in a *däbr* church, limiting it to five.[10] Those clergy allowed to give service to the church were exempted from the payment of taxes, while the rest of the *däbtära* were to pay land tax.[11]

Because the King had introduced a salary system[12], peasant communities paid taxes in the form of MT$[13]. This was not a completely new departure from the past; in some regions of northern Ethiopia taxes were paid in MT$ from the eighteenth century onwards.[14] Starting from the period of the *Zämänä Mäsafint*, the form of payment was dictated not by the produce of the region but by the military and monetary needs of the territorial princes.

King Yohannes (1872–1889) made no changes in the structure of taxes. The King had confiscated one-third of the communal land for the purpose of revenue allocation. But this measurement did not change the forms and rate of land tax payment. As one may infer from the land tax document of Medahni Alem *däbr* church of Mäkälé (Table 3), which was granted by King Yohannes, the King followed earlier principles and forms of tax payment. On two-thirds of the land possessed by the commune, the payment of due tax was fixed and assessed on the descent principle as before. In the *siso* land distributed to the clergy, the tax was paid based on percentage of the harvest.[15] The form and rate of extraordinary tax payments such as *fäsäs* continued as before. Indirect taxes (consumption tax, allocated for holidays of the church) were similar to those found in the documents of Tewodros.

Tewodros and Yohannes basically followed the same principles of assessment, forms of payment and rate of tax payment belonging to the *Rist Gult* and *Amisho Rim* systems. Even the reform in the forms of land tax payment by MT$ during the time of Tewodros and *wäqét* during the time of Yohannes was not new. What was different from the past was that more regions were included in the payment of tax to the kings and former privileges were abolished as done by Tewodros.

Menelik's reforms were basically different from Tewodros' and Yohannes'. Menelik operated within the *Gäbar Madäriya* system and his reforms were

[10] During the Gonder period and the Era of Princes *däbr* churches had around 120 clergymen when established by charter.

[11] See Täklä Iyäsus, *yäNegus Täklä Haimanot Tarik*, IES, manus. no. 254. p. 71.

[12] Salt and cloth were used to pay soldiers in lieu of salary. For payment in cash, see the copy of the letter of Tewedros kept at the National Library, Ministry of Culture and Sports, Addis Ababa. Document number 22.03.4. On the payment of amole-salt bar see Täklä Iyäsus, *yäNegus Täklä Haimanot Tarik*, IES, manus. no. 254. passim.

[13] See the tax documents of Tewodros in Pankhurst, R. and Germa Selassie Asfaw, eds., (1979).

[14] See Pankhurst, R. (1979/80).

[15] Interview with Malaka Genet Serse Dingel Arefe Ayne, Head of the Däbrä Gänät Medahini Alem Church, August 1993.

Table 3. *Gult Lands Given to däbrä gänät Medahni Alem Mäkälé by Yohannes IV in 1872/73*

Regions/districts	Regular Land Tax				Surtaxes
Adisu Sehun	*siso** (one-third) land		2 *ch´an mäba*	*quna ekul mar*	ekul frida
Elken	*siso* land	200 salt	*ch´an mäba*	*quna ekul mar*	*frida ekul*
Dur Anbäsa	*siso* land	500 salt	*ch´an mäba*	*quna mar*	one *frida*
Dägin B`ele´at	*siso* land	250 salt		2 *quna mar*	*ekul frida*
Waz	*siso* land	250 salt	*ch´an mäba*	1 *quna mar*	1 *frida*
Tehul	*siso* land	100 salt	4 *madga mäba*	*quna mar*	*ekul frida*
Al`asa	*siso* land	100 salt	4 *madga mäba*	*quna ekul mar*	*frida ekul*
Haräqo[i]			15 *ch´an*[ii]	8 *quna mar*	6 *frida*

Source: *Wärq zä-wängél* of *däbrä gänät* Mädahni Aläm, Mäkälé.
**siso* means that part of the confiscated land where cultivators paid *amisho* or *eribo* to the clergy. It is governed by the same tax assessment and forms of payment belonging to the *Amisho Rim* system.
Notes:
[i] The tax of Haräqol was assigned for the commemoration of the King.
[ii] Of the fifteen *ch´an*, one *ch´an* was pepper, 8 *ch´an teff*, and the remaining 8 *ch´an* was barley and *dagusa*.
The church was also granted custom tolls from the salt producing area (Arho) and market dues and tolls.

more of a structural change based on the principles of the *Gäbar Madäriya* system. During the reign of Menelik, three means of reform were introduced that changed the tax structure of the *Gäbar Madäriya* system. These reform means included standardization in the rate of land tax payment, creation of national uniform land tax payment, and an introduction of new extraordinary land tax payment. These issues are discussed separately in the following sections.

3.1.1. Standardization of Rate of Land Tax Payment

By definition, standardization meant that every one or everything should be treated in the same way. Menelik's tax reform policy had regional equity as an objective and made logistic considerations. In the *Gäbar Madäriya* system, though the payment of ordinary land tax was fixed, the basis and principles of assessment were not uniform. Payment of land tax proper was fixed during the second stage in the development of the system, and the level of payment was then fixed in consideration of the ideal needs of a soldier. The needs of an ordinary campaign soldier were identified and the quantification made on such bases was supposed to be met from a given size of land holding referred to by the general name of *gasha*.

One *gasha* land could be occupied by one owner-cultivator or by two or three. The rate of payment by a one owner-cultivator was calculated on the size of land held by the owner. In earlier times, the size of the land was measured by an eye estimation. This type of measurement did not distinguish differences in fertility, quality, drainage, altitude and exposure of the fields or soil type. The tax assessment thus created a considerable difference in the burden of the tax payment made on peasants holding the same size of land. Those peasants who had fertile land had the greatest advantage as the land could produce crops every year. Infertile land was fallowed every other year or, if the land were very poor, for two years out of three. Fertile land thus contributed more to most households than infertile land.

Another earlier problem of the *Gäbar Madäriya* system of taxation was that the forms of the tax payment (the honey part and the *hudad*-reserved land cultivation) were separated and had different bases of assessment. The labour aspect of the land tax could be considered as corvee, for the purpose of understanding. It included the labour for ploughing, sowing, weeding, harvesting, threshing, loading and transporting to the granary. This type of labour obligation was called *siso arash*, following the type of arrangement in cultivation of *hudad* land. Peasants of the surrounding area cultivated the reserved land based on different arrangements. Theoretically, if and when the peasant cultivated *hudad* land, depended on the availability of land and labour, but the system had no such consideration. In addition to the *hudad* obligation, peasants were paying honey for the land they owned and cultivated.

The government of Menelik made a cadastral survey in order to standardize payment of land tax. Cadastral survey was thought to redress the problem around the assessment and calculation of ordinary land tax payment. It is reported that in Shewa, land measurement began in 1883 (or 1876 E.C.).[16] Measured land came to be known as *qälad* land, named after the rope used for measurment. Considering the fertility of the land and the irregularity and ecology of the region, the following grades were fixed: one *gasha* measured 467 m. in width and 734 m. in length and was classified as first rate (*lem*, fertile land); land of fair fertility was graded as second rate and it measured 509 m. by 781m *lam-t´äf* (semi-fertile land); land that measured 667 m. by 1701 m. was classified as *t´äf*; bad and infertile land was rated as fourth class and was measured

[16] Gebre Selassie (1959 E.C.), p. 123. Mahteme Selassie wrote that land survey began in Shewa in 1887 E.C. (1894/5), see Mahteme Selassie (1962 EC), p. 105. Probably this was the second round. There is other information on land measurement from the early 1880s, and this was discussed in the background for purpose of land distribution to central stationed contingents who came from Gonder after the death of King Tewodros, see Haile Zalake (n.d.), *däjazmach Girmame yä-Hiwot Tarik*. IES. Amharic Collection. Addis Ababa. p. 25. Four years before the land measurement in Shewa, that is in 1872 E.C., the principal secretary of the King had given orders on the registration of land according to their tax obligation category. See Gebre Selassie (1959), p. 99.

801 m. by 1,355m.[17] In all cases, poor fertility was compensated for by increased acreage. If the land was measured and if the peasant had land less than the standard unit, he was not obliged to pay full land tax.[18] Those who had less than one *gasha* were given the extra land found in the area.[19] But a peasant could not hold more land than the measured land allowed by the government (7 times 11). In principle, the introduction of *qälad* measurement brought about standardization in payment of land tax.

The introduction of *qälad* measurement brought about changes in the rate and forms of land tax payment. According to the *qälad* principle, land tax was fixed as follows: one *gasha* land paid one *gundo mar* and two or three *dawula* of Grain, and this was called *fré gebr*. Formerly, the *gäbar* used to cultivate *hudad* lands in addition to the payment of fixed land tax in the form of honey, cloth, etc. The payment in kind and in labour had different forms of assessment. Payment in kind was related to the produce of the region and or military needs and the labour part depended on the number of household members. With the introduction of *qälad* measurement, *hudad* cultivation was commuted to three *dawula* of grain payment. At this juncture the payment in kind and labour merged to form a basic unit of land tax payment. The term merge is used to indicate that both in kind and labour obligations began to acquire the same basis of assessment, i.e., unit of measurement: a definite measured size of land and a specific type of soil was supposed to give a fixed amount of honey and grain tax payment. This was important since it avoided the problem of finding available land and labour for obligations of *hudad* cultivation.

Qälad measurement virtually abolished the practice of *hudad* cultivation which had been in existence for over a century. *Gäbar* began to pay a fixed land tax irrespective of price, produce of the region, or availability of land and labour situation. In documents studied in the district of Bacho, Tekalgn found a complete absence of *hudad* after land measurement in 1897.[20] Though he considered this feature as indicating a decrease in the possession of royal estate, the fact of the matter was that it indicated the end of the long practice of *hudad* cultivation when labour and in kind payment began to acquire the same basis of assessment. The introduction of *qälad* thus heralded the abolishment of labour for the cultivation of *hudad* land; however, this did not mean the elimination of all types of labour obligation. Peasants continued to grind cereals, build fences, and construct houses for governors; but these obligations were not part of the ordinary land tax payment, they were an additional imposition. Probably together with the new basis of land tax assessment, came another type of labour obligation on peasants imposed in the form of *senq*,

[17] For details see Mahteme Selassie (1962 E.C.), p. 106.
[18] See *Codified Laws*, art. no. 370.
[19] Ibid., art. no. 389.
[20] See Takalign Wolde Mariam, (1995), pp. 111f.

supply of provision to campaign soldiers and the palace. Again this type of obligation could be exempted in return for service as an auxiliary force.[21]

The objective of cadastral survey was not only to create the same basis of land tax assessment and equity in the distribution of land tax payment. It was also aimed at getting control over uncultivated (unused) and extra lands which the government could then distribute to its servants. Also, extra lands were sold, preferably to the owner who had one *gasha* of land. The former owner was given precedence when it came to buying the extra land.[22] Extra land was sold to the one who wanted to cultivate it and pay tax. The government (land surveyors or an official) could allocate it to whomever they liked.

With the introduction of *qälad* measurement, ordinary land tax payment pertaining to the *Gäbar Madäriya* system reached its third stage of development. As mentioned, the first stage belonged to the founder Nägasi when owner cultivators were only obliged to cultivate *hudad*-reserved land.[23] The second stage belonged to Asfa Wasen when the *gäbar* paid their proper ordinary land tax (payment of honey in addition to *hudad* cultivation). The third stage belonged to Menelik when honey payment and labour obligation acquired the same basis of assessment and when the *gäbar* were obliged to pay additional obligations including *senq*-provision supply and surtax payment.

Since land tax was paid in kind following the actual need of a soldier, military needs and the form of the economy were in harmony. The form of tax payment (in kind and in labour) was related to the form of the economy. Form of payment was interconnected with the actual current needs, including, for instance, various military needs such as rations for soldiers, palace banquets (flour, pepper, butter, honey, etc.), transport (*ch´an*), provisioning-*senq*, auxiliary services and weapons.

3.1.2. Creation of Uniform National Land Tax Payment

During the period of Menelik, individual registration and payment of land tax was not only standardized, but also became national in two senses. First, the land tax of the *Gäbar Madäriya* system included a major portion of the country. Secondly, an independent central administration was created to see to the collection, custody and distribution of tax payment. To say the standardized tax became national does not mean that it was universal within the realm. There was still particularism due to the existence of the *Rist Gult* and *Amisho Rim* systems. Yet there was an impressive attempt to impose the standardized land tax payment both in northern and southern Ethiopia.

[21] See Mahteme Selassie (1962 EC), p. 122 on the district of Qenbibit.

[22] See *Codified Laws*, art. nos. 351, 362, 366, 386, 388, 431.

[23] During this stage soldiers were paid mainly in the form of *madäriya* (state land).

In the *Rist Gult* regions of northern Ethiopia, the standardized rate had little effect in changing the descent type of land tax payment. In these areas the effect was felt or could be applied where the government had control over the land, such as *madäriya* lands confiscated from the community[24] and redistributed to the clergy or soldiers for cultivation by tenants. In principle, areas dominated by tenancy arrangements were propitious for implementing (or imposing) the standardized rate of land tax payment in northern Ethiopia.

There is evidence which indicates that grain payment was imposed in lieu of *hudad* land cultivation on communities belonging to the *Rist Gult* system. Formerly, cultivation of *hudad* land was a privilege given only to the local *shum*-chief. It was a type of additional obligation, not part of land tax payment. But starting from the period of Menelik, probabaly with the increase in the type and number of royal district and local tax officals such as the *mesläné*, peasants began to pay an extraordinary land tax payment referred to by different names in different regions. In Tigray it was called *hudad*, in Bägémder it was called *bäré ch´anqa*; this tax was assessed on the principle of *t´imad* (a land ploughed by a pair of oxen).[25]

In southern Ethiopia the introduction of a standardized rate of land tax payment was imposed through conquest following the tradition of the *Gäbar Madäriya* system. Individualized land tax payment was imposed as before through coercion (military means), mainly through confiscation of the land of the *balabat* (local chief), and through changing the status of the peasants from independent free owners to tenants and tax paying owner-cultivators (*gäbar*). There were stages in the introduction of the system. At first peasants paid a given amount, which was fixed following the amount paid customarily to the local-*balabat*, and this was called *qedéta*.[26] Later on, with the increase in the presence of imperial military power, *qedéta* was changed into the level and the rate of tax payment called *gasha*. At this stage, imperial provincial governors were installed in the various regions. Finally, the governor generals introduced the system of *qälad* (land survey) in their respective regions. At this stage, all the local *balabat*-chiefs were integrated into the system. Though

[24] See Menelik's letter written to *däjazmach* Gebre Selassie, *nebräed* of Aksum, dated April 12, 1900 EC. The document is deposited at the National Library, Ministry of Culture and Sports, Addis Ababa, document no. 7.06.1.

[25] See Gebre Wold Engda Worq (1948 EC), p. 58. During the time of Tewodros there was no *hudad* land cultivation in most of the regions of northern Ethiopia. In fact, the King at one time stopped the cultivation of *hudad* land ploughed by twenty-five pair of oxen and used it to supply the King's court. (Informant ato Ato Gäsäsä Bezabh, Mäkäle, August 1993). This was probably so, because the King's land tax administrators were paid in cash and did not need to cultivate the government's reserved land in lieu of salary.

[26] *Qedéta* was a tax or impost usually in-kind paid to a land owner by his tenant or to the headman or palace by the peasantry. This presupposition seems to be the case for Shewa, probably not for Yejju. It is said that *ras* Ali had introduced both the system of *madäriya* land and payment of land tax at the same time.

reforms of standardizing the rate of land tax payment and creating uniform national land tax payment were systematic, they were not introduced by parliamentary means.[27] In Ethiopia there were no territorial assemblies of the nobility and no representative institutions at the central level to which kings could resort to introduce taxes. However, there was an informal mechanism, and the traditional practice was that the King or the prince negotiated with the peasant community or governors of the provinces before sending military expedition.

3.2. Extraordinary Land Tax: Introduction of Tithe Payment

Another major change in the system of direct taxation during the reign of Menelik was the reform around the payment of extraordinary land tax. *Fäsäs* tax which was levied for the payment of the royal army, and the system of *täsäri* (billeting of royal troops) expanded in scale during the reign of Tewodros and Yohannes. During the reign of Menelik these extraordinary taxes were replaced by a payment called *asrat* (tithe).

Tewodros imposed the *fäsäs* tax on institutions hitherto exempted from payment. The King suggested that the clergy live on *asrat* tax (tithe), relinquishing their land ownership rights and collection of ordinary land tax to the state. The clergy disagreed and after long negotiations with the Abun, an agreement was reached by which church lands were to pay extraordinary tax, *fäsäs,* and relinquish their right of judicial fee collection to the state.[28] The King collected *fäsäs* and litigation money only from churches that had *rim* lands[29]; that means the tax was collected from alienated and privatized state lands of the *Amisho Rim* system[30].

[27] See Appendix B. There was resistance to the reforms both from the local nobility and peasants. For the period of Tewedros See Zänäb (1902), passim; For the period of Yohannes in the region of Wello see Asnake Ali (1983), chap. 1; Hussien Ahmed (1989), "The Life and Career of Shaykh Talha b. Ja`far (c.1853–1936)", in *Journal of Ethiopian Studies, 12, .XXII.* For the content of Yohannes' policy and military expeditions see Seltene Seyum (1972), "Yohannes IV Rise and Consolidation". B.A. Thesis in History, HSIU, Addis Ababa, pp. 15f; Gebre Medhin Kidane (1972), "Yohannes IV: Religious Aspects of his Internal Policy". B.A. Thesis in History, HSIU, Addid Ababa University, pp. 22f. For the period of Menelik see Bedru Ahmed (1984), "The Relations Between Western Gurage and the Kontab (ca. 1850–1937)". B.A. Thesis in History, A.A.U. Chapter 3; Abas Haji (1982), "The History of Arsi, 1850–1935". B.A. Thesis in History, A.A.U. Chapter 2; Gäbre Selassie (1959 EC), pp. 218–221; Caulk, Richard (1971), "The Occupation of Harar: January 1887", in *Journal of Ethiopian Studies; IX, 2.*

[28] See Zänäb (1902), p. 28.

[29] See Girma Tefera (1961 E.C). *Aba Tatäk Yä Quara Anbasa. Dagmawi Tewedros Negusä Nägäst Zä Ityopiya.* Addis Ababa. pp. 80–81.

[30] For an evidence see Tarekegn Yibabie (1988), p. 28.

Another form of extraordinary land tax payment was called *täsäri* (billeting), imposed probably in regions where emperors did not levy *fäsäs* tax. The King quartered his soldiers in peasant homes with the motto "peasants feed, soldiers eat".[31] By the *täsäri* system, a soldier was entitled to extract produce and service from peasants. Tewodros' successor, King Yohannes, maintained royal troops partly in the same way, billeting them in different regions.[32]

During the time of Menelik, the extraordinary land taxes, *fäsäs* and *täsäri*, were changed into *asrat* (tithe) payment. Menelik introduced payment of *asrat*-tithe in Shewa in 1892 for the remuneration of royal troops stationed in central regions[33]. *Asrat* was a universal tax paid by all who possessed and benefited from land use, and in principle no exception was made, even to local land lords (*balabat*) and government *madäriya* land holders. The tax was paid by the local chiefs and land lords (*balabat*), the *wäräda gendäbäl*, the provincial cavalry, and all who were given state lands such as the local government official, *mälkägna*[34], and government soldiers who possessed state land[35]. Holders of *samon* lands paid *asrat* to the government.[36] Those auxiliary corps recruited as *gendäbäl* soldiers[37], such as *dinkoan ch´an*, *gäbar* lands and *wärägänu,* paid *asrat* tax to the government. *Gäbar* peasants also paid *asrat* (tithe)[38] in addition to land tax and surtaxes. The *gäbar* in northern regions paid *asrat.*[39] Those exempted from *asrat* tax were tenants.

Asrat tax was introduced almost a decade after land measurement and, like the latter, the former had problems in expanding and being more widely applied in the different regions. There is not sufficient evidence to determine when it was introduced in each region and which one of them paid or were granted exemption. In the region of Tigray, *asrat* tax was paid during the time

[31] Zänäb (1902), pp. 32, 33, 34, 35, 42.

[32] On the *täsäri* system of King Yohannes see Afawark G/Iyasus (1905), *Dagmawi Menilik Negusä Nägäst zä-Ityopiya*, p. 16–17; *idem*., (1908), *Etiyopya: Guide du voyageur en Abyssinie*. Rome. pp. 230–232. Even though, this author had a biased judgement about King Yohannes, the facts he mentioned on billeting of royal troops was the practice of the time. On the *täsäri* policy of the King see also Mengstu Lemma (1959 E.C.), *Mäshafa Tezeta zä-aläqa Läma Haylu Wäldä Tarik*. Addis Ababa.

[33] *Asrat* was not a new type of tax introduced for the first time by Menelik. The term *asrat* was used in earlier documents in a different context. One-tenth of the communal land reserved and cultivated for the local *shum* (tax collecting offical) was refred as *medre asur* ("tenth land"). See Huntingford, G.W.B. (1965), p. 12. See also Pollera, A. (1913), *Il Regime delle Proprieta Terreria in Etiopia e nella Colonia Eritrea*. Rome. pp. 17–18. In the *Amisho Rim* system, lay officals who held *däbtära* land had the obligation to pay "one-fourth for the church (priest) and one-tenth for the *aläqa* (head) of the church". Tewodros also had suggested to the clergies of Gonder to collect *asrat* (tithe) and relinquish lands formerly alienated to the church. See Zänäb (1902), p. 28. Menelik drew on this experience and decreed tithe payment to solve remuneration of royal troops.

[34] See Mahteme Selassie (1962 E.C.), pp. 108, 127

[35] Ibid., p. 114

[36] See Gebre Wold Engda Worq (1948 E.C.), p. 25

[37] See Mahteme Selassie (1962 E.C.), pp. 111, 115.

[38] Ibid., p. 332; See also Gebre Wold Engda Worq (1948 E.C.), pp. 16, 18.

[39] See Mahteme Selassie (1962 E.C.), pp. 145, 150, 152, 153, 160.

of Menelik[40] replacing the *fäsäs* tax. In Wellega it was introduced by *däjazmach* Gebre Egzi Abher, first in order to maintain the church and later on for the payment of the *mälkägna*[41]. In Yejju, Rayya and Qobbo it was introduced by *ras* Welle in 1892/93.[42] The *asrat* tax spread fast in the north and in central Ethiopia, replacing the *fäsäs* tax. Like *fäsäs* and *täsäri* it was a royal tax levied for the provision of the royal army.[43] Regions whose land tax seemed to be heavy were temporarily relieved from the payment of *asrat*. Available information indicates that *asrat* tax was paid in most regions by the beginning of the twentieth century.

All the regions, however, did not have the same method of *asrat* tax assessment. Though the meaning of the term suggests a kind of levy which by definition was made up of one tenth of the produce of the land, it could have been of different amounts and paid in forms other than grain. In areas where there was no land measurement, the *asrat* tax was fixed by the principle of *t´imad* (number of plough oxen). In the region of Bägémder, where land was owned by the descent group, *asrat* tax was assessed by *t´imad* (pairs) of oxen.[44] In the region of Shewa and the south where land measurement was introduced, there was a similar method of *asrat* tax assessment. However, in these regions there were a number of problems around assessment and collection, and there were various attempts made to solve the problems.[45]

3.3. Composition of Surtaxes

Surtaxes were additional taxes or fees imposed on peasants for the purpose of covering part of the remuneration of royal tax officials. These extra levies included different varieties called *yä-bel*[46], *yä-ch´iqa qollo*, (payment given to a local tax official when installed in office), *mätin* (food provided to officials

[40] See Menelik's letter written to *däjazmach* Gebre Selassie, Nebred zä-Aksum, dated April 12 1900 E.C. The letter is deposited at the National Library, Ministry of Culture and Sports, Addis Ababa, document no 7.06.1.

[41] See Qäjela Märdasa (1985), "The Evolution of Land Tenure System in Mana-Sibu Wereda, Ghimbi, Wallaga: a Historical Survey to 1935". B.A. Thesis in History, A.A.U. p. 45.

[42] Feqadu Begna (1990), p. 58.

[43] While *fäsäs* tax was paid and collected at descent and territorial levels, *asrat* tax was assessed differently on percentage of cultivation.

[44] See Gebre Wold Engda Worq (1948 E.C.), p. 58

[45] On the various methods of *asrat* tax collection see Mahteme Selassie (1962 E.C.), pp. 333–340

[46] In the dictionary it is defined as money taken by an appointee to office, see Kane, T. L. (1990), *Amharic-English Dictionary. II*. p. 859. But in the document it was not clear which officials and who were paying what amount. In earlier tax documents, *bel* was written together with the tax of *asé qollo,* and one finds it in such statements as "*ase qollo* with the *bel*", see, Guidi (1905), p. 266. In the tax document of Tewodros we find similar statements like "*gebr* with the *bel",* see Pankhurst, R. and Germa Selassie Asfaw, eds., (1979), pp. 67, 71; *yä-nägarit bel* , ibid., p. 71; and, *yä shum bel* of the six *hageroch* (countries), ibid., p. 61.

on working visits), *yä- tsom qollo* (toasted cereal for land tax collectors in the *rist* regions), *yä- mät be`al* (tribute paid for holidays), etc.

The payment of surtax began in the *Amisho Rim* system (after 1593) as a type of remuneration for officials who administered taxes allocated for the King. As discussed above, ordinary land tax was then administered privately by the *rim* method, but extraordinary taxes such as *fäsäs* and *atsé qollo,* which were introduced as royal tax, were collected by new agents of the King (*känti-bas*, for instance). Surtaxes (extra payment) were imposed to supplement the remuneration of these officials.

The most important variety of tax was the one imposed on honey (*mar*) and cattle for slaughter (*frida*). There were a number of religious festivals and royal banquets which made honey and *frida* payment necessary. In some regions the honey tax was imposed on each village, whether or not it produced honey. The *frida* tax also was imposed on peasants, probably as a result of the small amount of revenue from livestock tax, or because of the absence of meat selling in a market. Like the honey tax, its purpose was to support local officials and clergies when they prepared feasts on holidays such as Epiphany, Christmas, Easter, etc. In the *Rist Gult* system, the tax was paid regularly every year, probably on festive occasions. The level of the tax was fixed and it was assessed territorially[47] or individually depending on the region. During the time of Tewodros and Yohannes, payment of *frida* tax was in money. The *frida* tax disappeared during the time of Menelik as more pastoralists began to be integrated into the fiscal system and when problems of keeping and feeding government livestock were solved through the expansion of *wärägänu* lands.

With the growth in the number of government tax officials, and the introduction of new taxes such as *asrat*, the variety of surtaxes increased as well. The introduction of *asrat* tax (tithe-payment) brought about new types of surtax payments such as *asrat lä-tsähafi* (one-tenth payment for scribers), fees for the *asrat* tax supervisor/collector[48], a tax for the *mälmay* and *bär-käfach* (land- and tax-surveyors)[49], and much later on during the reign of Menelik, additional levies were made to pay for postmen and telephonists[50].

It seemed that the government, in recognition of the low income of the functionaries, allowed some charges to supplement the inadequate income with customary fees. What was named here were just a few of the additional fees demanded from peasants.

[47] See Pankhurst, R. and Girma Selassie Asfaw (1979), p. 87.

[48] In the *Rist Gult* areas asrat tax collector was called *dambgna*. He was often a government soldier who was sent to supervise tax collection, and received two quna of grain per *awdma* (threshing ground). See Asfaw Tesema Werke (1969 E.C.), pp. 23–25.

[49] See Mahteme Selassie, (1962 EC), pp. 146, 150.

[50] Ibid., pp. 114, 115, 145, 146, 147.

3.4. Livestock Tax

Tax on cattle, sheep and goats as well as on mules and camels had a long tradition. For instance, the cattle-tax was introduced in 1540, and by then every peasant who had cows paid one in ten every three years.[51] Livestock tax was called *milmil*. This tax covered only those peasant households where livestock was raised in addition to their farming activity, or pastoralists whose main occupation was raising cattle. Often household officials (those in charge of the meat section) together with a surveyor (*mälmay*) and a local tax administrator called *ch´iqa*, went around households that raised sheep, goats and cows. They counted the number of animals and recruited one in ten as tax due the government. In the case of sheep and goats, it was only male sheep which were selected as tax, not female sheep or goats.[52] The livestock tax on the nomad population was based on the same principle of one in ten.

As far as peasant households were concerned, their capacity to raise livestock depended on the type of ecological zone they inhabited. Theoretically, the raising of livestock required ecological regions rich in water and abundant in pasture lands.[53] The availability of pasture land was also associated with land use rights. Abundant cattle were found in arid areas and pastoralists raised cattle adaptable to the environment.[54] In some areas where pasture lands were under the control of the local military administrator, *färäsägna*-cavalry, peasants were liable for paying tax for grazing on the land.[55]

Since 1855, succeeding Kings undertook different tax-technical measures, such as fixing the rate of land tax payment, standardization of land tax payment, merging of land tax payment obligations, introduction of tithe as regular and universal payment, etc. These measures elicited changes in the composition and rate of payments in the system of direct taxation. The determination of the tax policy was in the hands of the Kings and the major objective of the reforms was to increase government revenue and logistic ends. Government revenue was increased not only by discretionary measures such as increasing rate of land tax payment as was the case with Tewodros, but also by base-broadening as in the case of Menelik. These measures were synchronized with an attempt to introduce change and efficiency to the administration of taxes as well.

[51] See Beckingham, C.F. and Huntingford, G.W.B. (1954), p. 80

[52] See Asfaw Tesema Werke (1969 E.C.), p. 20

[53] For the various ecological zones and their suitability for cattle raising see Mesfin Wolde Mariam (1972), *An Introductory Geography of Ethiopia.* Addis Ababa.

[54] For the species and distribution of cattle in Ethiopia , see Alberro, M. and Haile Mariam (1982), "Ethiopian Cattle Indigenous Breeds", in *World Animal Review*, 41. pp. 2–34.

[55] See Mahteme Selassie (1962 EC), p. 145; Gebre Wold Engda Worq (1948 EC), p. 59.

3.5. Changes in the Administration of Direct Taxes

Administration of tax include the right of collection, supervision and custody of tax, as well as who collected, received and supervised taxes. It dealt mainly with the jurisdiction and responsibility of the tax officials both at the local/ regional and the central levels. In the period under discussion, the administration of taxes varied with the type of the fiscal subsystems and categories of taxes.

Restructuring of Local and Regional Direct Tax Administration in the Rist Gult System

In the *Rist Gult* and *Amisho Rim* systems, there were two types of tax administration which followed the arrangement form of revenue allocation. The first type was the private administration of ordinary land tax whereby the offices of administration were held as family property by the *gultägna*, the *aläqa* and in some cases the *ch´iqa shum*. The second type of administration was carried out by royal officials who were called *mesläné* and who were responsible for the administration of the domain of the prince and ordinary land tax alloted to the King or the prince.

The collection and custody of taxes at the local level were run by the office of *ch´iqa* (local tax collecting office).[56] The territorial unit over which the *ch´iqa shum* (office) had jurisdiction was usually the descent group who owned communal land (residing on a definite area), referred to as *adi* (meaning locality), or *däki* (children) or *got* (village), or *medr* (farm lands), etc. Each descent group had an official called *shum adi* or *ch´iqa* who was responsible for the administration of the locality and the collection of taxes. The peasant community elected one member of its *rist*-holder as *ch´iqa* officer to serve for one year. The office was theoretically rotating in nature so long as any *rist*-land owner of the locality was considered as an eligible candidate. During the *Zämänä Mäsafint*, in some regions this office became the patrimony of the local traditional families.[57] For those taxes which were assessed on the descent corporation as a whole, such as the ordinary land tax (*gebr*), the *ch´iqa shum* usually had a role in both assessment and collection. For the extraordinary land tax such as *fäsäs* which was allocated as royal tax and assessed by royal officials, the taxes would be paid directly into the district treasury with the direct involvement of the *ch´iqa shum* only in cases of default.

The *ch´iqa shum* paid an appointment fee (*yä-ch´iqa mar*) upon the assump-

[56] This office was introduced when payment of land tax was fixed by percentage of cultivation called *amisho* (one-fifth) during the period of quartering of displaced clergies in 1630s. The office is mentioned in the documents of King Fasilados (1632–1667), see B.L.Or. 518ff, 15v.

[57] The available documents do not make it clear as to how and where local tax collecting offices were privatized. In the region of Märäb Melash and Tigray, the office was hereditary, passing down to the eldest son. See Perini, R. (1905), p. 56; and Bruce, J.W. (1976), "Land Reform Planning and Indigenous Communal Tenures: A Case Study of the Tenure Chiguraf-Gwoses in Tigray, Ethiopia". Ph.D. Thesis, Faculty of Law, University of Wisconsin.p. 23.

tion of his office. In return, the *ch´iqa shum* received the privilege of cultivating *hudad* lands. The community set aside a small proportion of the community land, or collection of payment in lieu of *hudad*. In the Märäb Mälash it was called *grat goita*, in Tigray it was called *esir märét*, in Bägémder region *ch´iqa mägaräfiya*, in Yejju *ch´iqa märét*.[58]

In the *Rist Gult* system, at the district and provincial level, the private land tax administration was run by the *gultägna* and *aläqa*. Except for those held institutionally, *gult* administered by individuals were owned as an office by an aristocratic family and by noble kinship groups. *Gult* became property either by *de facto* ownership after a long period of administrative possession, or by royal grant. In return for private use and administration, the *gultägna* had an obligation to mobilize and command armed soldiers under his jurisdiction, supervise problems related to troop recruitment, and carry the responsibility of the administration of justice. In both the *Rist Gult* and *Amisho Rim* systems, administration of land tax was carried out by private means, and different functions were also fused into one office.

Kings and princes, however, had their own separated administration of tax and revenue. This was carried out by officials known as *mesläné* (meaning "like my-self"), and these officials were responsible for the administration of royal taxes and domains such as *wusti gulti* and other types. *Mesläné* were on the royal pay roll and received *qäläb*-ration payments. They were not granted *gult* as remuneration.

One of the major reforms made by Tewodros was his attempt to expand the *mesläné* type of royal tax administration and to abolish the private method of tax administration of the *gultägna*. These reforms were directed at securing central control over the administration of ordinary land tax and to use the revenues thus collected for payment of his salaried soldiers. The King declared a policy of *hagär bäge* (meaning "governorship in my hands"), a policy which abolished offices of hereditary governorship. "Saying the land is in my hands, he uprooted the *balabat* (local hereditary chiefs), (and) began to collect the *eribo* (one quarter payment) and *gämetä* (salt tax) of the land".[59] Through the system of *mesläné*, the King collected ordinary land tax used by local hereditary military governors.[60]

[58] In another study it is stated that the *ch´iqa shum* received a salary taking a small share of the collected revenue, never more than a tenth, and commonly only a twentieth, of the *fäsäs* and gäbäta *t´iimad* which he collected. Gesiotto, A. (1941/42), Breve Studio Sociale e Giuridico sul Tigrai Occidentale (con particolare riferimento alle regione di Axum e del Tembien)", in *Archivio Vittorio Socioloja per le Consuetudini qiurdiche agrarie, 8/9,* pp. 84–85.

[59] See Täklä Iyäsus, *yäNegus Täklä Haimanot Tarik*, IES, manus. no. 254. p. 70.

[60] It appears that in 1800 a similar policy that abolished private administration of land tax was applied in the region of Begemder by *ras* Gugsa, member of the Were Seh family, who occupied the office of the *rise mäkuanent*, head of the military nobility, between 1790s–1855. Although not clear, it is stated that *ras* Gugsa had dispossessed all *gultägna* and administered the land (ordinary land tax) through appointed officials. For further details see Pankhurst, R. (1966a), pp. 74–76.

To administer the land tax, he reorganized the provincial tax administration and gave new power to the office of the *mesläné*. Right after his coronation in 1855, Tewodros divided the central province, Bägémder, into 24 tax districts and appointed officials (*mesläné*) responsible for the collection of taxes and administration of the area.[61] In Tigray and in the provinces beyond the Märäb river (Hamassen, Säraye and Akalä Guzay) he appointed over 44 tax district officers (*mesläné*)[62] responsible to *däjazmach* Hailu and *däjazmach* Baryaw respectively.

In the provinces of Gojjam he appointed *balambäras* Wolqana as *mesläné* of Gojjam".[63] Later on, *ras* Engda was appointed as *mesläné* of the King.[64] But when the latter was removed and imprisoned on suspicion of disloyalty, *ras* Wube was appointed as *mesläné*".[65] He appointed officials in Shewa and Wollo; however there was no evidence of a constitution and an appointment of tax district officials as in Bägémder and Tigray.[66] In Shewa and Wollo there was no private administration of ordinary land tax; rather a royal tax administration belonging to the *Gäbar Madäriya* system.

Prior to the reign of Tewodros, *mesläné* (royal district tax collector) were managers of the royal or princely domain[67], and of extraordinary land tax collectors. Tewodros, however, changed the role of the *mesläné* from manager of royal estates and princely domains to district land tax collecting officers with administrative and judicial responsibility in the framework of direct taxation. Under the new structure, subordinate officials delivered taxes collected from their jurisdiction directly to the central treasury[68] and registered the tax under their name. The *mesläné* had the non-noble title of governorship, only honorific titles such as *ato* (Mr.) and *lig* (son, honourable).

Yohannes dropped the policy of *Hagär Bägé* and followed a policy which gave *gult* to appointed governors. He reinstituted *gult* formerly belonging to churches and local families.[69] He reinstituted former practices of private administration ordinary land tax. Only royal officials could administer the extraordinary land tax and the domains of kings. Yohannes changed the policy of Tewodros in order to get support from the local rulers, but after follow-

[61] For the list of the districts and their names see Girma Tefera (1961 E.C), pp. 65–66.

[62] For the names of direct and indirect tax administrators of the King see the tax documents of Tewedros, text and translation in Pankhurst, R. and Germa Selassie Asfaw, eds. (1979).

[63] See Täklä Iyäsus, *yäNegus Täklä Haimanot Tarik*, IES, manuscript no. 254. p. 62

[64] ibid. 66

[65] Ibid.66

[66] In Gojjam and in Wollo Dalanta, his officials were appointed as *mesläné*, see Shiferaw, B. (1990). p. 302, However, there is no evidence or report on the kind of tax districts like Tigray, Begemder, and in the provinces beyond Märab river.

[67] Tewodros himself was *mesläné* of the *rise mäkuwanet*, *ras* Ali, see Zänäb, (1902), p. 11.

[68] See the documents in Pankhurst, R. and Germa Selassie Asfaw (1979) ; Kolmodin, J., (1915), p. 145 trans.

[69] See Feseha Wolde Mikael (1936 E.C.), *yä Asé Yohannes Tarik*. Manuscript no. 22.01. National Library, Ministry of Culture and Sports. Addis Ababa. p. 42.

ing this policy, his revenue from ordinary land tax decreased at least by 30%.[70]

Local and Regional Direct Tax Administration in the Gäbar Madäriya System

As discussed in chapter two, under the *Gäbar Madäriya* system, ordinary land tax was not administered by an individualized private method like the *Rist Gult* system. Tax was administered through royal officials who had different types of responsibilities, jurisdiction, procedures and methods of remuneration. It should be noted that the *Gäbar Madäriya* system had different types of land ownership, principles of assessment, payment of land tax and revenue allocation.[71]

Tax administration at the local level was similar to that of the other two systems, but there were certain differences. The *ch´iqa* was no longer an office which belonged to the rotation system of the peasant community as in the *Rist Gult* and *Amisho Rim* system. In the period of Menelik, the office was occupied mostly by local *balabat*-chiefs and by the landed gentry (*märét-aläqa*). The local *balabat* were holders of *siso*-private land and were often recruited as cavalry. The *ch´iqa shum* was called *balagär t´äbaqi*, since he was supposed to protect the local community he knew from possible arbitrary exactions by the government soldiers. There was an increase in the number of *ch´iqa shum* as a result of the fiscal integration of southern provinces into the imperial tax administration system. In the *Gäbar Madäriya* system, *ch´iqa shum* had a very limited role in the administration of *madäriya*-state land.

One characteristic of the *Gäbar Madäriya* system was its elaborate structure which consisted of different types and an increasing number of officials belonging to the administration of the direct tax system. The introduction of the *asrat* tax (tithe) brought with it changes in the local tax administration. As a tax on production, it required a great number of government officials to work as tax assessors (*dänbägna*), scribers (*asrat ts´ähafi*), and receivers (such as *mälkägna* and *mesläné*). Principles of individual payment allowed the state to conduct land surveys, and to make constant revisions in land allocation. This process increased the number of tax assessors and land-meteries officers known as *bär-käfach* (land surveyors) and *mälmay* (tax assessors), who were assisted by one or two officials.[72]

At district and sub-district levels, the officer responsible for administration was generally referred to as *mälkägna*, who was a local official, at a level similar to that of the *gultägna*. The *mälkägna* supervised the collection of land

[70] See section 4.1.

[71] See Chapter Two.

[72] Mahteme Selassie (1962 EC), p. 146. For the method of remuneration of these tax officials read the works of Mahteme Selassie and Gebre Wold Engda Worq.

tax and administration of *madäriya*-state land in regions where taxes were paid individually and assessed on the basis of the size and fertility of the land. The office was mentioned in connection with administration of *mad bét* land and *gasha* land during the time of Negasi (1696–1703).

As remuneration, the *mälkägna* was given *hudad* land cultivated by corvee labour. The *hudad* land was either taken off from each *gäbar* or measured by *qälad*. This type of *mälkägna* had no right to use the land tax he collected. The land tax was supervised and collected by the *mälkägna* and was used by the *shaläqa*-governor and palace. In other words the *mälkägna* did not share the proceeds from the collected tax. In cases where land could not be reserved as *hudad,* as was the case in *qutr gäbar* regions, the *gäbar* peasant was obliged to pay a fixed quantity of cereal (24 *quna* of cereal), or make payments in lieu of *hudad* cultivation. This type of *mälkägna* was called *gäbar mälkägna*[73] or *gätär mälkägna*, and most of them were soldiers.[74] Those *mälkägna* who were given *gasha madäriya*-state land in lieu of payment were called *balä madäriya mälkägna*. The amount of *gasha* land they received depended on their rank. Those local traditional chiefs (*balabat*) who had their own *siso* private land and who were recruited as *mälkägna* were called *balabat mälkägna* or *siso mälkägna*. In *rist* areas they were called *ya-fär mälkägna*. *Mälkägna* was, therefore, a supervisor and collector of land tax which was due to the palace and the governor, and was thus called *asgäbari*. He was helped by the *ch´iqa shum*, local land owners who mediated between him and the tax paying peasants.

The office of the *mälkägna* was used entirely for the administration of ordinary land tax allocated for *ch´ifra* soldiers and clergy. That part of the ordinary land tax and reserve lands allocated for the royal or governor's kitchen was administered by another official called *mesläné*.[75] The *mesläné* was responsible for the collection of ordinary land tax allocated either for the King or governor; he was responsible for the management (cultivation) of crown *hudad* lands, was in charge of administering extraordinary land tax such as tithe (*asrat*), and he was also responsible for the administration of justice in his district. In regions allocated as *gana gäb* of the palace, the *mesläné* was appointed by the King; in regions allocated for the *shaläqa* he was appointed by the governor.[76]

The *mesläné* and the *mälkägna* had no control over the organization, administration, and deployment of campaign and auxiliary troops. The *mälkägna* could be a soldier or recruited as cavalry, but had no jurisdiction to adminis-

[73] See Mahteme Selassie (1962 EC), p. 162.
[74] See Gebre Wold Engda Worq, (1948 EC), p. 15.
[75] Note that there was a separated administration of revenue for the court of the King and governor, imperial troops and church, see Chapter Four.
[76] See Gebre Wold Engda Worq, (1948 EC), p. 36.

trate over soldiers as the *gultägna* were. Under the *Gäbar Madäriya* system, military administration was more or less separated from the administration of land tax and justice.

Large provinces and regions were administered by governors called *shaläqa*, meaning "chief of a thousand troops". In modern times it is the rank of major in the army. In regional administration, the *shaläqa* was a military man (or in few cases a civilian) who held gubernatorial office. There were two types of *shaläqa*: the first was known as (chief)-*shaläqa* or governor who had the title and rank of *ras* and *balä-nägarit däjazmach*. These were governors of large provinces with the power to assign titles that were one rank below themselves and to possess *ch´ifra* (a great number of soldier servants). These governors had the right to use *gebr* (ordinary annual land-tax), which was in principle due to the state, for the purpose of maintaining their *ch´ifra* and administrating the region.[77] The second type of *shaläqa* was the ordinary type of *shaläqa* who had a title of *yä-wuchi däjazmach, fitawrari* or equivalent ranks. Mostly these were military men who ruled over sub-provinces and districts under the chief-*shaläqa*. Under them were *mälkägna* and other categories of lower officials.

The *shaläqa*-governors were appointed by imperial decree (*awag*) and were given the responsibility for the military, judicial and taxation administration of a region. They had jurisdictional rights in the allocation of tax and state land following the principles laid down by the central government. The governor general administered justice through a judicial body called *wämbär*. It is probable that the governor and the *wämbär*-judges heard appeals on tax assessment and problems of payment. As regards the administration of justice, both the *mesläné* and the *mälkägna* were under the *wämber*.

Central Agencies of Direct Tax Administration

Reforms of land tax administration at the regional and local level were organized at the centre through the office of the *ts´ähafé tezaz* (the King's Secretary). The office was reinstituted by King Tewodros with a new responsibility for financial administration. Money taxation and the salary system necessitated the consolidation of revenue and thus the creation of a central office to receive and distribute funds.

During the reign of Tewodros, the office of the *ts´ähafé tezaz* was responsible for the registration of ordinary, extraordinary, livestock and indirect taxes collected from the regions through the offices of the *mesläné*. The King's secretary recorded the amounts of money received from each financial district, including the names of the officials, the local tax units and the type of taxes

[77] See Mahteme Selassie (1962 EC), p. 637.

collected.[78] For the purpose of financial administration, there were at least three central treasuries found at the Mäqedäla fortress, at Dabra Tabor (the "second" town after Gonder) and in the royal camp. The one at Mäqedäla was under the charge of three men who were members of the Mäqedäla council.[79] Each of them had a separate function of keeping and accounting the treasury, assisted by deputies titled *bäjirond* (meaning treasurer) with no seat at the council. Tewodros had declared that his property was to be stored at Mäqedäla.[80] The chief accountant of the Mäqedäla treasury worked together with two higher officials from the royal camp in the town of Dabra Tabor. The regular and irregular taxes channelled to the third treasury at the royal court were under the immediate supervision of the King himself. The Mäqdäla councillors were responsible for the payment of salaries and the supply of provisions to the civil and military officials as well as to soldiers in Mäqdäla and other *amba*[81], while the King was responsible for the immediate officials and for soldiers at the royal camp.

The revenue of the court of Menelik was administered by the various offices of the palace. There was the office of the *mädrä-gibi azazh* who was the chief superintendent of the palace, the palace estate and the state prison. Under him came the *azazh* responsible for providing and supplying the thousands of royal guards, soldiers, retainers, invited guests and others invited to the royal banquet. Under the *azazh* was the *wärägänu-shum* in charge of meat supply and herding royal cattle. Royal taxes paid in the form of honey, woven baskets, cattle or grain was collected by this office.[82]

There was the *ehil ena mar götara shum*, the official responsible for the supervision, collection and storage of taxes paid in grain, honey, butter and supply of wood. These taxes were collected from lands identified as *gana gäb*. The officials registered the name of the tax payer and the name of the country area in a book called *bahr mäzgäb*.[83] Under this officer, there were *ch´ifra*-soldiers, guards of *gotära*, key keepers, and women who measured grain and honey.

The *bägirond* was a treasurer in charge of finance which included among

[78] In the court of Yohannes there were four Chief Secretaries, see, Bairu Tafla, ed. (1977), A *Chronicle of King Yohannes IV 1872–1889*. Wiesbaden. pp. 129,131. Menelik had one chief Secretary whose office served not only for correspondence but mainly for revenue administration. The *ts´ehafé tezaz* of Menelik issued directive on registration of all categories of land in the region of Shewa, see Gäbrä Selassie (1959 E.C.) p. 99, the distribution of asrat tax (tithe) (see Mahteme Selassie (1962 E.C). p. 332; and kept records of land grants made as payment in lieu of salary. For further discussion see revenue administration of the court in Chapter Four below.

[79] See the inventories in Pankhurst, R. and Girma Asfaw (1979; Pankhurst, R. (1988), "An Unpublished Order of the Kings, Tewodros II, at the Institute of Ethiopian Studies" in *Ethiopian Journal of African Studies, V 5, N 1*.

[80] See Täklä Iyäsus, *yäNegus Täklä Haimanot Tarik*, IES, manus. no. 254. p. 67

[81] See the letters of Tewodros in Pankhurst, R. and Girma Asfaw (1979), in Part III.

[82] See Mahteme Selassie (1962 E.C), p. 165

[83] This book was also used to register allocation of land, after land measurement.

other things taxes paid in the form of money. There were different types of *bägirond*. First there was *bägirond* responsible for *guada* (imperial treasury including money). For instance, from the province of Jimma, which paid a fixed annual tax, this *bägirond* received different *dirb* cotton cloth (given usually to high ranking officials), *kuta* (double cotton cloth), *gasha* (shields) decorated with gold, and decorated swords.[84] The second *bägirond* was in charge of the *gemja bét* (storehouse) for the royal souvenirs such as the crown, medals, swords and other precious objects belonging to the King. Upon order from the King, he issued rewards such as clothes, medals and weapons to the nobility. He deposited taxes collected by agents from weavers and various types of smiths. In some cases, the *bägirond* served as head (*aläqa*) of the artisans who were in turn divided into various sections. For instance, he could be chief of the carpenters, chief of silver, copper, nickel-and gold-smiths, chief of leather goods makers, chief of embroiders of silk and cotton materials. The *dinkuan bét* (responsible for the procurement, maintenance and storage of the royal tents) was probably under the *bägirond* of *gemja bét*.[85] The third type of *bägirond* was in charge of the *eqa bét* (stores) whose peace and war time duty was to maintain mules and objects necessary for loading and transporting. In the court of King Menelik, for instance, this type of *bägirond* was also responsible for the lodging and food allowance (*dergo*) for official guests who came from northern and central parts of Ethiopia.

An important development in the financial organization of the state was the formation of a ministerial system by Menelik in 1907. The origin and background of this system lies in the gradual internal developments, particularly as regards fiscal and military administration. The introduction of *asrat* tax (tithe) for the royal army, creation of a uniform national land tax, and the concomitant need for land surveys, gave rise to an elaborate administrative network which demanded specialized agencies at the centre. Until 1907, much of the responsibility and jurisdiction in the administration of direct taxes was given to the office of the *ts´ähafé tizaz*. With the formation of the ministerial system in 1907 the administration and jurisdiction of taxes was distributed to different ministries, through which the government was able to consolidate the revenue and expenditure of the *Gäbar Madäriya* system.

The formation of a ministerial system clearly divided what was for the palace and what was for the state. What was for the King and the palace came under the Ministry of the Palace. The ministry had two major tasks: the security of the King and the household economy of the palace. As regards the latter, the Ministry was in charge of the administration and management of royal estates (*gana gäb* lands) and provincial taxes allocated as *mad bét* to the pal-

[84] See Mahteme Selassie (1962 E.C), p. 165

[85] See See Bairu Tafla 1974. "Civil Titles and Offices in the Reign of King Menelik II, 1889–1913, " in *IV Congresso Internazionale di Studi Etiopici, I.* Roma. p. 606.

ace. The following officials all came under this ministry: the *azazh*, the *eqa bét shaläqa*, the *baldäras*, the *mesläné*, the *wärägänu*, the *gotära shum*[86]. The imperial treasury was not under this ministry, but under the Ministry of Finance.

The Ministry of Finance was in charge of receipt, custody, disbursement and control of government finance and the private treasury of the King and the *alga* (throne). By ministerial regulation two basic divisions of the *bägirond* were made: those responsible for the *guada*, i.e., the private treasure of the King and the *alga*, and those responsible for the finance of the state. Accordingly, the private money of the King was supposed to pass from him to his heir and out of these money the King could make grants and give donations to churches and individuals. The finance of the state was that part of the money allocated for government administration.

Until 1907, much of the responsibility and jurisdiction in the administration of direct taxes was given to the office of the King's secretary at the central level, and the *shaläqa* at the regional level. With the formation of the ministerial system, revenues were centralized along departmental lines by different ministries. For instance, the Ministry of Agriculture was in charge of fixing land tax (*gebr*), livestock taxes, as well as taxes on agricultural enterprises. It was also responsible for the collection and distribution of the royal tax, *asrat* (tithe), for the army of the central government. It thus became the central agency for receiving and disbursing fixed grain payments to royal troops. The ministry made surveys of cultivated agricultural lands, forests, meadows and took a cattle census in each governorate; and in consultation with the government allowed tax exemptions for places affected by drought and epidemic diseases.[87]

The Ministry of Interior was in charge of the conducting the census in each governorate and of keeping the annual records dispatched to it. Based on the number of individuals and families found in the governorate, the ministry was given the responsibility for fixing personal and household taxes and sending the corresponding account of each governorate to the Ministry of Finance. By the new regulation, the task of land survey and measurement (*qälad*) and the distribution of state lands became the responsibility of this ministry. There were a group of *qälad t´ay* (land surveyors) headed by an *aläqa* in the ministry who were sent to measure lands. Ultimately, this ministry presented the survey

[86] The ministry also supervised the administration of posts, telephone and telegrams until this administration was raised to the level of an independent Ministry in 1910. See Mahteme Selassie (1962 E.C.), pp. 104–105.

[87] Other responsibilities of the ministry included the improvement of quality and quantity in agricultural production, cattle breeding, agricultural tools and forestry. The ministry was involved in the activities of the Bank of Agricultural Development and Commerce founded in 1909 by the King, with the Queen, three ministers and two other important officials as shareholders, Mahteme Selassie (1962 E.C), pp. 318–320.

to the King through the office of the *ts´ähafi tezaz*.[88] In other words the ministry was responsible for the allocation and supervision of land tax following the government principle which determined how much for soldiers, governors, clergy and central government. The right to fix the land tax was given to the Ministry of Agriculture.

The Ministry of Finance was authorised to collect all taxes fixed and imposed by the ministries including court dues imposed by the Ministry of Justice. The minister was also chief of the government store houses in the provinces and, in consultation with the King, he made appointments to their offices. The Ministry was also responsible for all bank activities of, for example, the Bank of Abyssinia, founded in 1905.

To facilitate an overall control and inspection of government funds, all the ministries were required by regulations to submit monthly account books indicating the revenues collected, and their income and expenditure to the Ministry of Finance. The Ministry of Finance in turn had to prepare a balance sheet every three months and submit it to the Ministerial council and to the King. The ministry thus functioned as a kind of a single budget office and as a central treasury of money. Its formation was an important step in the concentration of decision making, in the consolidation and preparation of a permanent type of government revenue, and in expenditure budget.

3. 6. The Structure and Administration of Indirect Taxes

3. 6.1. Composition of Indirect Taxes

If Mahteme Selassie and Gebre Weld were pioneers in discussing the system of direct taxation, Pankhurst was the first to collect and discuss data on trade.[89] Pankhurst discussed taxation on trade following five forms; "first a tax on goods brought to market, second a tax on articles actually sold, thirdly, a tax on supplies transported through internal customs posts, fourth, various systems of

[88] Ibid., p. 107. Before the establishment of this ministry, financial matters of the provinces (such as land survey and allocation) was the responsibility of the office of the *ts´ähafi tezaz*. Political affairs of the provinces were conducted through the *eqa bét shaläqa*.

[89] Pankhurst, R. (1964), "The Trade of Northern Ethiopia in the Nineteenth and Early Twentieth Centuries", *Journal of Ethiopian Studies, II: 1*; *idem*., (1968e), "The Trade of Central Ethiopia in the Nineteenth and Early Twentieth Centuries", *Journal of Ethiopian Studies, II:, 2*.; These articles are presented in a condensed form by the same author, (1968a). Again these articles are revised and published in his book, (1968c), *Economic History of Ethiopia*. Addis Ababa. pp. 346–459, 519–532. See also Pankhurst, R. (1985a). Among other authors see Abir, M. (1968); Garretson, P. (1974), "A History of Addis Ababa from its Foundation in 1886 to 1910". Dissertation, University of London; Bahru Zewde, (1976), "Relations between Ethiopia and the Sudan on the western Ethiopian Frontier". Dissertation; and Abdusamad, H. Ahmad (1980), "Trade and Politics in Gojjam 1882–1935". M.A. Thesis in History. A.A.U.

compulsory or semi-compulsory purchase, and fifth, import and export taxes collected either at the frontier or at some other usually well-defined palace".[90] These categories were extensively discussed in the literature mentioned, and it is not necessary to go into details to describe the structure of indirect taxes, but just to highlight the level of indirect taxation and the volume of trade by extracting samples from the various regions during the nineteenth century. The following discussion focuses on the components of indirect tax such as market dues (rural and urban market), custom tolls (regional trade), import and export (international trade), tax on production, and methods and reforms of indirect tax administration.

The first component of indirect tax was dues collected from domestic markets. It included commodities traded in rural and urban markets. In the countryside, the villages held periodic, often weekly markets. Agricultural products such as wheat, barley, millet, maize, *teff*, pepper, butter, and spices were brought to the market place. Horses, mules, sheep, and goats were also brought there. These products were exchanged for local craft products.[91]

In the towns, regular large and small markets were held throughout the week, and the crafts of the town were sold and bought wholesale and retail.[92] There was buying of agricultural products and selling of local luxury products and imported goods. Long distance merchants brought salt (from the north) and coffee, civet, ivory, gold (from the south), cotton (textile cloth) to the market from foreign countries. Markets were attended by peasants, craftsmen and merchants, the latter having been either hired by long distance merchants or by merchants who had some small capital of their own.[93] The scattered nature of production and the absence of a wholesale account and retail system[94], among other things, made it difficult to have a proper excise tax. Dues were levied at the time of sale (*delale*), and it included payment made by the seller on goods brought for sale, and payment made by the buyer when he left the market.[95]

The second major component of indirect tax was production tax related to goods manufactured or produced for domestic market consumption. Towns had craftsmen such as weavers, makers of swords and knives, tanners, leather workers, sandal makers, silver copper and gold smiths, metal workers, masons and stone cutters, wood cutters and carpenters, torch makers, tent makers, saddle, bridle, stirrups, spear and shield makers. Artisans were taxed on the goods

[90] Pankhurst, R. (1968a).

[91] See Abdusamad, H. Ahmad (1980), pp. 25–26

[92] Ibid. 27

[93] Shops were non existent (i.e., there was no show of the articles), for fear of plunder or taxation.

[94] For the system of rural market dues see the details described by Johnston quoted in Pankhurst, R. (1968a), p. 23.

[95] See Pankhurst, R. and Girma Selassie Asfaw (1979), pp. 10, 71.

they produced, and the tax collected from them was known as *täbib*. Weavers tax was identified by different names, e.g., *gud-guad* in Gojjam. Salt production at Teltel to the east of the Tigray massif, was taxed.[96]

The third component of indirect tax was that levied on goods in transit from one region to another. This type of trade was organized by big merchants who were responsible for the timing of departure, guidance, security matters, payment of customs tolls, and arranging of camping sites. The long distance merchants bought export commodities such as gold, civet, coffee and ivory from the local intermediary merchants (middlemen) who did not have the necessary capital and connection to trade with areas very far away from their own.[97] Goods in transit were taxed at the various custom posts referred to as *kélla*, and these were located at convenient places along the long distance trade routes. Ruppel mentioned that in the 1830s there were eleven posts between the ports of Massawa and Gonder in the south centre, while Ferret and Galinier state that there were no less than eighteen on that route. Blondeel, another contemporary, reported the existence of twenty-eight posts between Massawa and Enariya located in south western Ethiopia.[98] Dues levied at the various custom posts were not uniform, and were paid both in kind and money.[99] The tax bore little relation to the value of goods, the trader being in most cases merely charged on the number of his pack animals.[100]

The existence of so many customs posts, besides constituting a significant financial burden on commerce, led to much inconvenience and many delays. Blondeel commented that what was surprising about the system was not that trade suffered but that it existed at all.[101] Tewodros, Menelik and Haile Selassie had attempted to reform internal custom posts[102], but could not abolish it altogether[103].

The fourth category of indirect tax consisted of import and export taxes. In the first two thirds of the nineteenth century, exports and imports through Massawa remained fairly constant, each running at about a quarter to a third of a million dollars.[104] The estimation was based on the figures given by early nineteenth century travellers and the statistics subsequently collected by the Egyptian and Italian authorities. However, there was no *ad valorem* tax, (a single entry or exit tax which is expressed as a proportion of the value of the goods). As mentioned, customs were levied at the different tolls

[96] See Abdusamad, H. Ahmad (1980), p. 35

[97] Quoted in Pankhurst, R. (1968a), p. 26

[98] Blondeel made a list of the dues exacted at the 28 custom posts on the Masawa Enariya routes, ibid., 28

[99] Pankhurst, R. (1968c), p. 522

[100] Quoted in Pankhurst, R. (1968a), p. 29.

[101] Ibid, p36.38; see also Part V below.

[102] Internal custom posts were completely abolished during the Italian occupation 1935–41.

[103] See the details in Pankhurst, R. (1968c), pp. 360ff.

[104] For detail discussion see Pankhurst, R. (1968a), pp. 42ff.

within the country rather than at one fixed place either in the center or at the frontier.

Attempts were made to introduce *ad valorem* tax through bilateral international agreement such as the 1841 Anglo Shoan treaty, the 1843 French and Shewa treaty, the 1849 treaty between the British and the *ras* Ali, and the 1883 agreement between Italy and Menelik, which was revised in the 1889 Wuchale treaty, etc.[105] As noted by Pankhurst himself, these treaties were dead letters.[106]

The main reason for the absence of a single and fixed level of custom dues on import and export goods was related to the method of indirect tax administration and revenue allocation. As shall be explained below, indirect tax was administered by private method through farming out market dues and tolls. Market dues were also earmarked for payment of individuals and as sources of income for churches. Administration of indirect tax was thus privatized and localized, even during the time of Tewodros and Yohannes. It had changed in scale during the time of Menelik who acted within the *Gäbar Madäriya* fiscal system. Another factor was the growth of international trade in the fourth quarter of the nineteenth century. Colonization of neighbouring countries such as Sudan and Djibouti opened new outlets, and the adjacent colonial governments were encouraging expansion of trade with Ethiopia. After the battle of Adwa, colonial powers changed their policy from colonization by a military force to peaceful commercial penetration. Looked at from such a perspective, ad valorem tax was introduced by the end of the nineteenth century. The region of Harar had a long tradition of this type of tax, but in Addis Ababa the tax was introduced in 1900 by *nägadras* Hayle Giorgis.[107]

Internal reforms and external developments stimulated the expansion of long distant regional and international trade that passed through Gonder in the north west, through Adwa and Massawa in the north, Assab in north east, Addis Ababa in the centre, Harar, Djibouti and Somali coastal towns in the east, Borena and Lugh in the south, Enariya, Jiima, Kafa, Bongain in the south west, and Gore, Bure, Welega and Gambella in the west. These were regional trade centers during the second half of the nineteenth century through which import/export trade expanded. There is a detailed collection of data on the volume, patterns and direction of the import and export goods of these specified regions.[108]

The establishment of export and import duties during the time of Menelik was a major change in sources of government revenue. As regards the whole economy, as we shall see, there was no change from export of natural products

[105] Ibid., p. 45

[106] See Garretson, P. (1974), p. 318.

[107] See Pankhurst, R. (1968c), Chapter Nine on Trade.

[108] For discussion on changes in the export and import patterns in the period of our discussion see ibid., pp. 371f, 378f.

to export of proto industrial products such as wool or textile, or commercial agriculture products such as plantation and cattle farm. The commodities traded included items like civet, ivory, coffee and gold which came from south and south-west Ethiopia, and *amolé* which came from the eastern parts of Tigray.[109]

3. 6. 2. The Administration of Indirect Tax

Administration of indirect taxes depended on the type of fiscal organization of the state. In the *Rist Gult* system it was administered basically by private/ market methods (*shumät*), whereas in the *Gäbar Madäriya* system it was administered by the King's appointees (*mesläné*) and governors. In the *Rist Gult* system, rural market dues and custom tolls were farmed out to individuals who paid a fixed annual sum called *mäshomiya* to the King (or prince). Urban markets and *qäläfät* (long distance caravan trade), and important custom posts were farmed out to private merchants called *nägadras* (literally chief of merchants). Rural markets were farmed to local officials or private persons in return for an advance fixed payment called *shumät*. By such contracts, kings could get fixed and regular cash and escape the difficulty of levying and fixing a variety of merchandise found in a rural market. But there is no document which tells about the nature of this local contract between the tax-farmers and the King.

It was only dues from the domestic market (rural and urban) and caravan trade (custom dues) that was farmed out by princes and kings. Production tax, particularly tax from craft products such as *täbib* and from weavers were traditionally collected by officials of the prince, under the office of the *bäjirond*. Among other things, the *bäjirond* served as head of the artisans, e.g., chief of the carpenters, chief of silver, copper, nickel-and gold-smiths, chief of leather goods makers, and chief of embroiders of silk and cotton materials.

King Tewodros made no change in the private/market system of indirect tax administration. Offices for the collection of rural market dues and custom tolls were still sold (*mäshomiya*) and the King received the revenue from the sale of the office and not directly from taxes collected at the market place and tolls. In the documents, there is mention of *mäshomiya* fees for the *balagär* and *balgada* tax collector of Endärta[110], and payment in return for an appointment made to the post of tax collector at a salt toll (*yä-ch´äw bär*)[111]. District governors of Tämben were paying specified fees.[112]

[109] See Pankhurst, R. and Girma Selassie Asfaw (1979), p. 65.
[110] Ibid., p. 91
[111] Ibid., p. 45–46.
[112] See Ege, S. (1978), p. 144. There were two types of *mesläné*, one was responsible for the administration of land tax paid in the form of *hudad*, and the other was *mesläné* of the market. ibid.

During the reign of Tewodros, there were four types of higher officials responsible for the central administration of indirect taxes: (a) *shum* in charge of customs tolls (*kélla*), as for instance, *däjazmach* Sahlu who was at first appointed beyond Märäb Mälash, and later responsible for the province of Tigray, *däjazmach* Sahlu was also responsible for the collection of taxes from the production of salt in Tältäl; (b) the *shum* responsible for salt toll (*ch´äw bär*), as for example, *däjazmach* Baryaw who was responsible for direct tax collection and was once in charge of taxes collected from custom posts in the province of Tigray; in Bägémder, Haile Mercha and *shum* Tämben Wolde Girgis were in charge of the salt toll called *ch´äw bär* and customs tolls, called *kéllas*; (c) the *shum* responsible for the collection of taxes from artisans, as for example, *bäjirond* Wolde Täklé as *shum* and *ato* Bayru, *täkotatari* (inspector); (d) the *shum* responsible for taxes collected from caravan trades (*qäläfät*) as for example *däjazmach* Gäbrä Egziabher.

The reforms of Tewodros probably had undermined the independence of the *nägadras* by bringing customs tolls directly under royal control. Production taxes were collected as usual and the King had *bäjirond* for the artisan. The King's official, responsible for the collection of taxes from artisans, was *bäjirond* Wolde Täklé as *shum* and *ato* Bayru as *täkotatari* (inspector).

The administration of indirect taxes in the *Gäbar Madäriya* system was different from the *Rist Gult* and *Amisho Rim* system of Kings Tewodros and Yohannes. Market dues were collected by royal officials called *mesläné* (royal intendant), not by private/market administration.[113] Menelik's policy was a continuation of the royal administration of market dues. Government officials with the title of *nägadras*, *gäbeya qorach*, etc. were instituted to represent the state, and be responsible for the entire administration of indirect taxes (assessment, collection, custody and delivery). The *nägadras* was a government official responsible for the administration of indirect tax at the provincial level. The *nägadras* decided the amount of dues to be paid by the trader, and the *qärt chi´qa shum* received the market and customs dues and submitted the total amount collected to the governor's personal treasury where a *qärt ts´ähafi* registered the amount of money received. The *qäläb* payment to these customs officers in the provinces was paid in kind from the market dues collected in kind.

Another phase in the development of the administration of indirect tax was the formation of a ministerial system (1907) which gave rise to an independent ministry in charge of commerce. Thus, the Ministry of Commerce became responsible for the administration of internal and external trade including the collection of trade and custom duties. The minister, as chief of all the *nägadras*, supervised the activities of trade and customs officers. The minister was

[113] For administrative reforms in the region of Harar, see an autobiography titled *yä Nägadras Eshete Teketlew Hiwot Tarik*, IES, manus. no. 2000; See also Garretson, P. (1974), pp. 318ff.

also the principal head able to settle commercial disputes and, in consultation with the King, grant commercial concessions to foreign entrepreneurs. By regulation, the Ministry of Commerce submitted annual accounts of its revenue to the Ministry of Finance.

The kind of indirect tax administration belonging to the *Gäbar Madäriya* system was advantageous to the kings compared to the one in the *Rist Gult* system. In the former, kings could impose different indirect taxes which was inconceivable in the tax farming method of the *Rist Gult* system. Depending on the volume and on the items of trade, tax officials of the King could increase tax on various commodities, such as coffee, grain, cattle, etc., and levy ground tax (called *yä-bota qurach*).

To conclude, the issue of creating new resources by way of investigating the objects and administration of taxation was discussed. Reforms on the tax structure focused on increasing the number of taxes, conducting land surveys, introducing *asrat*-tithe payment, and encouraging foreign trade. The administration, too, was changed for the purpose of more efficient control and direction by the state. The various measures initiated to reform the system indicated the central ambitions of the Kings.

CHAPTER FOUR

The Structure, Size and Administration of Imperial Government Revenue, 1855–1913

The purpose of this chapter is to measure the results of the taxation refoms in figures in order to show the actual resources at the disposal of the kings. The purpose is to examine the contribution of each of the taxes to the total revenue. This aim is related to the assessment of the various degrees of tax burden: who paid for the expenditure of the state? How much was paid? Who was exempted or privileged? What type of sources was the state interested in, and why? These are familiar questions related to the structure, sources and size of government revenue. For questions of this nature, under normal circumstances, one has to investigate the various entries of the official financial accounts of the state.

In the historiographic tradition of Ethiopia, land and the obligations attached to its use are described as the economic bases of the state. The pioneers in the field, and following them many of the modern scholars, discuss the resources of the state in terms of the system of land tenure.[1] In the final analysis, this approach often leads the discussion to issues of land ownership and the legal status of the peasantry, often neglecting to study the amount of government revenue.

There are some attempts, however, made to address the issue of government revenue. Travellers in the second half of the nineteenth century had estimated the revenue of the state, often some aspects of the sources, but only from some regions, and with various differences.[2] Some estimates of travellers were made without citing sources and/or further comments, and therefore one hesitates to come to any conclusion based on such type of evidence. Other estimates are based on trade reports, and conclusions were drawn by looking at the volume of trade and level of taxation; again this was mainly for import and export tax purposes.

There are only two cases where government revenue was discussed on the basis of official documents. Pankhurst discussed the government revenue of Tewodros based on the tax documents which he and Girma Selassie Asfaw translated. He discussed revenue by region, and not by type, and that too was

[1] See, among others, Mahteme Selassie (1962 E.C.); Gebre Wold Engda Worq (1948 E.C.); Markakis, J. (1974); Mantel-Niecko, J. (1980); Donham, D and James, W. eds., (1986).

[2] Pankhurst use these sources for his discussion on trade and government revenue, see Pankhurst, R. (1968a), idem., (1968b); idem (1968c).

limited to ordinary land tax and tax on livestock following the model of the document.[3] It is quite understandable that revenue was not discussed by type since the issue required analysis of the prior tax structure system over centuries. Another attempt was made for the period of Menelik by MacGillivray, governor of the Bank of Abyssinia 1905–1911. He wrote a report on the revenue of Menelik as he saw it from the books of the various treasuries of the King. The figures he mentioned covered the period 1902–1904, and they were presented in terms of monetary forms (MT$ and *wäqét*-gold) and non-monetary forms such as salt, cloth and ivory.[4] Since the report is short, there was no detailed discussion on the sources of government revenue. Except in certain cases, the total figures did not tell where the money had come from, and what was included or excluded in the figures.

Though source material was a serious problem, lack of a systematic approach was also part of the problem for partial treatment of government revenue in the period under discussion. The first step in a discussion of government revenue ought to be the identification of the fiscal organization of the state. In this effort, some areas of concern include the identification of tax structure through the study of objects of taxation (land and/or market dues), methods of assessment (descent, proportional or land survey), forms of payment (in kind or money), and the level of payment. Once the system of taxation is studied, sources and size of government revenue could easily be analysed even if this had to be based only on available fragmented central accounts. Documents which showed entries of revenue are available only for the period of Tewodros, specifically for the years 1863–64.[5]

The second concern in discussing revenue is related to systematic presentation of the data. In this work the problem of revenue is approached by identifying fiscal systems that had their own peculiar properties.[6] Following the same line of thought, in what follows, the total amount of *Rist Gult* system and *Amisho Rim* system of northern Ethiopia are presented in a separate section. The data on the *Gäbar Madäriya* system of central and southern Ethiopia is also discussed in a separate section. To overcome the limits posed by problems of source material, a new set of figures is constructed based on cadastral documents and levels of ordinary land tax payments.[7]

As a general guide to the use and reading of the data given below, it is important to include a note of caution on the nature of the evidence. There are details in the notes of the tables that discuss what is included and not included in the available data. It is important to know that the data used for revenue

[3] See Pankhurst, R. and Girma Selassie Asfaw (1979); and, Pankhurst, R. (1985a).

[4] See FO 401/8, Inclosure 3 in N0.76, pp. 48–53; it is also quoted in Pankhurst, R. (1968c), pp. 533–540.

[5] See Pankhurst, R. and Girma Selassie Asfaw (1979).

[6] See Table 1 above.

[7] See Appendix A.

purposes does not purport to be either completely accurate or fully comprehensive. As consistent long term series data on government revenue is lacking, it is unthinkable to discuss fluctuation in revenue. In such instances, however, estimated figures are meaningful even in isolation. Since nothing more can really be expected from fragmented source material, the aim here is not a precise quantitative analysis and conclusion, but primarily administrative. The aim is to assemble in one place as many relevant figures as are available in the fragmented documents and classify them in a meaningful way in line with the points of inquiry outlined above.

4.1. Major Sources and Size of Government Revenue in the *Rist Gult* System

For the period of King Tewodros, there is an official manuscript which recorded actual receipts that reached the King's secretary, but this document is limited to the period of early 1860s, and covered only three regions (Märäb Mälash, Tigray and Bägémder).[8] It appears, however, that during this period the court and military expenses were largely drawn from the general central fund.[9]

The King had created a receiving centre in which revenues from direct and indirect taxes were deposited. As discussed in chapter three, the King followed the policy of *hagär bägé*, and on the basis of this policy, the central government levied and collected ordinary land tax. As a result, the government of Tewodros was able to know the full extent of its revenue[10], at least from certain regions.

In the regions of Tigray and Märäb Mälash (highlands of present day Eritrea) the number of tax paying localities as registered in the 1861 tax documents was in total 461 (*adi* and *gulti*). Of these, 98 descent localities were found in the region of Märäb Mälash and they paid a total of 44,604 MT$. There were 353 localities in Tigray which paid a total amount of 72,585 MT$. In the region of Bägémder, the tax registration showed only the northern part, and the number of tax paying descent localities in the northern part were about 30. The tax documents indicated that the northern part yielded about 47,000

[8] It appears that what was registered was only the revenue collected from the *Rist Gult* areas. The revenue collected from the *Amisho Rim* areas was not recorded, and might have been used at the local level.

[9] See the orders given by the King concerning cloth and grain payment for soldiers, in part three of Pankhurst, R. and Girma Selassie Asfaw (1979).

[10] He did not collect land tax from *gult* allocated for the use of the church. The latter negotiated with the King over the collection and use of the land tax, and agreed to pay an extraordinary land tax (*fäsäs*), and gave away their traditional right to collect judicial fee from their specified *gult*, see Zänäb (1902), p. 28–29.

Table 4. *Annual Revenue of the Central Government Collected from Direct and Indirect Taxes from the Regions of Märäb Mälash, Tigray and Northern Bägémder, 1863/4*

Revenu Sources	Regions & Amount			Percentage
	Märäb Mälash (Eritrea)	Tigray	Bägémder	
I. Ordinary Land tax				77%
a) *gebr*	44,604	69,504	34,740 & 4,626 Cloth	
b) *bel* of *nägarit*		33,563		
c) *gult* & Esir		2,340		
d) *shum bel*		141		
e) Others[a]		469		
Subtotal	44,604	106,017		
II. Indirect Tax				23%
mäshomiya		7,928	242 Cloth	
Toll (*mäshomiya*)		15,000	13,000	
täbib		1,000		
qäläfät		5,000		
Tältäl (tax on production of salt)		10,000		
Tältäl (*frida*)		600		
III. Surtaxes				
frida and *mar*	1,577	1,431		
Subtotal	1,577	40,959		
Total of Direct, Indirect and Surtaxes[b]	46,181	146,976	47,740 Thaler & 4,868 cloth	

Source: The tax documents of Tewodros, text and translation in Pankhurst, R. and Germa Selassie Asfaw, eds. (1979).

Notes:

Toll included salt toll *mäshomiya* and *yä-bär qäret.*

[a] It included ordinary land tax payments listed in different names such as payment of carpet, sheep, mule, *eqa bét* (storehouse) and Mäsqäl (Cross lands). See Pankhurst, R. and Girma A.W. (1979), pp. 45, 61–62, 68.

[b] There is a difference in the totals. In the tax document tax (*gebr*) of all Tegre, including caravan, toll, craftsmen, *bel* of *shum* and *nägarit* is 190 226 ½.

MT$, or about 20% of the total revenue.[11] The amount of imperial revenue registered in the tax documents was significantly less and limited to few regions. The tax documents did not register taxes of certain regions which were for certain periods under royal control. These included the whole region of Gojjam, and the districts of Wag, Lasta and Yejju.

[11] For the region of Bägémder much higher figure was quoted by Tewodro's European captives, see Blanc, H. (1868), *A Narrative of Captivity in Abyssinia: with some Account of the Late King Theodore, his country and People.* London.p. 310; Rassam, H. (1869), II, p. 16.

If one proceeds to look at where the money came from, the ordinary land tax, *gebr*, constituted about 77% of the collected taxes paid in money. As mentioned, the tax paid in *amisho* (western part of lake Tana) and the land tax paid in salt (eastern part of lake Tana) were not recorded. Following his policy of *hagär bägé*, the King had centralized the collection of *eribo* and *lemedew* taxes in the region of Bägémder. Probably the ordinary land tax paid in grain and *amisho* was considered as regional expenses used to maintain payment of troops in their respective districts.

Of the direct taxes, there is a part that was collected from taxes which was formerly allocated as expenses for provincial and local governors. The most significant item was *bel* of the *nägarit*. *Gult* land and *esir* land holders were also paying a fixed tax, even though it constituted a smaller amount of the total collection.

Indirect tax constituted 23% of the total revenue registered in the tax document. It included tax farming of rural market (*mäshomiya*). In regions where there was no tax-farming, the community paid surtaxes collectively known as *mar* and *frida*, and it was paid in the regions of Märäb Mälash. Other types included custom tolls, revenue from long distance trade (*qäläfät*) and production tax on salt and artisans. The indirect tax included neither the title nor the payment from the *nägadras* (head merchants) of Gonder, Adwa and other towns as was the case in the *Rist Gult* system. It appears that the document did not include indirect tax revenue from the region of Bägémder, Gojjam and Wollo. For instance, Rassam claimed that Celga (in Bägémder), one of the main custom posts on the western trade route, yielded 10,000 thalers per annum.[12]

From ordinary land tax and indirect tax, the King collected a total of 240,897 MT$ and 4,868 pieces of cloth in 1863/4. This amount was very large compared to the revenues of Gonderian kings of the mid eighteenth century. Gonderian kings had 3,000–4,000 *wäqét* gold annual income.[13] As discussed in chapter one, Gonderian kings had given away government revenue to churches, families, and private individuals during the eighteenth century.

In the tax documents of Tewodros, there was also a figure on livestock tax probably collected from those peasant households where livestock was raised in addition to their farming activity. In the tax document there is a list of over 13,400 head of cattle received by two officials of the King over a period of three consecutive days.[14] In other accounts, we are told that in the region of Bägémder the King is said to have levied a tax of no less than one-fifth of all cattle and sheep.[15] Such levies appeared irregularly depending on the needs of

[12] Pankhurst, R. (1990), p. 304

[13] See Pankhurst, R. (1983–84), pp. 71–76; idem., (1985a), p. 44

[14] See Pankhurst, R. and Girma Selassie Asfaw (1979), pp. 15f.

[15] Rassam, H., (1869), p. 16

the hour. In the chronicle, it is stated that the King's soldiers had plundered more than 15,900 cows which belonged to peasants supporting a rebel noble.[16]

The tax document did not record the extraordinary land tax levied in different forms. Soldiers of the King were billeted *täsäri*, living among the country people. King Tewodros quartered his troops in peasant houses.[17] The King had also collected *fäsäs* tax from some regions and from the church, and the size of this type of tax was not recorded in the document.

The central receiving account of Tewodros also did not include provincial tributes from Shewa and Gojjam. "From Shewa *mered azmach* Haile sent *gebr*: a great quantity of thaler, *shäma*-cloth, horse, mule and many other small things".[18] Again (in 1859) *mered azmach* Haile brought *gebr* from Shewa: 1,000 horses, 788 mules, 10,000 thalers, 1,000 *shäma* cloth, many slaughter cattle".[19]

Confiscation was another important source of revenue for the King. During the first part of his reign, King Tewodros seemed to have a policy of confiscating the treasury of the territorial aristocrats. In 1855, after he defeated *däjazmach* Wube of Tigray and Semen, Tewodros confiscated the treasury of the vanquished territorial prince, which according to Stern, was found to contain 40,000 MT$, besides "a great number of gold and silver plate,...".[20] In Bägémder, as Flad asserted, Queen Menen, mother of *ras* Ali Alula, was obliged to hand over her treasury of 30,000 MT$.[21] In Gojjam, the King confiscated the property of *däjazmach* Biru Goshu[22] and in Shewa also, the King might have sized undefined amount[23] of property.

Supplies of cash from punitive confiscation and fines were also obtained by Tewodros, though not on a regular basis. Abune Sälama was said by Flad to have been obliged to surrender 20,000 MT$ in 1863 for insulting the monarch, while two rich merchants of Qoräta were made to part with 20,000 MT$ and 10,000 MT$ each in 1865, and the rich Muslim merchants at Därita were reported by Massaia to have on one occasion provided 15,000 MT$. Gonder, whose inhabitants refused to pay the usual taxes was sacked in 1864 and 1868.[24]

His successor, King Yohannes had dropped the policy of *hagär bägé* and followed the traditional system of revenue allocation belonging to the *Rist Gult* system. The King followed this policy to get the cooperation of local nobility

[16] Zänäb (1902), p. 37.
[17] See Zänäb (1902), pp. 32, 33, 34, 36, 42
[18] Ibid., p. 30
[19] Ibid., p. 38.
[20] See, Pankhurst, R. (1990), p. 302; Zänäb (1902), p. 19
[21] Pankhurst, R. (1990), p. 302
[22] Zänäb (1902), p. 17
[23] Pankhurst, R. (1990), p. 303
[24] Ibid., p. 304

and the church which were the main forces that contributed to the decline of the power of Tewodros. According to the policy of the King, land tax administration was divided into that part belonging to the provincial governor called *yä nägarit gult* administered by aristocratic and local families, and *gult* belonging to the King called *yä nägash* or *wust gulti.*

Yä nägarit gult and *wust gult* were revenue sources for the upkeep of the imperial army of Yohannes. The King kept royal troops under the system of *täsäri*, billeting them in different regions.[25] The most important source of revenue for the army was the extraordinary land tax called *fäsäs*. In his letter addressed to the Ethiopian community in Jerusalem, the King wrote that the people were paying him "*fäsäs* and gold". *Fäsäs* was an extraordinary land tax paid by the community for the remuneration of royal troops stationed in the district. Gold could be that part of the land tax paid by and collected from some communities. Other than the income from extraordinary and ordinary land tax, the King also received regional contributions from the kings of Gojjam and Shewa.[26]

The total amount of land tax collected from the various localities could not reach the court of Yohannes. When compared to Tewedros, there was a decline in government revenue, and this was possibly due to Yohannes' policy of reinstituting former *gult* holders who were dispossessed by Tewedros. For instance, Yohannes collected about 35,927 MT$ from the region of Märäb Mälash, while Tewedros collected 47,155 MT$.[27] This means there was a 30 percent decline in revenue from the region of Märäb Mälash[28], and the same could have happened in the region of Tigray where there were a considerable number of *gult*. As stated in the tax documents, in 1863/4 Tewedros received from ordinary land tax payment about 69,504 MT$ from the region of Tigray. If one uses the rate of 30 percent reduction to indicate the consequence of the policy of reinstituting *gults*, Yohannes could then have recieved about 20,851 MT$ from ordinary land tax payment from the same region.[29]

It appears that Yohannes' income from indirect taxation (market dues and tolls) was less than that of Tewodros. As with the allocation of land tax, the

[25] On the *täsäri* system of King Yohannes see Afawark G/Iyasus (1905), p. 16–17; Afawarq G/Iyasus (1908), pp. 230–232. See also Aläqa Tesema, in *Mengstu Lemma Tezta*, p. 59

[26] Qoted in Pankhurst, R. (1968c), p. 536

[27] See Pankhurst, R. (1985a), p. 39.

[28] Pankhurst attributed the decline in the revenue to Egyptian incursion. However, by the early 1880s Egyptian presence was limited to boarder areas and it was not threatening the three major provinces from which the taxes were collected. The reason behind the decline in revenue was Yohanes' policy of reinstituting former *gult* holders. As we know from the account of Pollera, *gult* holders were entitled to share 10 percent of the proceeds from the total land tax collected from their respective *gult*. See Pollera, A. (1913), p. 17.

[29] There was a similar amount of estimation made for the region of Tigray in the year 1868 at the time when Yohannes was in control of the whole of Tigray before his coronation as King. See the figure as quoted in Pankhurst, R. (1968c), p. 536.

Tabel 5. *Amount of Annual Revenue Received by the Court of Yohannes in the 1880s*

Revenue Sources	Regions & Amount (in MT$)				
	Tigray	Märäb Mälash	Bägemder	Gojjam	Shewa
Ordinary land tax (*gebr*)	20,851	35,927	34,740		
Extraordinary land tax (*fäsäs*)[a]	279,505		92,824		
Indirect Tax (salt tolls at Teltel)	6,000				
Provincial Contributions[b]				10,000	80,000
Subtotal	306,356	35,927	127,564	10,000	80,000

Sources: Pankhurst, R. (1985), p. 39; Pankhurst, R. (1968c), 536; Pankhurst, R. (1968a), p. 40; Mahteme Selassie (1962 E.C.), pp. 148–149, 151; Pankhurst, R. and Germa Selassie Asfaw, eds. (1979).

Notes:

[a] There are no figures that show income in the form of extraordinary tax *fäsäs*. If one could judge by the period of Menelik, the districts in the provinces of Shere paid 13,090 MT$, Aksum paid 13,090 MT$, Enderta 53,360 MT$, Hult Awulalo 18,612 MT$, Temben 110,890 MT$, Agame 36,294 MT$, and Adwa 34,169 MT$. Total revenue from *fäsäs* tax was estimated to be 279,505 MT$ from the region of Tigray. *Fäsäs* tax was paid in Märäb Mälash, but there was no information provided on the total amount. Bägémder paid *fäsäs* tax since *ras* Ali and it spread during the time of Tewodros. From the documents of the Menelik period, the region paid a total of 45,412 *dawula* of grain; if the value of one *dawula* was two *birr*, this could have amounted to 92,824 MT$.

[b] In addition to the 10,000 MT$, Gojjam contributed three porters of gold and a great number of cattle.

King also waived some of his rights in the collection and use of revenues from indirect taxes.[30] It is reported that he received 6,000 MT$ out of 40,000 MT$ collected from salt tolls at the salt plains of Teltel.[31] There was also a royal trade in ivory, and the King himself had once hunted elephants in the lower regions of Märäb Mälash.[32] He had also sent royal merchants south to Wellega.[33]

It is hard to discuss the total revenue of Yohannes since there is no data or actual account book as there was for Tewodros, and no document of central receipt was kept at the King's palace in Mäkälé. Based on fragmented source material it is possible to designate the major sources of government income

[30] See the *gult* grant of Yohannes IV to Däbrä Gänät Mädhani Aläm of Mäkälé in 1872/73 (the document is attached to *Wärq zä-Wängél* (Golden Gospel) of the church; see also Tarekegn Yibabie (1988), p 33. The privilege of collecting customs from salt tolls was given to three other monasteries in Tämbein. Informant Malaka Genet Serse Dingel Arefe Ayne, Head of the Däbrä Gänät Medahini Alem Church, August 1993.

[31] Qoted in Pankhurst, R. (1968a), p. 40.

[32] See Fiseha Wolde Mikael (1936 E.C.), p. 24.

[33] See Nadew, *Yä ras Gobena Tarik*, manuscript deposited at the National Library, Ministry of Culture and Sports, Addis Ababa, document no. 23.01.5.

and the total amount of revenue received by the court. In the 1880s King Yohannes could annually raise around 559,847 MT$, an amount which could be used for the court and royal military expenditures.

4.2. The Structure and Size of Imperial Government Revenue in the *Gäbar Madäriya* System

Organization of the imperial government revenue of Menelik was different from that of the Kings Tewodros and Yohannes. In the case of Menelik there was more or less a clear division among the revenue of the court and the revenue allocated for the establishment of the military, and for civilian bodies (churches founded corporatively and privately, and *milmil* lands).

Why did the *gäbar Madäriya* system have a separate revenue for the army, and not the *Rist Gult* system? In the latter, custody and use of land tax was localized and privatized ever since the crisis of the sixteenth century. Land tax was mainly used as expenses for the various *gult* holders and the court received its meager income in the form of *wust gulit* and other domains. Of the ordinary land tax, there was little left for allocation to the army. Since the resource was meager and had different methods of administration, soldiers had never been allowed to collect and use land tax by themselves, except in the case of *amisho*, which also was privatized by means of *rim*. The army was largely remunerated by extraordinary taxes such as *fäsäs* and *täsäri*. Even if both extraordinary taxes were administered centrally, the revenue collected from *fäsäs* was deposited at the court to be distributed later, and this revenue was considered as one of the main incomes of the court and the army.

In the *Gäbar Madäriya* system, court revenue was completely separated from the revenue allocated for the imperial army. One reason was that in this fiscal system the state had direct control over the land tax, even though it was decentralized for the purpose of administration. Central and direct control over land tax, and for that matter over the whole system of direct taxation, enabled the state to prepare, at least in principle, different revenue budgets for the court, the army and the church. That part of the revenue budget prepared for the court was generally referred to as *mad bét* (literally kitchen), and this was separated from the revenue allocated for the army and the church.

4.2.1. Court Revenue of Menelik

The concept of *mad bét* is often confused with *gana gäb*, that part of ordinary land tax allocated to the royal kitchen in the form of *hudad* cultivation and honey payment. The concept of *mad bét* included various sources of reveneu such as ordinary land tax payment, fixed land tax from the provinces, and reserved crown lands (*wärägänu*). It also included provinces whose land tax and reveneu from trade were allocated to a palace such as Wällamo, and *milmil* lands.[34] The term *mad bét* was a broader concept which is used to refer to the revenue budget of the court. The term *gana gäb* refers to a form of arrangement for sharing the land tax base with local governors.

Gana gäb were districts whose ordinary and extraordinary land tax payments were allocated to the royal kitchen. In these districts, there were also *hudad* and *eribo* lands allocated for the royal kitchen, and the *hudad* land was cultivated by the neighbouring peasants and the *eribo* land by tenants. In this sense the districts allocated could be called crown lands, and following the calendar they were divided into twelve groups and each of them were assigned one month of the year during which they were supposed to supply grain and wood to the palace. These districts and the *hudad* land were managed by a royal official called *mesläné*. This official not only supervised the cultivation of *hudad* lands but also collected the land tax and *asrat* paid by *gäbar* of the *gana gäb* districts.[35] In the late nineteenth century, in central Shewa, there were 10,292 *gäbar* peasants paying 3,148 *dawula* and 52,605 *quna* grain, and 18,002 bundles of wood.[36] There was about 3,709 tenants cultivating a number of *hudad* lands and loading 18,585 *quna* grain and 3,709 bundles of wood.[37] If the grain from *hudad* land was not enough, the *mesläné* was entitled to take grain collected from *asrat* tax.[38] Often the *asrat* tax was collected from the districts and localities allocated as *gana gäb* to the palace kitchen.

In addition to *gana gäb* districts, the royal court also received land tax collected from far regions. Mostly it was the honey part of the land tax that was shipped to the court. The land tax collected and delivered from these regions in the form of honey, grain, and other in-kind was registered by the *ehil gotera shum* of the palace.[39] This official was responsible for the supervision, collection and storage of taxes paid in grain, honey, butter and supply of wood. The officials used to register the names of the tax payer and the locality in a book called *bahr mäzgäb* (this book is also used to register allocation of land after land measurement). The grain from government *hudad* land was used for the expenses for royal banquets and emergency *daragot*.[40]

There were also other reserved lands for raising government cattle and keeping government mules. These lands were known as *wärägänu*, *baldräs* and *eqa bét*. About 409 *gasha* lands (18,040 hectares land) were reserved as

[34] On *milmil* lands see section 4.2.3 below.
[35] See Maheteme Selassie (1962 E.C.), pp. 26–27.
[36] Ibid.
[37] Ibid.
[38] Ibid., p. 117.
[39] Ibid., p. 25f.
[40] Ibid.

wärägänu[41], about 16 localities were reserved as *baldräs*[42], and one district was reserved as *eqa bét*. The *bäjirond* of *eqa bét* (stores) had a duty to maintain mules and other objects necessary for loading and transporting.

Provincial contribution was another source of court revenue and there were three types; provinces which paid fixed tax revenue to the palace (*qurt gebr*), provinces allocated as belonging to the palace by royal decree, and annual presentation and contribution from some provincial governors. The exact amount of each type is difficult to know from the available reference material. Those provinces which paid fixed tax were Jima, Wellega, Awsa and Guba. For instance, in 1885, Abba Jifar of Jima had given Menelik 30 elephant tusks, 30 horns of civet, 30 mules, 60 horses, 100 large vases of honey, 100 sacks of coffee, 20 lion, leopard, and panther skins, and an unspecified amount of dollars.[43] The *balabat* in Wellega paid 1,000 *wäqét* annually.[44] There was no available data for Awsa and Guba countries. Wällamo under its traditional ruler, King Tona, had supplied Menelik with 5,000 *shäma*-cloth.[45]

The provinces of Wällamo and Illubabor were regarded as *mad bét* and *nägadras* Countries.[46] In the province of Wällamo there were about 19,361 *qutr gäbar* paying 19,361 *gundo* of honey and 58,083 *dawula* of grain, and in Illubabor, there were about 36,816 *qälad gäbar.*[47] Much later, *qurt gäbar* provinces contributed 28 bundles of cloth, estimated at 630 *birr*; 40 shields decorated with gold worth 2,191 *birr*; 15 types of highly selected swords worth 891 *birr*; 3,040 *gundo* of honey worth 21,280 *birr*; 5 Mesob worth 300 *birr*; 16 fully equipped horses, some of them decorated with gold estimated at 1,459 *birr*; 5 mules decorated with gold priced at 1,400 *birr*. Jima was paying a total of 29,065 *birr.*[48]

Finally, there was the contributions made by governor generals of the provinces who brought presentations once a year or any time they came to visit the King.[49] There is no evidence that the King was receiving provincial contributions from the *mäsafint hagär* (regional princes of northern Ethiopia). Other revenue sources of the court were *rist* (family estate of the dynasty), gifts, such as *gult* grant to Menelik by Yohannes[50], livestock tax[51], and nominal payment from the local *balabat* chiefs[52].

[41] Ibid., 23.
[42] Ibid.
[43] Quoted in Pankhurst, R. (1968a), p. 105.
[44] Gebre Wolde Engda Worq (1948 E.C.), p. 63.
[45] Quoted in Pankhurst, R. (1968b), p. 107.
[46] Mahteme Selassie (1962), p. 648; Tsehai Berhane Selassie (1980), p. 335.
[47] For the number of owner cultivators see Mahteme Selassie (1962), pp. 143, To get the estimated size of the annual revenue from the regions use the figures on table A-4, in Appendix A.
[48] Mahteme Selassie (1962), p. 165.
[49] See Gebre Selassie (1959 E.C.), passim.
[50] See Fekadu Begna, (1990), p. 75.
[51] See Pankhurst, R. (1967), pp. 47f.
[52] See for instance the nominal payment of the *siso balabat* in Mahteme Selassie (1962), pp. 107f.

Indirect tax was another major source of court revenue during the time of Menelik, as noted by Mahteme Selassie.[53] Market dues and custom tolls in principle belonged to the central government. Market dues were collected by the *nägadras* of the King from the capital Addis Ababa, and other district towns such as Addis Alem, Ankober and Roge, all in the region of Shewa.[54] Market dues were collected at the gates. For instance, there were five custom gates on each of the major roads leading to Addis Ababa. Any commodity such as coffee, ivory, salt, grain, sheep, hides, incense, and cotton goods were taxed at a 10% rate.[55]

Import-export tax was another source of central government revenue. Those engaged in the export of goods did not trade directly with the provinces. Commodities such as civet, coffee, and ivory were gathered by indigenous traders (e.g., *Jeberties*) who brought the items to the capital, Addis Ababa, and sold them to foreign merchants for export.[56] In 1899–1900, total revenue from the import-export tax of Addis Ababa was estimated at 450,550 MT$. The total revenue from import-export at the capital for the year 1905–6 amounted to 603,200 MT$. For Harar, import and export tax revenue amounted to 639,465 MT$ for 1899–1900, and about 124,682 MT$ for the year 1905–6.[57]

The court, through the *bäjirond*, collected tax from artisans and weavers. Except for those who worked as royal artisans, those weavers who worked for the market paid tax to government officials. There were about 1,200–1,400 weavers of this type in Addis Ababa, by the beginning of the twentieth century.

The court drew revenue from the monopoly export of gold, ivory, salt and coffee. Hunters were obliged to give Menelik the first tusk that touched the ground when an elephant was killed. Later on, hunting was monopolized and permission from the King was required to hunt elephants. The ivory which was brought as tax and tribute by regional governors was exported by two foreign agents of the King, Ilg and Chefneux, between 1890–1892, and then Savoure up to 1896. From the account of MacGillivray, Menelik's revenue from ivory was valued at 175,100 MT$ in 1902, 98,770 MT$ in 1903, and 201,280 MT$ in 1904, or 5%, 4% and 6% respectively of the total monetary revenue.[58] There was also a revenue obtained from coffee export.[59]

Menelik was also collecting income through grants of concession. In 1892, the King sold a number of monopolies. The coffee monopoly was sold to

[53] Ibid., p. 637.

[54] See Garretson, P. (1974), p. 322

[55] Ibid., p 325.

[56] Quoted in Garretson, P. (1974), p. 334

[57] See Pankhurst, R. (1968a), pp. 49f.

[58] See FO 401/8, p. 50. Note that there was no export tax on gold and ivory; in fact the former was duty free since these items were either royal monopolies or personal property of the King.

[59] Coffee was taxed in Illibabur, see Gebre Wolde Engda Worq (1948 E.C.), p. 65; For the region of Sidamo, see ibid., p. 74, For an estimation of export volume see Pankhurst, R. (1968c), pp. 437–451.

Table 6. *Amount of Annual Revenue Received by the Court of Menelik in the Years between 1902–1904, as Estimated by MacGillivray*

Year	Gold (in MT$)*	MT$	Salt	Ivory	Cloth	Total
1902	327,560	2,069,122	854,427	175,100	216,720	3,642,929
1903	384,840	903,887	904,988	98,770	128,485	2,420,970
1904	501,000	1,650,763	666,085	201,280	122,300	3,131,428

Source: FO 401/8, p. 50; Quoted also in Pankhurst, p. 538–539.
* The value of one ounce of gold was about 40 MT$. See Pankhurst, R. (1968c), p. 538.

Mohammed Aly for 65,000 MT$. In 1890 Chefnex obtained a salt monopoly over Lake Assala in return for the payment of 1,500 MT$ annually.[60] As a result of railway negotiations 45,000 MT$ was given as down payment and 5,000 MT$ was given per month.[61] Article three of the provision of the concession given to the Bank of Abyssinia stated that the bank would pay 10% of the profit placed in reserve, a 7% dividend would be paid to the shareholders, and a remaining 20% would accrue to the King.[62]

There were also other varieties of irregular and regular sources of income. Even though it is difficult to know how much it was, the *nägadras* collected a fixed fee from settling commercial cases. In 1895 Menelik exported 2,000 mules to Madagascar which he bought for 25 MT$ each, while he got 40 MT$ per head.[63] Also, the King lent out ca. 240,000 MT$[64] from which he collected interest.

There were various sources of court revenue and several taxation estimates. Reading the fragmented materials may help to understand the increase in court revenue over the period as a number of regions were integrated into the *gäbar Madäriya* fiscal system. By 1905, there was information on the financial situation of the court as reported by MacGillivray. He wrote on that part of the total revenue received in monetary forms (in gold, MT$, salt, ivory and cloth).

Except in the case of gold, MacGillivray never disclosed the sources of the revenue. He stated that the total revenue mentioned in terms of gold was received mainly from the provinces of Beni Shangul and Wellega.[65] Here again, to identify whether the amount of gold paid came from the fixed annual pay-

[60] See Garretson, P. (1974), p. 258.
[61] Ibid., p. 314.
[62] See Pankhurst, R. (1968c), p. 495.
[63] See Garretson, P. (1974), p. 259.
[64] Quoted in ibid., p. 315.
[65] It was not the province of Beni Shangul and Wellega which paid tax in gold. The traditional governor of the province of Jimma, Awsa, and governor of Guba were paying, among other things, fixed revenue in gold.

ment of the regions (*qurt gebr*) or from taxation imposed on gold extraction is problematical. In these regions alluvial gold was extracted by the localities and by companies which were given concessions. On the other hand, the *balabats* in the province of Wellega were paying one thousand *wäqét*-ounce annually as land tax to the central government.[66] It is therefore not clear whether the gold came from ordinary land tax, indirect tax on the extraction of gold, or tributes from provinces. The same is true for the revenue stated in salt. Did it come from salt in trade (as indirect tax) or from *milmil* lands which paid their tax in *amole* salt? The cloth payment came partly from the fixed land tax paid by the provinces of Jimma, Wellega-Neqemte, Wellega Qelem, Beni Shangul, Awsa and Guba. The ivory revenue came from ivory tax and ivory hunting by the palace.

The payment in cloth and in salt came mostly from *milmil* lands, which paid the tax attached to their land in the form of cloth, *bernos*-wool, *amole*-salt, farming implements, kitchen utensils, fuel, traditional weapons, food spices, etc.[67] For instance, salt was used as fodder to feed the great number of horses, mules and oxen of the palace.[68]

The total revenue calculated for the years 1902–1904 by MacGillivray of the Bank of Abyssinia, came largely from *milmil* lands, from provinces which paid fixed land tax (*qurt gebr*), and other tributes, and finally from the custom duties at Addis Ababa, Harar, Wällamo and other areas. In other words, the total revenue mentioned by him basically did not include revenue from ordinary and extraordinary land tax collected in honey and grain.

The court revenue of Menelik did not include the revenues of Queen Tayitu, who had a separate treasury. The Queen was given *gezat*, provinces to administer, such as Bulgo, Nono, Tebe, etc. in southern parts of Shewa[69], from which she collected revenue from land tax. The Queen also had *gult* lands in northern Ethiopia[70]. Queen Tayitu collected customs from a post at Doba near Weldiya of about 4,000 MT$ a year in 1906. The Queen also collected "considerable" revenue from another post on the northern route.[71] French reports for 1909 stated that Menelik had allotted one month's revenue (of Harar) out of every twelve to Queen Tayitu.[72] MacGillivray reported that the Queen's treasury contained over 600,000 MT$ in 1904.[73] He wrote that the Queen had received an amount of 154,880 MT$ for 1902, 219,918 MT$ for the year 1903, and

[66] It seems that this payment continued until the introduction of land measurement in the region in 1910. See also Gebre Wold Engda Worq (1948 E.C.), p. 61.

[67] Ibid., pp. 25–30; See also Mahteme Selassie (1962), pp. 115–116.

[68] See Gebre Wold Engda Worq (1948 E.C.), p. 28.

[69] See Gebre Selassie (1959 E.C), p. 338.

[70] Ibid., pp. 238.

[71] See Pankhurst, R. (1968a), pp. 40.

[72] Qouted in ibid., p. 50.

[73] FO 401/8, p. 50.

253,626 MT$ for the year 1904.[74] The Queen's treasury also contained about 40,000 MT$ worth of gold in bars and rings.[75] These total figures on the Queen's treasury presumably did not include the amount of grain and *gundo* of honey (ordinary land tax) collected from the *gezat* districts of the Queen. The Queen had her own army which she paid[76], and other expenses, particularly the construction of churches both in Ethiopia and in Jerusalem[77].

MacGillivray wrote that the King's treasury which he looked through was divided into three groups. Menelik's private treasury containing 1,000,000 MT$, the King's treasury containing 2,000,000 MT$ and the King's Public Treasury containing 60,000 MT$. This division seemed to follow the traditional line. Menelik's private treasury was called *guada*, and from this treasury the King made donations to churches, health centres, and gave charity and gifts to individuals. When the King died, the treasury would pass to his heir.[78] The second treausury was called *alga* (literally meaning throne), and was considered to belong to the royal family, and it too passed from one heir to the next. The third treasury was called *mängest* (state treasury) and was presumbaly used for public purposes. It appears that this division was fluid. With the formation of the ministerial system, came a clear division between the private and public treasuries. To this effect, the Ministry of Finance was given a regulation to constitute separate departments; the ministry was still in charge in the administration of the private and royal family treasuries.[79]

4.2.2. Revenue of the Imperial Army of Menelik

The revenue of the imperial army was separated from both the revenue of the court and the revenue allocated for the church. In the following discussion the figures calculated as revenue for the imperial army strictly excluded revenue sources of the court mentioned above and civil revenue allocated for the church and pensioners. There were two major sources of revenue for the imperial army: ordinary land tax (*gebr*) and extraordinary land tax (*asrat*-tithe). The details on the data and amount of revenue levied from ordinary and extraordi-

[74] Ibid.

[75] Ibid., p. 51.

[76] See Chapter Five below.

[77] See Gebre Selassie (1959 E.C.), pp. 125ff, 322. The buying of land and the construction of Däbre Genet church in Jerusalem had cost the Queen around 38,000 MT$. Maintaining the activity of the Ethiopian churches in Jerusalem was one area of expense for the Queen and before her Yohannes. For the amount of gold and money sent to the clergies in Jerusalem see the letters of the King attached as appendix in his chronicle, see Bairu Tafla (1977). For Menelik see his chronicle, Gebre Selassie (1959 E.C.), p. 315–319.

[78] Regional governor generals and court officials with a rank of *ras* had their own private treasuries. Menelik told MacGillivray that "many of (his) *rases* were much wealthier than (him). You (MacGillivray) should see their treasuries". FO 401/8, p. 52. This meant that some of his *rases* were millionaires; *ras* Makonnen, the governor of Harar, and the father of Haile Selassie, was "even richer than King Menelik". Ibid.

[79] See Mahteme Selassie (1962 E.C.), pp. 196–197.

Table 7. *Gross Estimate of Annual Revenue Collected from Ordinary and Extraordinary Land Taxes of the Gäbar Madäriya System*

Regions	No. of Tax Paying Units & Obligation Types	Ordinary Annual Land Tax (*gebr*)				Extraordinary Land Tax (*asrat*-tithe)
		shäma-Cloth[a]	*gundo* Honey	*dawula*	*birr*	*dawula*
Wello[b]						10,6287
	1,489 *gäbar gendäbäl*					
	64,244 *qutr gäbar*	264	4,288	4,288 G & 1,593 *quna* Butter		
	2,242 *madäriya*					
Shewa[c]						256,500
	12,237 *balabat*-chiefs					
	14,677 *gäbar gendäbäl*			29,354		
	18,979c, 20,237s *qutr gäbar*		18,979	117,641	80,948	
	25,838 *qälad gäbar*		25,838	64,595		
	45,045 *madäriya*		45,045	135,135		
Wellega	15,943 *qutr gäbar*		15,943	47,829		15,943
	2,757 *qälad gäbar*			5,514	19,299	96,495
Illubabor	36,816 *qälad gäbar*				368,160	128,856
Kafa	48,899 *qutr gäbar*			146,697	195,596	48,899
	14,648 *qälad gäbar*			21,972	102,536	51,268
Gomu Gofa	3,930 *qutr gäbar*			11,790	15,720	3,930
Sidamo	75,108 *qutr gäbar*			22,5324	375,540	75,108
	21,134 *qälad gäbar*				380,412	73,969
Arsi	3,641 *balabat* chiefs					38,231
	7,275 *qälad gäbar*			21,825	87,300	25,463
	10,266 *madäriya*		10,266	30,798		35,931
Harar	70,000 *qutr gäbar*			98,000	280,000	70,000
Total[d]			116,071	956,474	1,905,511	920,593

Sources: The data on the number of tax paying units are those that are reprocessed and calculated from the tables illustrated by Mahteme Selassie (1962 EC), pp. 133–143; the amount of payment is extracted from the detailed accounts on tax obligation lands discussed by Gebre Wold Engda Worq (1948 EC), pp. 17–19, and the whole of chapter two. For further details on the methods and steps of calculation see Apendix A.

Notes:

[a] The column *shäma*-cloth is almost empty, but it is kept as reminder that some of the ordinary land tax payments could have been paid in the form of cloth. See for instance, the case of *milmil* land in Shewa, and Harar, see Gebre Wold Engda Werq (1948 EC), pp. 25–30; 43–44.

[b] The whole figure including the tithe payment was taken as documented by Mahteme Selassie. The total figure did not cover the whole region, but only for the province of Wollo proper. Presumably, it did not include those grain payments made to the local *mälkägna*. In the present table, some figures indicating butter and honey payment are not listed here since it becomes difficult to convert them into *gundo*. For the details see Mahteme Selassie (1962 EC), p. 155.

[c] The figure on the size of the *asrat* tax was taken directly as documented in Mahteme Selassie (1962 EC), p. 332.

[d] The total number excludes the figure from Wollo. First there are different kinds of measurement for the tax paid in honey and butter and it is difficult to convert one into the other. Secondly, the total raw shows the size of imperial revenue, and the region of Wollo was under an independent control of *ras* Mikeal, later King Mikael from 1870s–1917, and its revenue could not be considered as imperial revenue. *Ras* Mikael was not a regional governor general appointed by King Menelik.

Table 8. *Annual Revenue Collected from the District of Jama, in the region of Wollo*

Revenue Sources	Amount in Kind	Amount in *birr*
Land Tax[a]		
	2720 *dawula*	5440
	124 *gundo* honey	1488
	116 *gundo* butter	1160
	6272 salt	
Handicraft	218	545
Livestock	1882	3293
Judicial fee & bet	500 /month	6200
Total		18126

Source: See Mahteme Selassie (1962 EC), p. 156.
Notes:
[a] 335 *gasha gäbar* paid 2,720 *dawula* of grain (5,440 *birr*), 124 *gundo* honey (1,488 *birr*) and 116 *gundo* butter (1,160 *birr*). 3,136 tenants (*tisägna*) paid 6,272 salt
The figures on the table do not include tax paying units for the clergy ca 294, *yä ch´iqa mar* ca 44, *gendäbäl* 39, as mentioned on a table shown on page 154 in the book of Mahteme Selassie (1962 EC).

nary land taxes are discussed in appendix A. In Table 7 one finds the amount of total land tax levied by the system for remuneration of imperial officers and soldiers.

This Table represents an estimation of ordinary and extraordinary land tax revenue of the *Gäbar Madäriya* system directly under the disposition of the central government by the end of the nineteenth century. The total figures exclude livestock taxes, surtaxes and *senq* obligations, and other types of labour obligations which in some cases were paid in the form of money. The amount of surtaxes, such as payment for holidays, supply of grass and wood was very considerable. The estimation is thus not a total revenue from direct taxation, and as such it is not possible to give the share of each tax from the total revenue of the state. The total figure does not include the regional revenue of Bale, some provinces in Wellega, Gomu Gofa, and provinces which paid fixed annual tax such as Jimma and Wellega. There may be other districts which are not found in the fragmented documents. It is, therefore, misleading to give in percentage the share of each region in the total revenue from the ordinary and extraordinary land taxes.

In addition to ordinary and extraordinary land taxes, there were also other sources of revenue for imperial troops. The example below is from the district of Jama, found in the province of Were Illu, in the region of Wollo. This district was divided into four localities and land measurement was conducted in the area. The governor of the district registered the types of revenue collected from the area as shown in Table 8.

What one concludes from Table 8 is that land tax, particularly in the form of grain payment or *hudad,* was the most important source of local government revenue and expenditure. The honey part of the land tax was also important if the *shaläqa* was allowed to retain part of it. Officials also had control over agricultural handicraft, probably the same was true for the rural market. Local officials also had control over and shared the livestock tax.

Surtaxes were another source of income for regional/local governments. Of the various types of surtaxes, the judicial fee, payments made in return for the administration of justice, constituted another important income source for local officials. What was not stated in the table was levies made for the purpose of celebration of certain occasions (such as New Year, Christmas, and Easter), and payment of additional fees to government officials (such as appointment fees).

4.2.3. Civilian Revenue

Revenues other than for the court and the army can be grouped together under the heading of civilian revenue. These were revenues earmarked for the church and officials who gave long service to the government. The revenues were collected independently by the respective beneficiaries, and there were different mechanisms affecting the size of revenue allocated for such ends.

It is beyond the scope of this chapter to discuss the various sources and the size of the revenues of the church in the period of our discussion. It is a subject of a separate study. In part one of this work, there is a discussion of the economic base of the church as outlined in the *Amisho Rim* system. Basically one sees the similarity and continuity in the forms and means of supporting church needs and service. Rather in an extraordinary manner, it had become a long tradition since the function and needs of the church are listed to the last detail for the purpose of earmarking revenue. To consider only the *däbr* church, for instance, there was a need for the payment of church officials, *däbtära*-cantors, keepers of treasury, and for service such as *zekr* (Memorial), *qurban* (Eucharist), *mäswat* (Holy Sacrifice), and for expenses such as incense, candles, etc. This is not surprising since the church was the source of land ownership and its needs were the forms by which confiscated state lands were given to noble families.

Basically the same old forms of revenue allocation and administration continued during the time of Menelik. After he came back from the national religious conference held in Borumeda in 1875[80], Menelik issued an order to regional governors to allocate two *gasha* lands from every *mälkägna* land for the construction of churches[81]. The clergy were given sate land (*madäriya*) in re-

[80] See Gebre Selassie (1959 E.C.), pp. 86ff. See also Caulk, R.A. (1972).
[81] See Nadew, *yä ras Gobena Tarik*

turn for service in the church. The amount depended on the type of the established church (*gädam*, *däbr*, *gätär* churches) and consequently on the size of the clergy. As with *madäriya* land, the clergy often leased the land to tenants. *Madäriya* lands were administered by the *aläqa* (head) of the church, who also had *madäriya* land for himself.[82] In 1890/91, Menelik made a regulation about the responsibilities of the officials, the ordinary clergy and how to apportion revenues collected from church services.[83] In this decree, the *aläqa* had no right to uproot the clergy from the state land unless they were caught committing a disgraceful act. Even in that case the lands could not be sold, but were reserved for someone else who could serve in the church in his place. Unlike soldiers who hold state land (*madäriya*), the clergy were allowed to collect judicial fees from their tenants, excluding cases which involved theft and murder.[84] To all intents, *madäriya* land was one source of revenue, and according to available data, there were about 11,416 state lands allocated for the clergy in the region of Shewa and Arsi.[85]

Gäbäz lands were another source of revenue earmarked to pay for incense, candles and memorial services. *Gebzena* land was allocated in 1894 and, according to the official document, the purpose of the allocation was to relieve the court of the expenditures allocated for incense, candles and for the preparation of holy sacrifices and memorials.[86] Menelik donated large estates to seven members of the royal families and relatives, and to six higher court officials. The aristocracy acquired the title of *gäbäz*, the financial office of the church, and administered all income for the church including taxes, donations and other offerings. This office was hereditary and passed from father to son.

The third type of revenue source for the church was what can be called *mälkägna* lands. These lands were extra state lands transferred into the permanent possession of private individuals who were obliged to support one of the activities and needs of the church assigned to them at the time of grant. The grantees were members of the lay and ecclesiastical nobility who got their permission directly from the court, and the lands were administered by higher court officials or princes with the title of *mälkägna*.[87] According to the studies

[82] See Mahteme Selassie (1962 E.C.), p. 545.

[83] EMML, 76 F291b

[84] The *aläqa* was also entitled to receive two thirds of judicial fee, money from *wurered* (bet), and inheritance, while the one remaining third was divided between the *liqe tebet* and *gebz*. Lands allocated for incense and candles were to be in the hands of the *gebz* which was a hereditary office. The *gebez* was also to keep ordinary land tax (*feré gebr*) and all money given to the church in the name of *sele*t. See EMML, 76 F291b.

[85] See table A-3 in Appendix A.

[86] For the translation and further comments on the document, see Haile Gebriel Dagne (1972), "The Gebzena Charter 1894" in *Journal of Ethiopian Studies, X: 1*.

[87] There are detailed studies of the land charters of *mälkägna* lands of the five churches in Addis Ababa. Among others, see Wudu Tafete Kasu (1989), "The Twin Churches of Raguel, 1889–1985". B.A. Thesis in History, A.A.U; Demeke Seifu (1989), "The Addis Ababa Urael Church (ca.1855 to 1974)". B.A. Thesis in History. A.A.U.

made in some churches of Addis Ababa, the Entoto Mariyam church had 503 *gasha* lands, the church of Holy Trinity 428, and the Raguel church 319 *gasha* lands.

There were various forms for transferring state lands to support the needs and activities of the church on quite a similar basis but for different activities. For instance, individuals who held 112 *gasha* lands registered their land as *zekr* by joining the Memorial House of King Menelik to provide cooked food and drinks to priests and the needy both monthly and annually.[88] Aside from state lands, the church was also allocated *asrat* tax as a supplement or for remuneration of priests. However, the most important source of revenue was state land held in perpetuity in private by members of the aristocracy and nobility.

Another category of "civil revenue" was that part of the state land/tax set aside for rewarding favourites and those with long government service, and this type of grant was called *milmil* lands. The land tax paid by this group was "light", paid in different forms and was fixed by royal permission.[89] This status was acquired by *däg t'inat*, long service to the government (*balä wuläta*). Most women nobility belonged to this group. In this category there was no uniformity of type and size of payment and/or obligation. Holders of the grant paid nominal land tax, and the status of the grant was approved only by the King because it was a kind of exemption from the payment of land tax. Often these kinds of privileges were given to those who gave long service to the state and to members of the higher nobility and aristocracy. Such grants could be as big as 20 *gasha* lands (882 hectors).

4.3. Changes in the Composition and Size of Imperial Government Revenue

There was a change in the composition of government sources of revenue particularly during the time of Menelik. Primarily the change was in the area of ordinary land tax which total size increased over time under central administration. In the *Rist Gult* system, ordinary land tax was administered by private means and government expenses were rigidly dependent on a given portion, no matter how it fluctuated over the years. Tewodros collected ordinary land tax through central administration by abolishing private method tax administration which was hitherto enjoyed by the class of *gult* holders. Yohannes abandoned this policy and thus reduced his revenue income from ordinary land

[88] See Mahteme Selassie (1962 EC), p. 523ff.

[89] There were twenty four types of *milmil* lands, see the details in Gebre Wold Engda Worq (1948 E.C.), pp. 25–30.

tax and he consequently supplemented his income by expanding the imperial control over regions hitherto not integrated into the royal tax system and by other means such as provincial contribution. Menelik was operating in a different fiscal system where the use of ordinary land tax was controlled and directed by a central administration. He increased the size of the collection of the ordinary land tax by means of land surveys and integration of the southern regions into the *Gäbar Madäriya* fiscal system.[90] Land surveys increased the number and variety of state lands used for remuneration of troops, retired soldiers and the clergy.

In the early 1870s, when the King's authority was limited in central Shewa and did not extend far beyond the Awash river, Menelik collected ordinary land tax from 18,979 *qutr gäbar* peasants, 12,181 *gendäbäl*, and a total of 14,368 *madäriya* land.[91] From these tax paying units, the King could collect 124,403 *dawula* of grain and 33,347 gundo of honey.[92] In a matter of two and a half decades, the imperial revenue from ordinary land tax alone rose to 88,742 *gundo* honey (i.e., a 166% increase), 874,487 *dawula* of grain (i.e., a 602% increase) and 1,905,511 MT$ which was a totally new income to the state.[93] The revenue was obtained by integrating the southern provinces into the *Gäbar Madäriya* fiscal system.

The introduction in 1894 of *asrat* tax, a one-tenth payment from the produce of the land, was another innovation of the period. This tax was universal and paid by all categories of people who benefited from the possession and use of land, including the local nobility and soldiers holding state land. Even the *tisägna* were liable in their contract to give an additional portion of their grain to help the land owner pay the *asrat* tax. In the *Rist Gult* system, extraordinary land tax had the form of *fäsäs* and *täsäri*; while the former was arbitrary, the latter was a burden to peasant households. *Asrat*, as a proportional payment of the produce, replaced the *täsäri* (billeting) form and the *fäsäs* tax in northern Ethiopia. *Asrat* not only avoided the negative sides of billeting, but also contributed to tax homogeneity. It created different alternative sources for remuneration of the regular army, other than the ordinary land tax. A decade after its introduction, the imperial government collected about 920,593 *dawula* of grain, an amount that covered the annual grain payment for 90,254 ordinary soldiers.

[90] For the size of the revenue obtained from the southern regions see table 7 above. Integration of each region in the fiscal system was tantamount to an increase in the size of government revenue. As to when each region was integrated into the system read the detailed accounts in Bairu Tafla (1987).

[91] Calculated from the table listed under the heading *rist* areas of Shewa, in Mahteme Selassie (1962 EC), pp. 139–142.

[92] The total figures on the revenue are obtained by multiplying the number of tax paying units by the amount and type of land tax payment shown in table A-4, Appendix A.

[93] See Table 7.

The share contributed by ordinary and extraordinary land tax was thus quite considerable. In the *Rist Gult* system, the revenue for the royal army came largely from the extraordinary land tax which was used both as payment and provision. In the *Gäbar Madäriya* system, there was a marked separation between payment and provision. Labour obligations (*senq ch´agn*) were imposed on the *gäbar* peasants with the aim of providing food, water, grass, etc. for campaign soldiers. Moreover the state itself could finance provisions and transport needs through tax exemption.

There was a change in the size and structure of revenue accruing from indirect tax. This was particularly noticeable in the import and export tax which was related to the growth of international trade since the 1880s. In the tax documents of Tewodros, the King was receiving 28,000 from custom tolls and 5,000 from *qelefät* (long distance trade), a total of 33,000 from three regions, namely Tigray, Märäb Mälash and northern Bägémder. Custom receipts from external trade were an important source of court revenue for Menelik. Based on knowledge of the volume of import and export trade and the level of taxation, one could estimate the amount of revenue the state was supposed to collect from import/export taxes at Addis Ababa and Harar. In 1899–1900, the value of import goods at Addis Ababa, for instance, was estimated at 2,977,000 MT$ and exports at 1,528,500 MT$.[94] Assuming a 10% *ad valorem* tax, the revenue amounted to around 297,700 MT$ for imports and 152,850 MT$ for exports, a total revenue of 450,550 MT$. Based on a similar method of calculation, the total revenue from import/export of the capital for the years 1905–6 amounted to 603,200 MT$. Pankhurst considered these figures tentative and looked at the very much lower sum of revenue collected at Harar, one of the two areas of revenue collection, Addis Ababa being the other. On the other hand, others estimated the customs revenue from Addis Ababa at 700,000 MT$ in 1907.[95] For Harar, import and export tax revenue amounted to 639,465 MT$ for 1899–1900, and about 1,246,829 MT$ for the years 1905–6.[96]

Notwithstanding the fragmented nature of the source material and the varying estimates of taxation, it is possible to detect a natural pattern in the increase of imperial government revenue over time. According to Tewodros' tax documents, the total revenue of the King amounted to a quarter of a million in 1863/64, excluding unrecorded revenue from direct and indirect tax from the areas

[94] On the volume of import and export see Pankhurst, R. (1968c), pp. 400f, 412.

[95] Quoted in Garretson, P. (1974), p. 320.

[96] See Pankhurst, R. (1968a), pp. 49f. In the early twentieth century, the right to collect and use indirect tax revenue was one of the major causes of conflict among the aristocracy and governor generals. The military nobility depended for its income on direct tax, while the aristocracy over and above land tax, drew much of their revenue from indirect tax. During the crucial phase when *ras* Teferi came to power, he concentrated his effort in the control of indirect tax collection and use. See Bahru Zewde, (1984). See also, Garretson, P. (1979), "The Naggadras: Trade, and Selected Towns in Nineteenthand Early Twentieth Century Ethiopia", in *The International Journal of African Historical Studies, 12*. pp. 416–439.

of west and eastern Bägémder, Wollo, and from other sources of revenue such as livestock, judicial fee and extraordinary land tax. In the 1880s King Yohannes could annually raise around 559,847 MT$, an amount which could be used for the court and royal military expenditures.

Government revenue had increased during the reign of Menelik. In 1904 he could raise from ordinary land tax 116,071 *gundo* honey, 956,474 *dawula* of grain and 1,905,511 MT$. From extraordinary land tax (*asrat*, a tithe) the imperial government could collect about 920,593 *dawula* of grain. Ignoring variation and effects of weight on price, and if one considered two MT$ as the price for one *dawula* of grain, and ten MT$ as the price for one gundo of honey[97], the total revenue from ordinary and extraordinary land tax in dollars amounted to 6,820,355 MT$. This figure excludes the regions of Bale, and many other districts.[98] From provincial contributions and customs revenue of Addis Ababa and Harar, the King received a revenue of 3,131,428 MT$ as calculated by MacGivillary. In fact this figure is net income of the court, excluding the share of indirect tax by regional governors, and excluding other sources of income such as commercial judicial fees. With such exclusion, the total court and army revenue of Menelik amounted to 9,951,783 MT$. This figure again excludes a considerable number of state lands which were used as remuneration for troops, the domain part of court revenue, the Queen's treasury, and "civilian" revenue.

[97] See Mahteme Selassie (1962. E.C.), p. 156.

[98] See the comment on Table 7, and see also the notes in Table A-3, in Appendix A.

Part IV
The Use of Existing Resources, 1855–1913

Introduction

Part IV deals with the priorities and items of government spending. What were the categories of expenditure? Was expenditure divided along functional lines such as defence, education, health, etc.? If not, what were the items of expenditure, and what was the size allocated to each of the items? What was given priority, and for what purpose? Was there permanent and nonpermanent categorizations of expenditure? Was there a system of accounting which balanced government expenditure against revenue?

These are points of consideration in a modern society which moves on a planned and budgeted line. Modern societies try to make informed decisions as to the probable cost of allocating funds. The society under discussion did not work under the rationale of a balance sheet. No accounting could ever stop the political and military ambitions of the Kings. War was a regular and pervasive activity of the state, and expenditures were primarily war expenditures. Kings of the period spent most of their time moving with their army from one region to the next.[1] The fact of the matter was that there was no clear line between war and peace, and consequently no difference between civil and military functions. In this sense it is not even meaningful to quantitatively discuss "total military expense", if it even is at all quantifiable in a society where war itself was the economy, the very means and purpose of allocating and distributing resources.

The purpose of discussing expenditure by type is not to see the place of war in the economy, which was an unquantifiable phenomenon, but to identify which part of the logistic system was more favoured by the expenditure allocation, and how that allocation elicited change in the composition and constellation of forces within the army itself. Was it the main force, auxiliary troops, cavalry, provisions or transport that was given priority? The aim is to see the planned nature of the logistic system, and the extent to which its components were ranked to bring about a desired effect, particularly in solving earlier military barriers. To facilitate discussion on structured changes, and to follow developments, it is important at first to describe the various components of the army, types of unit formation, and system of command. The nature of the evidence also makes it necessary to first discuss the number of troops mobilised for campaigns and engagements. Chapter five deals with the structure and size of the army, and chapter six deals with the manner and patterns of imperial government expenditure.

[1] See Appendix B.

CHAPTER FIVE

The Structure and Size of the Imperial Army, 1855–1913

5.1. Organization of the Imperial Army

This chapter tries to unravel the various components of the army, which constituted the main item and priority in government expenditure. Without a detailed understanding of the components and size of the army, it is difficult to rank the items and importance of military expenditures. The inquiry on structure of imperial troops includes identification of troop organization, command hierarchy, military administration, unit formation, and patterns of troop mobilization.

Though warfare was considered as a norm in the society, and even though the state was said to have had a long military tradition, no research was found that focused on the study of the imperial army as an independent subject. Discussions on the army focused mainly on troop movements, frequency of battles and/or their effects on society. If there was any mention on the composition of the army, it was often in the context of the internal organization of the *gibi*-palace[2] or it was limited to a review of the various military ranks and the functions of court troops[3]. Even then, this line of discussion centred mainly on court troops, and could not thus be projected to the regional government level, since courts of a regional governor were organized differently. At the royal court, at least, one could differentiate the "peaceful" activity from the military activity. But in the provinces, local officials had so closely integrated both functions that it became even more difficult to make any differentiation. This is particularly important in specifying the service base of the provincial troops or in the identification of the difference between regular and irregular troops. A good example is the *bét lij* troops of governors who served as household servants, police and participants in campaigns. The office of the *mälkägna* also had the responsibility for local land tax administration and cavalry service.

[2] See among others, Mahteme Selassie (1962 EC), Chapters 2 and 3; Tsehai Berehane Selassie (1980), chapter five; Asefa Balcha (1984); Ayele Taklahaymanot (1962), "Gerarchia Civile, Militare e Religiosa Nell' Antico Impero Etiopico", in *AEVUM*, *XXXV, 1–2*.

[3] See Habtämäriyam Seyum (1967), "Military Organization and Armament Acquisitions of Menelik II", B.A. Thesis in History, HSIU. Addis Ababa. The discussion in this thesis is based mainly on secondary literature, which consequently formed a biased view of 'traditional' forms of organization.

In some cases, the army was investigated in the context of land ownership.[4] Since this line emphasized the methods of remuneration, it gave no clear picture of how the identified means were related to the various components of the army. Method of remuneration by itself is not a sufficient criteria for making military class distinctions. In some studies the army was discussed in terms of military status such as cavalry and infantry.[5] Since these attempts often emphasized on the use of weapons, they tended to neglect the identification of the army in terms of its social identity, namely on the grounds of the recruitment of nobles and peasants. There were also attempts to cover all aspects of the army[6], but there was no structural relationship between the different themes used to organize the discussion.

A review of the literature highlighted the difficulty of analysing the structure of the army by using one or two models. There are a number of reasons why the army has not been studied as an independent topic. In the first place, military needs were met by all possible existing means that the form of the economy could accomodate, making military organization very flexible. For instance, troops were remunerated with cash in combination with grain; some were given the right to collect land tax, while others were given state-land. The forms of payment varied with the availability of the means and types of government revenue sources. This variation had an effect on military format.

Secondly, in the period under discussion there was a dynamism in the system of the military organization of the state, and the changes made could not be captured by the use of a few models. For instance, some offices or titles had changed the basis of their function while still keeping their former title and name and this created problems of definition. An example is the functional title *gendäbäl*. When it was first introduced by Negassi of Shewa (1696–1703), and much later until the time of Menelik, the term referred to government soldiers who were granted land in lieu of salary.[7] During the time of Menelik, *gendäbäl* was no longer a soldier who held *madäriya*-state land. Owner-cultivators were recruited as *gendäbäl* to serve as transport corps and supply provisions to the main army during campaigns.[8] In other words *gendäbäl* functioned as an auxiliary force.

In this chapter different criteria and conceptual categories were considered to help to identify the composition of the imperial troops. One major area of

[4] See Mantel-Niecko, J. (1980).

[5] See Pankhurst, R. (1968d), The History of Firearms in Ethiopia prior to the Nineteenth Century" in *Ethiopia Observer*, XI, 202–225. Merid Wolde Aregay (1980). Chapple, D. (1990), "Firearms Again: The Battle of Asem", in *Proceedings of the Fifth Seminar of the Department of History*. AAU. pp. 19–30.

[6] See Pankhurst, R. (1968c), Chapter XII.

[7] See section 2.3.

[8] See the definition and the use of the term in Mahteme Selassie (1962 EC), p. 110f.; Gebre Wold Engda Worq (1948 EC), pp. 21–23.

consideration was the manner of government expenditure and the administration of revenue allocated for the use of imperial troops.[9] Other criteria of identification included factors such as: the traditional Ethiopian categories which explain functional differentiation and their corresponding forms of institutional jurisdiction; the existing nature of power structure and the type of command; the service base in terms of regular or irregular format; the identity of troops defined in terms of military status such as cavalry as opposed to infantry; consideration of functional roles such as combat and/or auxiliary force; and, criteria used for mobile versus garrison troops.

Using the above considerations, an attempt was made to identify the composition of the imperial troops of Menelik. By imperial troops is meant troops commanded by court officials and general governors who were appointed by the King. This definition excludes the troops of regional princes (*mäsafint*) who, by virtue of their traditional rights, functioned independently of the Kings.[10] The imperial army of Menelik was divided into central and provincial troops.

5.1.1. Composition of the Central Troops (*mähal säfari*)

Central troops were called *mähal säfari*, literally meaning those stationed at the centre. Initially the term was given only to those divisions of regimental troops who were stationed in central regions of Shewa. Probably after the foundation of Addis Ababa in 1886, the term *mähal säfari* began to include body guard troops and departmental troops of the palace.[11]

The various components of the *mähal säfari* troops consisted of body guards, departmental troops (*ch'ifra*), and central contingents.[12] The first two categories performed household services, military needs and government administrative functions. They differed from one another by the nature of their functions and the power of jurisdiction assigned to them. The central contingents were a kind of provincial troop stationed in the vicinity of the King's town in the central province. The commanders of the *mähal säfari* troops were appointed directly by the King. They were recruited entirely from the household military servants of the King, and they had served for long periods and had proved loyal and meritorious.

[9] See Chapter Six below.

[10] The princes had a contractual agreement with Kings to provide assistance when called upon. King Tewodros, however, had at first gathered members of the regional ruling houses presumably as advisors, but later he imprisoned them all. In their place he appointed his own men to command the regional forces. He could not however avoid disobedience and disloyality of the forces. Yohannes and Menelik on the contrary tolerated the territorial princes and let them organize and command their own forces in return for imperial recognition.

[11] Märse Hazen Wolde Kirqos (1948 E. C.), pp. 51–52.

[12] It included also the troops of the Queen. The troops of Queen Tayitu, for instance, included guards, supporters, 600 riflemen, and artillery men, see Gäbrä Selassie (1959 E.C.), pp. 247, 262, 263.

Bodyguard troops were assigned purely military functions. They consisted mainly of *gasha jagré* and *zäbägna* (guard) troops. The *gasha jagré* were personal body guards of the King and accompanied him everywhere carrying his sword, shield and spear. During the period of Menelik there were about 1,500 troops commanded by the chief of the *gasha jagré*.[13] Count Pietro Antonelli, Italian agent and negotiator, reported that there were 2,000[14] of them. The *zäbägna* were guards responsible for the security of the whole complex of the palace. During the time of Menelik their number was 7,000.[15] These troops were armed with rifles and often they were called by the type of rifles they carried, e.g., *senadr yazh*, a body of troops armed with Remingtons[16]; *maläfia tämänga yazh*, troops armed with rifles of good quality.[17] Another category of the body guard troop was *färäs zäbägna,* literally meaning guards of horses and which was the household cavalry of the King. In 1887, Antonelli estimated their number at 1,000.[18]

Next to the body guard troops came the category of departmental troops assigned for government departments established for "civil" or "peace time" functions. There were various court departments whose functions could be divided into finance, justice, household, etc. Organizationally speaking, a department had a head, an independent existence and the right to address the Sovereign directly through the secretary. One such large category included all the household officers and servants of the palace under the *medrä-gibi azazh.* Under this title holder, there were various officials who were responsible for the household economy of the palace: *sega bét shum* (in charge of meat supply), *enjära-asalafi shum* (in charge of food supply), *t´äj-asalafi shum* (in charge of the drink called *t´äj*, mead), and the *fana-wägi shum* assigned to supply the palace with candles, lanterns and other means of light. *Asatabi shum* was in charge of the men who, in accordance with royal etiquette, helped the princes, aristocrats and nobility to wash their hands at the table. *Ehil mar götara shum* officials were responsible for the supervision, collection and storage of taxes paid in grain, honey, butter and supply of wood. Officers of these departments came under the *mädrä-gibi azazh* who was the chief superintendent of the palace estate and the state prison. In each of the departments mentioned there were at least three *shambäl ch´ifra* troops, one *shambäl* consisting

[13] See Mahteme Selassie (1962 EC), p. 29.

[14] A note extracted from the document is deposited at the National Library, Ministry of Culture and Sports, Addis Abab. Document no. 8.09.12. Probably, the orginal letter is found in Archivio Storico delléx-Ministero d'Africa Italiana. Antonelli letter to Ministereo degli Affari Esteri, Assab. dated 31.10.1888. (here after referred as Antonelli 1888).

[15] Mahteme Selassie (1962 EC), p. 29.

[16] It is derived from English Snider, a rifle used by British troops during the Mäqdäla campaign of 1868.

[17] For specific estimations of each rifle regiment see Antonelli (1888).

[18] Antonelli (1888).

of 450–500 troops.[19] Most of these categories of the royal household servants had auxilary functions in war times.[20]

Under the household offices of the palace came the palace department official called *baldäräs*, who was responsible for raising, classifying and tending horses, mules and other pack animals of the royal palace. Antonelli estimated the cavalry under the *baldäräs* as being 500.[21] The *baldäräs* was responsible for preparing saddles and other necessary equipment. Much later, assignments of the troops for this duty was estimated at five *shambäl* (total ca. 1,500) soldiers.[22]

Another important category was the various troops under the financial departments of the court. The treasurers in charge of finance were called *bäjirond*; there were different types which had their respective *ch´ifra*-troops. In war, the *bäjirond* of the *eqa bét* (warehouse guards in charge of the *eqa bét*) served as couriers and carried wounded soldiers. In 1887 their number was estimated at 3,000 and the troops were commanded by the *bäjirond*.[23] The *bäjirond* was also responsible for commanding the *barud bét* and *mädfäna* troops (gunpowder and artillery). Artillery men were also commanded by the *liqä mäkuas*, who dressed like the King, ostensibly to look like the King and lure enemies.

Finally there was an important category of troops which consisted of the *balämual* (Kings' favourites, or courtiers). They were mainly recruited from children of the nobility sent to court to learn etiquette and court administration. The force also included those individuals talented in different disciplines such as security, traditional medicine, foreign affairs. They were specially recruited troops and in most cases served as *baldäräba* to guests, as *endärasé* (representative) of the King. In 1887, their number was estimated by Antonelli as being 1,000.[24] Probably a decade later, their number increased to 5,000 and they were commanded by the *Elfin Askälkay*[25] who was responsible for the inner-chamber of the King and protocol of the palace. Other department heads of the palace, such as the *afä negus* (imperial justice) and the *tsähafé tezaz* (king's secretary), had their respective troops serving in their departments.

In addition to the court troops mentioned above, there were divisions of troops stationed in central Shewa. The divisions were established by Menelik in the late 1860s and consisted of the Gondere troops who came seeking employment after the death of King Tewodros. Regionally and ethnically speak-

[19] See Mahteme Selassie (1962 EC), pp. 24–27 , on the number of *shambäl* troops see ibid., p. 112.

[20] See section 5.1.4. below.

[21] Antonelli (1888).

[22] Mahteme Selassie (1962 EC), p. 23.

[23] Antonelli (1888).

[24] Ibid.

[25] See Mahteme Selassie (1962 EC), p. 21.

ing, these troops came from Tigray, Amhara, Agäw, Damot, and Gafat.[26] Gradually they also included troops from Oromo, Gurage and other ethnic groups.[27] In 1887 the number of Gondere forces was 20,000.[28] Another central contingent was called *näftägna,* free lance soldiers who roamed around and had corps formation. Initially these were soldiers belonging to a governor. They began to roam from place to place in search of employment when their commander (governor-general) died or gave up soldiering. These soldiers were not new recruits. They had their own weapons, had some specialisation as riflemen, and were accomplished soldiers in their own right. They were thus called *näftägna* (rifle men) and their number was 10,000.[29] Both the Gondere and *näftägna* troops were quartered at peasant houses in central Shewa until the introduction of the *asrat* tax (tithe payment). The third group of the central contingents was called *gendäbäl* who were *madäriya* land holders in central Shewa and in 1887 their number was 15,000.[30] Commemorating the 7th anniversary of the Battle of Adwa in 1903, there were 90,000 *mähal säfari* troops who paraded in Addis Ababa led by the King in person.[31]

5.1. 2. Types of Provincial Troops

Provincial troops were territorial regiments organised in the provinces at different levels and territories.[32] In the *Gäbar Madäriya* system, provincial troops were organized by a revenue sharing system called *gezat.*[33] Governors were given power to use the land tax of the province for the remuneration of personal retainers *(lolé)* and troops commonly known as *shaläqa-ch´ifra.* The number of troops depended on the military interest of the governor and richness of the province.

According to Mahteme Selassie, for instance, *ras* Wolde Giorgis of Kafa had raised 30,000 private soldiers (including *lolé* and *shaläqa ch´ifra*), *ras* Makonene of Harar had 30,000, *fitawrari* Habtegiorgis, commander-in-chief of the imperial army, had 17,000, *ras* Demesse had 5,000, *däjazmach* Balacha, governor of Sidamo had 5,000, *ras* Abate had 4500, and *ras* Lul Seged had 4,500.[34] The figures did not include the number of *qutr tor* (numbered soldiers)

[26] See Haile Zäläqa (n.d.), *Däjazmach Grmame Yä-Hiwät Tarik.* p. 25

[27] Bairu Tafla (1987), p. 239.

[28] Antonelli (1888).

[29] Ibid.

[30] Ibid.

[31] Gäbrä Selassie (1959 E.C.), p. 311

[32] In this work the discussion on provincial troops does not include the regions of the princes (*mäsafint hagär*) belonging to the *Rist Gult* and *Amisho Rim* systems. The topic discussed here is the *Gäbar Madäriya* system. For differences in the composition and methods of remuneration of troops among the subfiscal systems, see chapter one and two.

[33] For further discussion see section 6.2.

[34] Mahtämä Selassie (1962 E.C.). p. 638.

found in each of the governors' provinces. Personal retainers (*lolé*) and *shaläqa ch'ifra* troops recruited from the region were different from *qutr tor*. Mahteme Selassie referred to the former as private soldiers (*bét ashekär*) to distinguish them from the central government troops in the provinces.[35] *Qutr tor* was a force assigned by the central government at a time when a new governor was installed in the regions. As part of the order (*mängest dänb*), depending on his rank and the richness of the province, a governor was assigned to take with him a certain number of troops to the province. These troops were called *qutr tor*, and were additions to the personal retainers of the governor and to those that were recruited from the regions. The *qutr tor* were assigned by the central government and were thus directly answerable to the King.

There were mainly two sources for recruitment of *qutr tor*. Initially, the *qutr tor* were drawn from the central troops of the King (*mähal säfari)* who were stationed in central Shewa. In 1878, for instance, when Menelik appointed governors in the southern regions, the Gondere and the *näftägna* troops were dispersed into the provinces together with new governors.[36] These troops were billeted in central Shewa for the last 12 years before 1878. From the palace soldiers, the *barud bét* were stationed in Sidamo when *däjazmach* Balcha was appointed as governor of the province.[37]

Another source for the recruitment of the *qutr tor*, was the *lolé* and *ch'ifra*-troops of the provinces. When a governor general was removed from his region either by natural death or by reshuffling, except for the *lolé* troops, the rest of the troops came under the responsibility and jurisdiction of the central government. The court assigned some of the *shaläqa* troops to move to other regions along with a newly appointed governor. For instance, when *ras* Gabon Dashé, one of Menelik's generals, died in 1887, the King gave employment to the *ras*' soldiers by dividing them among the governors of Sidamo, Wellega and Illubabor.[38] When *ras* Makonene, governor of Harar died in march 1906, three thousand of his troops were given to *däjazmach* Teferi (Haile Selassie) when the latter was appointed as governor of the Sidamo region. Another three thousand were sent to the region of Wellega as *lig* Iyasu troops (central troops).[39]

[35] Ibid., 637.

[36] See Bairu Täfla (1987), pp. 755, 757.

[37] See Tsehai Berehane Selassie (1971), "The Life and Career of Däjazmach Balca Aba Näfso" in *Journal of Ethiopian Studies, IX: 2*, p. 180, fn.39; See also Mekonnen Tamru (1988), "The History of Garrison Town Gerawa (1889–1974)". B.A. Thesis. Department of History. Addis Ababa Univesrsity.

[38] For instance, the troops given to *däjazmach* Balcha in 1897 were made up of veterans of *ras* Gobena and others; previously these troops were with *ras* Lulseged, see Tsehai Berehane Selassie (1971), p. 207.

[39] See Haile Selassie (1965 E.C.), pp. 13, 20.

5.1.3. The Cavalry

Infantry troops were called *egräna*, and they consisted of *näftägna* (riflemen) and *warwari* or *gasha* (spear men). The cavalry was called *färäsägna*, the King's household cavalry was called *färäs zäbägna,* and those of the provincial cavalry were called *bälägär färäsägna* (or *wäräda gendäbäl*). The provincial cavalry was recruited at the district level and consisted mainly of *balabat* (local chiefs) of the districts. The *balabat* served as a cavalry force in exchange for tax exemption and received equipment (mainly horses) from the state. They had a status similar to the *mälkägna*, government appointed local administrators, and annually they paid one goat and *asrat* as tax to the government.[40] In peace time they served as soldiers of the local government in the nearby administrative towns and in war time they packed their own horses and mules and went to battle. They were armed and had their own male and female servants following them to battle. During the campaign of Adwa, the *wäräda gendäbäl* that followed the King were numbered at 7,000 and 8,000.[41] There were also regions like Yejju, Wollo and Yifat in Shewa which specialised in cavalry forces.[42]

5.1.4. Auxiliary Troops

Auxiliary troops accompanied the army on campaigns and performed various auxiliary tasks essential for the success of the campaign. Functionally speaking, there were two major categories of auxiliary troops: those responsible for provisioning and those responsible for the transportation system. Administratively, these auxiliary troops were organized by the court and some were recruited from the provinces.

The first category of auxiliary troops included those corps responsible for providing food and fodder to the army. At the court these troops belonged mainly to the office of the *medrä gibi azazh*. Those recruited from the provinces were called *gäbar zämach*, and were drawn from *gult* and *mad bét* lands. The provision corps were commanded by titled individuals who were assigned to perform specific provisioning tasks such as preparing grain, meat, drink, etc. The commanders were called *mesläné* who, during campaign times, acted as commissariat.

The second category of auxiliary troops consisted of the various corps responsible for the transport of military equipment and utensils. Generally they

[40] Mahteme Selassie (1962 EC), pp. 107–108; 111, 127.

[41] Gebre Selassie (1959), p. 226.

[42] *Ras* Mikael of Wällo had organized cavalry troops from *rist* peasants known as *qacha zämach*. In lieu of land tax, they took part in campaigns. See, Abebe Fisha (1987), "Land Tenure in Tahuladare Wäräda from 1799–1974". B.A. Thesis in History, A.A.U, p. 21.

were referred to as *gendäbäl*[43], but they were further qualified depending on the specific task of assignment. Again these categories of auxiliary corps were organized by the court and some were recruited from the provinces. At the court, there were three types of transport; for loading food stuff from the palace (office of the *baldräs*), for transporting palace treasury (*eqa bét*), and for transporting war materials such as ammunition and artillery. The office *baldräs* was responsible for keeping and raising horses, mules, donkeys, and mares necessary for loading and transporting food stuff. About 16 localities and countries were reserved as *baldräs*[44] and the office had five captain corps (about 1,500 soldiers) responsible for tending the animals. The *eqa bét shaläqa* (office responsible for accommodating guests and others who came to the palace for business) was in charge of supervising mules kept for transporting the central treasury. The office had 2,000 soldiers[45] and one district (Segele) was reserved as *eqa bét*[46].

Those responsible for raising mules that transported cannon and machine guns to the battle field were recruited from the peasants (called *bäqlo qälabi*) who had a good quality of land, and these lands were called *mädfna mäträys* (loading lands). Holders of these lands received a mule from the government and were allowed to retain nine *dawula* of grain from the *asrat* tax payment. During a journey to the battle field, they saddled the mule and travelled with the artillery troops.[47]

In addition to the provisioning and transport corps, there were auxiliary troops which had different functions. One such category consisted of those menial workers known as *balä wäg* (butchers, bakers, cooks, makers of *t´äj* and *t´äla asalafi*), and personal maids. Ranking officials brought with them male and female household servants. The women prepared food and drinks, while the men fetched firewood and forage for the animals. Another category of the auxiliary forces was the clergy who accompanied Kings with the Ark, a practice which had a long tradition.

The bulk of the auxiliary troops were recruited in exchange for tax-exemptions.[48] The task of auxiliary troops assumed clear definition and detailed specification during the reign of Menelik owing to the increase in the resources of the state.[49] When land was surveyed and obligations to the land were instituted, in principle, one-fourth of the surveyed land was allocated for recruitment of *gendäbäl* troops.

[43] Note that the term *gendäbäl* had different uses: it referred to *madäriya* land holders, then to *wäräda* cavalry troops, to troops in the transport corps, and finally to the groups of *bälämuwal*-constructors.

[44] See Mahteme Selassie (1962 EC), p. 23.

[45] Ibid., p. 33.

[46] Ibid., p. 118.

[47] Ibid., pp. 110–111, 114; Gebre Wold Engda Worq (1948 EC), p. 22.

[48] See section 6.2.2.

[49] See next page.

5.2. Size of the Imperial Army

In the above section on the composition of the army, estimated figures were used to show the size of each military class and contingent. Since the figures are incomplete and were represented various times, it would be misleading to give any total figure. Instead, the following figures are used as estimations derived from chronicles of the Kings, European travellers, and missionaries and diplomats who visited the country during the period under discussion. Estimations varied considerabely and it is again difficult to ascertain which were correct. Greater confidence in the estimation would require a statistical analysis based on information about the demographic situation of the regions, and on the extent of financial resources and political power or influence of the Kings.

According to the British counsul Plowden, King Tewodros had a force of 50,000 to 60,000 armed men in June 1855, immediately after his coronation. It is claimed that Tewodros at the height of his career had an army in excess of 150,000 men. King Yohannes IV (1872–1889) also commanded large forces. His army which was deployed against the Egyptians in 1875–6, according to his military adviser Kirkham, was numbered at 60,000 armed men. The British diplomat Gerald Portal, who visited Yohannes in 1887, declared that the King had something like 200,000 armed men.[50] The figures should be examined with consideration for the size of the population and the resource base which King Yohannes controlled at that time. It is obvious that the total revenue of Yohannes, which was estimated to run a little over half a million MT$ could not cover the annual expense needed for 200,000 soldiers.

The size of the Ethiopian force that participated in the battle of Adwa had been variously estimated and the number could not be confirmed as there was no record on the Ethiopian side. General Baraterie of Italy estimated the Ethiopian army at the beginning of the Adwa campaign at 75,000 to 80,000 men, while Ilg, the King's advisor, a few months later put it at 150,000 men, excluding irregular bands.[51] To commemorate the seventh anniversary of the battle of Adwa in 1903, Menelik held a military parade in Addis Ababa in the presence of invited guests, diplomats and merchants. His chronicler wrote that 390,000 riflemen marched through the city, and this number did not include troops from the regions of Harar, Tigray, Semien, Lasta, Bägémder, Gojjam (proper) and Damot. It seemed that this number did not include the auxiliary forces either.[52]

[49] For a list of auxiliary troops that marched with the main troops during the campaign of Adwa see Gebre Selassie (1959), pp. 226–230. See also Tsegaye Tegenu, (1996), "The Logistic Base and Military Strategy of the Ethiopian Army: the Campaign and Battle of Adwa, Septemebr 1895–February 1896". Paper Presented to the 100th Anniversary of Adwa, Institute of Ethiopian Studies. Addis Ababa University.

[50] The figures are qoted in Pankhurst, R. (1968c), pp. 552–561.

[51] Ibid.

[52] For the number of troops who participated in the parade see Gebre Selassie (1959 EC), pp. 308–311.

Excluding the troops of Damot, which were mainly recruited from areas of the *Rist Gult* system, the imperial provincial army that was raised from the regions of the *Gäbar Madäriya* system was estimated at 268,000. The *mähal säfari* commanded by the King was estimated at 90,000. Calculations based on the information of the chronicle suggest that a total number of 358,000 troops was raised from the *Gäbar Madäriya* regions alone.[53] Since the annual revenue which the imperial government could collect from these regions is known and can be calculated against these figures[54], it is possible to comment on the credibility of the total number of imperial troops mentioned by the chronicler.

The imperial government needed a total of 3,908,460 *dawula* of grain to cover the annual expenses for 358,000 troops. The imperial government could levy 956,474 *dawula* from ordinary land tax, and 920,593 from extraordinary land tax (*asrat*). Thus, annually a total of 1,877,067 *dawula* of grain was collected from ordinary and extraordinary land taxes alone. In addition, the government annually collected 116,071 *gundo* of honey as payment on ordinary land tax. Assuming that the average price for one *gundo* of honey was ten *birr*, and the price of a *dawula* of grain was two *birr*, the total amount of honey could purchase about 580,355 *dawula* of grain. The total of ordinary and extraordinary land tax revenue of the imperial government was valued as 2,457,422 *dawula* of grain, i.e., 63% of the total need. This amount could cover the annual grain expenses for 225,090 soldiers. The rest of the imperial soldiers, numbering about 132,910, could be remunerated by the system of *madäriya*-sate land.[55] The total number of the imperial army estimated by the principal secretary of Menelik for the year 1903 was within the resource capacity of the state, and so there was probably no exaggeration. For a total population, estimated to be ten million[56], this figure seems to make sense.

5.3. Military Administration and Command Hierarchy

At the center, at the royal palace, court troops were organized along functional lines generally outlined as civil and military. Body guard troops were organ-

[53] It is not possible to know the constitution of the 358,000 troops. The total figure does not tell how much of it was constituted of combat force, how many belonged to the transport and provision system, and how many were cavalry. One could not even know how many of the combat forces were paid by *qäläb* and *dämoz* collected from ordinary land tax, how many were paid from the *asrat*-tithe revenue, and how many of them were given *madäriya*, state-land in lieu of salary payment. These variations are not considered in the calculations made to comment on the credibility of the figure mentioned by the chronicler.

[54] See the discussion on government revenue in Chapter Four.

[55] Mahteme Selassie noted that most of government soldiers were given *madäriya*-state land from which they collected *qäläb*-grain payment, see Mahteme Selassie (1962 EC), p. 233.

[56] The population estimation was made by Gabrehiwot Baykadagn (1919), *The Political Economy of Ethiopia c 1910*. London. p. 45.

ized for the personal safety of the King and the security of the palace. Those in charge of the "peaceful" functions were organized along departmental lines, and each of the departments was supposed to carry out its assigned functions independently. Body guard regiments and the various departments had an independent existence, and through the department heads, each of them were responsible to the King. In time of need they co-ordinated and effected their work by a system called *baldäräba*. The system considered the parts as equal but, depending on the kind of task they would accomplish together, one of them would take the "initiative". For instance, during the time of *zämach* (campaign) or *guzo* (expedition) the *säyfä-jagré shaläqa* (captain of the sword-bearers) acted as *baldäräba* to the *blata-géta* (master of the pages and the chief in charge of the throne), as the "initiator" of the expedition. Functionally speaking the *baldäräba* system treated both equally. They had consultations to co-ordinate their respective sphere of activities and, depending on the nature of the task, e.g., *zämach* (campaign) or banquet, one of them would take the "initiative".

During campaigns or military parades body guards and department troops were commanded by their respective officers and department heads.[57] However, the chiefs of each department had no jurisdiction over the discipline and payment of the troops serving under their departments.[58] There were military state secretaries and personnel responsible for the central administration of the *gibi* troops. The commander-in-chief of the army was known by a military title *yä-tor abägaz* or *fitawrari*. In his absence the *ligaba* acted as a martial judge and a military liaison officer. The *ligaba* was assisted by the *agafari* who was also commander of one contingent of the imperial army. The *fitawrari*, the *ligaba* and the *agafari* were the administrators of the whole *shaläqa* regiment of the palace in cases concerning *qäläb*-payment, weapons, and personal quarrels among soldiers.

Central contingent troops stationed in the vicinity of the palace or in Shewa were commanded by *wuch'i däjazmach*. These title holders were given districts, but they were not entitled to raise troops using the tax levied from the districts.[59] They mobilised and commanded central contingent troops (*mähal säfari*) who were remunerated with land and *gäbar*. Although a *wuchi däjazmach* could not raise campaign soldiers, he was allowed to have his own private retainer.

Provincial troops were under the command of the regional governor called *wana shaläqa*. The governors had titles like *ras* or *däjazmach* conferred upon

[57] See Mahteme Selassie (1962 EC), p. 243.

[58] For an illustrating incident of conflict see Kebede Tesema, *Leyu Leyu yä-Tarik Mastawäsha*. Manuscript no. 2247. IES, pp. 3–5.

[59] For the title of *wuchi däjazmach* and districts which they governed see Mahteme Selassie (1962 EC), pp. 639, 657.

them depending on the size of their army and the wealth of their governorship provinces. They were allowed to assign ranks to those below them, which meant they were given the power to recruit soldiers and assign military ranks and titles in their *gezat*. A governor with a title of *ras*, had the right, in his own region, to appoint two or three *däjazmach* and as many *fitawrari, qägnazamach, grazmach, balamberas,* and *basha* as possible. He appointed the *däjazmach* either from his own *lolé* (retainer) or from the *qutr tor* given to him by the central government. A *däjazmach* thus appointed could command four or five *shambäl* (captain's forces). A *shambäl* is the comander of 300 soldiers. The other ranks, *fitawrari*, *qägnazmach* and *grazmach*, placed in a descending rank order, commanded from 300 to 50 forces.[60] That means a governor with a title of *ras* could organize between 2,700–4,000 soldiers. This was a minimum field combat force a *ras* had to summon and command in accordance with the requirements of a battle strategy. However, the numbers were often considerably larger than this. For example, Antonelli estimated that *ras* Gobena had 30,000 men while *ras* Darge commanded 15,000 men.[61] Since title and rank depended on the number of soldiers, there was fierce competition among governors to recruit as many soldiers as they could.[62]

As far as military matters were concerned, governors were under the *ligaba* of the King. The office of the *ligaba* transmitted verbal or written messages from the King or his chief secretary to all commanders and governors, and presented cases to the King.[63] The function of this office was so important and vast that at times the King appointed a trusted officer above the *ligaba*.[64] Problems of land allocation were referred to the *ligaba* of the Palace. The *ligaba*, for instance, administrated government land allocated to *madäriya* soldiers.[65]

With the formation of the ministerial system in 1907, central administration was given to the *fitawrari*, the Minister of War. He was the supreme commander of the King's army in charge of the army's divisional organization and training. Under the new regulations he also became responsible for the munitions, arms and grain storehouses of the army. He oversaw the proper administration of justice in the army and the promotion of officers. The Ministry distributed arms to soldiers and gave permits for the possession of arms. The

[60] See Mahteme Selassie (1962 EC), p. 649–50 note 1.

[61] Antonelli (1888).

[62] As an example see troops recruitment and administration by *fitawrari* Habte Giorgis in Mislu Gugsa (1974), "Estate Administration in part of present day Jibat and Mecha under Fitawrari Habte Girgis", B.A. Thesis in History. AAU. 33f.

[63] See Mahteme Selassie (1962 EC), p. 643.

[64] Ibid.,

[65] The case is mentioned in a report on land measurement, see *yä-Lul ras Kassa Hailu Astädadär Dänb: Segawin ena Mänfäsawi*, Manuscript no. 1190. IES. p. 301.

Minister of War was responsible for the production of arms and when the first munitions factory was established in Addis Ababa in 1912, he was responsible for financing and administrating it. Finally, the minister could give military orders to suppress any provincial rebellion against the central government.[66]

[66] See Mahteme Selassie (1962 EC), p. 223.

CHAPTER SIX

Composition of Imperial Government Expenditure and Methods of Imperial Troop Remuneration, 1855–1913

Government expenditure was problematic for two main reasons. First, no central account of government expenditure was available for the period under discussion.[1] The second problem was related to the state of the research and the consequent methodological problems. In the literature, expenditure was mentioned in relation to the discussion on the obligations attached to land.[2] This type of discussion fused rights of land ownership with the size and structure of taxes, complex administrative system, and with regional and time variations. It was difficult to know what amount was spent for what item and to achieve what objective. In this work, at least the problem of items of spending was clarified in the preceding chapter through the discussion on the various components of the army. Also, since the forms of government revenue administration were known, one could follow the same principle in identifying the forces that were served by the budgetary decisions.

As pointed out in chapter four, in the *Gäbar Madäriya* fiscal system, the government had direct and central control of the assessment and collection of direct taxes. This enabled the state to prepare, at least in principle, different revenue budgets for the court, the army and the church. There was more or less a clear division between the revenue of the court and the revenue allocated for the establishment of the military, and for civilian bodies. In this chapter, analysis of the items, priorities and levels of government expenditure follows the institutional line which the system used in the preparation and allocation of revenue. The purpose of examining government expenditure was to identify the parts of the logistic system which were more favoured by the arrangement forms of allocation.

6.1. Court Expenditure

The term court expenditure is here used broadly to encompass all central government expenditures, including money expended for the King's consumption,

[1] It is possible to find records of government expenditures and other relevant documents from the archive at the Menelik's palace, Addis Ababa. At the time of this research, documents in this archive were not accessible to researchers. To get at them required special permission from the Prime Minister's Office.

[2] As an example see Mantel-Niecko, J. (1980).

Table 9. *Menelik's Government Expenditure Calculated by MacGillivray, 1905*

Year	Gold	MT$	Salt	Ivory	Cloth	Total
1902	17,520	920,941	647,864	166,600	174,630	1,927,515
1903	93,080	645,977	686,679	170	119,970	1,545,876
1904	95,04o	933,450	421,274	175,950	48,785	1,674,499

Source: FO 401/8, p. 50.

royal banquets, household servants, feeding of court animals, allowances, rewards and charities. That part of court expenditure used for the payment of court troops and the purchase of weapons is discussed under the category of military expenditure.[3]

An account which provided a glimpse of central government expenditure during the period of Menelik was the one presented by MacGillivray. Court expenditure was presented in MacGillivray's chart in total cash equivalents of each form of payment. This method of presentation obscured the types of government expenditure. The author explained nothing about the purposes for which the government used the sums of money mentioned in gold, ivory, MT$, salt and cloth. For instance, as fragmented documents indicated, a great quantity of gold and ivory was used for the purchase of weapons. The MT$ was used for remuneration of court troops and for the purchase of weapons. The salt expenditure was used partly for the preparation of royal banquets and partly as fodder for court animals. Cloth could have been used as reward and payment for troops. The figures given by MacGillivray indicated only total court expenditure, not the items and types of court expenditure. To arrive at an understanding of the items of court expenditure, the present work closely studied the various functions of the palace departments and their institutional jurisdiction.

One item of court expenditure was the royal banquet. The royal palace was the central core in the organization of the state. It was, among other things, a form for the attraction of the nobility and organization of military force. Royal banquets had been one of the traditional means used for this purpose. Basically there were two types of royal banquet. The so called *elfign* (bed chamber) banquets were held daily for the royalty, higher ranking court nobility, governor generals and children of the nobility brought up at the court. The other was called *adarash* (hall) banquet held weekly and on significant holidays for the clergy, court troops and their commanders, and the total number of participants was estimated at over eight thousand.[4] For the preparation of the banquet, at

[3] See section 6.2.3. below.

[4] See Mahteme Selassie (1962 EC), p. 48; see also Gebre Selassie (1959 EC), pp. 131–137, passim.

least the following items were needed: a large quantity of grain, jars of honey, ram fattened for slaughter, castrated and fattened goats, young lambs, pepper, salt and butter.

Annually the royal court of Menelik expended around 350,000 *birr* for a banquet.[5] This was a considerable amount by the standard of the time. For instance, in the early 1920s an ordinary soldier was paid annually 23 *birr* and an officer with a rank of captain received abuot 146 *birr* annually.[6] The annual amount spent for the banquet could cover the annual expenses of a field combat force recruited and comanded by three different *ras*. Or the annual banquet amount was equal to the annual salaries of 97 expatriate teachers.[7]

Another expenditure item of the court was called *darägot*, a daily allowance given to important personalities who came to attend the court seeking promotion or simply to report to the King. They were *balabat*, *mäkwanent*, *mäsafint* and governors from distant regions. About 10 per cent of the annual income of the palace (be it collected in the form of grain or money) was allocated as *darägot*.[8] The distribution of the allowance was made through the office of the *eqa bét shaläqa*, a kind of liaison officer of the King. This court official was assigned as the *baldäräba* of the guests: he received them and saw to their accommodations and food. He informed the *azazh* of the palace that they must provide the guests with food and drinks. He had *ch´ifra*-troops under him assigned to accomplish the service.[9]

Another 10 percent of the income was spent for church administration, charity, monasteries, *däbr* churches, and religious vestments. Probably this percent did not include prizes and decorations for the military, and considerable gifts on occasions such as holidays, marriages, etc.[10] There is no information on the total amount spent for the administration of the palace, purchase of equipment, payment for women servants[11], expenses for the administration of reserved palace lands (*eqa bét*, *wärägänu*, etc.), and fodder for the animals belonging to the palace. There were no available documents to discuss the size of these court expenses.

[5] See Mahteme Selassie (1962 EC), p. 50.

[6] See table 10 below.

[7] An expatriate teacher at a school received an average of 300 *birr* per month at 1928 prices. See Mahteme Selassie (1962 EC), pp. 190–193.

[8] See Mahteme Selassie (1962 EC), p. 204.

[9] Later on, during the time of Haile Selassie, guests from far countries were directed to the house of the *mäkwanent*-nobility in Addis Ababa, thus cutting the budget for *darägot* (daily allowance).

[10] For the amount spent on royal marriages and decoration of princes and nobles, see Gebre Selassie (1959 EC). passim.

[11] A woman servant working in the palace received 17 *birr* and three cubic meters of cloth annually. For a further list of payments for other categories of palace workers see Paulos Gnogno (1984 E.C.), *Dagmawi At´é Menelik*. Addis Ababa, pp. 239f.

6.2. Military Expenditure

No central account was available showing the total amount spent on the various items of military expenditure. Using available fragmented source materials, an approach was developed for examining expenditures by looking at the logistic system and the administration of the revenue budget. Separate consideration of the various components of the logistic system (combat forces, auxiliary troops, cavalry, transport and provisioning, and weapons), allowed a breakdown of the subject. Examining of the system of allocation and administration of the revenue budget provided insights to the amount of revenue that was available to pay for the various units of the army, particularly for the remuneration of manpower. In this manner the discussion identified the pattern of change in the constellation of forces within the army between 1855 and 1913.

6.2.1. Manpower

It is often said that in Ethiopia every able body was practically a soldier, and the army was characterized as an ad hoc army which depended on *levée en masse*. This is not true; there had never been such a tradition and it could not have been so during the period under discussion. The misconception arises from the confusion about the method of remuneration (in kind and land) with a class of peasantry, and the lack of knowledge about the structure of the army, e.g., differentiation of the auxiliary troops (such as *gendäbäl* and *gäbar*) from the main combat troop as discussed in chapter five. In the *Gäbar Madäriya* system, the army was a state expenditure, and the government collected a considerable amount of revenue for the use of the army. The question considered here was how the total revenue collected to finance the army was allocated and administered, and what percentage of it was spent for manpower.

There were four types and methods of remuneration of the imperial army, namely, *qäläb* and *dämoz* (grain and salary payment), *qäläb*-grain payment, *qutr gäbar* (right to collect land tax from assigned owner-cultivator), and *madäriya* land (grant of state land). Soldiers who were remunerated by the first two methods were commonly called *qäläbtägna*, and those by the last two methods were called *teklägna*. This difference was important. Seen from the perspective of revenue administration, the first two types received their payment through an elaborate centralized administration, while the method of remuneration for the last two types gave soldiers the right to collect and use the payment directly from those owner-cultivators assigned to them or from the tenants cultivating state land. In other words, for the last two types, though the amount each received was centrally determined, there was no intermediary

Table 10. *Annual qäläb and Salary Expense of Court Military Official and Soldier*

Military Rank	Monthly Grain payment	Annual Money payment
shambäl (captain)	4 *dawula*	50 *birr*
mäto aläqa (commander of one hundred soldiers)	3 *dawula*	30 *birr*
hamsa aläqa (sergeant)	2 *dawula* and 7 *quna*	20 *birr*
Ordinary Soldier	17 *quna*	10 *birr*

Source: Mahteme Selassie (1962 EC), p. 233.

administration between the soldiers and the peasants/tenants.[12] Another difference was that the first two types were funded out of several sources of revenue such as ordinary land tax, extraordinary land tax (*asrat*-tithe) and revenue from indirect tax. The last two types were funded entirely from the ordinary land tax (*gebr*).

Qäläb-dämoz: Grain and Salary Payment

The type of remuneration called *qäläb*-and-*dämoz*[13], was used to refer to the income of soldiers who received their payment in a fixed quantity of grain and an additional sum of money paid annually. *Qäläb* and *dämoz* were centrally administered both at the court and regional levels. The jurisdiction belonging to the center was administered through the office of the *ts´ähafe tezaz*, the principal secretary "through whom all the King's expenses pass".[14] The *ts´ähafé tezaz*, gave orders for the distribution of tithe payment depending on the rank and number of family members of the soldier.[15] The tax was collected and deposited by the *mesläné*, a district military officer, assisted by *gätär mälkägna* (who was given *hudad* land in lieu of salary). At the office of the principal secretary, there were special secretaries responsible for registration of salary payment and allocation of state lands. Governor generals had their own *mesläné* and *mälkägna* who collected the land tax which was distributed as *qäläb* (grain payment) to soldiers. Secretaries of the governors were responsible for keeping records of grain payment and distribution.[16] Salary was paid both in kind (grain) and in cash. The monthly *qäläb* and the annual *dämoz* varied according to the rank, as shown in the table.

[12] It was to avoid arbitrary exaction by the soldiers that the central government placed the local *balabat* chiefs as local administrators (*balager t´äbaki*), meaning protector of the local peasants.

[13] Literally *dämoz* means a payment for a sweat coming out of the blood, i.e., payment for labour.

[14] See Mahteme Selassie (1962 EC), p. 646.

[15] Ibid. p. 332.

[16] See Asfaw Tesema Werke (1969 E.C.), p. 22; and *yä-Luel ras Kassa Haily yä-Astädadär Denb: Segawina Mänfäsawi bäkäfilu*, pp. 6, 8f.

There were various estimates of an ordinary soldier's income. According to Gebre Wold Engda Worq, the amount given to a soldier depended on the number of his household members, called *guaz tä-gasha* (wife, children and other dependants). The soldier received seven *quna* (ca. 35 kilo) of cereal for himself and five *quna* (ca. 25 kilo) of cereal for each member of the household[17] a total of 12 *quna* on a monthly basis. According to Mahteme Selassie, an ordinary soldier received 17 *quna* per month, with additional quna in certain cases. The grain payment was supplemented by salary. However, since money was not easily available, it was paid annually while grain was paid monthly. The money was sometimes collected from land tax but mainly from indirect taxes, and the *nägadras* of the province could participate in the payment.

The sources of revenue for *qäläb*-and *dämoz* were mainly of two kinds: ordinary land tax (*gebr*) and extraordinary land tax (*asrat*). The ordinary land tax was divided into the centre and the region, based on the one-third principle. According to this principle, in each governorate one third of the land tax was allocated for the central government and this was called *yä-mängest gäbar.* The rest was called *yä-shaläqa gäbar* and it was administered by the governor general. The principle was implemented at the time of the land survey. The *asrat*-tithe tax was, however, entirely for the central government, and the governor general received part of it if allowed to do so by the central government.

Grain Payment for Qit´a-bel Troops

The second type of remuneration was the allocation of grain payment for imperial soldiers who were stationed in central Shewa and in the provinces. The *qäläb-dämoz* payment discussed above was mainly for the court troops. Imperial soldiers who received only grain payment were called *Qit´a bäl* soldiers.[18] It appears that this method of payment started with the introduction of *asrat*-tithe payment. Before the introduction of tithe payment, central contingents were quartered in the houses of the rural peasants. Mostly these soldiers were *näftägna* who came from the north after the death of Tewodros. They were quartered in every house and they demanded ready made food and other labour services. When they became a burden, they were ordered to settle at a site, and peasants were ordered to pay *qedéta* (grain payment fixed at the level of local rent payment). But when the wives of the soldiers collected *qedéta*, they had to measure a greater quantity than the normal level, and this became a cause of conflict. Finally, the King ordered payment of tithe both to the relief of the peasants and soldiers.[19] Soldiers were stationed in garrison towns called

[17] Gebre Wold Engda Worq (1962), pp. 312–13
[18] Mahteme Selassie (1962 E.C.), p. 235
[19] Ibid., pp. 331f

kätäma and received their annual grain payment through their military officers. By the end of the nineteenth century, the annual revenue collected from *asrat*-tithe was estimated at 920,593 *dawula* of grain.[20] If a soldier received 17 *quna*[21] per month, which was about 10.2 *dawula* of grain per year, then the total tithe revenue could cover the annual grain payment for 90,254 *qit´a-bel* soldiers. But the *asrat* tax was not only allocated for the maintenance of *qit´a-bel* soldiers. About 20 percent of the collected tithe was allocated as fodder for government mules kept in the provinces by *gendäbäl* peasants.[22] Another one percent was reserved for provisions, while the remaing part was allocated to supplement incomes of the clergy.

Grant of Madäriya-State Land

The third type of remuneration method was the grant of *madäriya*-state land to soldiers who were given the right to collect the benefit by themselves. The size of the *gasha* land (ca. 42.5 hectares) given to the individual depended on rank and service years: three *gasha* for an ordinary soldier, ten *gasha* for *hamsa aläqa*, and 30 *gasha* for the *shambäl*.[23] The holder of the land could lease his land, cultivate it himself or sell it, but had no other right over the land.[24] The *madäriya* land owner had to find tenants (*tisägna*) who would sign a contract until his period of grant ended. Some *madäriya* land holders cultivated their share themselves[25], others retained the original tillers or brought in new tenants on a contractual basis[26]. When the land was given to a new *madäriya* holder, it was possible that a new contract could be signed and the *tisägna* could be evicted.[27] Even though soldiers and officers were given the same number of *gasha* land according to their ranks, the amount that each holder could collect varied depending on the kind of arrangements made. In some

[20] See Table 7.

[21] When converted and calculated into the metric system, one *qunna* is valued as five kilo, and one dawula contains 20 *qunna* (or 100 kgs). See Mantel-Niecko, J. (1908), pp. 74, and 95.

[22] According to Table A-3 in Appendix A, there were about 16,166 *gendäbäl* in the provinces, and each of them were receivng nine *dawula* of grain deducted from the *asrat* for the maintainace of government mules under their care. On the amount they received see Mahteme Selassie (1962 EC), p. 114.

[23] Ibid., pp. 114, 118

[24] See section 2.1.

[25] These soldiers who lived in their respective plots of land were referred to as *gäbar* because they gave military service in lieu of tax and paid *asrat* to the government. But they paid no judicial fee if they quarrelled over the land. See Bairu Tafla (1974), p. 6.

[26] The tenants, *t´isägna,* were of two types: the *mägazo* who, after paying the *asrat* on behalf of the landlord, provided the owner with one-third of the produce and kept the rest for himself, and the *eribo,* the tenant who provided the *madäriya* owner with a quarter of the produce. In this sense the amount of tax collected by the *madäriya* holder was similar to that of the *gasha* land holder. There were various categories of tenants who had distinctively different contractual rights. See Takalgn Wolde Mariam, (1995), pp. 52–53.

[27] See Mahteme Selassie (1962 E.C.), p. 157.

cases the holders of *madäriya* land could not get seed, oxen and labour so that the government was compelled to give them additional salary payments or part of the collected grain.[28]

In the region of Shewa, *madäriya* lands were administered centrally through the secretary of the King. In 1879/80, for instance, *ts´ähafé tezaz* Gebre Selassie issued a decree ordering registration of all land in Shewa including *madäriya* lands.[29] In the provinces, *madäriya* land was held under the local and district *mälkägna* and administered by the governor general.[30] Until 1907, *madäriya*-state lands were given mainly to provincial troops, not to the *mähal säfari* troops.[31]

In the region of Shewa there were about 32,536 *madäriya* lands for soldiers.[32] It is not known whether this number included or excluded *säqela* lands, reserved government lands not yet allocated for soldiers. It appeared that the number included only state lands held by soldiers who performed active military service. In other words, it did not include state lands allocated as pension for retired soldiers. Retrospectively, according to the directive given by the Ministry of War in 1933[33], state lands and military ranks attached to the obligation could pass from a father to a son officer if approved by the government. A son who reached the appropriate age to give military service, had the obligation to look after his father. If the officer had no son to take his place, he could retain one-third of his holdings, and the rest was given to the one who took over his position. Retired military men who held one-third of their state land were called *wuha senqu* (literally meaning a person who had nothing to eat but lived on water alone). This was said in reference to the small size of the land held compared to the previous holdings before they retired.[34] An ordinary soldier who had only one *gasha* of land could keep the land. If he had a son, he could transfer the holding and the son had the obligation to provide the pension for his father. *Mähal säfari* and *qitá-bel* troops, who had no state land but who were sustained by *qäläb* and *dämoz*, were given land when they retired. Arsi and Gibat was reserved for the *mähal säfar*, while *qitá-bel* soldiers received land from the provinces in which they gave service. In 1890 Menelik had declared that all *gasha* lands between Awayat and Awash be given as *rist* to the holders, and this pleased the *mäkwanent* and the soldiers.[35] Presumably, it was a form of providing pensions for soldiers.

[28] See the comment by Gebre Wold Engda Worq (1948 EC), p. 34.

[29] See Gebre Selassie (1959 EC), p. 99.

[30] See yä *Chercher Dänb*, Manuscript no. 734, I.E.S.

[31] On the mutiny of court troops and their demand for state land see Mersehe Hazen Wold Qirqos (1935 E.C.), *bä-Dagmawi Menilk Zämän Kayähutna Käsämahut*. Manuscript no. 267. IES. Addis Ababa. pp. 51–54.

[32] See Table A-3 in Appendix A.

[33] Mahteme Selassie (1962 E.C.), pp. 236–240

[34] See Gebre Wold Engda Worq (1948 EC), p. 15.

[35] See Gebre Selassie, (1959), p. 179

This decree was issued six years after the introduction of land survey in Shewa in 1876 E.C. (1883).[36]

Qutr gäbar: Right to the Collection of Ordinary Land Tax

The fourth type of remuneration was the method used to give soldiers the right to collect payment of ordinary land tax allocated to them by the government directly from owner-cultivators (*gäbar*). This was called *qutr gäbar* (numbered owner-cultivator), since in this case it was the peasant, not the land, which was assigned to the soldier. This type of remuneration was practised in regions where the land was not surveyed for various reasons. In some parts of southern regions, land was not measured because it was initially so abundant that holding of land had no return unless there was labour to work on the land. In this region the government preferred to count peasants (land tax paying units) and assign them to soldiers and officers.

The amount a soldier could receive depended on his rank and merit of service. A *shaläqa* (provincial governor) received from 200 to 300 *gäbar*, a *shambäl* had 70 *gäbar*, a *mäto aläqa* received 40 *gäbar*, a *hamsa aläqa* had 25 *gäbar*, and soldiers who served long received 10 *gäbar*.[37] In the literature this form of remuneration is not clearly explained. It is interpreted as if the peasants were given to the soldiers, which implies a complete jurisdiction over the subjects. The fact was that the soldiers were given only the right to collect the ordinary land tax paid by the peasants. Depending on the central order, they collected either the grain payment and/or the honey payment. Soldiers had no right to hear civil and criminal cases and were not entitled to judicial fees such as bet, blood money, divorce fees and appeal.[38] Just as ordinary land tax was allocated for the palace and the governor as *mad bét*, soldiers were also given the right to collect payment of ordinary land tax for themselves.

By the turn of the nineteenth century, there were about 317,340 *qutr gäbar* peasants whose land tax payment could be allocated to soldiers.[39] When compared to *madäriya*-state land, this was quite a considerable number. With time, however, this method of remuneration decreased as the government conducted land surveys in the *qutr gäbar* regions. There could have been many reasons for this, but one compelling reason was that the method of remuneration created differences among the soldiers themselves, even if they were allocated the same number of owner-cultivators. An ordinary soldier, for instance, was given ten *gäbar*-peasants. But the quality and size of the land held by a *gäbar,* and the labour (number of household members) of the *gäbar* differed from one

[36] Ibid., p. 123.
[37] Ibid., p. 162.
[38] See *Yä Leul ras Kassa Hailu Astädader Dänb*, p. 31
[39] See Table A-3 in Appendix A.

region to the other. This difference led to the income disparity among ordinary soldiers and officers, even though they were allocated an equal number of *gäbar*-peasants. The government, therefore, undertook land measurement to assess the capability of an individual to pay taxes based on size and fertility of the land and possession of property.

The expense of the cavalry *färäsägna* was not covered out of the collected annual land tax estimated at ten million. The King's household cavalry were called *färäs zäbägna* and were maintained by the domain system which included land of *baldäräs*.[40] As noted in chapter four, the ten million annual revenue did not include the income from the domains of the King. Those of the provincial cavalry called *bälägär färäsägna* (or *wäräda gindäbäl*) were recruited by grants of *madäriya*-state land, which was again not included in the annual revenue. Maintaining of cavalry was expensive and those who were recruited were mainly the *balabat* (local chiefs), and *balä madäriya mälkägna*, state land holder officials. In the region of Sälale, cavalry obligations became so hard for the *balabat* to bear that many of them gave away their land to commanding officers in exchange for exemption. This process was referred to in the chronicle of Menelik as *mäwras* (bequeathment). It became so acute that in 1904 the King decreed that the displaced *balabat* be reentitled to their lands.[41]

The method of remuneration in the *Gäbar Madäriya* system was different from the *Rist Gult* system. During the reign of both Tewodros and Yohannes, the organizational structure and methods of remuneration of troops were the same. Either the revenue for the military was integrated into the general revenue of the court, and/or the imperial troops were remunerated mainly by an extraordinary land tax levied for the maintenance of imperial troops. In the latter case, the forms were *fäsäs* and *täsäri*. The difference between the two Kings was not in the organization and payment of the army; it was in the administration (collection and use) of the land tax. With a centralized policy, Tewodros increased his court revenue, while Yohannes allowed the land tax revenue to be used by *gultägna* (lay and ecclesiastical officials), as a result of which his revenue from ordinary land tax was reduced (by 30%). In both cases soldiers were not allowed to collect and use the ordinary land tax by themselves or through their *aläqa*.[42] In the *Gäbar Madäriya* system, soldiers were allowed to collect and use ordinary land tax either individually or in corps

[40] About 16 localities and countries were reserved as *balderas* to feed the animals. See Mahteme Selassie (1962 EC), p. 23

[41] Bairu Tafla (1974), "Some Aspects of Land-Tenure and Taxation in Sälale under *ras* Darge, 1871–1900" in *Journal of Ethiopian Studies, XII: 2*, p. 6.

[42] Reinstituting *gult* holders to their former position does not mean allowing soldiers to collect land tax, as was indicated in the sense when Mahteme Selassie defined the term *gezat*, see Mahteme Selassie (1962 EC), p. 637.

through their commanders (*aläqa*).[43] This was one of the basic factors which made the *Gäbar Madäriya* system different from the *Rist Gult* system, and the reason was the very principle of tax assessment and payment. In the *Gäbar Madäriya* system, the organization of cavalry and recruitment of auxiliary troops was completely different from the *Rist Gult* system. In the latter case, it was dependent on the peasantry and *gultägna*. In the *Gäbar Madäriya* system, though the cavalry and auxiliary troops were recruited by grant of state land and partial exemption from payment of ordinary land tax, expenses were covered by the state.

6.2.2. Transport and Provision Expenses

A certain amount of the total imperial revenue was allocated for the recruitment of auxiliary troops who performed auxiliary tasks essential for the success of the campaign. Generally they were referred to as *gendäbäl*, but they were further qualified depending on the specific task of assignment. The auxiliary function of the troops was transportation of cannon and machine guns, tents, *täräda*-pole, and food stuff. Troops which had auxiliary functions were not paid in the form of grain or salary. They were recruited through partial exemption from the payment of ordinary land tax (*gebr*). Often owner-cultivators who had high quality land were selected and given government mules or horses which they were expected to raise in return for the partial tax exemption. A certain category of the *gendäbäl* also received annually about nine *dawula* of grain deducted from the *asrat*-tithe tax.[44]

Those *gendäbäl* responsible for raising mules that transported cannon and machine guns to the battle field were called *mädfna mäträys ch´agn*-loader. Those who transported government tents and *täräda*-poles during campaigns were called *täräda gendäbäl.* They were largely exempted from the payment of ordinary land tax. A *gendäbäl* paid only one *quintal* of cereals, ten liters of flour, or the equivalent in other goods.[45] In peace time, they served as messengers from one province to another, as and when required.[46] There were other types of *gendäbäl* called d*inkuwan ch´agn*. They were in charge of transporting government or governor's tents on the journey to a battle or on inspection of regions under the governorate. During peace time, they guarded the tent store for two months a year and patched and cleaned.[47] They paid only *asrat* tax to the government. There were others who loaded and transported the King's tent, and they were identified as *dästa* land holders. Often these were

[43] See also the comment of Gebre Wold Engda Worq on the collection of land tax, Gebre Wold Engda Worq (1948 EC), p. 36.

[44] See Mahteme Selassie (1962 EC), p. 114.

[45] Ibid., 110–111; Gebre Wold Engda Worq (1948 EC), p. 22.

[46] See Mahteme Selassie (1962 EC), pp. 110–111, 113.

[47] Ibid., p. 115

siso balabat (local chiefs) or a person who gave meritorious service to the government. For raising the mule they were also allowed to retain nine *dawula* of cereals from the annual *asrat* (tithe) tax payable to the government. If the mule they bought died, then they received another one from the government.[48] Skilled workers who performed public manual work and maintenance, were also recruited as *gendäbäl*. During a campaign they probably served as civil engineers by clearing and constructing roads.

The above type of *gendäbäl* were found in the regions where the land was surveyed by *qelad*. In *qutr gäbar* regions, because there was no *gendäbäl* recruitment, or since all land tax was allocated for soldiers, the *gäbar* had obligations additional to the ones that were normally covered by *gendäbäl*. In addition to the payment of ordinary and extraordinary land tax, peasants of these regions had the obligation of tending mules used for campaigns by the local governor and soldiers. Two *gäbar* were assigned to feed and raise one mule, and they were thus called *bäklo qälabi*.[49] If there was a reserved grass land, the *gäbar* cut the dried grass for the *mälkägna*; if not, he had to bring one bundle of dried grass every month. During war time, the *gäbar* had to take care of the transport mules loaded with honey, flour and other foodstuffs.[50]

Although the exact number is unknown, a large number of mules, horses and donkeys were raised at the provincial and local levels through the *gendäbäl* method of remuneration.[51] During campaigns, the task of feeding a large number of horses, cattle, sheep, mules and other transport animals was not part of state expense. Feeding was the responsibility of the *bäqlo täbaqi* himself. The provision which these animals required was considerable; if calculated, it would outstrip the supply needed for the troops. It appears that there was no fodder supply system prepared for the animals as for the provision of the troops. Usually campaigns were called after the rainy season was over and grass was abundant. During the campaign, tents were set up in areas where one finds abundant grass and water to feed horses of the cavalry force and the large number of donkeys, draught horses and mules that were used as transport animals to accompany the army. There were also sheep and beef cattle kept temporarily until they were slaughtered for consumption by the troops. It is not known if provincial cavalry forces were required to bring dried grass from their districts with them to the war. It seemed that the burden of feeding the cavalry was put on regions lying in the direction of the war.

[48] Ibid., p. 110.

[49] Gebre Wold Engda Worq (1948 EC), p. 22.

[50] See Mahteme Selassie (1962 EC), pp. 122f, 125, 162.

[51] The courts also kept a certain number of mules and horses for transport purposes, and this has been discussed in the section on court expenditure. As mentioned, those at the court received their fodder from the ordinary land tax paid to the court in the form of salt, and certain *dawula* of grain from the *asrat* tax. Those at the provincial level were largely recruited by tax exemption, supplemented with *asrat* (tithe).

There was no special budget or revenue allocated for provisioning. When the call for mobilization of the army was made, the court, the provincial governor and soldiers were expected to bring their supply with them. The superintendents of the palace, the *azazh*, had the responsibility of packing the provision of foodstuffs and drinks for the King.[52] The grain provision was drawn from the *ehil-ena-mar-gotera* belonging to the palace. During campaigns *gäbar* of the royal court and the governors were given five *quna* of grain to grind or one *gundo* of honey to load on their donkeys.[53] Supplying meat was undertaken by the system of *wärägänu*[54], which is here considered as the domain of the palace.[55] Government cattle were also raised by *gäbar*, owner-cultivators whose tax obligation was only to tend government cattle. During military campaigns they took the cattle and sheep with them and looked after them on the way to the battle.[56] In addition to the preparation made by the *azazh* of the palace, the district and local governors, *mesläné* and *gult-gäz,* who were responsible for the administration of land tax belonging to the palace, were ordered to prepare provisions at intervals during the march.

Except for the differences in scale, presumably the governor-generals had a form of provision system similar to that of the King. During the time of the campaign, soldiers were supposed to bring *senq* from their own sources which would last for about twenty days. The food consisted of *quanta* (dried meat), flour, *qita* (bread), *shimbra*-grain, *dabo kolo* and *bässo*. These food items did not spoil easily and could be kept for a longer period of time.

The system of provisioning was organized on the principle of self-sufficiency, but it had different sources. The court and the provincial governors depended largely on sources drawn from their *mad bét*. For the ordinary soldiers during the campaign, a *gäbar* who held one *gasha* land was obliged to grind five *quna* of grain or load one *gundo* of honey on his own donkey.[57]

6.2.3. Weapons

The first categories of weapons used in the nineteenth century were sharp edged weapons, namely sword, spear and shield. Swords were used for hand to hand combat, while shields were used only as defensive weapons. Soldiers carried two spears, one of which they threw from a distance, while the other was retained in hand for a closer encounter. Both the infantry and the cavalry were mostly armed with these weapons until the first half of the nineteenth

[52] For details see Mahteme Selassie (1962 EC), p. 51.
[53] See Mahteme Selassie (1962 EC), p. 110.
[54] Ibid., p. 23
[55] See court revenue in section 4.2.1. above.
[56] See Mahteme Selassie (1962 EC), pp. 117–118; Gebre Wold Engda Worq (1962), p. 312
[57] See Mahteme Selassie (1962 EC), p. 110.

century. However, spears and swords declined in importance with the increase of firearms in the second half of the nineteenth century.[58]

Tewodros, Yohannes and Menelik were enthusiastically interested in importing European firearms. His defeat by the Turko-Egyptian troops in 1848, convinced Tewodros "that the primitive mode of warfare of his country would have to be superseded by the more modern one if he were ever to accomplish the splendid designs of his ambition".[59] Right after his coronation he ordered for 20,000 English rifles[60], but since the ports were occupied by Egyptian and Turkish forces, that great quantity could not reach him. The Austrian consul at Massawa, who was the agent of Frisk and Co., was engaged in contraband traffic in fire arms and gunpowder to King Tewodros' enemy in 1861. The British were then strongly opposing any supply of arms to the King. Tewodros' request to buy arms and ammunition got no response.

The King then embarked on a plan to manufacture his own artillery. He founded a cannon manufacturing establishment which employed about 700 "clever men".[61] His factory produced 2 brass guns, four iron guns and nine brass mortars. The King had a total of 37 pieces of artillery including those made in Ethiopia. The Gafat factory was one of the expenses of the King, mainly covering salaries of the workers. After the first piece of cannon was made, the King promised to pay 1,000 MT$ to each of the missionary craftsmen, in addition to "his love and friendship".[62] The brass was collected from all parts of the country, including 30 vases from Meqdela, and was melted down.[63]

The supplies of arms and ammunition were destined to increase during the reign of King Yohannes. At the time of Napier's expedition, the British estimated that the future King Yohannes had 4,000 men, "very few" of whom were without firearms. Yohannes received a valuable addition to his supplies in 1868 when the Napier expedition on its return to the coast recompensed him for his friendship.[64]

Import of arms through Massawa became difficult in the year after 1868 when the Sultan of the Ottoman Empire transferred his sovereignty over the port to Kehediv Ismail of Egypt who had a plan for an extensive conquest of the area. Having decided on a policy of expansion, the Egyptians at once instituted a blockade of all arms and ammunition entering Ethiopia. However, until

[58] See Pankhurst, R. (1968c), pp. 557–561

[59] Qoted in ibid., p. 583.

[60] Natsoulas, T. (1984), "Prologue to Modern Ties between Greece and Ethiopia: the Efforts of Ioannis Kotzikas during the Era of Tewodros, 1845–1868", in *Northeast African Studies, VI.: 1–2*, p. 153.

[61] See Pankhurst, R. (1990), pp. 322, 333.

[62] Ibid., p. 325.

[63] Quoted in Pankhurst, R. (1990), p. 326.

[64] See Chapple, D. (1990). 19.

his removal, the Naib of Arkiko succeeded in carrying out a contraband trade in arms which was estimated to run at the rate of 4,000 rifles a year in 1870.

In the battles of Gundet, November 1875, and Gura, March 1876, the King defeated the Egyptian conquering army and confiscated something like 20,000 Remingtons and a considerable amount of artillery including 25 to 30 cannons. Only a decade later, King Yohannes became infinitely more powerful than King Tewodros.[65] After these battles, there were as many as 25,000 Remingtons and 15,000 other rifles in the country, a great change from the reign of King Tewodros. While Tewodros attempted to manufacture his own weapons, Yohannes acquired firearms through diplomatic venues and mainly from battles fought against the Egyptians. His requests to import firearms were ignored by the British, who were unwilling as so often before to alienate Egypt.[66]

The conditions during the reign of Menelik were different. An international system of states and a world economy were a reality on the Horn of Africa in the 1880s. Italy, France and Britain were no longer far away in Europe, but they were adjacent colonial neighbours. Italy established itself in the port of Assab, France had colonized the port of Obok, and the British were at Aden and advancing their interest in Northern Somaliland. It was a time when the strategic concept of balance of power and aggressive trade partnerships were shaping the government policies of the adjacent colonial powers. The Italians and the French were anxious to supply Menelik with arms as both wished to win his friendship for their own purposes, i.e., the former to help them against Yohannes, their enemy in the north, the latter to help them in their rivalry with England. As a result of these developments, the import of arms into Shewa became considerable and Menelik had the interest and capacity to afford payment.[67] To commemorate the 7th Anniversary of the battle of Adwa in 1903, about 390,000 riflemen marched into the city of Addis Ababa. 320,000 of these riflemen were under the command of the King. If one included the riflemen of the King's governor general of Harar[68], *ras* Mekonnen, the number of rifles under the disposition of the King was about 354,000, a figure not far from estimates of the period.

The weapons were purchased both by the King and the governor generals. By the principle of *gezat*, governor generals had control over the portion of the land tax collected from their respective regions for remuneration of *ch´ifra* troops and for the purchase of weapons. A number of governors, among them *ras* Mekonnen of Harar, were importing rifles by dealing with agents. The

[65] See Pankhurst, R. (1968c), p. 588.

[66] For detailed discussion see Zewde Gebre Selassie (1975).

[67] For details showing the quantity and quality of imported weapons over the years see Pankhurst, R. (1968c), pp. 579–605.

[68] *Ras* Mäkonnen, governor of Harar, had 30,000 troops excluding those troops given to him by Menelik. When the King left Harar he had fortified it with 4,000 troops, and if such troops are to be considered as *qutr tor*, then Mäkonnen had at least 34,000 troops.

King did not declare a monopoly over the import of weapons. It was Haile Selassie who forbade import of rifles without authorization and seal of the central government.[69]

6.3. Methods of the Central Control System

If there was no planned spending, it did not mean that there was no control over income sources or over collection and allocation of revenue. In all facets of administration there were principles upon which the system was based. As regards revenue, ordinary land tax was shared between the central government and the provincial government on *siso* (one-third) principle. For instance, in a regional territorial administrative unit under a chief governor, one-third of the land tax was allocated in principle for the use of the royal kitchen. Governor generals were given institutional jurisdiction over the administration of direct taxes, and this was known as *gezat*.[70] The *gezat* system marked a distinction in the relationship between the central and the regional governments' spending on the army. The center and the region were not financed from one treasury.

There were two basic ideas behind the principles of revenue allocation in the *Gäbar Madäriya* system. The first one was the desire to ensure the class harmony of the military nobility and the aristocracy. According to the principle of the system, the court had its own revenue assigned as *mad bét*; provincial governors also had their own *mad bét* for household expenses and *madäriya* -state lands for their *lolé* and *ashekär* soldiers. Government troops had their own land and tax from which they benefited directly. Each of them had their respective and well defined part of the revenue. The purpose of the administration was to implement this basic principle of division and resolve conflicts over the use and distribution of social surplus.

Another basic goal was to meet the logistic needs and functional requirements of the system. The principle of allocation and the various methods of remuneration were in harmony with a non monetary taxation system. Administration had to be decentralized to create an effective control over peasant labour and needed products to bring about a balance in the logistic components. The logistic system of the army was such that it required considerable labour input. On the remuneration side, for instance, cultivation of government reserved land required agricultural practices like ploughing, sowing, weeding, harvesting, and threshing; on the provision side, it needed grain grinding, collection and delivery of fire wood, cutting grass, among other things; and on the transportation side peasant labour was needed for loading and custody of war

[69] See the decree in *yä-Tor Mäsariya Dänb*. Addis Ababa. 1924 E.C. IES, Amharic Collection. See also Pankhurst, R. (1968c), p. 605.

[70] See Mahteme Selassie (1962 EC), p. 637.

materials. To meet the demand imposed by military needs, decentralization and local control seemed the practical options. Under the *Gäbar Madäriya* system, the government had full control over the revenue from the land tax, a fact attributed to individual registration, assessment and payment of land tax.

In the *Gäbar Madäriya* system, administration of revenue and expenditure as regards ordinary land tax was decentralized but never localized and privatized as in the case of the *Rist Gult* system. The allocation of revenue on institutional lines (court, army, church), and its administration (as *mad bét*, *gezat*), may impart an impression of fragmentation of jurisdiction over spending. In fact the *Gäbar Madäriya* system had a built-in mechanism which provided for central control over expenditures. Even though regional governors were allowed to collect ordinary land tax in their respective regions to finance military needs, the manner in which resources were used was centrally directed. In principle, governor generals were expected to recruit soldiers, auxiliary troops (*gendäbäl*) and cavalry; after that a fixed part of the land belonging to the local *balabat* was deducted. There were cases where governors were not allowed to transfer *gendäbäl* to *gäbar* lands and vice versa. In the codified law there were articles which prohibited governors from uprooting local *balabat*, who were often recruited as cavalry and local tax administrators. In the *Gäbar Madäriya* system, governor generals were appointed or dismissed by the King, and they were directly responsible to the King.

Nonetheless, the *Gäbar Madäriya* system was still insecure very much because of the society in which no differences were made between the private and the public parts. Governors abused funds and so it was not in their interest to keep any accounts on the preparation of revenue. There was also a lack skill in accounting techniques such as central accounting, and keeping inventories of provincial treasuries. As documents show, income and spending were not accounted for using the concept of double-entry book-keeping.

Besides accounting techniques, the system required an elaborate bureaucracy to ensure effective control. The formation of a ministerial system brought a certain degree of consolidation of government revenue and expenditure. When the ministerial system was established in 1907, a directive was given to the Ministry of Finance concerning expenditure allocations of government money received and deposited at the central treasury. The guideline stated that 45% of the money was allocated as *qäläb*-and-salary for soldiers, 10% for construction and artisan works, 10% for church administration, salaries for the clergy, school, and charity, 10% for *dergogna*, daily allowance for guests and job seekers, 8% for purchase of equipment, 5% for emergency, 12% for permanent deposit and not to be withdrawn for anything else.[71] These percentages hide a lot of both quantifiable and unquantifiable expenses. The 45% allocated

[71] Ibid., 204; see also how *ras* Hailu Kassa had allocated the grain revenue of his regions, in *yä-Luel ras Hailu Kassa Astädadär Dänb*, p7.

as salary did not include the expenditure allocated for troops in the form of *madäriya* state land. It did not include expenditure for cavalry and auxiliary troops (provisioning and transport). It excluded the larger part of the land tax revenue used by the provincial army and expenses for the purchase of weapons. The money that was said to be deposited could be spent for military purposes too. Although there was no planned budgetary system, the guidelines given to the Ministry of Finance indicated the desire for planned spending.

6.4. Changes in the Size and Composition of the Imperial Army

In the *Rist Gult* system, the *gultägna* and peasant community were the primary forces in providing the logistic base of the state. The *gultägna* was a traditional ruler who took most of the military responsibility in commanding and recruiting troops. In return the *gultägna* had literally privatized ordinary land tax. Soldiers of the Kings were maintained primarily by extraordinary land tax (*fäsäs*), which was introduced only in some regions. Peasants who owned land communally, paid the expenses for keeping *zämach* soldiers and for constantly supplying provision, in addition to the regular payment of ordinary and extraordinary land tax. The well entrenched peasant and *gultägna* interests could limit the level of a larger force that could be mobilized by the central government. Any increase in the number of soldiers, and thus in payment, meant reclaiming alienated land tax and/or increasing the burden of taxes on peasants. These were discretionary measures which could alienate the support of the *gultägna* and the peasants. Kings could not increase the land tax base either by introducing land survey or by registering the number of tax paying individuals. Doing otherwise would be out of the system, as land ownership and the principle of tax assessment and payment were controlled communally by descent.

Tewodros revolted and shook the system. Contrary to his predecessors, he followed a policy of increasing the number of his soldiers. To feed his troops, the King centralized the collection, custody and disbursement of land tax (*hagär bägé* policy), increased and imposed *fäsäs* tax in the regions and on the church. His move was not successful because the tax system was centralised at the expense of the local nobles and the clergy. The increase in regular (*fäsäs*) and irregular (*täsäri*) taxes led to the alienation of peasants. In his last letter written to the British military expedition force, he said that his countrymen turned their backs against him because he wanted them to pay tax.[72]

[72] See the letter in Rubenson, S. (ed.), *Tewodros and His Contemporaries 1855–1868. Acta Aethiopica V. II.*, p. 354.

Yohannes, his successor, did not resort to the centralization of ordinary land tax payment. He followed the earlier practice of the system, and reinstituted *gult* to the former holders.[73] He shared that part traditionally allocated as *wusti gulti* and *yä nägash* for Kings. His revenue from the ordinary land tax was not that big in size when compared to that of Tewodros. Indeed, there is no indication whether the King had followed a conscious policy of increasing the number of troops. Indirectly, through the appointment of provincial governors such as *ras* Alula (in the region of Märäb Mälash), he seemed to have been successful in increasing the size of the imperial army. It is difficult to say how his policy of resettlement (40 years policy) had increased the number of soldiers and the capacity to pay them. The provincial contributions he could get from Gojjam and Shewa were substantial enough to keep the royal army when supplemented by *fäsäs* tax.

It was Menelik who increased the size of the royal army and there were strong reasons for that. He operated within the *Gäbar Madäriya* system, which in principle allocated the collection and use of land tax for remuneration of imperial soldiers. The *abägaz* countries (in which there existed only *madäriya* land) became *gezat* (use of ordinary land tax for *ch´ifra*) during his time, which shows continuity in principle. In the earlier *Gäbar Madäriya* system, there was mainly one dominant method of remuneration of soldiers, the grant of state land. By the time of Menelik, there were four major types of remuneration.[74] The *gezat* policy was an efficient mechanism for increasing the size of the imperial army both at the centre and in the provinces.[75] From 60,000 men in 1855, the number of imperial soldiers increased to 354,000 men by 1903. With the increase in the number of soldiers, government expenditure for salary also increased.

Another dramatic change in the logistic system was the increased importation of rifles. From 20,000 rifles of poor quality in 1855, the number increased to half a million of relatively good quality firearms by the beginning of the twentieth century. This change became possible as a result of the formation of the world economy and the international state system on the Horn of Africa since the 1880s. An increase in importation of weapons meant a rise in government expenditure for weapons.

The expenditure for artillery had an impact on the composition of the army. Probably for the first time since the reign of Tewodros, there was an organized artillery corps called *barud bét* and *mädfäna* (gunpowder and artillery). These were artillery men and troops assigned to the corps of gunpowder and shell (ammunition) and they were commanded by a *bäjirond* (a treasurer in charge

[73] See Feseha Wolde Mikael (1936 E.C.), p. 42.

[74] See section 6.2.1. above.

[75] For the governors he appointed see Bairu Tafla (1987), pp. 755, 757, and Gebre Selassie (1959 EC), passim.

of finance and *Gemja Bét,* store house of the palace) and by the *liqä mäkuwas*, who was also commander of the royal cavalry.[76] By the end of the century, the artillery consisted of about eighty little mountain guns, of all calibres and systems. Nearly all were kept in Addis Ababa, though a few were distributed in the provinces.[77]

The focus of government expenditure was, thus, to strengthen the main field force both in number and armament. There was also a considerable improvement in the provisioning system. Formerly, court troops were quartered in peasant houses, but this was changed during the time of Menelik. The uniformity and standardization of land tax payment and the introduction of tithe had an effect on the provisioning system. Primarily it increased the *mad bét* budget of the court of Menelik and his provincial governors, enabling self-sufficiency in provisioning during campaigns. The advantage of self-sufficiency in provisioning had been clearly seen in the success of the march to the battle of Adwa. Over 100,000 troops were in the field for more than 150 days, excluding large numbers of auxiliary forces and the large herd of animals used as transport. Secondly, a new obligation to provide food, water, grass, etc. for a campaign soldier was imposed on the peasants, probably in the early 1880s when cadestral survey was in full swing in Shewa. Self-support and sufficiency acquired through adequate provisioning and payment spared peasants from the kind of horrible plunder reported by travellers in the first half of the nineteenth century.

Imperial government expenditures which gave priority to the creation of a standing field force had consequences. Primarily, it led to functional differentiation between auxiliary and combat troops. In the earlier system, both functions were performed by campaign soldiers who were recruited mostly by tax exemption. During the period of Menelik, however, a separate way of recruiting auxiliary troops and a different method of remuneration for field/combat troops came into effect. A permanent budget for permanent troops created professionalism within the main force. Field troops were not primarily cultivators but permanent soldiers who in return were paid *qäläb* and *dämoz*, and *madäriya* land. The transport corps (*gendäbäl*) were recruited through partial exemption in payment of land tax, and provision was carried out by *gäbar zämach*. Though the system was fluid, there appeared a functional differentiation between the main and auxiliary troops.

[76] The office of the *liqä mäkwas* was reinstituted with a new function during the reign of Tewodros. The office of *liqä mäqwas* was in existance during the Gonder period, see the precedence list of 1690s Varenbergh, J. (1915/16), p. 9, 28 text, 45 trans. King Tewodros gave the title to *likä mäkwas* John Bell, the English Consul, who later changed in service of the King, and when he died the office was given to *liqä makwas* Kidane Mariam. Stern, H.A. (1869). *The Captive Missionary: Being and Account of the Country and People of Abyssinia*. London. p. 199. Yohanes had four *Liqä Mäkwas* while Menelik had two. Bairu Tafla (1977), p. 127.

[77] Gleichen, Count (1898), *With the Mission to Menelik 1897*. London, p. 198.

The increase in artillery, rifle and infantry led to the decline in the role of the cavalry[78], the second effect of the fiscal priorities of the Kings. A third glaring effect on expenditures on troop payment and on importation of firearms was the formation of garrison towns (*kätama*) which became possible to defend by using considerable amounts of firearms.[79] The formation of *kätäma* was not a new phenomenon in the organisational system of the royal army in the provinces. With the expansion of the *Gäbar Madäriya* system in earlier times, royal capitals and fortified villages were often established along the frontiers to gain control over neighbouring districts.[80] However, the number of garrison town and the war tempo increased with the increasing importation of firearms. To mention a few, there were about twenty garrison towns in the Gurage region, three in Wällamo, nine in Sidamo, nine in the province of Hararge, five in the province of Arsi, eleven in Gamu Gofa, and more than four in the western parts of Wellega.[81] These fortified camps were built in strategic and inaccessible places to serve various functions, e.g., as a basis for further penetration into the outlying regions, for pacification, as posts for the collection of taxes, as temporary centres of administration. The function depended on the degree of resistance in the area and its economic and strategic importance. The garrisons were also used to maintain security at borders of the adjacent colonial powers.[82] The flourishing of *kätäma* created a functional dichotomy between garrison and mobile troops, but this difference was not sharply distinguished since garrison troops were often transferred from province to province.

[78] Qoted in Pankhurst, R. (1968c), p. 561.

[79] The role of firearms had been clearly demonstrated in its use against the cavalry force of the Arsi people and their "night attack" tactics during the process of fiscal and military integration of the region by King Menelik between 1882–1886. See, Abas Haji (1982), chapter 2.

[80] See, Ege, S. (1978), pp. 25, 97, 177; Darkwah, R.H.K. (1975), p. 192f; See also Pankhurst, R. (1985).

[81] See, Bedru Ahmed (1984); Rahmeto Hussien (1984), "The History of Azernet-Berbere until the Expansion of Shoa, during Menelik II". B.A. Thesis. Addis Ababa University; Pankhurst, R. (1985b), *History of Ethiopian Towns from the Mid-Nineteenth Century to 1935*. Stuttgart, pp. 191–201; There is more information in Nägädä, *Yä ras Gobena Tärik* (copy of this document is deposited at the National Library, Ministry of Culture and Sports, Addis Ababa, document number, 23.01.5.; Bairu Tafla (1987), passim and Gäbrä Selassie (1959 E.C.), passim.

[82] See documents in *Dagmawi Minilk kä-Täläyayu Hagäroch gar Yaderägut Yä -Wädagnet, yä-Negd, ena yä-Denber Wuloch*. Manuscript no. 2201. IES, pp. 28f. (hereafter, this manuscript is abbreviated as *Menelik's Treaties of Friendship, Trade and Boarder Delineation*).

Part V
Structural Problems of Economic Development and Government Economic Policy, 1855–1913

Introduction

Did the reforms of the fiscal military state lay the groundwork for a developing economy? How was revenue allocation used in the society? Did the allocation favour promotion of the benefits of the nobility, the peasants or the merchants? Was there any money available for encouragement of agricultural production? Did peasants receive material incentive to produce more? Part V continues the discussion of the objectives of revenue collection and expenditure distribution, and how the development of the economy was affected.

Although people in the contemporaneous world had different understanding, economic development is here refers to raising the population's material and social standard of living. During the period under discussion, economic policy was not based on a body of theory or on a planned economy which was intended for finding solutions to long term structural problems. Government actions, declared or otherwise, were intended to regulate economic relations and activities aimed at solving immediate and practical socio-economic problems.

Economic policy is a stated objective designed to promote the various sectors of the economy (agriculture, commerce and manufacturing) for the benefit of citizens or the state. Although the economic objectives were not explained by the state in a planned or publicly declared manner, it is possible to analyse the essence of the reforms by reviewing the intentional statements made by Kings and examining the ad hoc, yet regular measures that were taken. In the period under discussion economic objectives were usually stated during the time of coronation.

Empirical evidence for the present work was gathered from normative material such as government regulations, inventories, collections of instructions to provincial governors, and available government tax documents. References were also found in research results from dissertation papers, and Masters and B.A. theses. Some relevant published literature on the nature of economic history was used for general reference. Owing to the fragmented nature of the documents and the character of the country's non-market economy, explanations were most often qualitative statements and very few of them were based on statistical analyses.

CHAPTER SEVEN

Appraisal of Government Economic Reforms, 1855–1913

7.1. Essay on the Structure of Economic Problems

Chronicles mentioned the recurrence of famine, drought, and epidemics in Ethiopia, often without any attempt at identifying underlying reasons. Foreign travellers wrote accounts of the poverty and misery of the people, along with what they believed were the causes. Often the country's isolation from the outside world, warfare, technical limitations, problems of urban and trade development, were said to contribute to the miserable life of the people.[1] Others saw these factors as effects, and attributed the root cause to the system of land tenure and specifically to the absence of private ownership of land and to the consequent attitudes toward work, productivity and accumulation.[2]

The economic stagnation exhibited a complexity that did not yield itself to a single and simple explanation. The stagnation was linked to the nature of the social structure of the time which supported the given economic system. Changes in investment, production, and consumption did not occur in isolation from the social structure. Social compulsion was necessary in order to

[1] For quotations and comments see Pankhurst, R. (1966b), "Some Factors Depressing the Standard of Living of Peasants in Traditional Ethiopia", in *Journal of Ethiopian Studies, IV*; idem., (1972), "The History of Famine and Pestilence in Ethiopia Prior to the Founding of Gonder", in *Journal of Ethiopian Studies, X*.

[2] See Merid Welde Aregay (1984), "Society and Technology in Ethiopia 1500–1800", in *Proceedings of the Second Annual Seminar of the Department of History,* Addis Ababa University; idem., (1986), Land Tenure and Agricultural Productivity, 1500–1850", in *Proceedings of the Annual Seminar of the Department of History*, Addis Ababa University. Though not stated explicitly, the author defined land ownership in the sense of absolute right to use and abuse and, consequently, reduced the definition of feudalism to rent relationship (ownership). The definition of property and feudalism is another subject of discussion. In this case however, the author did not pursue the logic of rent ownership as a factor in increasing or decreasing production. Since absence of private ownership in land was assumed, the author emphasized the descent community and the predatory nature of the ruling class as main factors for stagnation of agriculture and technology. In that case what could be expected from the author was a discussion on the level and assessment of taxation, administration and allocation of revenue, and how they exactly influence an increase or decrease in production and productivity. These themes were taken for granted and were based on generalization without sufficient evidence. Even though the logical means by which he arrived at the conclusion was not explained, the judgement reached by the author was valid as would be expected from a veteran of the field.

realize surplus. Thus the fundamental task of this discussion is to examine how the social structure underpinning the production systems was related to increase or decrease in production output and productivity. No stress is laid either on population growth or on expanding markets as the sole factors for mobilizing labour. In the first place, such an explanation would require historical data on population size, prices, wages, and production which, given the non-monetarized form of the Ethiopian economy, was not available. All the elements which entered into production, such as land and labour, were not purchased on the market; and it was difficult to asses their price and identify problems of production based on the economic rationality and norms of a capitalist society.

In this work, the approach is rather structural, dealing with property relationships (i.e., manner and conditions of land ownership), and the fiscal system (principles of tax assessment and distribution, tax collection and administration, preferences for tax introduction), and their influence on the development of the economy.[3] This method of analysis is appropriate for an economic system which did not base itself on the play of market phenomenon. Structural problems include, for instance, major sources of income for the military nobility (such as taxation, state land, and allodial property), and forms of tax payment (in kind or money), etc., which were related to expenditure made for the items of consumption for the nobility. In what follows, a synthesis of the nature and cause of economic stagnation is presented based on a structural approach.

7.1.1. Agrarian Economy

Agronomists and ecologists have divided Ethiopia into a varying number of agro-ecological zones based on agro-climatic and land resource potential.[4] In this study, agricultural activity in Ethiopia is identified as being constituted of four major types of production systems based on the divergence in the nature of institutions (for instance, system of land ownership, taxation), farm methods (such techniques as ploughing, and crop rotation system) and the natural endowment. There was the descent communal system of production in the *Rist Gult* regions of the northern Ethiopia, the owner-cultivator (*gäbar*-household) system of production in the *Gäbar Madäriya* regions of central and southern Ethiopia, the *enset* (false banana) horticulture production system in the cen-

[3] In Part II of this book we have seen how these concepts related to and influenced the logistic system. Now it is in order to investigate their influence over the economy as a whole.

[4] For comments see, Dessalegn Rahmato (1992), "Peasant Agriculture under the Old Regime", in *An Economic History of Ethiopia. The Imperial Era, 1941-1974. V.I.* Draft Manuscript. Department of History, Addis Ababa University. p. 144.

tral-south, and pastoral (cattle and camel) production systems in the lowland areas along the border.[5]

In this section, these production systems are considered separately not only as subjects of studies in which one describes and explains types of crops grown and farming practices as related to a historical context, but as units of analysis full of socio-economic contradictions and conflicts. Because of problems with sources, it is beyond the scope of this study to provide a micro level definition and explanation of the productive practices of each production system and the historical interactions among them. Relative availability of literature and time makes it proper to focus on the descent communal and the *gäbar*-household production and reproduction systems[6] extending as far back as the crisis of the sixteenth century.

To begin with, culture and the peasants' innovative capacity were never factors which could explain agricultural stagnation in Ethiopia. On the contrary, there was a dynamism in peasant agriculture which in fact had reached its limit. This dynamism was not a response to market demands, or to a need for commercialization of agriculture. It was a response to fiscal and demographic pressures and to deterioration of non-renewable natural resources, such as soil. The creativity of this response expressed itself in the "experience and agronomic knowledge attained by the peasants in farming techniques, soil management, environmental protection, regeneration of the soil fertility, cropping strategy".[7] The principles of tax assessment and collection that were used, the objectives of government expenditures, and the type of ownership rights practiced were the principal factors that stifled innovative methods of crop farming (i.e. increase in production) and rural class differentiation (i.e., accumulation of land and investment of capital).

The Descent Communal System of Production

In the descent communal system of production, decisions about the allocation, disposition and use of arable, or grazing and forest land belonged to the village community as a body. Land could be redistributed among village members as a result of either population increase or natural calamities (like droughts, floods, famines, war and disease). Within the community, families had a basic right to cultivate land for their own use. However, households could not culti-

[5] Other authors distinguish four agricultural systems, namely, the seed farming complex, the *enset* planting complex, shifting agriculture and pastoral production. Ibid., p. 144. This approach makes a classification of the system emphasizing why and what peasants produce, not how they produce.

[6] On the system of production of *enset* see Shack, W. (1966). *The Gurage. A People of the Enset Culture*. London. pp. 50–83; For a general information on cattle breeding see Alberro, M. and Haile-Mariam, S. (1982). On camel see Tegegne Teka (1989), *Camel Pastoralism as Food System in Ethiopia*. IDR, Addis Ababa University. Addis Ababa.

[7] For a critical review of the positions and on dynamics of the peasant economy, see Dessalegn Rahmato (1992), p. 148–151, 168f.

vate and practise grazing as they pleased without reference to the community. Meadows. forest lands, mountains, rivers and lakes were not included within community ownership.[8] Clearing land in a hostile environment required capital, and even if the land was cleared, it automatically came under communal division and the divisible inheritance system. The opportunity for simple extension of cultivable land was under community control and it was also limited. For instance, the right to renew the use of lands abandoned by the holder as the aftermath of tax burdens was in the hands of the community and could be allocated to a newcomer.[9]

An increase in production through clearing and reclamation of land was thus difficult under the *Rist Gult* system. The pattern of fallowing was also controlled by community members[10], and a household could not increase production by reducing the amount of fallow as it pleased. The use of plough technology was supposed to enable the family labour to plant large areas and exploit unused and potentially cultivable land. But the kind of division and allotment of land along with the inheritance system, hindered even the simple accumulation of productive forces. Because of the limited opportunity for increasing and extending cultivable land, peasants resorted to intensive method of cultivation. Crop rotation and use of fertilizer were scopes and basic methods of intensive agriculture.[11] However, a sufficient amount of manure to be used as fertilizer could be obtained only if the farmer possessed a large area of pasture required to feed a large livestock herd; but the use of pasture land was again subject to communal constraints.

The system of land division and allotment exacerbated the problem of labour. In the crop rotation system, peasants used, among other things, *téff* and barley crops, which required more labour. Farmers had to plough the land many times in order to prepare the seed beds. Furthermore, sowing, weeding, threshing and harvesting were done by hand. While cultivation was by itself a full time job, the scattered nature of the farm fields consumed additional agricultural working time. The peasant households had the obligation to give some amount of labour service (cultivation of *hudad* or *grat*), to the local land tax collector.[12] In addition to cultivating crops and paying taxes, peasants also performed other tasks to provide themselves with clothing, tools, housing, and transportation.

Production also was affected by the number of work animals and equipment, and the amount of saving and investment. Raising livestock on a larger scale presented enormous difficulties in getting pasture land and fodder. The

[8] See Merid Welde Aregay (1986), 120.

[9] For exceptions see the discussion on *chiguraf-gwoses* in Bruce, J.W. (1976).

[10] See Hoben, A. (1973), p. 6

[11] See Dessalegn Rahmato (1992), pp. 148ff.

[12] There was an acute labour supply problem in the *Rist Gult* system particularly during the seventeenth and the whole of the eighteenth century, see Chapter Two footnote 46 above .

households had so little money left over from the heavy taxation[13] that they could not even cover all the expenses of social reproduction let alone save for further use. There was, if any, a very poor credit system. Even for that, the interest was so high that, in most cases, peasants who failed to pay back their debts were forced to leave their land. The situation was such that peasants could not invest in agriculture, and the nobility were interested mainly in military matters, not in increasing agricultural output and productivity.

Even if peasants could remain on their land holdings and manage to save, the very nature of the communal tax assessment and distribution discouraged households from investing in property use for fear of an additional taxation burden. At the lower village level, particularly in the division of land by allotment, the tax burden was distributed among community members by the number of plough oxen and other property holdings.[14] The privilege of tax exemption (of one *rist aläqa*) in return for participation in military campaigns (case of *zämach* soldier) could increase the burden of payment on other members of the community.[15]

The system of land ownership in the *Rist Gult* areas provided a kind of security to peasant land holdings. However its principle of tax assessment and collection was a hindrance to increasing production. Its system of ownership perpetuated small strips which did not allow consolidation of land or increase in the size of farm land. Since land was often allocated under the condition of residence, the system opposed in principle, trends toward the development of absentee landlordism. Internal constraints on the expansion of cultivable land in the face of demographic problems resulted in the system's developing acquisition of land by office and political affiliation and to litigation over land which in turn became the source of conflicts and tensions.

The type of land ownership in the *Amisho Rim* system was also so ambiguous that problems of litigation arose. Farm lands were left fallow if peasants and *amisho* collecting soldier were in conflict. The *Amisho Rim* tenure system failed to "indicate who does what, when and where". In the *Amisho Rim* system, ordinary land tax was paid on a portion of crops, and this system of levy could discourage both cultivation of fertile land and the introduction of novel crops which might otherwise have increased production.

The Gäbar-Household System of Production

Viewed from the perspective of plough-grain agricultural activities, the *gäbar*-household and the descent communal production systems were similar. For instance, the region of Shewa was said to "grow everything"; about forty-three

[13] For a vivid example see the letter of *gult wakil* (representative) of *wäyzero* Yewubdar, a daughter of the prince of Gojjam. Quoted in Fantahun Berihun (1973), p. 83.

[14] See Hoben, A. (1973), pp. 216f.

[15] For the region of Wag see Mahteme Selassie (1962 EC), p. 160.

species of grain[16], and it had its own system of crop and field rotation and irrigation[17]. Agro-ecologists called both systems of production the seed-farming complex. But there were differences in fiscal system and rights of land ownership settings for the production systems. As discussed in chapter two, the *gäbar*-household production system operated within a private land ownership system and individualized registration of tax payment. Consequently, the factors that affected the production system were different from that of the descent communal production system. Before the second half of the nineteenth century, it seemed that, at least theoretically, there were opportunities to increase production by clearing and reclaiming land. However, this opportunity expressed itself in the form of tenancy. There were three types of owners, namely the state (soldiers and clergy), the local *balbat*-chiefs, and the owner-cultivators. Ownership of land appeared to be complex since owner-cultivators were also part-tenants. The patterns of ownership concentration varied from district to district; to judge by late figures, in the district of lowland Tegult one-third of the cultivating population were tenants while 50 to 70 percent were owner-cultivators.[18] It appeared that the landlords were holders of state land, i.e., soldiers and clergies who had very little interest in investment and expansion of production. The share cropping system, which existed on one-third to one half of the harvest, may not have been a proper stimulus for tenants to produce more.

Apart from tenancy, demography was another major factor that affected the *gäbar*-household production system. A study in the district of Tegult indicated a pattern of population increase, in which doubling of the population had occurred within the last 700 years, in spite of the considerable toll from deaths caused by war and epidemic.[19] Population increase was also a problem in the *enset*-planting complex of the southern central Ethiopia. Peasants of this area adopted an intensive farming system to sustain themselves on tiny plots.[20]

Stagnation in agricultural production could be caused both by economic and non-economic factors. In this work the problem is examined from an economic context. Peasants could have been less vulnerable to population pressure, famine, pest infestation and other natural causes if their economy had been strong. Their standard of living depended on the surplus they produced, and the surplus product depended in turn on the volume of overall production. The volume of production also depended on how much land was under cultivation (given the extensive nature of the economy). An increase in the area under

[16] Graham, B. (1844), "Report on the Agricultural and Land Produce of Shoa", in *Journal of the Asiatic Society of Bengal, XIII*, part one, No.145 to 150, pp. 269ff.

[17] Stitz, Volker (1974), part three, pp. 237–346.

[18] For detail variations see, ibid., pp. 241ff, 253ff.

[19] Ibid., pp. 224ff.

[20] See Dessalegn Rahmato (1990), *A Resource Flow Systems Analysis of Rural Bolosso (Wollaita)*. Addis Ababa.

cultivation depended on the supply of labour and the types of land ownership (for instance, type of exclusion and use rights over arable and pasture lands). Since the supply of labour was, despite everything, available, it followed that the decisive role was played by factors belonging to uncertainty in forms of private ownership of land. In the face of such structural pressure, one response of the peasantry was to adopt methods of intensive farming (use of fertilizer, crop and field rotation systems).[21] Intensive farming even could not acheive its effects since the principle of tax assessment and collection, and the level of taxation and allocation of revenue were not favourable to simple accumulation and investment. The type of land ownership and the fiscal system were thus the root causes for the relatively constant level of agricultural output and labour productivity over the centuries.

7.1.2. Manufacturing and Mining

Concerning the causes for technological stagnation in Ethiopia, one formerly held view was that cultural contempt for manual labour was a major factor. But this view is no longer accepted on the grounds that this attitude was not unique to the Ethiopian society. What is more, it could have been an effect rather than a cause of technological stagnation. A comprehensive study which encompassed various aspects of technology (agricultural, building, metallurgic, military) attributed stagnation "to the weakness of the ruling class (in its) failure to create a legal system to protect property, (and in its) continuous warfare and absence of leisure".[22]

The assumption made here about the property of the ruling class was unfounded as shown by well documented and extensively discussed recent studies.[23] The transmission of family property among the ruling class did exist. War may have been another factor in technological stagnation but European history shows that war could also be a stimulus to technological development. On the other hand, it is true that "lack of test to material culture" and absence of dedicated patronage could affect the demand for and the growth of craft products.

The Ethiopian isolation thesis as a factor contributing to the country's economic stagnation is not accepted by Merid Welde Aregay since the country had uninterrupted import and export relations with Arabia, India and the Mediterranean world.[24] Factors of "isolation", however, could not be easily dismissed

[21] One other peasant response was resistance and rebellion as reported in the chronicles. See Bartricki, A. and Mantel-Niecko, J. (1971); Merid Wolde Aregay (1984), "Millenarian Traditions and Peasant Movements in Ethiopia 1500–1855", in Rubenson, S. (ed.), *Proceedings of the Seventh International Conference of Ethiopian Studies*. pp. 257–262.

[22] Merid Welde Aregay, (1984).

[23] Among others, see the works of Donald Crummey.

[24] See Merid Welde Aregay, (1984), p. 154

by reference to existing trade, particularly when one reads about the demand for artisans by successive rulers of Ethiopia since the reign of King Yeshaq (1413–1430). Basically the term technology does not refer to an output (product) of the system; rather, it means skills and methods related to the production and organization of goods and services in a society. Transmission of know-how as well as new methods of production were necessary for technological development and, in the period under discussion, this technological dissemination primarily took the form of the diffusion of skilled workers.[25]

A significant problem for dissemination and development in technology was the system of organizing craft production and reproduction. In the period under discussion, there were no professionally based craft associations or corporations which fostered the specialization and economic interest of craftsmen. There were two types of organizational forms which reproduced craft. The first one is tied to the rural areas, namely to villages and surroundings of towns that produced for utility values, not for exchange values. Those engaged in this activity were denied access to agricultural land as a result of land expropriation by Kings. This was clear in the case of the Wayto ethnic group of lake Tana, who were victims of the land "nationalization" policy of the *Amisho Rim* system. Deprived of their land which was allocated to soldiers, many of them migrated to other regions and ended up as hunters and craftsmen. Those who remained behind constructed boats and transported goods across the lake.[26] Another group of victims of the land policy of the *Amisho Rim* system were the Falasha (Ethiopian Jews), who were repeatedly attacked by the Gonderian Kings and were deprived of their lands. The Falasha community were described as the "only potters and masons in the country".[27] The very rule of survival led these craftsmen to establish a kind of network (informal association) and trustfully promote their trade taking ethnicity as a ground for organization. Consequently, in Ethiopia various professionals such as potters, blacksmiths, tanners and weavers were associated with ethnic groups.

The second type of craft production was organized around the households of princes and Kings. It was larger in scale and highly specialized and drew its capital demand from the court. This was, mostly, the production of articles of gold which, as ornaments, were valued at the court as symbols of prestige. In the Gonderian period, lowly paid gold and silver smiths of the court were organized under the title of *zan-sälämi*.[28]

The system of craft organizations was not favourable for technological adaptation and growth. In towns where craftsmen established informal and unin-

[25] Merid argued that foreign craftsmen were available, but what was lacking was dedicated patronage. Ibid., pp. 165f. More evidence is however needed on the scale of the migration of skilled workers, and their strategic importance in the production system.

[26] See Tecle Haimanot Gebre Selassie (1984), chapter two.

[27] Bruce quoted in Pankhurst, R. (1990), pp. 105–106.

[28] See Bartricki, A. and Mantel-Niecko, J. (1971), pp. 21–22.

stitutionalized relationships based on ethnicity, it was possible to sacrifice professionalism and further specialization because of cultural and social obligations. In other words it was hard to promote specialization and division of labour in network relations where there was no formal internal structure and regulation. Besides, income from what the artisans produced was for subsistance only and to acquire those foodstuffs and other things commensurate with their social rank. It could be possible that they did not aim to generate a surplus in order to produce larger quantities of goods for a subsequent cycle.

Those who lived in rural areas and in the vicinity of towns had no full time activity. They might have possessed small land holdings (usually rented) and could have worked as agriculturalists providing partially, if not entirely, for their own subsistence. Their relationship with the surrounding peasants was not exploitative. In some cases, such as in cloth making, they could even receive a semi-processed item from the peasant household in which they did further work. Generally in this type of organization, craft production was small-scale and seasonal. It tended to be relatively larger and more concentrated in the households of rulers (*mäsafint*), state officials and wealthy merchants.[29] But production here was generally meant for household consumption and not for sale.

In Ethiopia, craftsmen did not separate themselves from their rural and feudal household context. They did not appear as autonomous industrial households within the urban communities producing for sale to anybody who had money. The very manner in which craft production was organized (i.e., within an ethnic network and feudal household context), its tie to the countryside (i.e., domination by seasonal non-specialized craftsmen producing for household consumption), and its small-scale size, were causes for technological stagnation. In fact, feudal exploitation of the artisans was parallel to the exploitation of the peasants. The state preferred to tax their products, rather than to purchase on the market.[30] As there was a lack of demand from the state and the peasants, who were themselves partime artisans, there was no stimulus for craftsmen of urban communities to increase their production.

Although there was a royal organization for the production of ornaments and household iron utensils, there was no royal monopolization of mining production. Gold, iron and salt were produced in different regions such as Enariya, Wellega, and Tältäl. It is not known how the various operations involved in the production of these highly sought-after minerals were carried out. However, because gold was an alluvial deposit, it was relatively easier to extract it than other ores which required hammering the rock, and grinding and pounding it into powder.

[29] On the organization craft production at the palace and princes' houses see sources dealing with court structure and organization.
[30] See section 3.6.

There was thus no development of mining and iron smelting. This was nevertheless, not due to lack of techniques of iron making, but because the work required labour, capital and energy. For instance, iron production was a complex process that required skilled, lengthy and labour-intensive processes, and involved prospecting, mining, smelting and forging. Considering the intensive nature of agricultural production, the mode of military organization (main and auxiliary forces), the various functions and needs of the church, there was a limited number of workers left for the mining sector.

Even if labour was available, there was no working capital and no forces to raise a large sum of money to finance technological innovation. Considering court expenditures, and the state of merchant capital, there was no accumulation of funds of the size required as working or as fixed capital for the manufacture of goods. Sources of energy on which the manufacturing economy would depend for growth was another problem area. Apart from human and domestic animal labour, water power and wind-power, there existed only organic substances, above all, wood. The court and prince's houses demanded wood to construct wooden huts that were later demolished during the long military campaigns.[31] Wood and coal were obtained as tax from the peasants. For instance, districts in Hammasen sent coal as tax payment to the Kings' smithy in Adwa during the time of Yohannes[32]; Menelik also received coal as tax payment[33]. Lack of capital accumulation, the labour demanding mode of the logistic system, and the lack of stimulus from the agricultural sector were decisive factors that were responsible for the lack of urban-based simple commodity production.

7.1.3. Trade

With all the structural problems surrounding the agricultural and manufacturing sectors, it is not difficult to imagine the limit thus placed on expansion of trade. Manufacturing was tied to the countryside, and the agricultural sector did not have much surplus for sale. Quite a sizeable amount of the surplus was supplied to the market after the payment of ordinary land tax (*gebr*), tithe (*asrat*), surtaxes, obligations and, in the case of tenants, after rent (*eribo*), family needs and seed for the next harvest. The products that left the farm and the household were disposed of within the local market. This type of market was dominated by producers who had no cash profit motives, but carried out simple exchanges. In the rural market, the seller was identical with the producer and the buyer with the consumer. Because producers were able to sell

[31] Travellers and chroniclers have mentioned the destruction of forests to construct temporary huts during the long marches of the army.

[32] Perini, R. (1905), p. 64.

[33] See Gebre Wold Engda Worq (1948 EC), p. 28.

directly to the consumer, small traders could not mediate between those two sides and make a profit by selling at a higher price than that at which they had purchased. So there was no retail trade of consumption products and, consequently, the class of small retail traders was undeveloped.[34]

It could have been possible that a small proportion of the total supply that remained from the local market flowed to other regions for the benefit of more distant towns. Here again, there were problems of transportation and security. Mainly camels and mules were used for transportation, the latter being more suitable along the rugged mountainous routes. Security was a special problem along the long caravan routes where bandits waylaid merchants. Long distance trade merchant groups were comparatively well organized and developed. They operated in regional markets and on a large-scale international import/export trade.[35] Long distance trade needed organization and professional groups. Caravan trade was organized by a big merchant with the title *nägadras* (head of merchants).[36]

Towns, however, were less dominated by mass staples (consumption food) such as sugar, spices, grains, meat, wine, beer, and coffee. The type of agricultural production systems helped peasants and nobles to become self-sufficient in foodstuffs such as grain and meat. Merchants did not deal in proto-industrial products (such as wool and cloth), or in consumption of mass staple products. Long distance merchants traded not in necessity products such as grain, but primarily in naturally extracted items such as civet, ivory, wax, gold. In Gojjam for instance, long distance merchants brought to market towns salt (from the north) and coffee, civet, ivory, and gold (from the south), and cotton, and textile cloth from (foreign countries).[37]

The class of merchants was also affected by factors other than the lack of non-commercialization of agriculture and the lack of specialization between manufacture and agriculture in the division of rural labour. The system of indirect tax administration, which was farmed out to individuals in return for a fixed payment, led to arbitrary taxation of the domestic market.[38] The great number of custom tolls, and insecurity along the roads, particularly during the Era of Princes, had affected long distance trade. The situation is summarized by Blondeel's apt remark "what was surprising about the system was not that trade suffered but that it existed at all".

[34] In Ethiopian historiography there is no study made of the social base of trade activity. No studies were conducted on the activities of the groups engaged in trade, about their carrier, their commercial activities, their number, their strategies and network, financial resources, etc. We only find reference made to their status based on foreign observation and accounts.

[35] Foreign trade in Ethiopia can be divided into two types: trade among its neighbours (regional trade) and trade with the outside world, particularly with Europe and Asia (international trade).

[36] See Abdusamad Haj Ahmad (1980), p. 38.

[37] Ibid., p. 30.

[38] See section 3.6.

One other factor that affected the demand for commodities was the problem caused by the vicissitudes in town development. Most towns were established as political centers and places surrounding an endowed church. In the period of the Era of Princes, a number of towns were established as seats of provincial lords.[39] The population of these capitals (the lowest population being 1,800) consisted of, among others, soldiers, ecclesiastics, craftsmen of all kinds, and merchants engaged in long distance trade.[40] These capitals were also visited by provincial governors who came with their entourage to meet with and to pay homage and tribute to the prince. This type of town often declined with a shift in power. However, there were important commercial centres such as Gonder which survived political instability. But with the exception of Gonder (with a population approaching 100,000 in the 1770s), the populations of the towns were too low to exert any kind of insurmountable demand for food and energy.

If regional trade was so limited in scope and organization so as not to inject any dynamic change, much could not be expected in the way of developing an international trade. Until the last decades of the nineteenth century, Ethiopia's foreign trade with Europe and Asia was limited in scope, volume and frequency.[41] There was no trade in capital and goods. Foreign trade did not have much impact on the internal market by way of presenting an opportunity for development.

If there was any significant economic link with Europe, it was mainly in the area of currency, namely, the import of MT$, the development of which can be traced back to the late eighteenth century and early nineteenth century.[42] The introduction of MT$ is considered a major event in an economy dominated by barter and use of primitive money. However, Kings had no monopoly over the MT$ trade and the country had no regulatory control over the amount of money in circulation. The country was either starved for currency or flooded with it. Compounding the problem was the value of the MT$ which fluctuated with world silver prices.[43]

The problems of agriculture, manufacturing and trade discussed above were so interwoven that it is difficult to improve any one sector without also consid-

[39] Pankhurst, R. (1982), *History of Ethiopian Towns from the Middle Ages to the Early Nineteenth Century*. Wiesbaden. p. 319. See also Crummey, D. (1987), "Some Precursors of Addis Ababa: Towns in Christian Ethiopia in the Eighteenth and Nineteenth Centuries", in *Proceedings of the International Symposium on the Century of Addis Ababa*. November 24–25, 1986. Addis Ababa. pp. 9–31.

[40] Ibid., pp. 320ff

[41] There were European commercial agents, particularly in the period between 1830s–1855, see memorandums in F.O.1/13, pp. 191–201; F.O.1/13, pp. 232–234, 235–236, and F.O. 401/1, *Correspondence respecting the Circumstances which led to the Establishment of a Consulate at Massowah*: 1846–47. See also Rubenson, S. ed. (1987), *Correspondence and Treaties 1800–1854*. Illinios and Addis Ababa.

[42] See Pankhurst, R. (1979/80), pp. 19–48.

[43] Shaefer, Charles G.H. (1990), chapter three.

ering the others. Of all the sectors, agriculture was, owing to the intensive cultivation practices of peasants, the most dynamic. Nevertheless, it had to constantly cope with inherent problems imposed by the system of land ownership, taxation and demography.

7. 2. Government Economic Reforms, 1855–1913

The net result of the structural problems of the economy in Ethiopia was that there was a relatively constant level of production output and labour productivity. The economic state was vulnerable, and even proved fragile when faced by natural disaster (such as drought, locust invasion, and pestilence). Food crisis and famine became a constant feature of the society, further compounded by incessant warfare among the princes. After the crisis of the sixteenth century, the society developed a philosophy of social protest known as millenarianism. It was a prophecy about the coming of a Messiah—a King who was to come in the later days and rule the world in righteousness, peace and prosperity.[44] Since the crisis of the sixteenth century, many Kings and princes claimed to be the promised Tewedros[45], and probably attempted reforms to get the support of peasants. When Kassa Hailu, a nobleman from the province of Quara, was annointed as King in 1855, he took the name Tewedros, thus once again reviving the Messiah vision of social reform. The following discussion, may show the contradictions in objectives of the fiscal military state, between being a Messiah of social protest (i.e., addressing socio-economic problems) and a Messiah of the military nobility (overcoming earlier logistic problems of the army).

7.2.1. Agriculture

Concerning agrarian production relationships, the objective of Tewodros's policy was to maintain full agricultural employment and assurance of security in property rights, particularly of land. One of the measures the King took was to reinstitute the *rist* land, as was expressed in his declaration of "*bäyä abateh geba*" (literally meaning, go to your father's land). In Shewa, for instance, the King declared that peasants could own the land of their fore-fathers, while those without any hereditary right to land were told to follow the King. This

[44] This prophecy is written in the Ethiopian apocalyptic work called *Fukaré Iyäsus*. According to this book, Christ himself would bring a king called Tewodros to power after a long period of corruption, war, famine, lawlessness and perversity. For a general discussion see Merid Welde Aregay, (1984).

[45] See, Mered Wolde Aregay, (1990) "Ye Tewedros Alamawoch Kayet Endemenchu" in Taddese Beyene, Pankhurst, R. and Shiferaw Bekele (eds.), *Kasa and Kasa,* I.E.S., Addis Ababa University. pp. 69–115.

declaration caused litigation since the peasants had been uprooted by the tenancy system and they had no chance to claim back land. This policy brought similar problems in Hamasen. The King, upon the request of the nobility, reversed his policy, and declared *yä* Iyasu *yebqa*, (literally meaning, let that be as declared by King Iyasus). It referred to the land policy formulated by and since the times of King Iyasu I (1682–1706), with an *Amisho Rim* type of land ownership, like the one in Hamasen, and a *Gäbar Madäriya* type of land ownership in Shewa.

Unable to reinstitute the *rist* holdings, the King instead took another measure which aimed at encouraging land clearance. This policy was known as *hagär maqnat*, (literally meaning "to open up a land", or to first cultivate a virgin land). It was based on the traditional concept expressed in terms of land use referring to the first occupant, clearer and cultivator of the land called *aqni abat*. King Tewedros distributed cattle to each (*aqni*) household ready to cultivate new land.[46]

King Yohannes followed a different policy, mainly focusing on settlement rights. In 1888, King Yohannes and *ras* Alula jointly issued an edict dealing with the position of squatters. The King in Tigray, and his governor general, *ras* Alula in the province of Hamassen, issued an edict "man is free, land is tributary", and went on declaring that every land holder, by whatever title, who paid tribute for the land in his possession would thence forward be considered to hold his land by right of *rist* (i.e., permanent heritable tenure). This measurement laid down that forty years of undisputed occupation of land constituted legal ownership, tantamount to *rist*.[47] As contemporary circumstances illustrate, through this policy the state interferred in the land ownership system to avert landless peasants from being uprooted from their holdings particularly as a result of loans and mortgaging of land.[48]

Menelik did not resort to the policy of reinstitution of land ownership to the landless peasants. Instead, he continued to follow the *Gäbar Madäriya* system of Shewa, which encouraged tenancy and private individual holdings of land. In the early 1880s, the King introduced land measurement by *qälad* and classi-

[46] See the letter of Tewodros in Pankhurst, R. and Germa-Selassie Asfaw (1979), p. 151. The term *hagär maqnat* is translated as 'uniting the country', but in the context of the letter it means "to cultivate a virgin land, to clear a land for cultivation".

[47] Various reasons were propounded for the introduction of such policy, see Pankhurst, R. (1966a), p103; Bruce, J. W. (1976). pp. 77f.

[48] During the beginning of the seventeenth century, the practice of enslaving peasants (enserfment) as a result of failing to pay back debts (through a credit system) was legally abolished by King zä-Dengel who promulgated the famous decree that "man is free, it is the land which pays tax". Quoted in Chernetsoy, S.B. (1974), "The History of the Gallas' and the Death of Zädengel, King of Ethiopia (1603–1604)", in *IV Congresso Internazionale di Studie Etiopici, 10–15 April 1972*. Roma, p. 806. See also, Täklä Iyasus, *Yä Ngus Tälä Haymanot Tarik*. Manus. no. 254, p. 35. The edict reappeared in the chronicle of King Iyasu I (1682–1706). During the Gonder period labour was acquired through raiding of boarder lands. See, Taddesse Tamirat (1986).

fied and registered lands in the region of Shewa. In the south, the *qälad* system classified and registered noble holdings exempted from tax and put the rest of the land under state possession, thus depriving the *balabat* of their traditional privilege and right to collect taxes from the *gäbar* peasants who now came under state control and use. What had been considered as state land was distributed to peasants paying land tax, who were in fact owner-cultivators; the rest of the land was kept as *madäriya* (state land).

There is no study describing the immediate effect of the *qälad* system on agricultural output and labour productivity. One visible consequence of the *qälad* system was the concentration of abundant land in state ownership. There were areas where land was measured two or three times as governors were more interested in land survey. The land amassed was distributed to the aristocracy and military nobility in the form of *milmil*, *madäriya*, and *mälkägna*, *wuha senqu*, etc., which made the land in effect, become the private property of the holders when sanctioned by the King.[49] According to one contemporary social critic, the nobility had augmented about 100,000 *gasha* land as private property and *madäriya* land in lieu of payment. He calculated that if the land tax for one *gasha* was 15 *birr* (by the price rate of early 1930s), the government had lost 1.5 million *birr* as tax[50]. In addition, the land thus accumulated was not cultivated by the holders.

Because of heavy taxation, the *gäbar* too could not accumulate capital. A *gäbar* family of five members, farming one *gasha* of semi-fertile arable land through a rotation system, produced fifty *dawula* of grain.[51] From this it paid three *dawula* of grain, and one *gundo* of honey (i.e., about five *dawula*) as ordinary land tax, and five *dawula* of grain as *asrat* (extraordinary land tax). There were also various surtaxes such as one *birr* for wood, one *birr* for holidays, three *birr* for grass, two *quna* of grain for the *asrat* collector, (a total of approximately three or four *dawula*) as surtax. Through taxes, the peasant lost about 17 *dawula* of grain. For household consumption, the peasant needed a minimum of 15 *dawula* grain per year. The peasant also had to save a significant proportion of *dawula* for the next year's crop, as well as to use it to cover other extraordinary expenses such as feasts and holidays. In the end, it was very little the peasants brought to the market.

The labour of the peasant was utilized for government and private purposes by government officals. In areas where the peasant cultivated *hudad* land in lieu of paying grain as tax, the peasant contributed his physical strength, his implements and his work animals for one out of every three working days. It is not difficult to understand why the principle of *hudad* cultivation had pushed

[49] See revenue allocation in sections 4.2.2. and 4.2.3. above.

[50] See Asbe Hailu, "selä mängest gudat", in *Brehanena Selam*, July 1926.

[51] If a *gäbar* who had semi-fertile land paid five dawula of grain as tithe, it meant that his farm produced fifty dawula of grain. On the amount of tithe payment see section 3.2. above.

the peasant to an extreme point. The *gäbar*-peasant also served as provision supplier, and had thus to grind grains and transport them to the required destination. In addition, he had extraordinary labour obligations arbitrarily imposed by governors (such as fencing, constructing houses, transporting the private property of the governor, building churches, etc.). Peasants' obligations of tax payment in kind and service limited his freedom in terms of working arrangements, working time, and choice of cultivation.[52]

In the *Gäbar Madäriya* system, peasants' investments in agricultural production depended on the amount of labour available from the household and on the local possibility of enlarging the arable land. As discussed above, the tax obligations of the peasants and the principles of *qälad* measurements were factors that restricted production investment. The *Gäbar Madäriya* system simply reproduced the class of the peasantry without making any changes in the possibility of accumulation. On the contrary, the system presented tenancy as an alternative opportunity for those who became landless as a result of debt or other household demographic problems.

Before the time of Menelik, agricultural production in the *Gäbar Madäriya* system was faced mainly with the problems of population pressure. During the reign of Menelik, accumulation of land and the system of taxation were constraints on the simple accumulation needed for an increase in agricultural product. On the other hand, the introduction of the *qälad* system encouraged private ownership of land, reinforced by law. For instance, *balabat* were given unrestricted rights to dispose of their *siso* land. It was possible for them to raise rent from their land from its custmory level to whatever amount they were able to extract. In general, the system differentiated between the owner and the ruler, and among property owners. Theoretically, this type of ownership was an indespensable condition for productive investment and accumulation of wealth. But as was explained in the section above, the system had no immediate impact on increasing production. In the long run, however, the system created favourable conditions for large scale farming.

The system enabled the state to encourage plantation agriculture.[53] Menelik also encouraged coffee production.[54] But plantation agriculture and cattle farms did not spread widely. Even if the system had the potential to produce tenancy and consolidation of small farming, peasants continued to give prior-

[52] Among others, see the often quoted critic of Asbe Hailu in the newspaper *Brehanina Selam*, 1927.

[53] See documents in *Dagmawi Minilk kä-Täläyayu Hagäroch gar Yaderägut Yä -Wädagnet, yä-Negd, ena yä-Denber Wuloch*. Manuscript no. 2201. IES, pp. 28f. (abbriviated as *Menelik's Treties of Friendship, Trade and Boarder Delination*); See also Pankhurst, R. (1968c), pp. 184–208. In the early 1920s, for instance, governor generals of some provinces engaged in the production of coffee on plantations. *Däjazmach* Demesew, governor of parts of Wellega, planted 50,000 coffee trees on ten gasha of land. See the newspaper *Berehanena Selam*, March 15, 1928.

[54] Pankhrrst, R. (1968c), p. 210.

ity to food crops. There was no government policy as regards restriction on grain production in favour of stock-farming, tobacco or coffee plantation. It was the peasant household which made the decision, and peasants continued to give priority to food crops. In fact, *teff* production was widely introduced in the south as a result of Menelik's expansion policy.[55]

For the period under discussion, there is little information about the state's policy as regards the system of land use. It seems that methods of cultivation, soil management, use of suitable farming tools, and cultivation of crop patterns were the responsibility of the peasant household and the community. However, there were some state reforms that had spill-over effects on the system of land use. Menelik introduced the eucalyptus tree, primarily for fire wood[56], and these trees were later used to combat soil erosion caused by centuries of deforestation.

The objectives of introducing reforms, in land use systems in particular and in agriculture in general, were stated explicitly in the decree which established the Ministry of Agriculture in 1907.[57] This ministry was responsible for the improvement of the quality and quantity of crop production, cattle breeding, agricultural tools and forestry. The ministry also made surveys of cultivated agricultural lands, forests, meadows and conducted cattle census in each governorate and, in consultation with the government, allowed tax exemption for places affected by drought and epidemic diseases. The ministry was in charge of agricultural contracts and the running of agricultural schools. It fixed taxes on land, livestock, and agricultural enterprises.

7.2.2. Reforms in Manufacturing and Mining

The reforms in agriculture were not of the kind which would encourage an increase in surplus nor release the labour tied to the land. Manufacturing and mining received no stimulus and demand from agriculture. In other words, there was little drive inspired by local enterprise and interest that would precipitate the development of large scale factory machine based production. The drive came only from the state which had the capacity to organize the labour force and supply the capital required for large scale manufacturing. Since 1855 royal workshops were established based on local handicrafts, and the state also tried to inspire large scale manufacturing through grants of concessions.

In 1861, Tewedros established a cannon and mortar gun-manufacturing plant at Gafat, near his capital, Debre Tabor. This factory was destroyed during

[55] See B.A. thesis in history dealing with southern regions, among others, see Raga Abdissa (1984), "A Brief Survey of Land Tenure System in Qellem, Western Walläga, ca. 1880–1944". B.A. Thesis in History, AAU.

[56] Pankhurst, R. (1968c), p. 246; Paulos Gnogno (1984 E.C.), pp. 293–297.

[57] See the regulations given to the Ministry in Mahteme Selassie (1962), pp. 318f.

the British military expedition in 1868. Menelik also tried to establish an ammunition factory at Addis Ababa.[58] However, the factory could not continue producing for a long period due to the deliberate embargo imposed by adjacent colonial powers.

Menelik also continued the tradition of household craft production organized by the court, but on a larger scale. In 1908 the King issued a decree that safeguarded the status of craft workers, and the King had already established a craft workshop (*tägbarä`ed mäsriya bet*).[59] In addition to the royal work shop[60], the King attempted to establish wood work factory[61]. The King also encouraged establishment of mills and leather, soap and other small-scale factories around Akaki, near Addis Ababa, mainly through grant of concessions.[62] During the reign of Menelik, there was a concerted effort to develop the mining sector through concession.[63] Concessions were also given for the construction of a hydro electric power station over the falls of the Nile and Akaki for the commercialization of energy.[64]

Generally, the state showed interest in the promotion of the manufacturing and mining sectors, although not for the purpose of obtaining large scale commodity production. In the manufacturing sector, the interest was related to the development of a military industry and self-sufficiency for court consumption. In the mining sector, there was a clear interest in revenue. Concessions on gold extraction were made between the company and the King himself and it was agreed that the revenue was to be given to Menelik himself and his heirs. Other companies paid a fixed sum or portion of the annual revenue to the state. The drive for manufacturing and mining was not motivated by local enterprise and interest, nor did it involve large scale factory machine based production. Lack of stimulus to local manufacturing, both from the state and from the agricultural sector, made traditional craft so vulnerable that the tradition of mining and smelting of iron and cloth making died out due to the availability of cheap and better tools and cloth on the market.

In the manufacturing sector, a basic problem was the lack of stimulus from the agricultural sector in the provision of both labour and food surplus for the

[58] See the decree to establish the factory quoted in Mahteme Selassie (1962), p. 225, see also Paulos Gnogno (1984 E.C.), p. 355.

[59] For list of the items of production of royal workshop see Mahteme Selassie (1962 EC), p. 416–420.

[60] On the amount of salary payment to employees of the royal craft, see ibid., p. 239f.

[61] See *Menelik's Treaties of Friendship, Trade and Boarder Delineation*, pp. 68f.

[62] On the concession on mills see ibid., pp. 29–30; Shiferaw Bekele, (1989), "Aspects of the History of Dire Dawa (1902 to 1936)", in *Proceedings of the Fourth Seminar of the Department of History*. AAU., p. 87; Garretson, P. P. (1974), pp. 279, 285; *Menelik's Treaties of Friendship, Trade and Boarder Delineation*, pp. 61f.

[63] See Garretson, P. P. (1974), p. 258f;

[64] See *Menelik's Treaties of Friendship, Trade and Boarder Delineation*, pp. 57f; For Harar province see. ibid., 37–38.

towns, which in turn led to the absence of labour specialization. Agriculture was dominated by the *rist* system which tied the labour force to the land, while the extensive process of mining required labour. Towns could not develop as manufacturing centers because of the low supply of surplus production brought to the market, and the rural nature of craft production. The Kings tried to encourage manufacturing but under the same system of household organization, (i.e., royal manufacturing centers) and all ventures in this direction were inspired by military interest rather than an ambition to industrialize.

7.2.3. Domestic, Regional and International Trade

7.2.3.1. Safety, Transportation and Communication Facilities

In the second half of the nineteenth century, particularly during the last decades of the century, there was considerable growth in the volume and frequency of regional and international trade caused by a combination of internal and external factors. Among the factors that illustrate deliberate government intervention were pacification of the regions and the ensuring of security for trade promotion and other economic activities which were the concern of all of the three Kings. During his coronation, Tewedros issued an edict: "everyone should return to his lawful avocation, the merchant to his store, and the farmer to his plough". During this time there were a large number of demobilized soldiers of the territorial princes who roamed the countryside, and in many places there were outlaws and bandits.[65] Establishment of peace was a condition for the promotion of trade and agriculture. The King severely punished professional highway robbers, as in the case of the people of Tisba. Consequently, in some areas market days were held without the incident of a murder.[66]

King Yohannes had also issued a decree that stabilized areas during his coronation ceremony[67], but there is no information on concrete measures undertaken. Quite in a different context and situation, Menelik was also preoccupied with abolishing robbers and bandits. A number of imperial decrees were sent to provinces making the people of the areas responsible for vigilance against robbery. A significant measure in the promotion of internal trade was the establishment of camping sites (*mänähariya*) for merchants of long distance trade. The King ordered the selection of safe places for the overnight stay of merchants. The places were selected for their supply of water and availability of pasture.[68] At the sites, merchants were granted safety and provincial

[65] See Crummey, D. (1984); and Caulk, R.A. (1984), "Bad Men of the Borders: Sum and Shifta in Northern Ethiopia in the Nineteenth Century", in *Proceedings of the Second Annual Seminar of the Department of History*. AAU. Vol. I. Addis Ababa.

[66] See Pankhurst, R. (1990),

[67] Fiseha Wolde Mikael (1936), p. 42.

[68] For details on the number and location of the sites, see Mahteme Selassie (1962), pp. 424–432.

governors were made responsible for their areas. At such places, the merchants were required to register their goods, and if a merchant was robbed at the *mänähariya* site he was repaid by the governor. If he was robbed on the way, the country people were liable for his reimbursement.[69]

The King and provincial governors and military officials not only thus protected merchants, but also took measures to improve the commercial infrastructure. Traditionally the construction of public works was the responsibility of the community. During the second half of the nineteenth century, there was a state program and involvement in public works, particularly in the transport and communication system. Transport was an important feature of trade. Since the state benefited from trade through taxation and involvement in foreign trade, improving the transport system appeared a necessity. Though limited, there were development works of road networks linking rural and urban areas. Initially the motive for road construction had been to assist military operations. King Tewedros constructed a road for the transportation of his artillery.[70] During the time of Menelik, road construction was considered a means of encouraging trade and developing the country for its own sake.[71] There was road building in the provinces and bridges for heavy tracks were also built.[72]

During the period of Menelik there was a change in the modes of land transport. A concession was given to construct a railway line from Djibouti to Addis Ababa.[73] Menelik also gave a concession to the ox-cart enterprise for organizing two-wheeled ox cart service from Dire Dewa to Addis Ababa until the completion of the railway line.[74]

The development of the transport system was not financed by the state.[75] The railway was financed by foreign capital[76] and road construction was carried out by peasant labour. Menelik ordered an obligatory payment of tax, one *birr* per head of cattle around 1907. Peasants complained about the collection of this levy, and governors from Wollo, Begemder and Tigray reported this to the King. Finally it was decided to levy, collect and deliver the money to the center over two years. With this money the King constructed, among other things, bridges over the Blue Nile, and other rivers.[77] In 1893,

[69] Kebede Tesema, *Leyu Leyu yä-Tarik Mastawäsha*, p. 12.

[70] See Pankhurst, R. (1990).

[71] See Pankhurst, R. (1968c), pp. 248–9.

[72] Guluma Gemeda (1989), "An Outline of the Early History of Jimma Town", in *Proceedings of the Fourth Seminar of the Department of History*, AAU. p. 39.

[73] For details see Shiferaw Bekele (1982), "The Railway, Trade and Politics: A Historical Survey (1896–1935)". M.A. Thesis in History. AAU.

[74] See Garretson, P. P. (1974), p. 300; Shiferaw Bekele, (1989), p. 87.

[75] In Egypt, public works programmes were financed by state borrowing, and because the state could not repay its debt, it led to British colonization. See Zeleza, T. (1993), *A Modern Economic History of Africa, I. The Nineteenth Century*. Oxford. pp. 345–354.

[76] See the discussion by Shiferaw Bekele (1991), "The Ethiopian Railway and British Finance Capital, 1896–1902", in *Africa, 3*. pp. 351–374.

[77] See Paulos Gnogno (1984 E.C.), p. 352.

Menelik built the metal bridge across the Awash river to assure year round use of the route.[78]

During the formation of the Ministerial system in 1907, the responsibilty for developing the transport system was given to the Ministry of Public Works. This ministry was also in charge of the construction of roads, railways, bridges, dams, irrigation canals, government buildings, the palace and churches. The ministry could contract with engineers and workers and supervise the execution of the contracts.

During the time of Menelik, a modern postal, telephone and telegraph system was installed. In 1897 construction of telephone lines between Addis Ababa and Harar started. When the ministerial system was established in 1907, the administration of Post, Telephone and Telegraph was headed by a director working under the supervision of the Ministry of Palace. By 1910, an independent Ministry of Posts, Telephone and Telegrph was set up.

The changes in the structure of the transport system and the establishment of a communication system did not contribute to the expansion of domestic trade. It did not stimulate production or facilitate the formation of integrated national markets.[79] Its development, however, was a precondition for the regions' integration into the world capitalist market.

7.2.3.2. Development of Privileged Trade Monopolies and Enterpots

The internal developments discussed above were synchronized with external influences, particularly in the direction and structure of foreign trade. One major phenomenon was the spread of European colonialism in the Horn of Africa, particularly since the third quarter of the nineteenth century. With the opening of the Suez Canal in 1867, there was an increasing interest in colonial trade and the acquisition of trading posts along the Red Sea. European colonization of neighbouring countries such as Sudan, Djibouti and Somaliland opened new outlets, and the adjacent colonial governments were encouraging expansion of trade with Ethiopia. For instance, the collapse of the Mahdist state and the subsequent British colonization of Sudan, as well as the opening of the various Nile confluences, saw an expansion of a western Ethiopian outlet.[80] This development brought new partners and new demands for goods .

However, a qualitative change occured after the battle of Adwa in 1896. Until the battle of Adwa, Europeans concentrated on colonization by means of military force; at this point there was more diplomacy at work than commerce. Italy's aggressive military colonization affected the development of trade in the north. After the battle of Adwa, however, colonial powers changed their policy from colonization by military force to a peaceful commercial penetra-

[78] See Garretson, P. P. (1974), p. 248.
[79] Refer to the critical analysis of Gebre Hiwot Bykädagn in section 8.3 below.
[80] See Garretson, P. P. (1974), p. 250.

tion and there arose an increasing interest in trade with Ethiopia on the side of European countries and merchants. Adjacent colonial countries encouraged and expanded trade.[81] The establishment of a civilian governor, Martini, in Eritrea encouraged trade in the north[82] and galvanized the import/export trade. The Ethiopian government became interested in collecting tax and in this respect it did its best to exploit the expansion of trade.

The changes in the direction and structure of export goods were also accompanied with changes in trade partners. Until the third quarter of the nineteenth century, foreign trade agreements were bilaterally conducted between the princes and Kings of Ethiopia on the one hand, and the European countries through their commercial agents and adventurers on the other.[83] During the reign of Menelik, trade agreements were not only among and at the level of governments, but also between companies and the Ethiopian government and aristocrats. With these kinds of partnerships, a new form of trading system emerged that may be called the privileged trade monopoly system. It referred to the running of import-export trade on a large scale and to the degree to which the companies were allowed to dominate the trade as stated in the agreement.[84]

Some of the concessions are mentioned in the sections on the manufacturing sector, and in the discussion about transport and finance. Ivory, and to a certain extent gold, were a royal monopoly.[85] There were also foreign trade monopolies in gold, coffee, beeswax, ivory and, after 1909, rubber.[86] During this time, no government monopolies were set up for the sale of agricultural and other produce. For instance, there was no prohibition against private trade in cereals. Privileged monopolies were limited to the export of certain items. There was no policy of control over the domestic market.

The growing expansion of international trade led to an increase in the number of foreign merchants.[87] The big merchants in Ethiopia, foreigners of different national origin, were called *tujar*, meaning "the King's traders". The King provided them with special permits to trade as wholesalers, and with loans to finance their activities. The merchants were tied to the King and some aristocrats as clients, debtors and partners. This prevented them from becoming an independent social class and hindered their accumulation of capital. As appendages of the state, the merchants were very vulnerable to any crisis that

[81] For British Somali land see Garretson, P. P. (1974), p. 247.

[82] Ibid., p. 253.

[83] For Tewodros see Rubenson, S. ed. (1994), *Tewodros and His Contemporaris 1855–1868. Acta Aethiopica, II.* Addis Ababa and Lund. For emperor Yohannes see Zewde G. Selassie (1975).

[84] On the list of concessions see among others, *Menelik's Treaties of Friendship, Trade and Boarder Delineation*, pp, 2–3, 7–11, 31–32, 34–36.

[85] See the discussion on aristocratic capital in section 8.2. below; see also Garretson, P. P. (1974), pp. 261–262.

[86] See Ibid., pp. 257–259, 275.

[87] See Paulos Gnogno (1984 E.C.), p. 369f.

hit the state such as the intervention of foreign powers and costly military reforms and expenditures. Most foreign merchants resided in Addis Ababa, a town which very soon developed into a trading center from which import and export were directed.

Priorities were given to enforcing the trade that passed through Addis Ababa and crossed the border through eastern outlets to increase the central government's custom revenue.[88] During the 1880s and early 1890s, but not really until 1896, the bulk of the vital trade of the South and West (areas which consistently produced exportable items due to the role of ecology) was transferred from its northward route to the east so that it could pass first through the new capital and then through Harar, and neighbouring areas, to finally reach Red Sea ports.[89] Formerly, exports of coffee, hides, rubber and other commodities had gone through Gambela, but after 1908 they were re-routed through Addis Ababa.[90]

A multiplicity of different interests, at times coinciding, at times conflicting, lurked behind the development of Addis Ababa as an entrepot since 1886.[91] For revenue reasons, the state wanted Addis Ababa to serve as a central point for transit trade in import and export[92], and merchandise in transit was often compelled to pass through Addis Ababa. Each of the more important nobles organized caravans from their provinces which passed through Addis, presented tribute, were taxed and headed for the coast.[93] Addis Ababa was chosen as the point of exit and entry because transport and communication facilities as well as financial institutions were found there. Major commercial houses of Harar, like that of Mohamed Aly, were forced to move their head offices from Harar to Addis in 1808/9.[94]

Other than Addis Ababa, there were also regional trade centers through which import/export trade expanded during the second half of the nineteenth century. These were Gonder in the north west, Adwa and Masswa in the north, Assab in the north east, Harar, Djibouti and Somali coastal towns in the east, Borena and Lugh in the south, Enariya, Jiima, Kaffa, Bonga in the south west, and Gore, Bure, Wellega and Gambella in the west.[95]

[88] Ibid, p. 254.
[89] Ibid., p. 241
[90] Ibid., p. 281
[91] For the history on the foundation and development of Addis Ababa see *Proceedings of the International Symposium on the Century of Addis Ababa, November 24–25, 1986*. Addis Ababa.
[92] The town of Harar was another custom post for import-export trade. For the complexity of the import taxes between Addis Ababa and Harar see Pankhurst, R. (1968a), pp. 45–46.
[93] Garretson, P. P. (1974), p. 255.
[94] Ibid., p. 252.
[95] On the volume, patterns and direction of the import and export goods of these specified regions see the detailed collection of data by Pankhurst, R. (1968c), Chapter IX.

7.2.3.3. Finance: New Currency and Establishment of Banking System

Trade was conducted through the use of MT$ and an "imperfect currency"[96] such as *amole* salt, pieces of cloth, and cartridges. MT$ was introduced during the eighteenth century, but since it had no denominations (small change or divisional units), and had supply problems, imperfect items of currency were often used instead.

Of the two forms of currency, the MT$ was durable and could be stored without its value being spoiled. It was hoarded as a way of saving money. Although the MT$ was valued, its availability and fluctuation had an effect on the economy. For a long time Kings had no control over the supply of MT$. "Lack of regulatory control over the amount of money circulating in Ethiopia meant that the economy was either starved for currency or was flooded with it. Compounding this problem was the value of Ethiopia's silver-based currency, MT$, which fluctuated with world silver price. The result was that Ethiopia suffered from double dependency".[97]

In 1893, Menelik decided to mint new money. At first, from 1896–1903, the majority of the coins were struck in Paris and then shipped to Ethiopia, but only in the capital were they fully accepted as currency.[98] In 1903 machinery for a mint arrived and was under the direct supervision of two Armenians who were directly paid by Menelik.[99]

His monetary policy and reform was designed to replace the MT$ and solve the problem of currency dependency by increasing its availability. Secondly, Menelik's coins were advantageous in that they were easily divisible (*alad*-half *birr*, *rub*-quarter, *tämun*-one-eighth, *mähaläk*-one-sixteenth, and *béssa*-one-thirtysecond) and could be used conveniently in retail trades. Its divisibility could replace the "imperfect curency" and the problems associated with it. But as to holding value and for further exchange, it had problems of acceptance. To this end, Menelik promulgated an *awaj*-decree prohibiting the use of salt and cartridges as currency and thus promoting the popularity of the new coinage.[100] In a way, enforcement of this decree facilitated monetarization of the economy.

Another major monetary and policy reform of the period was Menelik's decision to establish a joint stock bank. On March 10, 1905 the King gave a 50-year concession to the Britsh owned National Bank of Egypt, a banking monopoly in Ethiopia. The company was called Bank of Abyssinia. There was a conflict of interest between the bank and the government about the policy

[96] "Imperfect currency (is) a form of money, with all the appearances and properties of money" Braudel, F. (1982), *Civilization and Capitalism, 15th–18th Century. II. The Wheels of Commerece.* p. 444.

[97] See Schaefer, C.G.H. (1990), pp. 131–132.

[98] See Gebre Selassie (1959), p. 271; Pankhurst, UR. (1968c), pp. 478–486.

[99] See Garretson, P. P. (1974), p. 237.

[100] See Mahteme Selassie (1962), p. 198f.

and performance of the Bank. As was seen from later developments, the government and the Bank had opposing views as regards regulating money supply. The government prohibited silver export, while the bank opposed currency restriction because it hindered the Bank from selling MT$ and conducting world business.[101] Much of the profit came from the rights originally given to the bank and from the concession to import MT$ at the cheap government rate. However, loans were given to reputable traders, not to manufacturers of items such as cartridges and rubber.[102].

In 1909 the aristocrats led by Queen Tayitu established a counter bank named Commerce and Agricultural Development Bank. This bank was supposed to stand as a rival to the Bank of Abyssinian and aimed to promote domestic economic development. The purpose of the Commercial and Agricultural Development Bank was "to counter the influence of the foreign controlled Bank of Abyssinia by attracting Ethiopian depositers and by controlling the loan market. Capital and profit were to be directed toward infrastructural development which was to benefit the polity and the people".[103] The Bank was envisaged as a development agency, that is, it was established to develop agricultural, industrial and commercial interests by providing loans. It is said that the Queen had the intention of controlling imperial loans and the imperial treasury through the disguise of the bank.[104] The Queen tried to collect money loaned out by Menelik (outstanding loans) to both foreigners and Ethiopians, and to finance the new bank[105], and this led to a conspiracy which finally ousted the Queen from power[106].

With the establishment of a ministerial system, all financial matters were given to the Ministry of Finance. This Ministry was in charge of receipts, custody, disbursement and control of government finance, the private treasury of the King, and activities carried out by the banks (including the Bank of Abyssinia).

In the period under discussion, economic policy was relatively in the hands of the central government. Before it, in the *Zämänä Mäsafint*, economic life was

[101] Ibid., pp. 86ff.

[102] For an in-depth critical analysis of the Bank see Gabra Hiwot Bykadagn (1919), *Mängistna Yähizb Astädader*, IES. The title reads in English as follows: Government and Public Administration. However, the book acquired a new title when the whole text was translated into English by Tenkir Bonger: Gabrahiwot Baykadagn, *The Political Economy of Ethiopia c 1910*. London. Chapters Eleven to Fourteen.

[103] See Schaefer, C.G.H. (1990), p. 203.

[104] Prouty, C. (1986), *Empress Taytu and Menelik II: Ethiopia, 1883–1910*. London. p. 323.

[105] On Menelik's loan see section 8.2. below.

[106] See Garretson, P. P. (1974), p. 293. *lij* Iyasu had ordered an inventory of government property and auditing of government accounts, including those loans and that remained with the aristocracy and nobility. See Gebre-Igziabiher Elyas (1994), p. 48, text. p. 342f translation. Probably his measurement to take stock of government property partly contributed to his downfall.

fragmented and regional princes had the power to conclude diplomatic and trade agreements with foreign powers, thus providing traders with the opportunity to freely compete amongst one another. Since the time of Tewedros and particularly during the reign of Menelik, Kings had been behind the making of economic policy and the giving of special privileges. However, there were still problems around the formulation of economic policies and the implementation of various measures. First it had to match the fiscal interest of the state but, in most cases, reforms were not calculated to see how they influenced economic growth. Inefficient systems (such as inequality of customs tax, noblity exemptions) were allowed to operate. Secondly, policies had to coincide with the interest of the entrenched military nobility who frustrated the implementation of agreements which were not in their interest.[107]

[107] Even though government concessions were given with revenue in mind, it should be also known that in many occasions and undertakings, Menelik had expressed his good will and intention to promote the economic welfare of his people. He made this very clear in all negotiations, including the provision of credit to peasants by the Bank of Abyssinia, the construction of a railway line far into western boarders of Ethiopia, and in the number of social reforms he introduced such as in education and health. See MacGillivray report in FO 401/8, p. 51, see also the letters of Menelik compiled and commented in Paulos Gnogno (1984 E.C.), pp. 236–430. Even the King's intelligence security had an insignia on their hat to warn the people to watch what they discuss and with whom they gossip. Between the King and the people, however, there was a well entrenched class of aristocracy and military nobility.

CHAPTER EIGHT

The Question of Economic Dynamism

Two important economic developments were marked during the making of the fiscal military state. First, there was rapid evolution in the scope and organization of trade; and secondly, there was a speedy process of wealth accumulation by the aristocracy. Agriculture had sustained its former dynamics in the form of intensive cultivation. Agricultural dynamics were limited mainly to farming techniques, water management and use of fertilizer. The equilibrium was often interrupted by natural catastrophe such as the "Great Famine of 1888–1892". Intensive agriculture could not change to a different scale for various reasons. First, the fiscal system (distribution in the burden of taxation) discouraged investment in agricultural improvement (as in the case of the *rist* areas). Secondly, types of communal land ownership prevented primary accumulation. Thirdly, the level of taxation left no space for sufficient surplus accumulation and savings (as in the case of the *Gäbar Madäriya* regions). Did the dynamics in trade and aristocratic capital give momentum to agricultural dynamics and inject change in the manufacturing sector? This chapter presents a bird's eye view of the economic dynamism of a stifled transition, which, as a rule, followed from the character of contradictory objectives of governments in the first phase of absolutism.

8.1. Trade and Development of Towns

Government intervention (in terms of safety, transport and communication, establishment of market areas, military garrisons, changes in the administration of indirect taxation, currency measures), introduction of crops (such as *teff*, maize, pepper), and external developments (particularly concerning change in the commercial philosophy of adjacent colonial countries) led to the evolution of regional trade both in scope and organization.[1]

There was, however, a limit to the reforms. They could not enlarge the ca-

[1] For a quantifiable data on the various types of commodities, their relative value, on volume trade (transport and routes), and geographical context, readers may see Pankhurst, R. (1968c), Chapter IX on Trade.

pacity of trade or translate it into a kind of economic development. The reform in the area of transport was insufficient to match the volume and frequency of trade and it did not reduce transport costs. Although direct government administration of indirect tax was practiced, the system was inefficient and corrupted.[2] There were innumerable local tariffs and other fiscal barriers.

Notwithstanding an expansion in the volume and frequency of foreign trade, the government made no attempt to introduce systematic economic regulation to protect the economic welfare of its citizens. Menelik's government gave monopoly concessions to trading, mining and manufacturing companies, which by virtue of their privilege had relative control over the movement, exchange and prices of commodities. The government had no systematic regulation to protect citizens from the side effects of the increase in foreign trade and monopolization concessions. In 1893 small merchants demanded the abolishment of monopolies, and pledged to raise two million MT$ to be paid as compensation to the government.[3] In 1902 Harar merchants protested against the coffee monopoly which was a profitable item of trade in Harar.[4] In 1906, small merchants protested and demanded reform in bank policy. The monopoly over currency given to the Bank of Abyssinia hindered merchants from importing MT$, since the bank imposed a 10% tax on imports of MT$. Merchants also protested against the caravan monopoly of Abubäkar, who made arbitrary charges.[5] Addis Ababa merchants resented privileges of tax exemption for customs officials who engaged in trade.[6] The King instituted a commercial tribunal to hear the cases.

In certain cases, the King interfered to defend the interests of local traders. For instance, when concessions were given to gold extracting companies, there was an article in the agreement which prohibited the companies from excluding local gold extractors. In 1894 Menelik made a pact with *ras* Welde Giogis and *däjazmach* Tesema Nadew indicating that they would send the coffee collected as tax from the provinces of Kaffa and Illibabour to Addis Ababa.[7] Governors were also allowed to purchase coffee for export, but not to the extent of excluding small traders.[8] Menelik also imported raw materials useful for weavers.[9]

As pointed out in the preceding chapters, the driving motive behind foreign trade and concession was the fiscal interest. Monopolies were created, particu-

[2] See the administration of justice, *lebashay*: a local method of catching a thief, led to the expropriation of small merchants, see Garretson, P.P. (1974), pp. 279f.

[3] Ibid., p. 276

[4] Ibid.

[5] Ibid., p. 279f.

[6] Ibid., p. 282.

[7] On document numbers see Ibid., p. 261.

[8] Ibid, 262

[9] See Paulos Gnogno (1984 E.C.), pp. 339–340.

larly at times of financial need. For example, the monopolies were sold to foreigners coinciding with the Great Famine (1889–1891) and on the eve of preparation for the battle of Adwa. Grants were made immediately after the famine, and again immediately before the battle of Adwa (1905/6). The King also had a monopoly over the export of ivory and gold, and these items were not subjected to export duties.[10] Custom duties were not uniform, as for instance between Addis Ababa and Harar. The rates varied considerably between 3% and 8%, and the classes of goods were not categorized.[11] As regards foreign trade, the government had no common and coherent policy to regulate its dynamic effects. This policy had been examined and formulated for the first time by Gebre Hiwot Bykedagn. In fact, most factors which limited the capacity to expand were structural (such as the military provisioning system, forms of land tax allocation and collection, and organizational forms of manufacturing) which in one way or another were related to the ruling classes' economic philosophy (i.e., self-reliance) as can be demonstrated by looking at the development of towns.

One aspect of the growth in the scope of regional trade was the increase in the formation of towns, particularly in the southern Ethiopia. There were different views as to the cause of the formation of towns, some regarding it as a political development, particularly as a consequence of the establishment of *kätäma*, military garrison towns.[12] Others considered aspects such as the revival of long distance trade[13], earlier settlement, and development of local politcal power. There were divergent factors, however, which led to the foundation and development of towns. Military settlements on extensive land had an effect in many ways. Peasants visited towns in order to pay tributes. The population of the towns also increased as many came to settle seeking protection. The construction of lines of communication, the introduction of *teff* and cereals (such as maize, pepper)[14], ruthless suppression of robbers by governors, and state ownership of land facilitated the establishment of market places, introduction of currency, establishment of *kella* at strategic places like cross roads. Although there were divergent factors, there was one particular factor applicable to all: towns did not grow as a result of agricultural specialization and neither could they induce comercialization of the sector. The city of Addis Ababa was a conspicuous example.

[10] See section 4.2.1.

[11] See Pankhurst, R. (1968a), pp. 51ff.

[12] See among others, Akalu Wolde Michael (1973), "Urban Development in Ethiopia (1889–1925)", in *Journal of Ethiopian Studies, XI: 1.*

[13] See Benti Getahun (1989), "Shashemane: Foundation and Early Growth up to the Italian Occupation", in *Proceedings of the Fourth Seminar of the Department of History*. AAU; see also Guluma Gemeda (1989).

[14] See Shimeles Bonsa (1990), "The History of Butajra Town to 1974. B.A". Thesis in History, AAU. p. 34.

Addis Ababa was founded and developed as a collection of large military camps (*säfär*), with empty spaces between them.[15] In a course of three decades since its foundation in 1886, the population of the city reached 60,000.[16] In spite of its size and the "type" of the population, (due to the system of revenue allocation and collection), Addis Ababa did not exert weight on the market. The military nobility, soldiers and clergy who resided in the town were remunerated by methods of state land allocation or collection of land tax.[17] Governors who resided in the town had their own *mad bét* in the vicinity of the city as in the case of Habte Giorgis, the Minister of War. The *mad bét* of the King and the Queen were also in central Shoa.[18] That meant, for the consumption of grain, the royal court and the various camp sites were not dependent on the market. In their compounds and in the relatively empty spaces of the city, residents also kept animals for the production of meat and milk.[19] The food supply of Addis Ababa was not ensured through the market, nor were there institutions such as a municipality responsible for the supply of food and control of price. The city had only one large market where various kinds of commodities were sold, and which was characterized by a relatively low volume of commercial activity, and barter exchange.[20]

Thus, to sum up, government intervention to promote trade and the concomitant development of towns with a relatively large size of population whose items of diet consisted chiefly of grain and meat from cattle and sheep did not, contrary to expectations, lead to trade in necessities. This was a significant constraint on agricultural specialization and commercialization. The revenue allocation and collection system and the forms of tax payment stifled the potential to develop demand in items of food consumption; and in this context, price was not the 'invisible hand' that allocated the cost of production and determined specialization in agriculture.[21]

Expansion of foreign trade had no effect on the agrarian sector. As there was

[15] For a review of the literature and a discussion of this unique feature of the city, see Bahru Zewde (1987), "Early Safars of Addis Ababa: Patterns of Evolution", in *Proceedings of the International Symposium on the Century of Addis Ababa, November 24–25, 1986*. Addis Ababa. pp. 43–55.

[16] Quoted in Chapple, D. (1987), "Some Remarks on the Addis Ababa Food Market up to 1935" in *Proceedings of the International Symposium on the Century of Addis Ababa, November 24.25, 1986.* Addis Ababa. p. 143

[17] See section 6.2.1.above; Chapple, D. (1987), pp 148ff. see also the detailed study on the strategy and means of feeding the town of Addis Ababa, by Tekalign W. Mariam (1995).

[18] See section 4.2.1.

[19] See Chapple, D. (1987), p. 143.

[20] Ibid. p. 144ff.

[21] Earlier we noted that the level of taxation and system of land ownership did not lead to the primary accumulation process, thus affecting the volume of agricultural surplus. Intensive agriculture remained constant. That was the supply side. Now, in spite of the developments of marketing towns, the demand side was affected by the forms of tax payment and by the tax allocation system, which were based on the philosophy of self-reliance.

no grain trade across regions, there was no trade in basic food stuff. Trade focused on exporting primary items such as coffee, wax, civet, hide and skin, which were not produced on a large scale. Without entering the debate on the effect of "non equivalent exchange", it can be said that there was profit and revenue obtained from the import-export trade. But, was foreign trade an opportunity or a pressure? Who benefited from this trade? How can one characterize the accumulation of wealth? Could this wealth and its beneficiaries serve as development forces? These questions led to investigating the second aspect of dynamism of the period, namely, the type and management of aristocratic wealth.

8.2. Aristocratic Capital

Accumulation of aristocratic wealth is an aspect of the dynamics of the period, and in this section the structure of aristocratic patrimony and the essential elements that conferred economic value and power are examined. The aim of the discussion is to make a general assessment of the major sources of aristocratic revenue, and their relative importance to the continuity of aristocratic power. Basically, the issue discussed here is the system of management of aristocratic patrimony and its economic priorities.

However, there were no account books kept that recorded the income and spending of the aristocracy and it is, therefore, difficult to discuss the economic role of the aristocracy. Except for some biographical studies that often emphasized the political aspect, there is no literature on aristocratic families and patrimonies. The generalizations here are thus based on fragmented source materials such as wills, church documents, fragmented central revenue accounts and bank reports. Considering the limits on available source materials, the problem was approached by looking for probable answer to the legal sources of ownership and for methods of wealth acquisition. Except at a general level, there was no discussion on the system of management of aristocratic patrimony. The will document used to view the components of patrimony belonged to *ras* Tesema Nadew, who was governor general and board member of the Bank of Abyssinia and who later acted as prime minister.[22] The main problem of this document was the difficulty in finding quantifiable evidence for the various components of the property. Some forms of property rights were stated in terms of the names of localities while others had units of measurement such as *gasha* land.

As a whole, the document consisted of two major categories of property divided on the basis of the legal characteristic (the type of acquisition and

[22] The full title of the document is *Yä Ras Tesema Nuzazé*, manuscript no. 1639. IES. Addis Ababa.

transmission) of ownership. The first category can be called the family estate and it consisted of both indivisible and divisible property acquired by inheritance, purchase and royal favour. The second category referred to that part of the income derived from holding title and government office. The family estate consisted of various elements such as land, houses in towns, and liquid assets such as money deposited at the house or in the bank. It seemed that the larger component of the aristocratic patrimony consisted of estates acquired by means of royal grant (such as *gebzena* and *mälkägna*) and by holding government offices (such as *madäriya* land). The bulk of the revenue came from the *gebzena* and *mälkägna* lands, which they literally owned. It should be noted that given the prevailing forms of land ownership, to found churches was the safest and most predictable way of keeping aristocratic property. The aristocracy also collected direct and indirect taxes by possession of government offices. They also derived income from their engagement in business activities.

Land was not the only source of income for the aristocracy of the period. The expansion of trade and development of towns presented an opportunity for alternative forms of investment. One area of interest was investment in urban land and housing and, since sale of land to foreigners was prohibited, the aristocracy benefited by renting out land to foreigners.[23] Some bought stores in Addis Ababa, and others like *ras* Hailu of Gojjam, in defiance of aristocratic attitudes, went as far as setting up a cinema, and a European type hotel with a night club.[24] Aristocratic investment was made not in the development of the productive sector, but rather in the service sector.

The aristocracy were also engaged in lending out money, particularly to those who could repay and had good guarantors. Menelik himself loaned substantial amounts of money to various lords, not only to help them build large and expensive houses in Addis Ababa, but also, perhaps, to enable them to carry on trade if they felt so inclined. In 1905, MacGillivray reported that the King had about £45,000 out in loans, but his *rases* also lent sizeable amounts.[25]

The aristocracy acted as silent partners in trade or commercial engagement by furnishing capital to merchants, by giving protection, and by procuring privileges and monopolies from the King. Menelik was heavily involved in the import and export trade by lending money to foreign companies. For example, he either had to lend G.M. Mohammedally & Co. nearly two million pounds sterling prior to 1901 or become a sleeping partner.[26] In regions where there were a great number of custom tolls, merchants were working together with princes to procure special privileges of tax exemption. Long distant merchants

[23] See Scehaefer, C.G.H. (1990), p. 250.
[24] Quoted in ibid., p. 289.
[25] See FO 401/8, p. 51. see also Garretson, P.P. (1974), p. 239.
[26] Quoted in Scehaefer, C.G.H. (1990), p. 289, see also FO 401/8, p. 51.

who dominated the activities of the important trade centers of Gojjam, where import and export took place, were given a letter of exemption or written permits addressed to the tax collector at the custom post. The permit clearly stated the name of the *nägadras*, the number of loaded mules and asses, the type of commodities, the place of destination, and the date the *nägadras* left.[27]

Another new element in the economic history of the aristocracy was their holding of shares and joint ventures in commercial, financial, manufacturing and mining concerns. The Bank of Abyssinia had sold shares in London, Paris, New York, Rome, Vienna, Cairo and Addis Ababa. Out of the 100,000 shares of stock, about 6,180 were owned by Ethiopian aristocrats. It was probable that the aristocrats also had small shares in the railway company, which had sold a total of 34,700 shares. The King held the largest number of shares in mining companies.

Beginning with the period under discussion, the acquisition and ownership of all alternative investments (rural land, urban real estate, share holding, credit giving) became constant features of the aristocratic economic history. The question is what role did the aristocracy play in economic development? This is not a simple question to answer and requires, above all, an examination of the management system of aristocratic patrimony. Available fragments of documents gave the impression that the aristocracy did not manage their property directly to reinvest in land for the purpose of increasing their income. For instance, for whatever valid reason one could come up with (such as market outlet), the extensive rural land held by royal favour was unexploited. It was not until the late 1920s that they even engaged in commericalized agriculture such as coffee plantations to increase their "land income".

Instead of reinvesting and improving agriculture for more revenue, they tried to diversify the sources of their revenue by taking advantage of their position. Engagement in business activity was one example. It is difficult to tell whether the aristocracy profited more from state revenue or from business engagement. It could be concluded that aristocratic power and status were based on holding government office and titles rather than building economic strength via direct management of property, exploitation of wage labour, reinvestment in agriculture, engagement in trade, etc. During the period under discussion, consumption (holding of great and regular banquets) and military build-up were the guiding purposes of aristocratic economic behaviour.

Aristocratic investment was not made in the productive sectors of the economy. One aspect of investment was in urban land and housing. Their engagement in foreign trade did not encourage export of proto-industrial products (wool and textile) or commercial agricultural products (such as plantations and cattle farms), or provision of raw materials for manufacturing of, say, cloth.

[27] See Abdusamad H. Ahmad (1980), pp. 46f.

This can be evidenced by looking at the items and structure of export trade. Throughout the nineteenth century, the commodities were items like civet, gold, coffee and ivory from the south and southwest, and *amolé* from Tigray. By about 1910 the products of Gojjam (like hides and skins, honey and wax, butter, and pepper) were highly demanded in Asmara and much later in Metema. By 1918, as a result of the completion of the Addis Ababa-Djibouti railway, these commodities were demanded by foreign companies which were beginning to station their agents in Addis Ababa. From this time on, the trade in these commodities continued to boom.[28] Even if there was a change in the structure of the export products, the trade items were not dominated by exports of agricultural products or finished products which required intensive capital and labour.

8.3. Social Critics and Development Ideas

The discussion in the above two sections and in previous chapters suggests that the orientation of economic dynamics was moving rapidly to increase the revenue capacity of the state and create diversification in the aristocratic sources of revenue. Expansion of trade, development of towns, and increasing the aristocratic patrimony did not bring change in the structure and output of production. Like peasant agriculture earlier, the new dynamics operated within the limits of the structure outlined by the interest of the aristocracy and the objectives of the state. Government involvement in the economy and its activism was aimed at increasing the revenue potential and logistic capacity of the state, and not the productive capacity of the economy. Intentionally or not, government motives could have been a catalyst for economic development if other conditions, such as the private economy had strongly prevailed. In a country where the development of the merchant class was structurally suppressed, the aristocracy happened to be an alternative historical force of development. However, the aristocracy could not be an agent of change, as the class was more interested in the tradition of keeping military power and of founding of private or corporate churches[29] than in improving and increasing the strength of its economy. Peasants could not improve their condition through the process of primary accumulation and commercalization owing to the structural limitations on agriculture. Instead their position now became tougher because they had shouldered the weight of the fiscal military state.

The contrasting discrepancy between the orientation of the dynamics on the one hand and the continued poor economic reality of the population on the other, did not escape the attention and understanding of the contemporary in-

[28] Ibid., p. 46.
[29] See the sections 4.2.2. and 4.2.3 above.

telligentsia and social critics. One among them was Afewerk Gebre Iyesus (1867–1946) who had been to Italy and who was an author of several articles and novels. In his book *Guide da Voyageur*, published in 1908, he criticised the military nobility (excluding the King) for using various mechanisms to extract the surplus from the people in order to fatten themselves and live idly. To him, soldiers knew nothing other than plundering and harassing peasants and leading a parasitic life. It was no wonder, therefore, that peasants abandoned their farms, and that some joined the army not out of pleasure but to escape being plundered and tortured.[30]

Of all the social critics and intellectuals of the period, Gebre Hiwot Baykadagn (1885–1918) stands as the first among class thinkers. He explained and criticised the system, not on the basis of moral grounds, but on a corpus of economic doctrines, which can be summed up as the theory of "non equivalent exchange".[31] For the first time, the economy of the country and the reforms of Menelik were examined based on the theory of labour-value which consequently led to a conclusion promulgating a systematic formulation of development strategy. During the short period of his life, he lived twelve years in Europe (mostly in Germany), and it must be assumed that he had acquainted himself with the works of Ricardo and Karl Marx, among others.

In 1912 he published an article titled "Emperor Meneilk and Ethiopia". After a brief survey of Ethiopian history and comparing its economy with adjacent colonial countries, the author suggested a structural reform of the state and economy: separation of the private income of the King and the revenue of the government, salary payment in lieu of tax and land allocation, separation of the civil and military administration, fixed tax payment assessed on one's property, population registration, commutation to money payment, expansion of schools and standardization of the written and spoken language, drawing up of a new constitution, training and disciplining the army, currency reform, abolishing the numerous internal custom tolls, central supervision of provinces, and freedom of religious worship.[32]

[30] See Afewerk Gebre Iyesus (1908), pp. 212–2179.

[31] Here, this term is used consciously to avoid confusion around the different meanings implied by the concept "unequal exchange", as used by dependency theory. The concept of "non equivalent exchange" presupposes the Marxian labour-value theory "which defines the center of price formation as being directly or indirectly related to the socially necessary amount of abstract human labour needed to reproduce a commodity, which in principle can be measured in labour time, i.e., independently of a given prices". For further clarity see Szentes, Tamás (1979), "A Brief Survey on the Theories of International Trade", in *Studies on Developing Countries. No. 102.* Budapest. pp. 45–48. There is an arguement which upholds that trade alone is not the means for the occurrence of unequal exchange between different pre-capitalist societies. For unequal exchange to take place, there must be some form of surplus appropriation by economic means. See Nováky, G. (1990), *Handelskompanier och kompanihandel. Svenska Afrikakompaniet 1649–1663. En studie i feodal handel.* Uppsala.

[32] See Gebre Hiwot Baykadagn (1910), *Emperor Menelik and Ethiopia*, Manuscript no. 2224. IES. Addis Ababa.

In his second work, titled "Government and Public Administration"[33] and published in 1919, Gebre Hiwot Baykadagn presented his reform ideas coherently in terms of development strategy and concrete economic policy which he arrived at after critical analysis of the reforms of Menelik and the economic level of the country. For his analysis, Gebre Hiwot Baykadagn took the theory of labour and value, assumed price as the measure of value, and considered labour power, technology, transaction costs, and labour supply as determinants of values and prices.[34]

Based on formulation of such an economic theory, he analysed in separate chapters the role and effects of Menelik's reforms concerning the Bank of Abyssinia, the introduction of currency, and the construction of the railway.[35] He emphasized that even though such reforms were necessary[36], their intention was to facilitate foreign trade. As discussed in chapter seven above, fiscal considerations were the motive behind these reforms, along with the fact that the government took no concerted measures to protect the economy from the effects of international trade.

In this respect, Gebre Hiwot Baykadagn sounds like the mercantilists of Europe who advocated the reduction of import by what is today called a policy of import substitution.[37] Like them, he advocated restriction on import consumption goods through a higher rate of tax and encouraging import of capital goods by lowering the tax rate and by industrialization.[38]

Non-equivalent exchange was disadvantageous to the peasants in Ethiopia. "Since their needs are brought from afar (or since what they need for themselves was not produced nearby), the effort needed to buy the goods will have to increase eight times. Since very little of what they get from their work is left for themselves they will be burdened with hardship. If the government bought all the goods it needed from workers in the rural areas, the tax which the peasant pay will have been returned for him. However, things, have not been like this".[39]

Gebre Hiwot Baykadagn put the peasantry at the center of his development strategy and pointed to a number of policy measures with the objective of

[33] See Gebre Hiwot Baykadagn (1919), *Mängest ena Yähizb Astädader*, IES. The book is translated into the English language by Tenkir Bonger and it is titled as Gabrahiwot Baykadagn, *The Political Economy of Ethiopia c 1910*. London. It should be noted that this title is the translator's interpretation of the book, not the original title of the author. With such reservations, the quotation sited in following paragraphs are adopted from the translated work.

[34] See the translator note in Gabrahiwot Baykadagn, *The Political Economy of Ethiopia c 1910*, pp. xif

[35] See ibid., Chapters Six to Fourteen.

[36] See, for instance, ibid., p. 37

[37] Regardless of the period in which it was applied, there was one criteria of mercantilist economic policy. The objective of the mercantilist was always development from an agrarian base to an industrial and commercial power, coupled with the attempt to secure a bigger share in the profits of international commerce for one's own citizens, see Klaveren, J. (1969), p. 142.

[38] Gabrahiwot Baykadagn, *The Political Economy of Ethiopia c 1910*, pp. 57–59.

[39] Ibid., p. 61.

creating a prosperous peasant whose demand and exchange could promote domestic industrialisation. He suggested that the first task in this direction be the distribution of land to peasants.[40] He argued that monopolization of land by a few people, and cultivation of land by tenants could not encourage production, since tenants did not improve the land as it was not theirs.[41] He also suggested abolishing conditions attached to private ownership of land and advocated the selling of land. Probably Gebre Hiwot Baykadagn had in mind the communal ownership of the *rist* system and the conditional private ownership of the *Gäbar Madäriya* system. He might have envisaged that security and protection for small property rights would encourage the process of primary accumulation and differentiation among the peasantry. Gebre Hiwot Baykadagn also suggested introducing a light direct taxation system, facilities for education, and credit as part of creating a prosperous peasant class.

Gebre Hiwot Baykadagn identified the revenue interest of the state with the development of the rest of society. He stressed the interrelationship between the needs of the state and the economic ability to support those and other needs. He advocated refashioning the *Gäbar Madäriya* fiscal system[42] and the reform polices of Menelik in a way that would stimulate the development of the peasant economy.

Gebre Hiwot Baykadagn's idea of development was further propagated by Deresa Amente, another intellectual of the 1920s. If not advocating the same line, there were other intellectuals who discussed the plight of the peasants and urged further reforms. Critics like Asnbe Hailu, Hirry Welde Selassie, and Takele Wolde Hawriyat also discussed reform ideas by contributing articles to the *Brehanena Selam* newspaper.[43] At this time Japan became a model for the kind of transformation to be adopted in Ethiopia, a point of view completely divergent from the ideas of Gebre Hiwot Bykedagn. It was at various levels of understanding and views of development, that the intellectuals were working with the aristocracy. This could be one of the reasons why their ideas could not produce a dramatic effect in the King's reform plans. However, their ideas had influenced ("enlightened"), those aristocrats such as *ras* Teferi, who supported the expansion of education and tax reforms out of their concern for efficient management of aristocratic patrimony and efficient administration of revenue.[44] This was the background for the demilitarization of the Ethiopian society and the bureaucratization process during the time of Haile Selassie.

[40] Ibid., p. 33.

[41] Ibid. p. 57.

[42] Ibid., Chapter Seven.

[43] See *Brehanena Selam* news paper, july 1926, july 1928, and febrary, 1931.

[44] See *Chärchär Dänb*, Manuscript no. 734, IES, Addis Ababa; Haile Selassie (1965 E.C.). The best detailed document on the management of aristocratic patrimony and attempts at an efficient administration of revenue is the 500 page document titled as *yä-Luel Ras Kassa Hailu Astädader Dänb*.

Part VI
Conclusion

The First Phase of Ethiopian Absolutism: 1855–1913

The nature and essence of the period under discussion was marked more by rapid transformation than by fixed and settled structure. Changes, rather than continuity, were the norms. Attempts were made to identify these changes as they unfolded in state and society and to explain why and how they occurred in the way they did. The key arguments, methods and conclusions were discussed in the theoretical sections and at the beginning and end of each chapter. At this point the author briefly surveys the study's premises, approaches and major findings, contrasting them with other societies under similar conditions.

The basic idea in the mode of analysis used in this work can be summed up as follows. There were changes and developments in the mode of military organization and techniques of warfare as a consequence of the internal population migration and settlement which took place in most parts of present Ethiopia since the second decade of the sixteenth century. The new military needs and capacity brought about the developments of two new types of fiscal systems which coexisted and operated along with the old one. The fiscal systems are here called triangular fiscal system consisting of subsystems called the *Rist Gult* system, the *Amisho Rim* system and the *Gäbar Madäriya* system. These three had their own particular properties and operated concurrently as the logistic basis of the regional aristocratic power. One of the subsystems, the *Gäbar Madäriya* system, had all the capacity to meet military needs and accommodate the interests of the aristocracy. This system developed into the fiscal military system country-wide as new opportunities and pressures appeared during the second half of the nineteenth century. The formation of the capitalist world economy and the international state system were qualitatively new phenomena which begun to affect the historical development in the Horn of Africa.

The essence, the structural properties and the orientation of the dynamics of historical changes since the making of the fiscal military state and society have been identified and interpreted as Ethiopian absolutism. Viewed both from theoretical and empirical standpoints, this historical period had two orderly stages, namely the phase of the fiscal military state (which lasted from 1855–1913), and the phase of enlightened absolutism (which covered mainly the reign of Haile Selassie). This work was limited to the first phase of absolutism, which was defined and explained through the construction of a resource system model of an absolutist state.

The historical category and the general theory of absolutism was used to identify and explain the essence of change within Ethiopia at a particular historical phase. The different possibilities for interpreting absolutism and its direct relevance to the observable empirical evidence were commented upon in the theoretical sections. Some authors defined absolutism in terms of actions and events from an above or a below perspective. Some defined absolutism structurally by analysing relations and rules that were drawn out over centuries and could not thus be reducible to individuals. Whatever the existing differences, historically, absolutism has never been defined from a geographical context and on the basis of cultural similarity or dissimilarity (i.e., ethnicity, religion, locality, linguistic affiliation, dress, housing and life style). Scholars of any perspective define absolutism at the level of knowledge and theory. They differ on the theoretical knowledge (nature of the objects of inquiry) and on methodology (manner of explaining the practice).

In the present work, absolutism was interpreted as an ephemeral historical phenomenon structurally linked to the social transformation belonging to the last stage of feudalism. As a theory of interpretation, it dealt with three *necessary* and changing *conditions* comprised of *the feudal mode of production*, *an international state system* and *the world economy*. Describing the necessary conditions told only *why* the absolutist state was expected, not *how* it actually occurred. In this study the mode of links among the necessary conditions was used as theory to explain the coming and existence of an absolutist state. A resource system model was constructed to show the mechanisms working towards the making of an absolutist state and to analyse the dynamics of a state and society in transformation. Absolutism is thus used not as an empirical category but as a theoretical model explaining a transitional period. Accordingly, absolutism can take place anywhere and anytime so long as those necessary and changing conditions (historical space-and-time or events) are fulfilled, and the resource system model defining it could explain observable empirical evidence.

In Ethiopia the aristocracy had their own independent traditional base anchored regionally, and used both ideological and military means for extraction of surplus. They used the church as an ideological shell for the smooth and continued transfer of resources. What was specific to Ethiopia was that the church itself served as one form and source of aristocratic land ownership. The church was not only part of society's control system, but also part of the social distribution of the resources. Its function was very much affected by and dependent on changes in the distribution of social surplus. In the final analysis, the underlying mechanism of resource extraction, therefore, lay with the military means. In fact, those mechanisms (such as confiscation of property, dismissal and appointment to an ecclesiastical and military office) were enforced by military means. In the Ethiopian context, campaigns were typically non-economic forms of surplus extraction.

Since the crisis of the sixteenth century, court and provincial governorships were in the process of being militarized. There were changes in the mode of military organization and techniques of warfare. These changes and the consequent increase in military capacity led either to dependency on the peasants and local lords, or was achieved at their expense by way of land and office confiscation. There was no capacity to increase and diversify sources of aristocratic revenue. The peasant economy had reached its peak of dynamism and could not go beyond that level. Trade and manufacturing were underdeveloped and could not expand to give more yield. Growing needs for resources in an economy of scarcity, and in a society hit by periodic environmental crises led to constant violence, rebellion, political instability and poverty. Aristocrats never stopped increasing their patrimony and military strength. Finally, this brought change in the reorganization of the fiscal system, particularly in central regions which were highly affected by the synthesis of population migration and settlement. By the beginning of the eighteenth century, the *Gäbar Madäriya* system emerged in these regions based on the principle of private ownership rights in land, individualized registration, payment of land tax based on the size of one's holding, freedom of labour contract and tenancy arrangements, cadastral survey, administration of revenue by royal officials, and a revenue sharing system based on centrally laid dawn principles and state ends. The *Gäbar Madäriya* system harmonized the acquisition and distribution of resources and the mode of military organization, techniques and frequency of warfare which came as consequences of the crisis of the sixteenth century.[1]

The principles and properties of the *Gäbar Madäriya* system developed at country-wide concurrently with the formation of the European colonialism on the Horn of Africa during the second half of the nineteenth century. This new phenomenon of colonialism presented a challenge and an opportunity for the speedy development of the internal conditions and process. For the first time Kings and princes feared losing territory to an external enemy that had a modern army. Also, they were presented with opportunities of diplomatic channels and development of international trade that could be exploited to defend and promote aristocratic interests.

From 1855 onwards, successive Kings had undertaken administrative and

[1] The peasant economy supporting a great number of clergy and soldiers, the kind of aristocratic patrimony and logistic system of the state, in short the dynamics explained under the concept of the triangular fiscal system make Ethiopia different from most precolonial African states. Trade, particularly long distance trade, is considered as the economic base of precolonial African states, and the rise and decline of states is associated with the rise and decline of trade. On the trade thesis and the formation of states in precolonial Africa, see among others, Salim, A. I. ed., (1984), *State Formation in Eastern Africa*. London.

different tax-technical measures to increase government revenue and the logistic capacity of the state. The major source of government revenue was from agriculture and a share was contributed by ordinary and extraordinary land tax. With the coming of colonialism on the Horn of Africa there came a process of state integration with the capitalist world economy. Consequently, the revenue from international trade in the form of import and export duty increased, particularly during the reign of Menelik. An increase in international trade with Europe led to qualitative development of internal reforms by way of introducing new transaction currency, banking and transportation facilities, and privileged monopolies.

Reforms followed the line of aristocratic interests in wealth and government needs for revenue. The magnitude and effect of these internal reforms can be understood readily when compared and contrasted with the patterns and the various processes of the colonization of Africa. The 'secret' of Ethiopian independence cannot be answered only through an account on the diplomatic skill of the Kings and warrior tradition of its people. The survival of Ethiopian independence owes much to the types and nature of internal reforms actively implemented by Kings Tewodros (1855–1868), Yohannes (1872–1889), and Menelik (1889–1913). These Kings did not obtain credit from international financial institutions, nor subsidy from friendly states to finance internal reforms.[2] For instance, the development of the physical infrastructure during the time of Menelik was financed by internally generated revenues. In contrast, the rulers of Egypt turned to loans from foreign merchants and countries to finance modernization of the military and construction of infrastructure for the export economy. The mounting debt led to colonization of Egypt. West Africa was colonized as the consequence of fierce rivalries of mercantile classes who could petition for European involvement. In Ethiopia import and export trade was strictly controlled by the state, and the driving motive behind foreign trade and concession was the fiscal interest of the state. Merchants were finacially and politically dependent on princes and Kings. Mining capital which became the source of colonization of southern Africa, obtained concessions on a limited scale, particularly for the type of minerals for which the Ethiopian government sought to procure more revenue such as on the extraction of gold. Even in such a case there was a monopoly by the King. East Africa was colonized not as a result of existing trade links and mining capital, but through intensified inter-European rivalries. In the case of Ethiopia, pre-emptive colonization by means of force was rebuked time and again owing to increased capacity in the logistic system of the state.[3]

[2] These opportunities were present to the absolutist states of Europe; see Webber, C. and Wildavsky. A. (1986), pp. 250–260.

[3] For the various processes and patterns of colonization in Africa, see Zeleza, T. (1993), pp. 343–422.

Government revenue was spent largely on military needs and demands. The focus of government expenditure was on strengthening the main field force both in number and armaments. Import of fire arms changed the composition of the army. First, it led to the formation of artillery corps and facilitated the formation of garrison towns; this led to the decline in the importance and size of cavalry.

There was a similarity in the objectives of government expenditure between Europe and Ethiopia, but there was a difference in the items and priorities. Expenses for war debt was big in Europe and this was related to the source of the revenue. In Ethiopia there was no expenditure for war debt. European absolutist states were maritime powers and had expenditures for this purpose, which was not the case in Ethiopia. The preference in policy objectives and reforms also came as a result of differences in the mode of military organization. In Ethiopia the court was organized along regimental lines which was intended for service in both peace and war times.[4] Court troops were remunerated by allocating land tax and grant of state land in lieu of salary. In Europe, there was a class of mercenaries who were paid in cash and this required the search for and accumulation of silver and gold.

Whatever the methods of remuneration and the type of reforms chosen, the intent of the aristocrats' measures, both in Europe and in Ethiopia, was strengthening of their position and ensuring their survival in a new situation. In Ethiopia, the aristocracy benefited from government expenditures by holding military offices and titles. The larger component of the aristocratic patrimony consisted of estates acquired by means of royal grant and by holding of government offices. Following tradition, the founding of churches was the safest and most predictable way of keeping aristocratic property. The aristocracy had also derived an income from their engagement in business activities. However, the aristocracy did not manage their property directly to reinvest in land for the purpose of increasing their income. Aristocratic investment was not made for productive purposes and sectors of the economy. Investment in urban land and housing, holding of great and regular banquets, and military build-up were the guiding principles of the aristocratic economic behaviour. The aristocracy could not, thus, play a significant role in economic development.

Trade had increased in scope and organization but its contribution was not realized in promotion of economic development. Most factors which limited the capacity to expand were structural, such as the military provisioning sys-

[4] There is a difference in the principle of organization of the central governments of Ethiopia and European absolutist states. In some absolutist states of European countries such as Sweden, Russia and Prussia, the central government was organized on collegial principle. Government was divided into blocks of activities such as mining, manufacturing, commerce, municipal administration, etc. Each college could make appointments and collect funds. On the organization of the central government of the fiscal military state of Ethiopia see sections 3.5., 3.6.2., 4.2.1., 6.1. and Chapter Five above.

tem, forms of land tax allocation and collection, and organizational forms of manufacturing, which in one way or other were related to the ruling classes' economic philosophy (i.e., self-reliance).

During the period under discussion, economic policy was primarily in the hands of the central government. Kings were behind the making of economic policy and the giving out of special privileges.[5] Considering the fragmented power of the princes, centralization of economic policy was an achievement in itself. However, there was no developed and organized class of private owners such as merchants and manufacturers which could benefit from the reforms. Merchants and artisans were not a class in themselves. Although no one as yet knows about their demography, they were not economically organized, and their life experience was identified with the community and region in which they lived. As such, they lacked the capacity to act as an independent group. They were a product of the fiscal system, and for their development they were dependent on the political system.[6]

In the absence of alternative forces, the aristocracy happened to be the historical driving force in economic development. But aristocratic interests and government objectives focused on military build up. The consequent fiscal and economic reforms could not change the structural problems of economic development. For the fiscal military state, the strategy was to maximize revenue and expenditure. The "safety and growth" of the state was the objective of the fiscal policy and resources for the state were created regardless of local interests and economic consequences. Some Ethiopian intellectuals criticised the system as reactionary. Some of them were realists; they presented a development strategy aimed at creating a prosperous peasant class whose demand and exchange would promote domestic industralization.

The centralization and consolidation of power and the resource system during the second half of the nineteenth century gave a particular characteristic to the type of social system. In this study this type of social system is labelled as the fiscal military system, a specific socio-economic system belonging to the last stage of Ethiopian feudalism. The case of the fiscal military system of Ethiopia illustrated that the first phase of absolutism was not a social type that would create avenues for capitalist development. In Ethiopia as well as in Europe, the system strengthened the military and economic wealth of the aristocracy; one difference being that in Europe, there was a development of merchant capital. In both cases, however, this type of dynamic change did not lead to the development of capitalism, primarily because the interests and objec-

[5] The wide range of issues discussed under the question of dynamism of the economy was one factor which distinguished the Ethiopian society of the period from other precolonial African countries.

[6] In Europe, craftsmen were organized through the guild system, and merchants had a professional organization and municipalities to defend their interest. These types of institutions were absent in Ethiopia.

tives of the fiscal military state were intended to promote the logistic system of war.

Indeed, there was a difference in the challenges and opportunities presented to the aristocrats in Ethiopia. It was a period of monopoly capitalism, a system which had a capacity to conquer markets, create dependency, and forcefully integrate into the market system. European aristocrats and merchant capitalists did not face the same pressure and challenge. Yet there was no orientation to capitalist development, as can be seen by the cases of Spain and France. In fact the whole period of the first phase of European absolutism is summed up as the age of crisis, not of economic growth.[7]

Nevertheless, the first stage of absolutism had a role in the development of an exchange economy. Centralization of power was used for the promotion of the interests of merchant capitalism such as in the development and securing of private property. Its war characteristic represented a form of market for the production and sale of weapons and provision. Its financial interest, particularly the need for loans, led to the introduction of technical changes in the financial system. The dynamics were constrained structurally by the objectives of the state and the interests of the aristocracy. The developments did not necessarily lead to capitalism. Capitalism is here defined in terms of the domination of the production process (labour power and means of production) by capital, and physical transformation of the means of production, and new sets of commodities. Transition to capitalism belonged to the second stage of absolutism, namely, the period of enlightened absolutism, which developed in the second half of the eighteenth century.[8] In Ethiopia the enlightened absolutist state was crystalized during the reign of Haile Selassie I.[9]

[7] Vries, J. D. (1976). Not only the title of the book but also the period of the crisis reflects the very essence of the fiscal military state.

[8] For further explanation see the model outline of Enlightened Absolutist state, see the theoretical section 2.3 in Part I.

[9] See section 3.1. in Part I.

Glossary

Adi	villages, localities.
Alga	throne, seat of government; core of regional aristocratic rule.
Aläqa	chief; campaign commander; head of *däbr* church.
Amisho-Märet	farm lands from which one-fifth of the produce is paid to a soldier or a clergy.
Amisho Rim system	one of the three fiscal subsystems which was formed after the crisis of the sixteenth century; see table one.
Asrat	tithe, extraordinary land tax paid in the form of one-tenth of the harvest.
Azazh	superintendent of the palace, responsible also for packing provision for the court troops.
Balabat	local hereditary chiefs ; notable; local land lord.
Bétä Ahegurat or *Bétä gebr*	regions allocated as sources of court revenue and the military during the period of the autocratic state, 1150–1540.
Bét Lij	literally, "Children of the House"; a unit made of young men drawn from the nobility and who grew up in the court; household troops of provincial governors.
Balä Rist	a peasant who owned a hereditary farm land by birth or descent right.
Balä Rist Zämach	a *Balä Rist* recruited to participate in a campaign in return for land-tax exemption.
Bäjirond	treasure.
Ch´an	a measure of grain equivalent to 30 *quna* in Shewa. A *quna* varies from region to region and from period to period but it is valued here as weighing 5 kgs. A *dawula* holds 20 *quna*, ca. 100 kgs. *Madega* is a medium sized jar holding between 8 and 10 *quna*.

Ch´ifra	troops assigned to the various departments of the palace or provincial governors; retainer and soldiers; court department troops.
Ch´ika Shum	a local land tax administrator (collector).
Ch´äwa	territorial regiments belonging to the autocratic state 1150–1540; in the *Amisho Rim* system, chäwa were campaign troops
Dawula	a leather bag measured to carry ca. 100 kilograms
Däjazmach	"Commander of the rear"; military title given to provincial governors who were entitled to possess private *ch´ifra*; commanders of *qutr Tor.*
Frida	an ox not used for farming but selected and fattened for meat; fatten cattle for slaughter; indirect tax on meat.
Färäsägna	cavalry.
Fäsäs	an extraordinary land tax levied for royal troops imposed on a district.
Gana Gäb	that part of ordinary land tax allocated to the royal kitchen in the form of *hudad* cultivation and honey payment.
Gasha land	gasha means shield; in the Amisho Rim system, gasha land was a state land allocated to campaign soldiers and commanders, and it consisted of an average of eight farm lands; in the Gebar Madäriya system it referred to a unit of land measured with a rope called *qälad* usually about 42 hectors.
Gäbar	owner-cultivator; a peasant who had the obligation to pay ordinary land tax in the form of honey and labour, in addition to the preparation of *Senq*-provision for a soldier, a governor or a king, and payment of surtaxes.
Gäbar Madäriya system	one of the three fiscal subsystems formed after the crisis of the sixteenth century; it emerged from 1696 and developed into the fiscal military system in the second half of the nineteenth century; see table one.
Gebr	an ordinary annual land tax.
Gendäbäl	earlier it was holder of state land; later it changed to indicate the status of auxiliary troops responsible for the transport of military equipment and utensils.
Gezat	a regional territorial administrative unit under a governor general (*shaläqa*).

Grazmach	"commander of the left wing", a title given to local governors.
Gult	jurisdictional and beneficial right to ordinary land tax granted to churches; after the crisis of the sixteenth century it became a private method of ordinary land tax administration by hereditary kinship families; grant of right to use *Gebr* institutions and individuals.
Gultägna	administrator of Gult; local hereditary land tax administrator and commander of campaign soldiers levied by the Rist Gult system.
Hagär Bägé	literally meaning "governorship in my hands"; abolishing of private method of ordinary land tax administration.
Hudad	selected land worked by owner cultivators and tenants; this land was assigned for the supply of the palace and government officials (*shaläqa* and *mälkägna*).
Kätäma	a garrison town.
Lolé	retainers.
Mad Bét	literally meaning kitchen, often used to refer to selected regions whose tax and land was allocated for the use of the palace and governors; revenue budget allocated for the court and regional governor generals, it included various sources such as ordinary land tax (*gana gäb*), fixed land tax from provinces (*qurt gäbar* regions), reserved crown lands such as *wärägänu*.
Madäriya land	state land; a temporary piece of land grant made to an individual in return for active military service.
Mesläné	literally meaning "like myself"; an economic intendant of the king or provincial governor (royal intendant) responsible for royal tax districts; a district governor responsible for administration of justices and collection of tax;
Milmil	lands whose tax obligation was light. It was often given to those military nobility who gave long service to the government.
Mähal Säfari	central troops, palace troops.
Mälkägna	a subdistrict governor responsible for the administration of *Gäbar* lands, and for the collection of tax and supervision of state land; a local government tax administrator; a subdistrict official.

Mäkwanent	court military officials.
Mängest Mätäkiya	state land used to "plant or uproot" soldiers.
Näftägna	riflemen, literally, musketeer.
Nägadras	chief of merchants, administrator of indirect taxes.
Nägarit	military territorial administrative units; judicially independent regional centers of power responsible for the government and administration of a territory.
Quna	a woven basket holding five kilograms of grain.
Qurt Gebr	regions which were allowed to pay a fixed annual tax revenue to the palace.
Qutr Gäbar	owner cultivators whose land was not measured after *qälad*; soldiers were given the right to collect ordinary land tax from these owner cultivators, and the number of *qutr gäbar* given to a soldier depended on his rank.
Qutr Tor	literally, numbered soldiers; provincial troops assigned by and answerable to the king's court; central government troops stationed in the provinces.
Qälad	a rope used for the measurement of land, cadastral survey.
Qäläb	ration, payment in-kind.
Qägnazmach	"commander of the right wing", a title given to local governor.
Ras	literally "head"; title given to a governor-general of a region.
Rim	a beneficial title to state land allocated for the maintenance of church services and functions.
Rist Gult system	one of the three fiscal subsystems; it was formed since 1150 and developed as part of a subsystems after the crisis of the sixteenth century; see table one.
Senq	provision prepared by a *gäbar* for a military campaign or for a journey.
Semon	land assigned for the clergy.
Siso	literally meaning one-third; land left to the local chief or descent community upon state confiscation or measurement of land.
Shaläqa	literally meaning "commander of thousand army", a regiment commandant, a provincial governor-general.
Shaläqa Mätäkiya	land assigned for the remuneration of troops recruited by governor generals.

T´imad	a pair of plough oxen; a land ploughed by a pair of oxen.
T´isäna	a tenant.
Ts´ähafé Tezaz	the king's principal secretary.
Täsäri	quartering of royal troops among the country people, extraordinary land tax paid in the form of billeted royal troops.
Wusti Gulti	*gult* of a principal (a king), a territory which was in a direct dependence on the sovereign.
Wäräda Gendäbäl	provincial cavalry consisting local hereditary chiefs and government officials.
Wärägänu	reserved lands for raising and keeping government cattle and mules.
Yä märét aläqa	representative of kinsmen who owned *rist* land, he paid government tax in his name.
Zämach	campaign soldier; peasant soldiers recruited to participate in campaigns in return for tax exemption.
Zämänä Mäsafint	Era of Princes.

APPENDIX A

Estimation of Total Direct Tax Revenue Collected Annually between 1890s–1910s

Notes on Data and Method of Calculation

This appendix deals with the total amount of ordinary and extraordinary land tax collected in the *Gäbar Madäriya* system of central and southern Ethiopia. The figures presented are estimates arrived at by reconstructing raw and separated data used by other writers for different purposes. There are two central issues around which the data and the techniques of calculation revolve: i) Who paid the taxes? and how many payers were there? and ii) how much did they pay? and how much money did the system supposedly collect?

Who paid the taxes?

The central and southern parts of Ethiopia were under the *Gäbar Madäriya* fiscal system. In this system, there was individual registration of land tax payment, and the tax was calculated according to the size of the land or possession of property by the owner-cultivator. In other words, the central government had a direct control over the tax paying individual and knew who was paying and who was exempted. For instance, at the palace of Menelik, there was a document called *baherä mäzegäb* which registered the name of the tax payer, the amount and type of tax paid, the locality from which the tax payer came, and the year of payment.[1] The *baherä mäzegäb* was also a kind of cadastral book which registered types of land owned by the *balabat*, the *gäbar* owner-cultivator, and the state (*mätäkeya mänqäya*).[2] Unfortunately this document is not available to reconstruct the total revenue of the central government.[3]

In the absence of this document, and for that matter any other document of the central treasury that would list receipts and expenses, another method was used to make an estimation of total annual revenue raised by the system. Before discussing the methods of identification of the tax payers and the techniques of calculation, it is important to comment on the nature and accuracy of the data used for constructing the estimations.

[1] See Mahteme Selassie (1962 EC), p. 25.

[2] Ibid., p. 107.

[3] The document is found deposited at Menelik's palace, but access to the archive requires a special permission from the Prime Minister Office.

The total figures used for the *Gäbar Madäriya* system are derived from reprocessed data documented in the book by Mahteme Selassie (*Zekrä Nägär*). The author of the book was a higher court official during the 1940s and he gathered the data from a reliable source materials, presumably from the *baherä mäzegäb* deposited at the palace of Menelik. The nature and purpose of the data used in the book *Zekrä Nägär* are quite different from the ones here. Mahteme Selassie used the data for the purpose of showing the number of tax obligation (paying) lands both in the surveyed and unsurveyed regions. For instance, in the regions surveyed by *qälad* measurement, the data are categorized as *siso*, *gäbar*, *gendäbäl*, *samon*, *mälkägna siso*, *madäriya*. The data therefore included a number of local landlords (*balabat*-chiefs) who had no obligation to pay an ordinary land tax (*gebr*) on the *siso* land they owned as private property. Besides, the different land-tax categories tell more about the principles and functions allocating of ordinary land tax and distributing land, not the actual size of land tax payment. This had to be further qualified with other sources.

One final comment is that, except in a general case, there was no statement of the specific time when the data was collected. For instance, it was stated that land survey and registration started in Shewa in 1894/95, but no date was given for other regions. It is known that in some parts of Wellega, land survey was conducted in 1910. Surely there was a time variation in the data used in the work of Mahteme Selassie. The date of collection seemed to fall in the period ranging from the 1880s to 1910/20.

With such limitations affecting the accuracy of estimation, the discussion now turns to data that would help identify a reasonable estimation of the number of persons who had obligations to pay land tax. The number was sorted out primarily following the basic division of surveyed and unsurveyed regions belonging to the *Gäbar Madäriya* system. Those areas which were surveyed were various districts in the region of Shewa, Arsi, parts of Sidamo, Sibu and Gudru from Wellega, Limu and Konta from Kafa, and Illubabor.

Those districts surveyed by *qälad* are here referred to as *qälad gäbar* and the figures are mentioned in number of *gasha*, a unit of measurement which indicates an actual size of land and soil fertility. One *gasha* equals 44.2 hectares. According to the principle of land measurement each peasant had to get equal *gasha* of land. But this did not mean all of them had an equal size of land. It all depended on the availability of extra units of land in areas which could later be distributed to those who had less. Mahteme Selassie calculated his data with this knowledge and he used codes such as *nu*, *ru*, and *me* letters (Ethiopian alphabet) to refer to half, one-fourth and one-sixth of measured units of land (*gasha*). He rounded up the amounts in the total figures. The codes used by Mahteme Selassie, and the very principle and purpose of land

Table A-1. *The Type of Land Tax Payment Obligations and the Number of Tax Paying Peasants in Regions Measured by qälad*

Types of Obligation and Status of the Land	Regions						
	Shewa	Illubabor	Wellega	Arsi	Kafa	Sidamo	Total
siso	8,629			3,528			12,157
dästa	911			113			1,024
qälad gäbar	25,838[a]	36,816[b]	2,757[d]	5,493[c]	14,684[d]	21,134[d]	106,722
gendäbäl	2,496						2,496
wäräda gendäbäl	413						413
samon	4,030			494			4,524
mängest mätäkiya	13,863			10,266			24,129
shaläqa mätäkiya	2,876						2,876
Other kind of *gebr*	1,397			11			1,408
Extra Found	3,061			3,983			7,044
wärägänu	242						242
hudad	53						53
Expenses Unknown	2,530			2,441			4,971
ch´ibesta	46						46
t´äf	434						434
Total	66,819	36,816	2,757	26,329	14,684	21,134	168,539

Source: Mahteme Selassie (1962 EC), pp. 133–138.
[a] The figure is calculated from the table of Mahteme Selassie listed on pages 133–138. It includes those names of localities supposed to lie in the region of Shewa and those number of *gasha* lands listed on the total column, namely, Farsi 588, Chafu 735, Dgugur 709, Jilena Resi 423, Jibat 2,118, Alaba Dar 853, a total of 5426 *gasha* lands.
[b] This figure is written in the table on page 143 of *Zekre Neger* under the title unsurveyed land, but in brackets the number is stated as indicating areas measured by *qälad.*
[c] The figure included not only that part of Arsi stated in the column but also those *gasha* of land transferred from the region of Sidamo to Arsi and their number was 4,642.
[d] The figure listed in the total coulmn of Mahteme Selassie for the regions of Wellega, Kafa and Sidamo have been considred as number of *qutr gäbar.*

survey (*qälad*), indicate that all figures mentioned in surveyed area are stated in *gasha* units.

For the purpose of estimating the total size of the land tax, the figures mentioned under the categories of *qälad gäbar*, *gendäbäl*, and *mätäkiya-mänqäya* are considered. The others, *siso* and *dästa,* belonged to the *balabat* and made only a nominal payment not related to the size and fertility of the land. *Samon* belonged to the church, and since this was considered as the budget for the church, it is excluded from the total tax levied for central expenses. The other figures are not sufficiently decisive for an estimation, and are thus ignored.

Now to the regions where land was not surveyed by *qälad*. In the region of Shewa, unsurveyed districts included Moret, Bulga, Yifrat, Jiru and Gedem,

Table A-2. *The Type of Land Tax Payment Obligations and the Number of Tax Paying Peasants in Regions where no Land Survey was Conducted*

Regions	*qutr gäbar*	*aqni siso*	*gendäbäl*	*wäräda gendäbäl*	*samon*	*mängest mätäkiya*	*shaläq mätäkiya*	Others	Total
Shewa[a]	20,237	471	–	1	144	767	60	54	21,734
Shewa *rist* areas	18,979	1,460	12,181	340	6,748	162	1	1,059	40,930
Sidamo including Borena	75,108								75,108
Wellega (Abgar)	15,943								15,943
Kafa	48,899								48,899
Gomu Gofa	3,930								3,930
Total	183,096	1,931	12,181	341	6,892	929	61	1,113	206,544

Source: Mahteme Selassie (1962 EC), pp. 139–142, 143.
[a] In this raw the figures are for the provinces and disitricts of Gurage, Wellamo, Wurubare and Dobi.

which Mahteme Selassie called *rist* countries[4], Kembata and Gurage in the southern parts of Shewa. Parts of the region of Sidamo, parts of Harar, the provinces of Kulo, Konta, Gämu and Borana were also unsurveyed.[5] There could be different reasons why land was not surveyed in these regions. In these regions the fixed ordinary land tax payment (*gundo* of honey/or *birr* and three *dawula* grain payment) was not standardized on the basis of a definite land size unit, *gasha*, as in the case of *qälad* surveyed regions. In these regions, when peasants were allocated to the *shaläqa* governor or *mälkägna*, they were counted in number and the tax they paid was assessed by the number of oxen, houses (probably household members) and other properties.[6] In those areas where land was not surveyed the figures show the number of eligible persons who paid tax individually (thus called *qutr gäbar*), not *gasha* lands.

Of the figures, shown important for our discussion are the categories of *qutr gäbar*, *gendäbäl*, *mängest mätäkiya* and *shaläqa mätäkiya*, as in the case of *qälad* regions. It is, therefore, important at this stage to make a total list based on the type of payment and service obligation.

The total figures in the table are presented by types of obligation, and in principle the ordinary land tax paid by each category contained two main parts. The first part was called *fré gebr* and was paid in the form of *gundo* of honey and a certain quantity of grain. The second part was referred to as "labour

[4] Ibid., pp. 139–142.

[5] Gebre Wold Engda Worq (1948 EC), pp. 65, 67, 71; Mahteme Selassie (1962 EC), pp. 124, 126, 161–3.

[6] In the nomad regions such as Adal and Käräyu, the tax was assessed according to the number of cattle and stables, See Mahteme Selassie (1962 E.C.), p. 127; Gebre Wold Engda Worq (1948 EC), p. 19.

Tabel A-3. *Number of Land Tax Paying Units belonging to the gäbar madäriya system presented by Region and Types of Obligation*

Regions	*balabat* Local landlords		*gäbar*, Owner-cultivator			*t'isägna* Tenants		Total
	siso & dästa	*wäräda gendäbäl*	*gäbar gendäbäl*	*qutr gäbar*	*qälad gäbar*	*madäriya*	Clergy Land	
Wollo[a]			1,489	64,244		2,242	7,262	75,237
Shewa[b]	11,483	754	14,677	39,216	25,838	32,536	10,922	135,427
Wellega[c]				15,943	2,757			18,700
Illubabor					36,816			36,816
Kafa[d]				48,899	14,648			63,547
Gomu Gofa[e]				3,930				3,930
Sidamo				75,108	21,134			96,242
Arsi	3,641				7,275	10,266	494	21,676
Harar[f]				70,000				70,000
Bale[g]								
Total	15,124	754	16,166	317,340	108,468	45,045	18,678	521,575

Source: Tables A-1 and A-2 above.

[a] Wollo: The figure for Wollo was taken from the data calculated in the 1927 registration book (see Mahteme Selassie (1962), p. 155.

[b] The figure for Shewa excludes those numbers obtained from areas dominated by *Rist Gult* system, particularly, the district of Menz. According to the calculation based on the tables of Mahteme Selassie, there were about 1,208 *balä rist*, and 5,406 *akafay*. Since these numbers refer to *Rist Gult* areas, they are ignored for the calculation of total land tax revenue in Shewa. Again in Shewa one finds tenants, and their numbers are inferred from the type of contracts: *t'isägna* (9,843), *täguwazh* (4,362), and *erbo afsash* (563), a total of 14,768. The tenant worked for the land owner, and in this case it is assumed that the land owner was state land holder called *balä madäriya*. Even if the government codified laws which regulate tenant-landowner relationship, it was very unlikely that the state registered all tenants working for any-one land lord. It is presumed that in the state register book called *baherä mäzegäb*, it was only those tenants working on government land which were registered, not tenants belonging to private landowners. The total figure 14,768 was thus considered as *madäriya* land belonging to the state. Added to this figure are 53 *hudad* lands which were here considered to fall within the category of *madäriya* lands. Finally, the figure for Shewa also excluded 6,071 numbers registered as unknown and extra expenses.

[c] From the region of Wellega we have no data for the following provinces Leqemt, Qelem, and Beni Shingual. Some of these provinces paid a fixed annual tax to the royal *mad bét*.

[d] From Kafa, there is no data for the province of Jima. In this province land was not surveyed and government soldiers were not given counted *gäbar*. The province was administered by its traditional ruler who agreed to pay a fixed annual land tax to the *mad bét* of the palace.

[e] The region of Gemu Goffa is extensive and the number given in the table is too small for the area. In the book of Gebre Wold Engda Worq, it was stated that there were measured lands and one fertile *gasha* land paid 12 *birr*, see Gebre Wold Engda Worq (1948, EC), p. 71; but we have no figure for the number of *gasha* land in the region.

[f] The data for the region of Harar comes from the total number of *gäbar* counted during the time *däjaz-mach* Teferi was governor of Harar. Around 1910 when Teferi was appointed as governor of the region, he made a count of *gäbar* peasants who could pay tax, and their number was 70,000. See Haile Selassie (1965 EC), p. 21.

[g] No data for the region of Bale.

Note: The number of *madäriya* lands registered in the cadestral book were only those state lands used as *mänqäya* and *mätäkiya*, and in the case of land cultivated by tenants it could be *hudad* lands. There are other types of lands such as *shum shir* and *säqäla* lands which could not be registered. Obviously the large part of unused reserved state lands which were often in the hands of the local administrator and tax collector, (i.e., *mälkägna*) might not have been recorded in the document. What was recorded were mainly lands that had tax obligation.

obligation", which was in essence provision obligation (*senq-ch´agn*). Basically these were the elements which constituted the obligation attached to the land or *gäbar*-peasants. However, there were lands whose obligation was paid only in one form and these lands were called *milmil*.[7] There are no data which show the total number of *milmil* lands, and the total figure above does not include these lands.

How Much was Paid ?

Once the question of who was paying is clarified, the next step is to know how much they paid. Again there is neither a central account nor a local tax pay roll which could tell who paid and how much in relation to the size of land held or property possessed. In such circumstances, it would be helpful to try to identify the amount and kind of payment attached to each of the tax obligation categories mentioned in the tables, namely, *qälad gäbar*, *qutr gäbar*, *gäbar gendäbäl* and *madäriya*. There were regional and local variations in each category, and the details are explained in the book of Gebre Wold Engda Worq. There is no space here to summarize tax obligation payments by regions; instead the following table is constructed as a standared of land tax payment.

In this table and those above, there is detail on division of the land obligation types and payment only for the region of Shewa and Arsi. For instance no number of *gäbar gendäbäl* and *madäriya* lands were given for the regions of Wellega, Kafa and Sidamo, and Illubabor even though these regions were measured by *qälad*. The figures due from the regions are mentioned in the total column table of Mahteme Selassie. Detailed break-downs for other regions were not available in the palace record. Governor generals who had full authority over the regions used to notify the palace only of the total figures of their respective regions, while they kept detailed accounts in the provincial registration book.

Payment of an Extraordinary Land Tax (asrat)

In the *Rist Gult* system, extraordinary land tax was paid in the form of *fäsäs* and *täsäri*. This tax was later replaced by *asrat*, a tithe payment, introduced in Shewa by Menelik in 1894/5. It is not exactly known when it spread to other regions, even though the tax was said to be national and universal. From the documents it was clear that by the beginning of the twentieth century it was paid in most regions.

It was also difficult to know the actual size of tithe payment. Since it was a proportional payment (a tenth part out of the crops produced), it is difficult to know exactly how much was collected each year. The size varied with cultivation and harvest. In a good year of harvest the amount could be high, while it

[7] See Gebre Wold Engda Worq (1948 EC), pp. 25–3, Mahteme Selassie (1962 EC), pp. 115–116

Table A-4. *Amounts and Kinds of Land Tax Payment and Service Obligations of the Gäbar Madäriya System*

Regions	Types and Amounts of Land Tax Payment & Service Obligation											
	qälad gäbar			*qutr gäbar*			*gäbar gendäbäl*			*madäriya*[c]		
	GH	Daw	*birr*	GH	Daw	*birr*	GH	Daw	*birr*	GH	Daw	*birr*
Wollo[a]												
Shewa	1	2.5		1c	3cs	4s		2		1	3	
Wellega		2	7	1	3							
Illibabur[b]			10									
Kafa		1.5	7		3	4						
Gomu Gefa			12		3	4						
Sidamo			18		3	5						
Arsi[b]		3	12		–	–		–		1	3	
Harar					1.4	4						

Source: Gebre Wold Engda Worq (1948 EC), pp. 17–20, and chapter two; for Harar see Mahteme Selassie, (1962 EC), p. 162.

Notes: GH means *gundo* of honey, Daw means *dawula, birr* = MT$.

[a] The region of Wollo is consididred as *qutr gäbar.* Depending on the locality, one full *gäbar* paid four bar of salt (or four cups of honey), and three *dawula* of grian, in addition to labour obligation (Gebre Wold Engda Worq (1948 EC), p. 47–48). Since the total annual land tax of the region is given in the book of Mahteme Selassie (1962 EC), p. 155, there is no need to make any kind of estimation.

[b] According to the documents, in the region of Illubabur and Arsi there was no *qutr gäbar.*

[c] Often one *madäriya* land is one *gasha*, and if fully cultivated it is done by two or three tenants. The share from it depended on the provision of ox, plough, and seeds. The variation meant a lot to the holder of the land and for the cultivator. From the interest of this work, and considering *madäriya* land as central government expense, *madäriya* land could be considered as having similar type and size of payment as the *qälad gasha* land held by a *gäbar.* One *gundo* of honey and three *dawula* of grain payment is taken as a standard for calculation of *madäriya* land.

could be less in bad harvest times. If many lands were left fallow, the size would also decrease. In addition to some natural problems, there was also the problem of measurement. Corrupted tax officials could assess the crop as less which led to a decrease in revenue from the tax.[8]

To calculate an estimation for the total amount of tithe, two of the methods used to find practical solution to the problems of tithe were considered: i) a fixed payment of *dawula* grain based on the quality of the land classified as *läm* and *täf*[9]; and, ii) payment of a fixed amount of tithe on the number of plough oxen (*t´imad*)[10]. The first method belonged to regions measured by *qälad*, and the second method was applied for unsurveyed regions (*qutr gäbar* regions).

[8] For the various kinds of problems associated with the assessment and collection of *asrat* tax see Mahteme Selassie (1962 EC), pp. 332–33.

[9] Mahteme Selassie (1962 EC), p. 333

[10] For the various regions see Gebre Wold Engda Worq (1948 EC), passim.

According to Mahteme Selassie, in *qälad* areas one *gasha* fertile land paid, ten *dawula*, *läm-täf* (average soil fertility) *gasha* paid five *dawula*, and *täf gasha* land paid two *dawula*. In this work the *läm-täf* average number is considered , i.e., three and half *dawula* is considered as the average number for the calculation of *asrat* tax for *qälad gäbar* lands. Holders of *madäriya* land paid *asrat* tax[11], and the same figure is used to calculate the total amount. *Gendäbäl* land holders were basically exempted from the payment of tithe. Feeding of a government mule year-in and year out was expensive, and each *gendäbäl* was given nine *dawula* of grain out of the collected *asrat*.[12]

Wärada gendäbäl (provincial cavalry) and *siso balabat* (local chief) paid *asrat*.[13] Their share of *gasha* land ranged between three and six[14], and in their case three *gasha* was considered an average. Each of the local lords thus paid a total of ten and half *dawula* as tithe.

In *qutr gäbar* regions *asrat* tax was mainly assessed by *t´imad* (number of oxen held by the cultivator). In the region of Illubabor, a *gäbar* paid 30 *quna* (1.5 *dawula*) per pair of oxen[15]; in Gomu Gofa a *gäbar* paid one *dawula* as tithe, and Gebre Wold Engda Worq noted that the taxation in the regions was administered by the directives given from Shewa[16]. It could be possible that the *qutr gäbar* regions in Shewa paid a tithe of one *dawula* each, and this standard was taken for the calculation of *asrat* tax in *qutr gäbar* regions. The total amount of ordinary (*gebr*) and extraordinary (*asrat*) land taxes is shown in table 7 in the main text in section 4.2.2.

[11] Mahteme Selassie (1962 EC), p. 114
[12] Gebre Wold Engda Worq (1948 EC), p. 21–22, Mahteme Selassie (1962 EC), p. 110
[13] Mahteme Selassie (1962 EC), pp. 108, 111
[14] Ibid. p. 108.
[15] Gebre Wold Engda Worq (1948 EC), p. 23
[16] Gebre Wold Engda Worq (1948 EC), p. 71

APPENDIX B

Frequency of Troop Movements and Conflicts, 1855-1913

No	Authority/ Leader	Objectives of Expedition	Date, Duration & Place of Battle	No of Participants	Remarks (death, etc.)	Source
Tewodros 1855–1868						
1	Tewodros	Campaign in Wollo to subdue governors.	July–Oct. 1855, at Läga, Qerqura, Gimba		Fought and defeated both Ali Dega, and Sidaq Danqa, the 7th House of Wollo.	Z, 19–22
2	Tewodros	Campaign to Shewa, to subdue the prince.	Oct 14, 1855– Feb. 1856, at Gib-Washa, Gishe, Bäräkät,		Fought against *Balabat* of various districts and lost many soldiers.	Z, 22–24, TM, cha. 15
3	Tewodros	Campaign to Gojjam.	Feb. 1856–July 1856, through different districts		Lost many troops by epidemic "Näftäna Fängel".	Z, 26
4	Tewodros	From Gojjam to Gonder	July 1856			
5	*Ras* Ingda	Fought against Tädla Gualu.	August 1856			Z, 27
6	Tewodros	Campaign in Wollo.	Nov. 1856, Korebe, Mäqdäla, Gishen, Wadla, Yejju, Dälanta		Chased Amede Bäshir wh fled; fought against Liben.	Z, 29–30
7	Tewodros	Marched to Begemder.	Nov. 1856			Z, 30–31
8	Tewodros	Campaign in Gojjam against bandits.	Dec. 1856–Feb. 1857, Agta, Tälba, Baso			z, 31
9	Tewodros	Quartering of soldiers: *täsäri.*	Feb 1857		This was done for the first time.	Z, 32
10	Tewodros	Campaign in Wag, Wadla and Wollo	March–April 1857		Against governors such as Amede	Z, 32–3

11	Tewodros	Campaign to Tigray, against Agew Niguse and Agaw Täsäma.	1860		The rebels had killed the king's governor, and escaped.	TM, 232
12	Tewodros	Campaign to Shewa through Wollo.	1860		Many people killed.	TM, 196
13	Tewodros	March against Agaw Neguse in Tigray.	1861		Rebels were captured and killed.	TM, 241
14	Tewodros	Marched against Shewa.	1862, 1864, 1865		Against Bezabeh who was his appointed governor.	Ru, 173
15	Gobeze	Invaded Tigray	1866, Adwa		Defeated *ras* Bariau.	GS, 21
16	Tisso Gobeze	Attacked chiefs of Chilga and governor of Belessa.	January 1868		All sides suffered great losses; victory to Tisso Gobeze.	GS, 22
17	Gobeze	Against governor of Wägära.	31 March, 1868, Wägära		Defeated Tiso Gobeze.	GS, 22
18	Tewodros	Against British military expedition.	1868		Was defeated and committed suicide.	
Yohannes 1870/72–1889						
19	Kassa	Kassa rebelled.	1865/6, Tserae	–	Defeated governor Gäbrä Mikael.	GS, 25
20	*Däjazmach* Teklä Giorgis, *däjazmach* Deres, *däjazmach* Sahlu	Tewodros decision to invade Tigray.	1866	–	No Battle; epidemic ravaged the army.	GS, 25
21	Kassa	To gain more control.	May 1867, Kilete Awlalo	–	The governor was defeated.	GS, 25
22	Kassa	Against Tewodros governors in eastern Tigray.	August 1867, Gura	–	Azmach Bariau, governor of Tigray was defeated.	GS, 26
23	Kassa	To control Hammasen.	1867	–	Peaceful submission of *däjazmach* Hail Habal family of Tsazzega, and of *däjazmach* Wolde Mikael of Hazzega.	GS, 26
24	King Täklä Giorgis	Marched to Wadla and Yejju.	end of 1868	–	The rebel leader Faris Ali fled.	GS, 31

No	Authority/ Leader	Objectives of Expedition	Date, Duration & Place of Battle	No of Participants	Remarks (death, etc.)	Source
25	King Täklä Giorgis	Marched to Dämbia to quell uprising instigated by Gebre Medhen.	end of 1868	–	Little success for the king; the rebels controlled Belesa and Wägära.	GS, 32
26	Täklä Giorgis	Marched to Gojjem.	end of 1868	–	Desta Gualu fled; Adal appointed as governor.	GS, 32
27	King Täklä Giorgis	Marched against Kassa of Tigray.	July, 1871, at Asem, Adwa, two hours battle.	Täklä Giorgis's 60,000 against Kassa's 12,000.	King Täklä Giorgis was defeated; over 500 killed, 1,000 wounded.	GS, 33
28	*Blatta* Gebre Medhin, *fitawurari* Tesfai & *däjazmach* Gabru	Sent by Yohannes to crush Kassa Golja rebellion in Hammasen.	Dec.1871, near Däbrä Sina	6,000 royal troops.	The rebels were surprised but managed to escape.	GS, 35
29	Kassa	Campaigned against Rayya and Qobbo.	1871 & 1872	–	At first appointed the Rayya elders; later appointed *ras* Bitwadad Gäbrä Kidan as governor.	FeB, 54
30	Yohannes	Marched to Gonder.	Feb.20, 1873	At the head of 30,000 men.	*ras* Woregna, governor of Amhara submitted to Yohannes.	GS, 44
31	*Wagshum* Täfari, governor of n. Chachaho	Marched to suppress rebellion of *ras* Ali Bru.	1873, Wadla Dalanta	–	*ras* Ali, governor of Yäju, was defeated and killed.	FeB, 55
32	Yohannes	Marched to Gojjam to suppress rebels.	Dec. 1873	–	*Ras* Adal, the governor, fled; the king appointed Desta as governor with title of *ras*.	GS, 45
33	Adla	Opposed Desta's appointment.	July 1873	–	Klled *ras* Desta and reconciled with the king.	GS, 45
34	Yohannes	Marched to Yejju.	January 1875	–	Aba Wataw, the hereditary ruler, submitted.	GS, 45
35	Yohannes	Marched against Azabo Oromo.	March 1872	–		GS, 48

36	*Ras* Adal	Ordered by the king to suppress rebel.	At Shimagle Giorgis		The rebel, *ras* Wolde Mariam was defeated.	GS, 56
37	Yohannes	Marched to Gundet to resist Egyptian aggression.	5–6 November, 1875, at Gundet, one hour battle.	50,000 men led by the King.	Egypt lost 800 men and their commanders were killed; on Ethiopian side, 521 killed, 335 wounded.	GS; 61f; RU 322–3
38	Yohannes	Marched to Gura against Eygptian aggression.	7-10 March, 1876, at Gura three days battle.	King's troop numbered 45–50,000, Egyptian force 11,000 with 5,000 additional troops.	Seven Egyptian battalion was routed (ca. 3270 dead); Yohannes lost 3,500–4,000 men.	RU, 328–9
39	Yohannes	Marched to Shewa to subdue Menelik.	January 1878	Yohannes had 75,000 fighting men; Menelik had 70,000 fighting men	Menelik submitted peacefully.	GS, 92f
40	Yohannes	Marched to Werielu to meet Menelik.	July 1882			
41	*Ras* Gebre Medhin, Shum Dahna Fanta	To relieve Egyptian troops in Qallabat.	1884		The Mahdist forces were defeated, and the relief operation succeeded.	GS, 171
42	*Wagshum* Gebru, Bäjirond Lewte	To relieve Egyptian troops Qallabat.	June 1885	Ethiopians lost 600 men	Mahdist forces were again defeated.	GS, 174f
43	*Ras* Alula	To relieve Egyptian troops.	Sep.1885, at Kufit.	Of the 10,000 men, *ras* Alula lost 1550 men	Mahdist troops were defeated.	GS, 177f
44	Yohannes and Menelik	Campaigned in Adal.	end of 1886		Wollo for the first time came under control.	GS, 197
45	Mahdist troops	Invaded Dämbia and killed it's governor.	January 1885		They further advanced into the interior.	GS, 204

No	Authority/ Leader	Objectives of Expedition	Date, Duration & Place of Battle	No of Participants	Remarks (death, etc.)	Source
46	King Täklä Haimanot	Against Mahdist invasion.	Jan. 1887, at Tabarek, Qallabat	With 100,000 men; 16,000 Mahdist.	Mahdist were defeated.	GS, 204
47	*Ras* Alula	Campaigned against Italian invasion.	Jan. 1887, at Dogali	With 5,000 men.	500 Italian reinforcement troops were routed.	GS, 223
48	Yohannes	Against Italian Invasion.	February 1887	Over 100,000 men.	Withdrew after six weeks of siege	GS, 236f
49	Mahdist troops	Invaded western Ethiopia far into the interior.	Jan. 1888, plundered Gonder, burnt 240 churches	Had 19,000 troops.	Defeated King Täklä Haimanot troops.	GS, 239
50	Yohannes	Marched to Qallabat, after his campaign to Gojjam.	March 9, 1889, one day battle	Over 100,000 troops; Mahdist had 60–70,000 troops.	The emperor was wounded, and the news of his death in the morning led to collapse of Ethiopian's defence.	GS, 249
Menelik 1865–1913						
51	Menelik	Fought against Bezabh who robbed the Shewa Alga-throne.	26 August 1865		The victory gave Menelik 1,000 musketeers and one cannon.	TGS, 58; HM, 26
52	Menelik	Marched to break Kebrat Amba .	31 May, 1866, at Merhabete.		Many people died of the siege war; Menelik got muskets	TGS, 66; HM, 26
53	Menelik	Marched to Mäkdäla.	30 Nov. 1866, at Wärä Ilu.	Commanded 30,000 men.	No battle, for he exhausted provisions.	HM, 28f
54	Menelik	Marched from Wäre Ilu to Wollo.	Dec. 1867			
55	Menelik	Pacification of Wollo; founded military garrison town-Kätäma.	late 1868, at Wärä Ilu and Enawari		Also fought against governor of Mästiyat and her son Aba Wattow.	HM,
56	Menelik	Marched against Aba Watow and Mastiyat who defied his lordship.	Nov. 1871			BA, 2f

57	Menelik	Marched to Begemder.	Nov. 1871	With Shoan and Wollo troops.		HM, 35
58	Menelik	Led expedition to northern Gurage	May–June 1875, Qebena		The people submitted without resistance.	DK, 99
59	Menelik	Second campaign to Gurage.	Oct. 1875		Achieved costly victory, returned with war captives and many cattle.	DK, 102
60	Menelik and Mohammed Ali	Fought against Abba Wataw	late 1871		Could not dislodge him out of Mäqdäla fortress.	BA, 3; HM, 36
61	*Ras* Gobena	Campaigned and imposed taxation in regions above Awash.	starting June 1876			Tgs, 69, Nad, 3
62	*Ras* Gobena	Campaigned in the direction of Gurage and Kambata.	in 1876			Nad, 3–4
63	*Ras* Gobena	Quelled the rebellion instigated by Bafana.	1876 Entot			Nad, 5
64	Menelik and Mohammed Ali	Fought and captured Abba Wataw.	July 1876		Aba Wataw was imprisoned and Mohammed Ali declared as Imam of Wollo.	BA, 3
65	Menelik	Marched to Begemder, for *ras* Adal of Gojjam; captured rifles of Begemder.	Feb.–May 1877		No battle, marched through Gojjam.	TSG,
66	*Däjazmach* Wole, Menelik's Yejju governor	Fought against rival family members.	21 March, 1877		He was victorious.	TGS,
67	*Däjazmach* Grmame, Afä *negus* Bedane, *azazh* Engda of Menelik	Fought against the rebel Merd Azmach Mikael.	May 1877, at Ankober		The rebel was captured.	TGS, 77
68	Menelik	Marched to Wärä Ilu because Mohammed conspired and burned the town.	12 July, 1877		He failed to capture the Imam who escaped to Yohannes.	TGS, 78
69	Menelik	Marched to Wollo together with Aba Wataw.	Oct. 1877			TGS, 80

No	Authority/ Leader	Objectives of Expedition	Date, Duration & Place of Battle	No of Participants	Remarks (death, etc.)	Source
70	Menelik	Marched to Merhabete and encircled the Amba.	Nov. 1877		The rebel Mäshäsa Seifu was captured together with rifles; the governorship was given to *däjazmach* Darge.	TGS, 80
71	Yohannes	Marched to Shewa to subdue Menelik.	Jan. 1878		The Liche agreement was signed between them.	TGS,
72	Menelik	Marched to Wärä Ilu and Yejju, and met Yohannes.	1878/79			TGS, 97
73	Menelik	Marched south of Shewa.	29 Oct.–17 Nov. 1878		Many dwellings burnt and many captured	TGS, 71
74	*Ras* Gobena	Campaigned in the regions beyond Gibe river in the direction of the Gibe states and Wellega.	1878–1882			Nad, 5
75	Menelik and *ras* Mikael	Campaigned to Dämbäl, near lake Zway.	Dec. 1879		Captured many cattle.	TGS, 99
76	Menelik	Marched to Timuga.	1881		To capture those who robbed merchants; to pacify the region.	TGS, 100
77	Menelik and Täklä Haimanot	Fought against each other over control of southern provinces.	6 June 1882, at Embabo, eight hours battle		in King Täklähaimanot force over 900 men dead and 1,000 wounded; disarmed,	Caulk
78	*Ras* Gobena	Campaigned in the direction of western Wellega, Illubabor until Gimira.	1883			Nad, 7
79	Menelik and *ras* Mikael	Launched military expedition to quell a series of revolts caused by forceful religious conversion.	1884, 1885–86		*Ras* Mikael was appointed as governor-general of Wollo.	BA, 5
80	*Ras* Darge	To quell a rebellion in Gurage.	Lent season of 1885, at Maräqo		Was successful.	BT, 28

81	*Däjazmach* Wolde Ashenge, *däjazmach* Grmmame and *balambäras* Makonnen	Ordered by Menelik to suppress Gurage resistance.	1886	Were successful.	Asm,
82	*Däjazmach* Wolde Gabriel	Led expedition against Harage.	1886, camped at Hirna	The Imir of Harar terrorised them with cannon, and fled.	Asm, 773f
83	Menelik	Campaign to Harar.	6 Jan. 1887, at Chalanqo	The Imir suffered defeat and fled.	Asm,
84	*Ras* Gobena	Campaigned to western most Wellega against Mahdist invasion.	17 Oct. 1888, at Dabus, near Assosa, whole day battle	5,000 Mahdist dead and 1,235 rifles confiscated.	Nad,
85	*Ras* Gobena	Mobilised his Wellega troops and camped near Entot to guard the town until Menelik returned from Hara.	Jan.– Feb. 1877		Nad, 10–11
86	Menelik	Mobilised the troops beyond Awash and marched to Gonder to face Mahdist invasion.	1888	No battle, Menelik came through Gojjam.	Nad, 11–12
87	Menelik	Deployed troops on three fronts along river Abay to withstand possible attack on Shewa by King Yohannes.	1888 when Emperor Yohannes marched to Gojjam	The king left to Meqdala to fight against Mahdist.	Nad,
88	*Ras* Mäkonnen and his command officers	Pacified Hara and established garrison towns.	1887–1891		Tbb, 17–20
89	*Ras* Gobena, Fit. Habtä Giorgis, *däjazmach* Grmame	Campaigned to suppress Gurage resistance.	Aug. 1889, Jebdu Meda at Agamja	3,048 Gurage resistans forces died; 28 officers and many soldiers died in the Menelik force.	Nad, 15–16
90	*Däjazmach* Wolde Girgis Aboye and *däjazmach* Lemma	Expedition against Kollo and Konta.	1891	Destroyed 36 fortified camps.	TGS, 181; HM, 139
91	*Däjazmach* Lul Sägäd	Campaigned against Sidamo.	1891		Tse, 20

No	Authority/ Leader	Objectives of Expedition	Date, Duration & Place of Battle	No of Participants	Remarks (death, etc.)	Source
92	*Däjazmach* Basha Abboye	Campaigned against Gemu.	1891			Asm, 847
93	*ras* Darge and his son *däjazmach* Asfaw	Conquered Bale.	1891			TGS, 182
94	King Täklä Haimanot of Gojjam	Campaigned to Kafa, after the Great Famine.	1891			TGS, 181
95	*Däjazmach* Tassama	Campaigned in western Illubabur in the direction of Gambela.	1891, after the Great Famine			TGS, 181f
96	*Ras* Makonnen	Campaigned against Ogaden.	1891–92		Sent 10,000 cattle to Menelik.	TGS, 182,195; HM, 137f
97	*Ras* Wolde Giorgis, governor of Kulo, Limu and Kafa	Campaigned at the frontiers of his region.	1893			TGS, 218
98	Menelik	Campaigned in the areas around lake Zway.	1893		Pacified the area and encouraged trade.	TGS, 202
99	Menelik	Campaign against Wälamo.	June 1894, at Dlba		First attacked by 3,000 men, next by the King of Wälamo, but defeated.	TGS, 219f
100	*Ras* Mengasha	Campaigned against the advancing Italian force.	January 1895, near Senafe	*Ras* Mangasha had 12,000 man	The Italians defeated the *ras* army and controlled Tigray.	HM, 156
101	Menelik	Mobilised his force and marched to Tigray to resist Italian invasion.	The march started from Addis Ababa in october 1895.	The King moved with his own army; earlier he had sent the governors' army.	Before the final battle, the King and the army had travelled for almost five months.	TGS, chap. 60
102	*Ras* Wolde Giorgis and *ras* Tesema	Camped against Awsa to quell rebellion instigated by the Italians.	January 1896		The Awsa force was defeated.	TGS, 236–7

103	*Fitawurari* Gebeyhu and others	Fought the Italian outpost.	December, 1895, at Alage		The Italians were defeated and the troops moved to Mäkälé.	TGS, 239–242
104	Menelik	Attacked the Italian fortification at Mäkälé.	19–22 December 1895		Italians were defeated but given free passage to regions with main force.	TGS, 245–249
105	*Ras* Sebehat and *däjazmach* Hagos, *Balabat* of Agame	Cut the telegraph line and attacked the supply line of Italian forces.	January 1896, at Enki-Chäw		360 Italians were killed and many surrendered.	TGS, 254–255
106	*Däjazmach* Wold.., son of *däjazmach* Bahata Hagos	Cut the supply line of the Italians coming from Massawa.				
107	Menelik	Final battle against the Italians.	29 Feb. 1896, at Adwa	Menelik force 80–100,000; Italians 17,700.	4,000 Italians and 2000 *askaries* died; Menelik lost 4,000–6,000; he captured eight cannons and many rifles.	TGS, chap.63 & 64; Berk. 346
108	*Fitawrai* Habte Giorgis	Conquered Borena as far as Dollo and Lug.	1896–1897		He founded military garrison.	TGS, 277
109	*Ras* Wolde Giorgis, *däjazmach* Täsäma & *däjazmach* Demsew	Campaigned against the Kng of Kafa in three directions.	in 1897,		The campaign lasted nine months until the King was captured; many people died.	TGS, 276–7
110	King Tkla Haimanot	Expanded his frontier to the western most part.	1898		Founded garrison town.	TGS, 284
111	*Ras* Wolde Giorgis	Expanded his frontier further south.	1898			TGS, 284
112	*Däjazmach* Tessema	Expanded the frontier beyond Gimira.	1898			TGS, 284
113	*Ras* Makonnen and *däjazmach* Damsaw	Expanded frontier in western Wellega.	1898			TGS, 248

Source: GS= Zewde Gabre Selassie (1977); TGS= Gäbrä Selassie (1959 E.C.), Z=Zänäb (1902); Ru= Rubenson, S. (1976); TM= Täklä Sädiq Mäkuria (1981 E.C.); FeB= Feqadu Bena (1990); Nad= Nadew, History of Ras Gobena; DK= Darkwah, R.H.K. (1975), Asm= Bairu Tafla (1987); BT= Bairu Tafla (1975).

Comments: This work does not exhaust the number of troop movements made by King Yohannes during his rise and consolidation of power in the region of Tigray, between 1868–1872. For details see Feseha Wolde Mikael (1939 EC), and Seltene Seyum (1972).

Bibliography

A. Unpublished Sources

1. Unpublished Documents

Ethiopia

Institute of Ethiopian Studies, Addis Ababa

Dagmawi Menelik kä-Täläyayu Hagäroch gar Yaderägut yä -Wädagnet, yä-Negd, ena yä-Denber Wuloch. Manuscript no. 2201. IES. (abbreviated as *Menelik's Treaties of Friendship, Trade and Boarder Delineation).*

EMML, 76 F291b (*Ethiopian Manuscript Microfilm Library*. Addis Ababa/Collegeville, Minnesota. Catalogued by by Getachew Haile), 76 F291b.

Menelik's Treaties of Friendship, Trade and Boarder Delineation, (see *Dagmawi Minilk kä-Täläyayu Hagäroch gar Yaderägut yä -Wädagnet, yä-Negd, ena yä-Denber Wuloch*. Manuscript no. 2201. IES.)

yä Ras Tesema Nuzazé, Manuscript no. 1639. IES. Addis Ababa.

yä-Luel Ras Kassa Hailu Astädadär Dänb: Sgawi ena Mänfäsawi, Manuscript no 1190. IES. Addis Ababa.

Chärchär Dänb, Manuscript no. 734, IES. Addis Ababa.

National Library, Ministry of Culture and Sports, Addis Ababa

Antonelli, Count Pietro (1888). A note extracted from an original account, document no. 8.09.12. Probably, the orginal letter is found in Archivio Storico del Ministereo dell´ Africa Italiana. Antonelli letter to Ministereo degli Affari Esteri, Assab. dated 31.10.1888.

A letter of Tewodros, document number 22.03.4.

Menelik's letter written to *däjazmach* Gebre Selassie, *nebred* zä-Aksum, dated April 12 1900 E.C, document no 7.06.1.

Däbr Churches, Tigray Region

Wärq zä-wängél of *däbrä* Selassie Chäläqot, Chäläqot.

Wärq zä-wängél of *däbrä* Gänät Mädahni Aläm, Mäkälé.

"*Report submitted by a Committee established to investigate and to make recommendations on solving the continues litigation problem arising between Amisho (one-fifth) paying peasants and Amisho (one-fifth) receivers". July 2, 1954 E.C*. In the possession of *ato* Gäsäsä Bezabh.

Wärq zä-wängél of the Adwa Mikael church. (This document is copied and coded by Crummey, D. as 92.I.16.19)

Great Britain

Public Record Office (Foreign Office) and British Library, Orient (B.L.Or.), London

B.L. Or. 518	B.L. Or. 776	B.L. Or. 820	F.O. 401/1
B.L. Or. 604	B.L. Or. 777	B.L. Or. 821	F.O. 1/13
B.L. Or. 636	B.L. Or. 799	B.L. Or. 828*	F.O. 401/8.
B.L. Or. 659	B.L. Or. 813	B.L. Or. 829*	Bodl. Bruce 88.

Bibliothèque Nationale, Paris

D' Abbadie 118 (cf, Antoine d´Abbadie (1859), Catalogue raisonné des mss. éthiopiens. Paris, pp. 133–136).

2. Unpublished Chronicle

yä Tewodros Tärik, IES, Manuscript no. 91.

3. Manuscripts

Principal Manuscripts

bä-Itiyopia Tintawi yäferd mäzgeb yätägägnä fttabher hegawi dreget, 1945. Manuscript, Addis Ababa (abbreviated as *Codified Laws*).

Codified Laws (see, *bä-Itiyopia Tintawi yäferd mäzgeb yätägägnä fttabher hegawi dreget*, 1945. Manuscript, Addis Ababa).

Nägädä, *Yä Ras Gobena Tärik* (copy of this document is deposited at the National Library, Ministry of Culture and Sports, Addis Ababa, document number, 23.01.5).

Secondary Manuscripts

Asfaw Tesema Werke (1969 E.C.), *yäRas Gugsa Wäle Tarik*, IES, Manuscript no. 998.

Feseha Wolde Mikael (1936 E.C.), *yä Asé Yohannes Tarik*. Manuscript no. 22.01. National Library, Ministry of Culture and Sports. Addis Ababa.

Haile Zalake (n.d.), *Dejazmach Girmame yä-Hiwot Tarik*. IES. Amharic Collection. Addis Ababa.

Kebede Tesema, *Leyu Leyu yä-Tarik Mastawäsha*. Manuscript no. 2247. IES.

Mersehe Hazen Wold Qirqos (1935 E.C.), *bä-Dagmawi Menilk Zämän Kayähutna Käsämahut*. Manuscript no. 267. IES. Addis Ababa.

yä Nägadras Eshete Teketlew Hiwot Tarik, IES, Manuscript no. 2000.

Gebre Hiwot Baykadagn (1910), *Emperor Menelik and Ethiopia*, Manuscript no. 2224. IES. Addis Ababa.

B. Published Sources

1. Published Documents

Conti Rossini (1954), "Documenta ad Illustrandam Historiam: I. Libre Axumae", in *Corpus Scriptorium Christianorum Orienalium, Vol. 54 text, Vol. 58, French version.*

Euringer, S. (1933/34), Die Geschichte von Närga. Ein Kapitel aus der abessinischen Kulturgeschichte des 18. Jarhunderts" in *Zeitschrift fur Semitistik und verwandte Gebiete, Band 9, Band 10* , 1935.

Guidi, I. (1905), "Il racconto di Näraga" in *Rendiconti della Reale Accademia dei Lincei*. Roma, Serie V, XIV.

Huntingford, G.W.B. (1965), *The Land Charters of Northern Ethiopia*. Addis Ababa, p. XI.

Pankhurst, R. and Germa Selassie Asfaw, eds., (1979), *Tax Records and Inventories of Emperor Tewodros of Ethiopia (1855–1868)*. London.

Säratä Gebr. For the list of documents and for partial translation of *Säratä Gebr* see Kropp, M. (1989a), "The Seràtä *Gebr*: A mirror view of daily life at the Ethiopian Royal court in the Middle ages" in Taddese Beyene (ed.) *Proceedings to the 8th International Conference of Ethiopian Studies, I.* Addis Ababa, p.219

Säräte Mängest. On the list where one finds the documents of *Särate Mängest* see Huntingford, G.W.B. (1990), *The Historical Geography of Ethiopia. From the First Century AD to 1704.* Oxford, pp. 8–9. For translation of the document see Bairu Tafla and Scholler, H. (1976), "Sera`ata Mangest. An Early Ethiopian Constitution", in *Verfassung und Recht in Übersee. A Quarterly on Law and Modernization, Vol. 9, No. 4.* pp. 487–499. The text is traslated into the German language by Varenbergh, Joseph (1915/1916), "Studien zur Abessinischen Reichsordnung", in *Zeitschrift fur Assyriologie, band XXX.*

yä Tor Mäsariya Dänb issued on May 1924 E.C. deposited at IES, Amharic collection.

yä *Tor Särawit Dänb*, 1927 E.C. Addis Ababa. Deposited at IES Amharic Collection.

2. Printed Chronicles

Annale Iyasu II et Iyoas, in *Corpus Scriptorium Christianorum Orienalium,(*CSCO) *vol.61.*

Bairu Tafla, ed. (1977), *A Chronicle of Emperor Yohannes IV 1872–1889.* Wiesbaden.

Blundell, W. (1922), *The Royal Chronicle of Abyssinia, 1769–1840.* Cambridge.

Conti Rossine, C. (1907), *Historia Regis Sarsa Dingel (Malak Sagad).* Louvain.

Dombrowski, F.A. (1983). *Tänäsee 106: Eine Chronik der Herrscher Äthiopiens, B. II.* Wiesbaden.

Gabrä Selassie Walda Aregay (1959 E.C.), *Dagmawi Menelik Neguse Nägäst zä-Etyopia*, Addis Ababa.

Gebre-Igziabihr Elyas (1994), *Prowess, Piety and Politics. The Chronile of Abeto Iyasu and Empress Zewditu of Ethiopia (1090–1930).* Köln.

Pankhurst, R., ed. (1967b), *The Ethiopian Royal Chronicles.* Addis Ababa.

Täklä Iyasus, *yä Negus Täklä Haimanot Tarik*, Manuscript no. 254, IES.

Zänäb, (1902), *yä Tewodros Tarik* : ("*The Chronicle of King Theodore of Abyssinia").* Litman, E. (ed.). Leipzig.

3. Autobiography

Haile Selassie (1965), *Heywäté ena yä Ityopiya Ermega, I*, Addis Ababa.

C. Oral Sources

All of the informants are residents of Mäkälé, capital town of Tigray region. Lengthy interviews were held at Mäkälé town in August 1993.

Ato Gäsäsä Bezabh, age 78, served as judge at the High Court of the Region of Tigray; was a relation of Emperor Tewodros through the descendants of his father and Emperor Yohannes IV through the descendants of his mother.

Fitawrari Eyasu Asbäha, age 75, served as provincial governor in the region of Tigray during the reign of Haile Selassie.

Mälakä Gänät Serse Dingel Arefe Ayne. Age 67. He is the head (*aläqa*) of the Däbrä Gänät Medahini Alem Church of Mäkälé. He served in the church in different capacities since the age of 28.

D. Published Accounts of Travellers

D' Abbadie, A. (1980), *Douze ans de séjour dans la Haute-Éthiopie (Abyssinie)*, Vaticano.

Almeida (1632), "The History of High Land Ethiopia or Abyssinia", in Beckingham, C.F. and Huntingford, G.W.B. (eds.), 1954.

Blanc, H., (1868), *A Narrative of Captivity in Abyssinia: with some Account of the Late Emperor Theodore, his country and People*. London.

Bruce, J. (1790), *Travels to Discover the Sources of the Nile in the Years 1768–1773. V 5*, Edinburgh.

— (1790), *Travels to Discover the Sources of the Nile. II.* Edinburgh.

Cecchi, A. (1886). *Käfa ena Tarikua, 1390–1897,* (an abbreviated Amharic translation. Original title reads Cecchi, A. (1886), *Da Zeila alle Frontiere del Caffa, 3 vols.* Roma.)

Dimothéos, S. (1871), *Deux ans de séjour en Abyssine, ou vie morale, politique et religieuse des Abyssines, V.I.* Jerusalem.

Gleichen, C. (1898), *With the Mission to Menelik 1897.* London.

Harris, W.C. (1844), *The Highlands of Aethiopia. III*, London.

Parkyns, M. (1855), *Life in Abyssinia.* London.

Pearce, N. (1830). *The Life and Adventures of Nathaniel Pearce, written by himself during a residence in Abyssinia from the Years 1810 to 1819; together with Mr. Coffin's Account of his Visit to Gonder.* J.J. Halls, ed., I. London.

Plowden, W.C. (1868), *Travels in Abyssinia and the Galla Country, with an Account of a Mission to Ras Ali in 1848.* London.

Rassam, H., (1869), *Narrative of the British Museum to Theodore, King of Abyssinia, V.2.* London.

Stern, H.A. (1869). *The Captive Missionary: Being and Account of the Country and People of Abyssinia.* London.

E. Newspapers, Addis Ababa

Berehanena Selam, March 15, 1928.

Brehanena Selam newspaper, July 1926, July 1928, Febrary, 1931.

Brehanina Selam, 1927.

F. Unpublished Theses

Abas Haji (1982), "The History of Arsi, 1850–1935". B.A. Thesis in History, AAU.

Abdusamad H. Ahmad (1980), "Trade and Politics in Gojjam 1882–1935". M.A. Thesis in History. AAU.

Abebe Fisha (1987), "Land Tenure in Tahuladare Wäräda from 1799–1974". B.A. Thesis in History, AAU.

Asefa Balcha (1984), "The Court of Negus Mikael: An Analysis of its Structure and a Description of the Role of "Ayteyefe" Hall. B.A. Thesis in History. AAU.

Asnake Ali (1983), "Aspects of the Political History of Wallo: 1872–1917". M.A. Thesis in History, AAU.

Bahru Zewde, (1976), "Relations between Ethiopia and the Sudan on the western Ethiopian Frontier". Dissertation. School of Oriental and African Studies, University of London.

Bedru Ahmed (1984), "The Relations Between Western Gurage and the Kontab (ca. 1850–1937)". B.A. Thesis in History, AAU.

Berry, L.V.B. (1976), "The Solomonic Monarchy at Gonder, 1630–1755. An Institutional Analysis of Kingship in the Christian Kingdom of Ethiopia". Ph.D. Thesis. Boston University.

Bruce, J.W. (1976), "Land Reform Planning and Indigenous Communal Tenures: A Case Study of the Tenure Chiguraf-Gwoses in Tigray, Ethiopia". Ph.D. Thesis, Faculty of Law, University of Wisconsin.

Demeke Seifu (1989), "The Addis Ababa Urael Church (ca.1855 to 1974)". B.A. Thesis in History. AAU.

Ege, S. (1978), "Chiefs and Peasants: The Socio-Political Structure of the Kingdom of Shawa in about 1840". M.A. Thesis. Bergen.

Fantahun Berhane (1973), "Gojjam 1800–1855". B.A. Thesis in History, HSIU.

Fekadu Begna, (1990), "Land and the Peasantry in Northern Wallo 1941–1974: Yajju and Raya and Qobbo Awrajas". M.A. Thesis in History. AAU.

Garretson, P. (1974), "A History of Addis Ababa from its Foundation in 1886 to 1910". Ph.D. Dissertation, University of London.

Gebre Medhin Kidane (1972), "Yohannes IV: Religious Aspects of his Internal Policy". B.A. Thesis in History, HSIU.

Habtamariam Seyoum (1967), "Military Organization and Armament Acquisition of Menelik II", B.A. Thesis in History, HSIU.

Haddis Gebre-meskel (June 1992), "A Survey of Representative Land Charters of the Ethiopian Empire (1314–1868) and Related Marginal Notes in Manuscripts in the British Library, The Royal Library and the University Libraries of Cambridge and Manchester". Ph.D. Thesis submitted to School of Oriental and African Studies, University of London.

Mekonnen Tamru (1988), "The History of Garrison Town Gerawa (1889–1974)". B.A. Thesis in History. AAU.

Merid Wolde Aregay (1971), "Southern Ethiopia and the Christian Kingdom, 1508–1708, with Special Reference to the Galla Migrations and their Consequences". Ph.D. Thesis, University of London.

Mislu Gugsa (1974), "Estate Administration in Part of Present Day Jibat and Mecha under Fitawrari Habte Giorgis". B.A. Thesis in History, AAU.

Qäjela Märdasa (1985), "The Evolution of Land Tenure System in Mana-Sibu Wereda, Ghimbi, Wallaga: a Historical Survey to 1935". B.A. Thesis in History, AAU.

Raga Abdissa (1984), "A Brief Survey of Land Tenure System in Qellem, Western Walläga, ca. 1880–1944". B.A. Thesis in History, AAU.

Rahmeto Hussien (1984), "The History of Azernet-Berbere until the Expansion of Shoa, during Menelik II". B.A. Thesis in History. AAU.
Schaefer, Charles G.H. (1990), "Enclavistic Capitalism in Ethiopia, 1906–1936. A Study of Currency, Banking, and Informal Credit Networks". Vols. I & II. Dissertation in History, Illinois, University of Chicago.
Seltene Seyum (1972), "Yohannes IV Rise and Consolidation". B.A. Thesis in History. HSIU.
Shiferaw Bekele (1982), "The Railway, Trade and Politics: A Historical Survey (1896–1935)". M.A. Theis in History, AAU.
Shimeles Bonsa (1990), "The History of Butajra Town to 1974. B.A". Thesis in History, AAU.
Tarekegn Yibab (1988), "The History of Mahdara Maryam ca. 1596–1939". B.A. Thesis in History, AAU.
Tecle Haimanot Gebre Selassie (1984), "The Wayto of Lake Tana: An Ethno-history". M.A. Thesis in History. AAU.
Tekalign W. Mariam (1995), "Land Tenure, Urban Supply and Regional History: A Political Economic Approach to the History of Shoa and the Provisioning of Addis Ababa", Ph.D. Thesis, Department of History, Boston University.
Tesema Ta`a (1980), "The Oromo of Wallaga: A Historical Survey to 1910". M.A. Thesis in History, AAU.
Tsehai Berhane Selassie 1980. "The Political and Military Traditions of the Ethiopian Peasantry." Ph.D. Dissertation, University of Oxford, Faculty of Anthropology and Geography.
Worku Tafara (1977), "Judicial Administration in Ethiopia: A Reform Oriented Analysis". Thesis on Law, Northewestern University, School of Law, Chicago
Wudu Tafete Kasu (1989), "The Twin Churches of Raguel, 1889–1985". B.A. Thesis in History, AAU.

G. Printed Books and Articles

1. Theory and Methodology

Anderson, M.S. (1987), *Europe in the Eighteenth Century, 1713–1783.* Third Edition. London.
— (1988), *War and Society in Europe of the Old Regime, 1618–1789.* Leicester.
Anderson, P. (1974), *Lineages of the Absolutist State.* London.
Astarita, T. (1992), *The Continuity of Feudal Power. The Caracciolo di Brienza in Spanish Naples.* Cambridge.
Black, J. (1991), *A Military Revolution? Military Change and European Society 1550–1800.* London.
Bonney, R. (1987), "Absolutism: What's in a Name", in *French History, 1: 1.*
— (1991), *The European Dynastic States, 1494–1660.* Oxford.
Braudel, F. (1982), *Civilization and Capitalism, 15th–18th Century. II. The Wheels of Commerce.*
Braun, R. (1975), "Taxation, Sociopolitical Structure, and State-building: Great Britain and Brandenburg-Prussia", in Tilly, C. (ed.), *The Formation of National States in Western Europe*. Princeton.
Collins, J. (1988), *Fiscal Limits of Absolutism. Direct Taxation in Early Seventeenth Century France.* Berkeley.

— (1994), *Classes, Estates and Order in Early Modern Brittany.* Cambridge.

Dahlgren, S., Lindkvist, T. and Stadin, K. (1993), "Skattesystem i förändring—en kommentar", in *Historisk tidskrift, 1.*

Dickson, P.G.M., (1987), *Finance and Government under Maria Theresia, 1740–1780. II.* Oxford.

Downing, B.M. (1992), *The Military Revolution and Political Change. Origins of Democracy and Autocracy in Early Modern Europe.* Princeton.

Eltis, D. (1995), *The Military Revolution in Sixteenth-Century Europe.* London.

Finkel, C. (1988), *The Administration of Warfare: the Ottoman Military Campaigns in Hungary, 1593–1606.* Wien.

Habermas, J. (1991), *The Structural Transformation of the Public Sphere. An Inquiry into a Category of Bourgeois Society.* Cambridge.

Henshall, N. (1992), *The Myth of Absolutism. Change and Continuity in Early Modern Europe.* London.

Hickey, D. (1986), *The Coming of French Absolutism: The Struggle for Tax Reforms in the Province of Dauphine, 1540–1640.* Toronto.

Hobsbawm, E. and Bourn, D. (1976), "Feudalism, Capitalism and the Absolutist State", in *Communist Review, pamphlet 66,* summer 1976.

Jansson, T. (1988), "Rättsuppfattningar och sockenrätt. Tsarer mot baroner och baroner mot bönder i strid om lokaladministrationen i estlandssvenska områden vid 1800-talets mitt", in *Scandia,* 54, 1.

Kennedy, P. (1988), *The Rise and Fall of the Great Powers: Economic Change and Military Conflict from 1500 to 2000.* London.

Kettering, S. (1986), *Patrons, Brokers and Clients in Seventeenth-Century France.* Oxford.

Klaveren, J. (1969) "Fiscalism, Mercantilism and Corruption" in Coleman, D. C. (ed.), *Revisions in Mercantilism.* London.

Kriedte, P. (1980), *Peasants, Landlords and Merchant Capitalists. Europe and the World Economy, 1500–1800.* Leamington.

Kunisch, J. (1986), *Absolutismus.* Göttingen.

Ladewig Petersen, E. (1975), "From Domain State to Tax State. Synthesis and Interpretation", in *The Scandinavian Economic History Review,* XXIII: 2.

— (1983), "War, Finance and Growth of Absolutism: Some Aspects of the European Integration of Seventeenth Century Denmark", in Rystad, G. (ed.), *Europe and Scandinavia: Aspects of the Process of Integration in the 17th Century.* Lund.

LeDonne, J. (1984), *Ruling Russia: Politics and Administration in the Age of Absolutism, 1762–1796.* Princeton.

— (1991), *Absolutism and Ruling Class. The Formation of the Russian Political Order 1700–1825.* New York.

Lindegren, J. (1984), "The Swedish 'Military State', 1560–1720", in *Scandinavian Journal of History,* X: 4.

— (1992), *Maktstatens resurser.* Unpublished manuscript. Department of History, Uppsala University.

— (1993), "Two thousand years of warfare", in *The Roots of Western Civilization. Two Thousand Years of Warfare.* Hilversum.

Litchfield, B. (1986), *Emergence of a Bureaucracy. The Florentine Patricians 1530–1790.* Princeton

Lublinskaya, A.D. (1968), *French Absolutism: The Crucial Phase, 1620–1629.* Cambridge.

— (1980), "The Contemporary Bourgeios Conception of Absolute Monarchy", in *Economy and Society, 1: 1.*

Lüdtke, A. (1980), "Genesis und Durchsetzung des "modernen Staates". Zur Analyse von Herrschaft und Verwaltung", in *Archiv für Sozialgeschichte. Bd. XX.*

Mettam, R. (1990), "France", in Miller, J. (ed.), *Absolutism in Seventeenth Century Europe*. London.

Mousnier, R. (1970), "The Exponents and Critics of Absolutism" in Cooper, J. (ed.), *The New Cambridge Modern History, IV.* Cambridge.

Nilsson, S. A. (1990), *De stora krigens tid. Om Sverige som militärstat och bondesamhälle*. Uppsala.

Nováky, G. (1990), *Handelskompanier och kompanihandel. Svenska Afrikakompaniet 1649–1663. En studie i feodal handel.* Uppsala.

Oestreich, G. (1969), *Neostoicism and the Early Modern State*. Cambridge.

— (1969), *Geist und Gestalt des Frühmodernen Staats*. Berlin.

Parker, D. (1971), "The Foundation of French Absolutism 1610–1630" in *Past and Present, n.53.*

— (1983), *The Making of French Absolutism*. London.

Parker, G. (1988), *The Military Revolution. Military Innovation and the Rise of the West, 1500–1800.* Cambridge.

Pickl, Othmar (ed.) (1980), *Krieg, Militärausgaben und wirtschaftlicher Wandel. Proceedings of the Seventh International Economic History Congress*, Edinburgh, 1978.

Pryor, J.H. (1985), "The Historical Foundation of a Feudal Mode of Production", in Leach, E., Mukherjee and Ward, J. (eds.) *Feudalsim: Comparative Studies.* Sydney.

Ranum, O.A. (1963), *Richelieu and the Councillors of Louis XIII. A Study of the Secretaries of State and Superintendents of Finance in the Ministry of Richelieu 1635–1642*. Oxford.

Redlich, F. (1964), *The German Military Enterpriser and His Work Force, 2 vols.* Wiesbaden.

Roberts, M. (1956), *The Military Revolution.* Belfast.

Runciman, W.G. (1980), "Comparative Sociology or Narrative History? A Note on the Methodology of Perry Anderson", in *Archives Européennes de Sociologie,* tome xxi, n.1.

Salim, A. I. ed., (1984), *State Formation in Eastern Africa.* London.

Schumpeter, J. (1951), *Die Krise des Steuerstaates*. Wiesbaden.

Scott, H.M. ed., (1990), *Enlightened Absolutism.* London.

Szentes, Tamás (1979), "A Brief Survey on the Theories of International Trade", in *Studies on Developing Countries. No. 102*. Budapest.

Tilly, C (ed.) 1975, *The Formation of National States in Western Europe*. Princeton.

— (1984), *Big Structures, Large Processes, Huge Comparisons.* New York.

Vries, Jan de (1976), *The Economy of Europe in an Age of Crisis, 1600–1750*. Cambridge.

Wallerstein, I. (1974), *The Modern World-System. Capitalist Agriculture and the Origins of the European World-Economy in the Sixteenth Century.* London.

Webber, C. and Wildavsky, A. (1986), *A History of Taxation and Expenditure in the Western World.* New York.

Wright, G.H. (1971), *Explanation and Understanding*. London.

Zanden, J.L. (1993), *The Rise and Decline of Holland's Economy. Merchant Capitalism and the Labour Market.* Manchester.

Zeleza, T. (1993), *A Modern Economic History of Africa, I. The Nineeteenth Century.* Oxford.

2. Ethiopia

Abir, M. (1968), *Ethiopia: the Era of Princes. The Challenge of Islam and the Reunification of the Christian Empire, 1769–1855*. London.

— (1980), *Ethiopia and the Red Sea: the rise and decline of the Solomonic dynasty and Muslim-European rivalry in the region*. London.

Addis Hiwot, (1975), *Ethiopia: From Autocracy to Revolution*. Review of African Political Economy. London.

Afawark G/Iyasus (1905), *Dagmawi Menilik Negusä Nägäst zä-Ityopiya*. Rome. (IES, Amharic collection, catalogue no. 10919).

— (1908), *Etiyopya: Guide du voyageur en Abyssinie*. Rome.

Akalu Wolde Michael (1973), "Urban Development in Ethiopia (1889–1925)", in *Journal of Ethiopian Studies, XI: 1*.

Alberro, M. and Haile Mariam (1982), "Ethiopian Cattle Indigenous Breeds", in *World Animal Review*, 41.

Aläqa Tayye Gabra Mariam, (1922), *Yä Ityopia Hezb Tarik*. Hudson, G. and Tekeste Negash, translators. Uppsala.

Ayele Taklahaymanot (1962), "Gerarchia Civile, Militare e Religiosa Nell' Antico Impero Etiopico", in *AEVUM, XXXV, 1–2*.

Bahrey (1522), "History of the Galla", in Beckingham, C.F. and Huntingford, G.W.B. eds., 1954, *Some Records of Ethiopia 1593–1646*. London.

Bahru Zewde (1984), "Economic Origins of the Absolutist State of Ethiopia (1916–1935)" in *Journal of Ethiopian Studies, 17*;

— (1987), "Early Safars of Addis Ababa: Patterns of Evolution", in *Proceedings of the International Symposium on the Century of Addis Ababa, November 24–25, 1986*. Addis Ababa.

— (1991), *A History of Modern Ethiopia, 1855–1974*. London.

— (1992), "Haile Selassie: from Progressive to Reactionary" in *Preproceedings of the Sixth Michigan State University Conference on Northeast Africa*. Compiled by Hinnant, J. and Finne, B. Michigan.

Bairu Tafla (1974), "Civil Titles and Offices in the Reign of Emperor Menelik II, 1889–1913," in *IV Congresso Internazionale di Studi Etiopici*, Roma, I.

— (1974), "Some Aspects of Land-Tenure and Taxation in Sälale under Ras Darge, 1871–1900" in *Journal of Ethiopian Studies*,

— (1987), *Asma Giyorgis and His Work: History of the Galla and the Kingdom of Shäwa*. Stuttgart.

Bairu Tafla and Scholler, H. (1976), "Sera`ata Mangest. An Early Ethiopian Constitution", in *Verfassung und Recht in Übersee. A Quarterly on Law and Modernization, IX: 4*.

Bartricki, A. and Mantel-Niecko, J. (1971), "The Role and Significance of the Religious Conflicts and Peoples Movement in the Political Life of Ethiopia in the Seventeenth and Eighteenth Centuries", in *Rassegna di Studi Etiopici, XXIV*. 1969–1970. Roma.

Beckingham, C.F. and Huntingford, G.W.B. (eds.) (1954), *Some Records of Ethiopia 1593–1646*. London.

— (eds.), (1961), *The Prester John of the Indies, I*. Cambridge.

Benti Getahun (1989), "Shashemane: Foundation and Early Growth up to the Italian Occupation", in *Proceedings of the Fourth Seminar of the Department of History*. AAU.

Caulk, R.A. (1971), "The Occupation of Harar: January 1887", in *Journal of Ethiopian Studies; IX, 2*.

— (1972), "Religion and the State in Nineteenth Century Ethiopia", in *Journal of Ethiopian Studies, X, 1.*

— (1984), "Bad Men of the Borders: Shum and Shifta in Northern Ethiopia in the Nineteenth Century" in *Proceedings of the Second Annual Seminar of the Department of History (AAU), Vol.I.* Addis Ababa.

Chapple, D. (1987), "Some Remarks on the Addis Ababa Food Market up to 1935" in *Proceedings of the International Symposium on the Century of Addis Ababa, November 24.25, 1986.* Addis Ababa.

— (1990), "Firearms Again: The Battle of Asem", in *Proceedings of the Fifth Seminar of the Department of History.* AAU.

Chernetsoy, S.B. (1974), "The History of the Gallas' and the Death of Zädengel, King of Ethiopia (1603–1604)", in *IV Congresso Internazionale di Studie Etiopici, 10–15 April 1972.* Roma.

Crummey, D. (1975), "Cächaho and the Politics of the northern Wällo-Begemder Border", in *Journal of Ethiopian Studies, XIII: 1.*

— (1978), "Orthodoxy and Imperial Reconstruction in Ethiopia, 1854–1878", in *Journal of Theological Studies, XXIX, 2.*

— (1978), "Gondarine *Rim* Land Sales: An Introductory Description and Analysis", in Hess, R. (ed.), *Proceedings of the Fifth International Conference on Ethiopian Studies.* Session B.

— (1983), "Family and Property amongst the Amhara Nobility" in *Journal of African History, XXIV, no.2.*

— (1984), "Banditary and Resistance: Noble and Peasant in Nineteenth Century Ethiopia", in *Proceedings of the Seventh International Conference of Ethiopian Studies,* Rubenson, S. (ed.). Uppsala.

— (1987), "Some Precursors of Addis Ababa: Towns in Christian Ethiopia in the Eighteenth and Nineteenth Centuries", in *Proceedings of the International Symposium on the Century of Addis Ababa.* November 24–25, 1986. Addis Ababa.

— (1988), "Theology and Political Conflicts During the Zämänä Mäsafint: the case of Esté in Begemder" in *Proceedings of the Ninth International Congress of Ethiopian Studies, Moscow.*

— (1989), "Three Amharic Documents of Marriage and Inheritance from the Eighteenth and Nineteenth Centuries" in Taddase Beyene (ed.) *Proceedings of the Eighth International Confrence of Ethiopian Studies, vol 1,* Addis Ababa.

— (1993), "Medieval Ethiopian Land Grants, 1200–1540" A paper presented to the symposium on "State, Land and Society in the History of Sudanic Africa", Center for African Studies, University of Illinois, Urbana, April 22–24.

Crummey, D. and Shumet Sishagne (1991), "Land Tenure and the Social Accumulation of Wealth in Eighteenth-Century Ethiopia: Evidence from the Qwesqwam Land Register" in *International Journal of African Studies, vol.24, no.2.*

— (1988), "The Lands of the Church of Däbrä S`ähay Qwusqwam, Gonder" in *Proceedings of the Tenth International Confrence of Ethiopian Studies.* Paris.

Crummey, D., Shumet and Daniel (1991), "A Gondariane Land Grant in Gojjam: The Case of Qäranyo Mädhane Aläm" in *Proceedings of the XIth International Confrence of Ethiopian Studies,* Addis Ababa.

Darkwah, R.H.K. (1975), *Shewa, Menelik and the Ethiopian Empire, 1813–1889.* London.

Dessalegn Rahmato (1990), *A Resource Flow Systems Analysis of Rural Bolosso (Wollaita).* Addis Ababa.

— (1992), "Peasant Agriculture under the Old Regime", in *An Economic History of Ethiopia. The Imperial Era, 1941–1974. V.I.* Draft Manuscript. Department of History, Addis Ababa University.

Dombrowski, F.A. (1985), *Ethiopia's Access to the Red Sea.* Koln. pp. 21ff.
Donham, D. (1986), "Old Abyssinia and the new Ethiopian empire: themes in social history", in Donham, D. and James, W. (eds.), *The Southern Marches of Imperial Ethiopia.* Cambridge.
Ethiopia: a Cradle of History (1989), Addis Ababa.
Fekadu Begna (1990), The Wello Territorial Army, 1943–1974", in *Proceedings of the Fifth Seminar of the Department of History.* Addis Ababa University.
Gebre Hiwot Baykadagn (1919), *Mängistna Yähizb Astädader,* IES.
Gebrehiwot Baykadagn (1919), *The Political Economy of Ethiopia c. 1910.* London.
Garretson, P. (1979), "The Naggadras: Trade, and Selected Towns in Nineteenth and Early Twentieth Century Ethiopia", in *The International Journal of African Historical Studies, 12.*
Gebre Wold Engda Worq (1948 E.C.), *Yä-Ityopia Märetna Gber Sem.* Addis Ababa.
— (1962), "Ethiopia's Traditional System of Land Teneur and Taxation", in *Ethiopia Observer,* V, 4.
Gebru Tareke (1991), *Ethiopia: Power and Protest. Peasant revolts in the twentieth century.* Cambridge.
Gesiotto, Adolfo (1941/42), Breve studio sociale e giuridico sul Tigrai Occidentale (con particolare riferimento alle regione di Axum e del Tembien)", in *Archivio Vittorio Scialoja per le Consuetudini giurdiche agrarie, 8/9.*
Girma Tefera (1961 E.C). *Aba Tatäk Yä Quara Anbasa. Dagmawi Tewedros Negusä Nägäst Zä Ityopiya.* Addis Ababa.
Graham, B. (1844), "Report on the Agricultural and Land Produce of Shoa", in *Journal of the Asiatic Society of Bengal. V. XIII,* part one, No.145 to 150.
Guidi, I. (1901), *Vocabolario Amarico-Italiano.* Rome.
Guluma Gemeda (1989), "An Outline of the Early History of Jimma Town", in *Proceedings of the Fourth Seminar of the Department of History,* AAU.
Haile Gebriel Dagne (1972), "The Gebzena Charter 1894" in *Journal of Ethiopian Studies, X: 1.*
Halldin Norberg, V. (1977), *Swedes in Haile Selassie's Ethiopia 1924–1952. A Study in Early Development Co-operation.* Uppsala.
Hoben, A. (1973), *Land Tenure among the Amhara of Ethiopia: The Dynamics of Cognatic Descent.* Chicago.
Hultin, Jan (1977), "Man and Land in Wallaga, Ethiopia", in *Working Papers of the Department of Anthropology, no. 10.* University of Gothenburg.
Huntingford, G.W.B. (1990), *The Historical Geography of Ethiopia. From the First Century AD to 1704.* Oxford.
Hussien Ahmed (1989), "The Life and Career of Shaykh Talha b. Ja`far (c.1853–1936)", in *Journal of Ethiopian Studies, 12, .XXII.*
Kane, T. L. (1990), *Amharic-English Dictionary. I–II.* Wiesbaden.
Kolmodin, J., (1915). *Traditions de Tsazzega et Hazzega.* Uppsala.
Kropp, M. (1989a), "The Seràtä *Gebr*: A mirror view of daily life at the Ethiopian Royal court in the Middle ages" in Taddese Beyene (ed.) *Proceedings to the 8th International Confrence of Ethiopian Studies, vol.1.* Addis Ababa.
— (1989b), *Die Äthiopischen Königschroniken in der Sammlung des Däggazmc Haylu.* Frankfurt am Main.
Lange, J.W. (1982), *History of the Southern Gonga (Southwestern Ethiopia).* Studien zur Kulturkunde, 61. Wiesbaden.
Lapiso G. Delebo (1983 E.C). *Yä-Ityopya Yä-Gäbar Serä`at ena Jimer Kapitalizm 1900–1966.* Addis Ababa.
Levine, D. (1974), *Greater Ethiopia: The Evolution of a Multiethnic Society.* Chicago.

Mahteme Selassie Wolde Maskel (1962 E.C.), *Zekrä Nägär*. Addis Ababa.
— (1957), "The Land System of Ethiopia", in *Ethiopia Observer, I.*
Marcus, H. (1975), *The Life and Times of Menelik II: Ethiopia.* Oxford.
— (1994), "Haile Sellassie's Leadership", in *New Trends in Ethiopian Studies. Papers of the 12th International Conference of Ethiopian Studies. Vol.I.*
Markakis, J. (1974), *Ethiopia: Anatomy of a Traditional Polity.* Oxford.
Markaksi, John and Asmelash Beyene (1967), "Representative Institutions in Ethiopia", in *Journal of Modern African Studies, V: 2.*
Marse Hazan Walda Kirqos (1948 E.C.), *Yä Amarigna Säwasäw.* Addis Ababa.
McClellan, C. W. (1988), *State Transformation and National Integration: Gedo and the Ethiopian Empire, 1895–1935.*
Mengstu Lemma (1959 E.C.), *Mäshafa Tezeta zä-aläqa Läma Haylu Wäldä Tarik.* Addis Ababa.
Mered Wolde Aregay, (1974), "Political Geography of Ethiopia at the Sixteenth Century" in *IV Congresso Internazionale di Studie Etiopici, 10–15 April. Tomo I.* Roma.
— (1980), "A Reappraisal of the Impact of Firearms in the History of Warfare in Ethiopia (c.1500–1800)", in *Journal of Ethiopian Studies, XIV.*
— (1984), "Society and Technology in Ethiopia 1500–1800", in *Proceedings of the Second Annual Seminar of the Department of History,* Addis Ababa University.
— (1984), "Millenarian Traditions and Peasant Movements in Ethiopia 1500–1855", in *Proceedings of the Seventh International Conference of Ethiopian Studies*, Rubenson, S. (ed.).
— (1986), Land Tenure and Agricultural Productivity, 1500–1850", in *Proceedings of the Anual Seminar of the Department of History,* Addis Ababa University.
— (1990) "Ye Tewedros Alamawoch Kayet Endemenchu" in *Kasa and Kasa,* Taddese Beyene, Pankhurst, R. and Shiferaw Bekele (eds.) I.E.S., Addis Ababa University.
Mesfin Wolde Mariam (1972), *An Introductory Geography of Ethiopia.* Addis Ababa.
Mohammed Hassen (1990), *The Oromo of Ethiopia. A History 1570–1860.* Cambridge.
Molla Tikuye (1994), "The Rise and Fall of the Yajju Dynasty (1784–1980)", in Bahru Zewde, Pankhurst, and Taddese Beyene (eds.), *Proceedings of the Eleventh International Conference of Ethiopian Studies, I.* Addis Ababa.
Nadel, S.F. (1946), "Land Tenure on the Eritrean Plateau", in *Africa, 21, 1.*
Natsoulas, T. (1984), "Prologue to Modern Ties between Greece and Ethiopia: the Efforts of Ioannis Kotzikas during the Era of Tewedros, 1845–1868", in *Northeast African Studies, VI.: 1–2.*
Pankhurst, R. (1961), *An Introduction to the Economic History of Ethiopia, from early times to 1800.* London.
— (1964), "The Trade of Northern Ethiopia in the Nineteenth and Early Twentieth Centuries", *Journal of Ethiopian Studies, II: 1.*
— (1965), "The History of Currency and Banking in Ethiopia and the Horn of Africa from the Middle Ages to 1935", in *Ethiopia Observer, 8.*
— ((1966a), *State and Land in Ethiopian History.* Addis Ababa.
— (1966b), "Some Factors Depressing the Standard of Living of Peasants in Traditional Ethiopia", in *Journal of Ethiopian Studies, IV.*
— (1967), "Tribute, Taxation and Government Revenues in Nineteenth and early Twentieth Century Ethiopia, Part I", in *Journal of Ethiopian Studies, V, 2.*
— (1968a), "Tribute, Taxation and Government Revenues in Nineteenth and early Twentieth Century Ethiopia, Part II", in *Journal of Ethiopian Studies, 6, 1.*
— (1968b), "Tribute, Taxation and Government Revenues in Nineteenth and early Twentieth Century Ethiopia, Part III", in *Journal of Ethiopian Studies, 6, 2.*

— (1968c), *Economic History of Ethiopia*, 1800–1935. Addis Ababa.
— (1968d), The History of Firearms in Ethiopia prior to the Nineteenth Century" in *Ethiopia Observer*, XI.
— (1968e), "The Trade of Central Ethiopia in the Nineteenth and Early Twentieth Centuries", *Journal of Ethiopian Studies,II:, 2.*
— (1972), "The History of Famine and Pestilence in Ethiopia Prior to the Founding of Gonder", in *Journal of Ethiopian Studies, X.*
— (1979), "An Eighteenth Century Ethiopian Dynastic Marriage Contract Between Empress Mentwab of Gonder and Ras Mikael Sehul of Tigre", in *Bulletin of the School of Oriental and African Studies, XIII, 3.*
— (1979/80), "The Advent of the Maria Theresia dollar in Ethiopia. Its Effect on Taxation, and Wealth Accumulation, and other Economic, Political, and Cultural Implications", in *Northeast African Studies,I:3.*
— (1982), *History of Ethiopian Towns from the Middle Ages to the Early Nineteenth Century.* Wiesbaden.
— (1983–84), "Ethiopian Taxation Prior to the Time of Menelik: A Collection and Analysis of Estimates, Part I", in *Northeast African Studies, 5, 3.*
— (1984), "Wag and Lasta: An Essay in the Regional History of Ethiopia from the 14th Century to 1800", in Rubenson, S. (ed.), *Proceedings of the Seventh International Conference of Ethiopian Studies*. Uppsala.
— (1985a), "Ethiopian Taxation Prior to the Time of Menelik: A Collection and Analysis of Estimates, Part II," in *Northeast African Studies, VI: 1.*
— (1985b), *History of Ethiopian Towns from the Mid-Nineteenth Century to 1935.* Stuttgart.
— (1988), "An Unpublished Order of the Kings, Tewodros II, at the Institute of Ethiopian Studies" in *Ethiopian Journal of African Studies, V 5, N 1.*
— (1990), *A Social History of Ethiopia.* Addis Ababa.
Pankhurst, Rita and Pankhurst, Richard (1978), "A Select Annotated Bibliography of Travel Books on Ethiopia, Part One and Pat Two", in *African Journal, IX, 2*, and 3 respectively.
Paulos Gnogno (1984 E.C.), *Dagmawi Até Menilik.* Addis Ababa.
Perini, R. (1905), *Di Qua dal Mareb.* Florence.
Pollera, A. (1913), *Il Regime delle Proprietà Terreria in Etiopia e nella Colonia Eritrea.* Rome.
Prouty, C. (1986), *Empress Taytu and Menelik II: Ethiopia, 1883–1910.* London.
Rubenson, S. (1969), *King of Kings Tewodros of Ethiopia.* Addis Ababa.
— (1976), *The Survival of Ethiopian Independence.* London.
— ed., (1987), *Correspondence and Treaties 1800–1854.* Illinios and Addis Ababa.
— ed., (1994), *Tewodros and His Contemporaries 1855–1868. Acta Aethiopica, II.* Addis Ababa and Lund.
Sergew Hable Sellassie (1972), *Ancient and Medieval Ethiopian History to 1270.* Addis Ababa.
Shack, W. (1966). *The Gurage. A People of the Enset Culture.* London.
Shiferaw Bekele (1989), "Aspects of the History of Dire Dawa (1902 to 1936)", in *Proceedings of the Fourth Seminar of the Department of History.* AAU.
— (1990a), "Reflections on the Power Elite of the Wärä Séh Mäsafint (1786–1853)", in *Annales d'Ethiopie, XV*;
— (1990b), "Kassa and Kassa: The State of Their Historiography", in *Kasa and Kasa. Papers on the Lives and Images of Tewodros II and Yohannes Iv (1855–1889)*, Taddese Beyene, Pankhurst, R. and Shiferaw Bekele (eds.). IES. Addis Ababa.

— (1991), "The Ethiopian Railway and British Finance Capital, 1896–1902", in *Africa, 3*.
— ed., (1992), *An Economic History of Ethiopia. The Imperial Era, 1941–1974. V. I.* Draft Manuscript. Department of History, Addis Ababa University.
— (1992), "The Land Question in the Ancien Regime" in *An Economic History of Ethiopia. The Imperial Era, 1941–1974.* Draft Manuscript. Department of History. AAU.
Stitz, V. (1974), *Studien zur Kulturgeographie Zentraläthiopiens*. Bonn.
Taddese Beyene, Pankhurst, R. and Siferaw Bekele, eds., (1990), *Kasa and Kasa. Papers on the Lives, Times and Images of Téwodros II and Yohannes IV (1855–1889).* Addis Ababa.
Taddesse Tamirat (1972), *Church and State in Ethiopia, 1270–1527.* Oxford.
— (1986) "Process of Ethnic Interaction and Integration in Ethiopia History: the case of Agew", in *Journal of African History*, 29.
Takalign W. Mariam (1986), "Land, Trade and Political Power Among the Oromo of the Gibe Region, A Hypothesis" in *Proceedings of the Third Annual Seminar of the Department of History*. AAU.
Tegegne Teka (1989), *Camel Pastoralism as Food System in Ethiopia.* IDR, Adiis Ababa University. Addis Ababa.
Tekeste Melake (1990), "The Genesis and Growth of the Imperial Body Guard of Ethiopia up to 1960", in *Proceedings of the Fifth Seminar of the Department of History.* Addis Ababa University.
Tekeste Negash (1986), "Land Tenure and the Organization of Surplus Appropriation on the Eve of the Colonial Period", in *No Medicine for the Bite of a White Snake: Notes on Nationalism and Resistance in Eritrea, 1890–1940.* Uppsala.
Tekle Tsadik Mekuria (1981 E.C), *Asé Tewodros ena yä-Ityopya Andenät.* Addis Ababa.
— (1982 E.C), *Asé Yohannes ena yä Ityopya Andenät.* Addis Ababa.
— (1983 E.C), *Asé Menelik ena Yä-Ityopya Andenät.* Addis Ababa.
Triulzi, A. (1981), *Salt, Gold and Legitimacy. Prelude to the History of a No-Man's Land Belä Shangul, Wallagga, Ethiopia (ca. 1800–1898).* Napoli.
Tsegaye Tegenu (1994), "The Taxation System of Ethiopia, 1855–1868", in *Proceedings of the Eleventh International Conference of Ethiopian Studies*, Bahru Zewde, Pankhurst, R. and Taddese Beyene (eds.), *I.* Addis Ababa.
— (1994), "A Revolution from Above? Change in the Fiscal and Military Organization of the Ethiopian State, 1855–1913", in Marcus, H. (ed.), *New Trends in Ethiopian Studies. Papers of the 12th International Confrence of Ethiopian Studies, I.*
— (1996), "The Logistic Base and Military Strategy of the Ethiopian Army: the Campaign and Battle of Adwa, Septemebr 1895–February 1896". Paper presented to the 100th Anniversary of Adwa, Institute of Ethiopian Studies. Addis Ababa University.
Tsehai Berehane Selassie (1971), "The Life and Career of Däjazmach Balca Aba Näfso" in *Journal of Ethiopian Studies, IX: 2.*
Tzadua, P. (1968), *The Fetha Nagast. The Law of the Kings.* Addis Ababa.
— (1974), "Organization of the Central Administration in Ethiopia", in *Studies in Ethiopian Government and Administration*, Mimeographed, compiled by Asmelash Beyene, HSIU. Addis Ababa.
Villari, G. (1938), "I´gulti´ della Regione di Axum" in *Rassegna Economici dell'Africa Italiana. XVI*;
Waldron, Sydney (1984), "The Political Economy of Harri-Oromo relationship, 1559–1874", in *North East African Studies., nos. 1–2.*
Zewde Gebre-Sellassie (1975), *Yohannes IV of Ethiopia: A Political Biography.* Oxford.

Index

This index excludes names of Kings Tewodros, Yohannes, Menelik and the analytical concept "fiscal military state".

Acta Universitatis Upsaliensis
STUDIA HISTORICA UPSALIENSIA

Editores: Rolf Torstendahl, Torkel Jansson & Jan Lindegren

1. *Gustaf Jonasson:* Karl XII och hans rådgivare. Den utrikespolitiska maktkampen i Sverige 1697–1702. 1960.
2. *Sven Lundkvist:* Gustav Vasa och Europa. Svensk handels- och utrikespolitik 1534–1557. 1960.
3. *Tage Linder:* Biskop Olof Wallquists politiska verksamhet till och med riksdagen 1789. 1960.
4. *Carl Göran Andræ:* Kyrka och frälse i Sverige under äldre medeltid. 1960.
5. *Bengt Henningsson:* Geijer som historiker. 1961.
6. *Nils Runeby:* Monarchia mixta. Maktfördelningsdebatt i Sverige under den tidigare stormaktstiden. 1962.
7. *Åke Hermansson:* Karl IX och ständerna. Tronfrågan och författningsutvecklingen 1598–1611. 1962.
8. Hundra års historisk diskussion. Historiska föreningen i Upsala 1862–1962. 1962.
9. *Sten Carlsson:* Byråkrati och borgarstånd under frihetstiden. 1963.
10. *Gunnar Christie Wasberg:* Forsvarstanke og suverenitetsprinsipp. Kretsen om Aftenposten i den unionspolitiske debatt 1890–mars 1905. 1963.
11. *Kurt Ågren:* Adelns bönder och kronans. Skatter och besvär i Uppland 1650–1680. 1964.
12. *Michael Nordberg:* Les ducs et la royauté. Etudes sur la rivalité des ducs d'Orléans et de Bourgogne 1392–1407. 1964.
13. *Stig Hadenius:* Fosterländsk unionspolitik. Majoritetspartiet, regeringen och unionsfrågan 1888–1899. 1964.
14. *Stellan Dahlgren:* Karl X Gustav och reduktionen. 1964.
15. *Rolf Torstendahl:* Källkritik och vetenskapssyn i svensk historisk forskning 1820–1920. 1964.
16. *Stefan Björklund:* Jordbrukskris och borgerlig liberalism. 1964.
17. *Håkan Berggren & Göran B. Nilsson:* Liberal socialpolitik 1853–1884. Två studier. 1965.
18. *Torsten Burgman:* Svensk opinion och diplomati under rysk-japanska kriget 1904–1905. 1965.
19. *Erik Wärenstam:* Sveriges Nationella Ungdomsförbund och högern 1928–1934. 1965.
20. *Torgny Nevéus:* Ett betryggande försvar. Värnplikten och arméorganisationen i svensk politik 1880–1885. 1965.
21. *Staffan Runestam:* Förstakammarhögern och rösträttsfrågan 1900–1907. 1966.
22. *Stig Ekman:* Slutstriden om representationsreformen. 1966.
23. *Gunnar Herrström:* 1927 års skolreform. En Studie i svensk skolpolitik 1918–1927. 1966.
24. *Sune Åkerman:* Skattereformen 1810. Ett experiment med progressiv inkomstskatt. 1967.
25. *Göran B. Nilsson:* Självstyrelsens problematik. Undersökningar i svensk landstingshistoria 1839–1928. 1967.
26. *Klaus-Richard Böhme:* Bremisch-verdische Staatsfinanzen 1645–1676. Die schwedische Krone als deutsche Landesherrin. 1967.
27. *Gustaf Jonasson:* Karl XII:s polska politik 1702–1703. 1968.
28. *Hans Landberg:* Statsfinans och kungamakt. Karl X Gustav inför polska kriget. 1969.
29. *Rolf Torstendahl:* Mellan nykonservatism och liberalism. Idébrytningar inom högern och bondepartierna 1918–1934. 1969.
30. *Nils Runeby:* Den nya världen och den gamla. Amerikabild och emigrationsuppfattning i Sverige 1820–1860. 1969.
31. *Fred Nilsson:* Emigrationen från Stockholm till Nordamerika 1880–1893. En studie i urban utvandring. 1970.
32. *Curt Johanson:* Lantarbetarna i Uppland 1918–1930. En studie i facklig taktik och organisation. 1970.
33. *Arndt Öberg:* De yngre mössorna och deras utländska bundsförvanter 1765–1769. Med särskild hänsyn till de kommersiella och politiska förbindelserna med Storbritannien, Danmark och Preussen. 1970.
34. *Torgny Börjeson:* Metall 20 – Fackföreningen och människan. 1971.
35. *Harald Runblom:* Svenska företag i Latinamerika. Etableringsmönster och förhandlingstaktik 1900–1940. 1971.
36. *Hans Landberg, Lars Ekholm, Roland Nordlund & Sven A. Nilsson:* Det kontinentala krigets ekonomi. Studier i krigsfinansiering under svensk stormaktstid. 1971.

37. *Sture Lindmark:* Swedish America 1914–1932. Studies in Ethnicity with Emphasis on Illinois and Minnesota. 1971.
38. *Ulf Beijbom:* Swedes in Chicago. A Demographic and Social Study of the 1846–1880 Immigration. 1971.
39. *Staffan Smedberg:* Frälsebonderörelser i Halland och Skåne 1772–76. 1972.
40. *Björn Rondahl:* Emigration, folkomflyttning och säsongarbete i ett sågverksdistrikt i södra Hälsingland 1865–1910. Söderala kommun med särskild hänsyn till Ljusne industrisamhälle. 1972.
41. *Ann-Sofie Kälvemark:* Reaktionen mot utvandringen. Emigrationsfrågan i svensk debatt och politik 1901–1904. 1972.
42. *Lars-Göran Tedebrand:* Västernorrland och Nordamerika 1875–1913. Utvandring och återinvandring. 1972.
43. *Ann-Marie Petersson:* Nyköping under frihetstiden. Borgare och byråkrater i den lokala politiken. 1972.
44. *Göran Andolf:* Historien på gymnasiet. Undervisning och läroböcker 1820–1965. 1972.
45. *Jan Sundin:* Främmande studenter vid Uppsala universitet före andra väldskriget. En studie i studentmigration. 1973.
46. *Christer Öhman:* Nyköping och hertigdömet 1568–1622. 1973. (Ej i bokhandeln)
47. *Sune Åkerman, Ingrid Eriksson, David Gaunt, Anders Norberg, John Rogers & Kurt Ågren:* Aristocrats, Farmers and Proletarians. Essays in Swedish Demographic History. 1973.
48. *Uno Westerlund:* Borgarsamhällets upplösning och självstyrelsens utveckling i Nyköping 1810–1880. 1973. (Ej i bokhandeln)
49. *Sven Hedenskog:* Folkrörelserna i Nyköping 1880–1915. Uppkomst, social struktur och politisk aktivitet. 1973. (Ej i bokhandeln)
50. *Berit Brattne:* Bröderna Larsson. En studie i svensk emigrantagentverksamhet under 1880-talet. 1973.
51. *Anders Kullberg:* Johan Gabriel Stenbock och reduktionen. Godspolitik och ekonomiförvaltning 1675–1705. 1973.
52. *Gunilla Ingmar:* Monopol på nyheter. Ekonomiska och politiska aspekter på svenska och internationella nyhetsbyråers verksamhet. 1870–1919. 1973.
53. *Sven Lundkvist:* Politik, nykterhet och reformer. En studie i folkrörelsernas politiska verksamhet 1900–1920. 1974.
54. *Kari Tarkiainen:* "Vår gamble Arffiende Ryssen". Synen på Ryssland i Sverige 1595–1621 och andra studier kring den svenska Rysslandsbilden från tidigare stormaktstid. 1974.
55. *Bo Öhngren:* Folk i rörelse. Samhällsutveckling, flyttningsmönster och folkrörelser i Eskilstuna 1870–1900. 1974.
56. *Lars Ekholm:* Svensk krigsfinansiering 1630–1631. 1974.
57. *Roland Nordlund:* Krig på avveckling. Sverige och tyska kriget 1633. 1974.
58. *Clara Nevéus:* Trälarna i landskapslagarnas samhälle. Danmark och Sverige. 1974.
59. *Bertil Johansson:* Social differentiering och kommunalpolitik. Enköping 1863–1919. 1974.
60. *Jan Lindroth:* Idrottens väg till folkrörelse. Studier i svensk idrottsrörelse till 1915. 1974.
61. *Richard B. Lucas:* Charles August Lindbergh, Sr. A Case Study of Congressional Insurgency, 1906–1912. 1974.
62. *Hans Norman:* Från Bergslagen till Nordamerika. Studier i migrationsmönster, social rörlighet och demografisk struktur med utgångspunkt från Örebro län 1851–1915. 1974.
63. *David Gaunt:* Utbildning till statens tjänst. En kollektivbiografi av stormaktstidens hovrättsauskultanter. 1975.
64. *Eibert Ernby:* Adeln och bondejorden. En studie rörande skattefrälset i Oppunda härad under 1600-talet. 1975.
65. *Bo Kronborg & Thomas Nilsson:* Stadsflyttare. Industrialisering, migration och social mobilitet med utgångspunkt från Halmstad, 1870–1910. 1975.
66. *Rolf Torstendahl:* Teknologins nytta. Motiveringar för det svenska tekniska utbildningsväsendets framväxt framförda av riksdagsmän och utbildningsadministratörer 1810–1870. 1975.
67. *Allan Ranehök:* Centralmakt och domsmakt. Studier kring den högsta rättskipningen i kung Magnus Erikssons länder 1319–1355. 1975.
68. *James Cavallie:* Från fred till krig. De finansiella problemen kring krigsutbrottet år 1700. 1975.
69. *Ingrid Åberg:* Förening och politik. Folkrörelsernas politiska aktivitet i Gävle under 1880-talet. 1975.
70. *Margareta Revera:* Gods och gård 1650–1680. Magnus Gabriel De la Gardies godsbildning och godsdrift i Västergötland. I. 1975.
71. *Aleksander Loit:* Kampen om feodalräntan. Reduktionen och domänpolitiken i Estland 1655–1710. I. 1975.
72. *Torgny Lindgren:* Banko- och riksgäldsrevisionerna 1782–1807. "De redliga män, som bevakade ständers rätt". 1975.
73. *Rolf Torstendahl:* Dispersion of Engineers in a Transitional Society. Swedish Technicians 1860–1940. 1975.
74. From Sweden to America. A History of Migration. Red. Harald Runblom & Hans Norman. 1976.
75. *Svante Jakobsson:* Från fädernejorden till förfäders land. Estlandssvenskt bondfolks rymningar till Stockholm 1811–1834; motiv, frekvens, personliga konsekvenser. 1976.
76. *Lars Åkerblom:* Sir Samuel Hoare och Etiopienkonflikten 1935. 1976.
77. *Gustaf Jonasson:* Per Edvin Sköld 1946–1951. 1976.
78. *Sören Winge:* Die Wirtschaftliche Aufbau-Vereinigung (WAV) 1945–53. Entwicklung und Politik einer „undoktrinären" politischen Partei

in der Bundesrepublik in der ersten Nachkriegszeit. 1976.

79. *Klaus Misgeld:* Die „Internationale Gruppe demokratischer Sozialisten" in Stockholm 1942–1945. Zur sozialistischen Friedensdiskussion während des Zweiten Weltkrieges. 1976.
80. *Roland Karlman:* Evidencing Historical Classifications in British and American Historiography 1930–1970. 1976.
81. *Berndt Fredriksson:* Försvarets finansiering. Svensk krigsekonomi under skånska kriget 1675–79. 1976.
82. *Karl Englund:* Arbetarförsäkringsfrågan i svensk politik 1884–1901. 1976.
83. *Nils Runeby:* Teknikerna, vetenskapen och kulturen. Ingenjörsundervisning och ingenjörsorganisationer i 1870-talets Sverige. 1976.
84. *Erland F. Josephson:* SKP och Komintern 1921–1924. Motsättningarna inom Sveriges Kommunistiska Parti och dess relationer till den Kommunistiska Internationalen. 1976.
85. *Sven Lundkvist:* Folkrörelserna i det svenska samhället 1850–1920. 1976.
86. *Bo Öhngren:* GEOKOD. En kodlista för den administrativa indelningen i Sverige 1862–1951. 1977.
87. *Mike L. Samson:* Population Mobility in the Netherlands 1880–1910. A Case Study of Wisch in the Achterhoek. 1977.
88. *Ugbana Okpu:* Ethnic Minority Problems in Nigerian Politics: 1960–1965. 1977.
89. *Gunnar Carlsson:* Enköping under frihetstiden. Social struktur och lokal politik. 1977.
90. *Sten Carlsson:* Fröknar, mamseller, jungfrur och pigor. Ogifta kvinnor i det svenska ståndssamhället. 1977.
91. *Rolf Pålbrant:* Arbetarrörelsen och idrotten 1919–1939. 1977.
92. *Viveca Halldin Norberg:* Swedes in Haile Selassie's Ethiopia 1924–1952. A Study in Early Development Co-operation. 1977.
93. *Holger Wester:* Innovationer i befolkningsrörligheten. En studie av spridningsförlopp i befolkningsrörligheten utgående från Petalax socken i Österbotten. 1977.
94. *Jan Larsson:* Diplomati och industriellt genombrott. Svenska exportsträvanden på Kina 1906–1916. 1977.
95. *Rolf Nygren:* Disciplin, kritikrätt och rättssäkerhet. Studier kring militieombundsmannaämbetets (MO) doktrin- och tillkomsthistoria 1901–1915. 1977.
96. *Kenneth Awebro:* Gustav III:s räfst med ämbetsmännen 1772–1799 – aktionerna mot landshövdingarna och Göta hovrätt. 1977.
97. *Eric De Geer:* Migration och influensfält. Studier av emigration och intern migration i Finland och Sverige 1816–1972. 1977.
98. *Sigbrit Plaenge Jacobson:* 1766-års allmänna fiskestadga. Dess uppkomst och innebörd med hänsyn till Bottenhavsfiskets rättsfrågor. 1978.
99. *Ingvar Flink:* Strejkbryteriet och arbetets frihet. En studie av svensk arbetsmarknad fram till 1938. 1978.
100. *Ingrid Eriksson & John Rogers:* Rural Labor and Population Change. Social and Demographic Developments in East-Central Sweden during the Nineteenth Century. 1978.
101. *Kerstin Moberg:* Från tjänstehjon till hembiträde. En kvinnlig låglönegrupp i den fackliga kampen 1903–1946. 1978.
102. *Mezri Bdira:* Relations internationales et sous-développement. La Tunisie 1857–1864. 1978.
103. *Ingrid Hammarström, Väinö Helgesson, Barbro Hedvall, Christer Knuthammar & Bodil Wallin:* Ideologi och socialpolitik i 1800-talets Sverige. Fyra studier. 1978.
104. *Gunnar Sundberg:* Partipolitik och regionala intressen 1755–1766. Studier kring det bottniska handelstvångets hävande. 1978.
105. *Kekke Stadin:* Småstäder, småborgare och stora samhällsförändringar. Borgarnas sociala struktur i Arboga, Enköping och Västervik under perioden efter 1680. 1979.
106. *Åke Lindström:* Bruksarbetarfackföreningar. Metalls avdelningar vid bruken i östra Västmanlands län före 1911. 1979.
107. *Mats Rolén:* Skogsbygd i omvandling. Studier kring befolkningsutveckling, omflyttning och social rörlighet i Revsunds tingslag 1820–1977. 1979.
108. *János Perényi:* Revolutionsuppfattningens anatomi. 1848 års revolutioner i svensk debatt. 1979.
109. *Kent Sivesand:* Skifte och befolkning. Skiftenas inverkan på byar och befolkning i Mälarregionen. 1979.
110. *Thomas Lindkvist:* Landborna i Norden under äldre medeltid. 1979.
111. *Björn M. Edsman:* Lawyers in Gold Coast Politics c. 1900–1945. From Mensah Sarbah to J.B. Danquah. 1979.
112. *Svante Jakobsson:* Osilia–Maritima 1227–1346. Studier kring tillkomsten av svenska bosättningar i Balticum, i synnerhet inom biskopsstiftet Ösel-Wiek. 1980.
113. *Jan Stattin:* Hushållningssällskapen och agrarsamhällets förändring – utveckling och verksamhet under 1800-talets första hälft. 1980.
114. *Bertil Lundvik:* Solidaritet och partitaktik. Den svenska arbetarrörelsen och spanska inbördeskriget 1936–1939. 1980.
115. *Ann-Sofie Kälvemark:* More children of better quality? Aspects on Swedish population policy in the 1930's. 1980.
116. *Anders Norberg:* Sågarnas ö. Alnö och industrialiseringen 1860–1910. 1980.
117. *Jan Lindegren:* Utskrivning och utsugning. Produktion och reproduktion i Bygdeå 1620–1640. 1980.
118. *Gustaf Jonasson:* I väntan på uppbrott? Bondeförbundet/Centerpartiet i regeringskoalitionens slutskede 1956–1957. 1981.
119. *Erland Jansson:* India, Pakistan or Pakhtunistan? The Nationalist Movements in the North-West Frontier Province, 1937–47. 1981.

120. *Ulla-Britt Lithell:* Breast-feeding and Reproduction. Studies in marital fertility and infant mortality in 19th century Finland and Sweden. 1981.
121. *Svenbjörn Kilander:* Censur och propaganda. Svensk informationspolitik under 1900-talets första decennier. 1981.
122. *Håkan Holmberg:* Folkmakt, folkfront, folkdemokrati. De svenska kommunisterna och demokratifrågan 1943–1977. 1982.
123. *Britt-Marie Lundbäck:* En industri kommer till stan. Hudiksvall och trävaruindustrin 1855–1880. 1982.
124. *Torkel Jansson:* Samhällsförändring och sammanslutningsformer. Det frivilliga föreningsväsendets uppkomst och spridning i Husby-Rekarne från omkring 1850 till 1930. 1982.
125. *Per Jansson:* Kalmar under 1600-talet. Omland, handel och krediter. 1982.
126. *Svante Jakobsson:* Fattighushjonets värld i 1800-talets Stockholm. 1982.
127. *Runo Nilsson:* Rallareliv. Arbete, familjemönster och levnadsförhållanden för järnvägsarbetare på banbyggena i Jämtland–Härjedalen 1912–1928. 1982.
128. *J. Alvar Schilén:* Det västallierade bombkriget mot de tyska storstäderna under andra väldskriget och civilbefolkningens reaktioner i de drabbade städerna. 1983.
129. *Bodil Nävdal-Larsen:* Erik XIV, Ivan Groznyj og Katarina Jagellonica. 1983.
130. *Birgitta Olai:* Storskiftet i Ekebyborna. Svensk jordbruksutveckling avspeglad i en östgötasocken. 1983.
131. *Ann Hörsell:* Borgare, smeder och änkor. Ekonomi och befolkning i Eskilstuna gamla stad och Fristad 1750–1850. 1983.
132. *Ragnar Björk:* Den historiska argumenteringen. Konstruktion, narration och kolligation – förklaringsresonemang hos Nils Ahnlund och Erik Lönnroth. 1983.
133. *Björn Asker:* Officerarna och det svenska samhället 1650–1700. 1983.
134. *Erik Tiberg;* Zur Vorgeschichte des Livländischen Krieges. Die Beziehungen zwischen Moskau und Litauen 1549–1562. 1984.
135. *Bertel Tingström:* Sveriges plåtmynt 1644–1776. En undersökning av plåtmyntens roll som betalningsmedel. 1984.
136. *Curt Ekholm:* Balt- och tyskutlämningen 1945–1946. Omständigheter kring interneringen i läger i Sverige och utlämningen till Sovjetunionen av f d tyska krigsdeltagare. Del 1: Ankomsten och interneringen. 1984. Andra upplagan 1995.
137. *Curt Ekholm:* Balt- och tyskutlämningen 1945–1946. Omständigheter kring interneringen i läger i Sverige och utlämningen till Sovjetunionen av f d tyska krigsdeltagare. Del 2: Utlämningen och efterspelet. 1984. Andra upplagan 1995.
138. *Sven H. Carlson:* Trade and dependency. Studies in the expansion of Europe. 1984.
139. *Torkel Jansson:* Adertonhundratalets associationer. Forskning och problem kring ett sprängfullt tomrum eller sammanslutningsprinciper och föreningsformer mellan två samhällsformationer, c:a 1800–1870. 1985.
140. *Bernt Douhan:* Arbete, kapital och migration. Valloninvarndringen till Sverige under 1600-talet. 1985.
141. *Göran Rydeberg:* Skatteköpen i Örebro län 1701–1809. 1985.
142. *Habib Ben Abdallah:* De l'iqta' étatique à l'iqta' militaire. Transition économique et changements sociaux à Baghdad, 247–447 de l'Hégire/861–1055 ap. J. 1986.
143. *Margot Höjfors Hong:* Ölänningar över haven. Utvandringen från Öland 1840–1930 – bakgrund, förlopp, effekter. 1986.
144. *Carl Johan Gardell:* Handelskompani och bondearistokrati. En studie i den sociala strukturen på Gotland omkring 1620. 1986.
145. *Birgitta Olai:* "... till vinnande af ett redigt Storskifte ...". En komparativ studie av storskiftet i fem härader. 1987.
146. *Torkel Jansson:* Agrarsamhällets förändring och landskommunal organisation. En konturteckning av 1800-talets Norden. 1987.
147. *Anders Florén:* Disciplinering och konflikt. Den sociala organiseringen av arbetet: Jäders bruk 1640–1750. 1987.
148. *Tekeste Negash:* Italian Colonialism in Eritrea 1882–1941: Policies, Praxis and Impact. 1988.
149. *Lotta Gröning:* Vägen till makten. SAP:s organisation och dess betydelse för den politiska verksamheten 1900–1933. 1988.
150. *Ove Pettersson:* Byråkratisering eller avbyråkratisering. Administrativ och samhällsorganisatorisk strukturomvandling inom svenskt vägväsende 1885–1985. 1988.
151. *Knut Ohlsson:* Grosshandlare, bönder, småfolk. Trönös skogsnäringar från och med det industriella genombrottet. 1988.
152. *Eva Österberg & Dag Lindström:* Crime and Social Control in Medieval and Early Modern Swedish Towns. 1988.
153. *Marie C. Nelson:* Bitter Bread. The Famine in Norrbotten 1867–1868. 1988.
154. *Gísli Ágúst Gunnlaugsson:* Family and Household in Iceland 1801–1930. Studies in the relationship between demographic and socioeconomic development, social legislation and family and household structures. 1988.
155. *Elsa Lunander:* Borgaren blir företagare. Studier kring ekonomiska, sociala och politiska förhållanden i förändringens Örebro under 1800-talet. 1988.
156. *Ulla-Britt Lithell:* Kvinnoarbete och barntillsyn i 1700- och 1800-talets Österbotten. 1988.
157. *Annette Thörnquist:* Lönearbete eller egen jord? Den svenska lantarbetarrörelsen och jordfrågan 1908–1936. 1989.
158. *Stefán F. Hjartarson:* Kampen om fackföreningsrörelsen. Ideologi och politisk aktivitet på Island 1920–1938. 1989.
159. *György Nováky:* Handelskompanier och kompa-

nihandel. Svenska Afrikakompaniet 1649–1663. En studie i feodal handel. 1990.

160. *Margareta Åman:* Spanska sjukan. Den svenska epidemin 1918–1920 och dess internationella bakgrund. 1990.
161. *Sven A. Nilsson:* De stora krigens tid. Om Sverige som militärstat och bondesamhälle. 1990.
162. *Birgitta Larsson:* Conversion to Greater Freedom? Women, Church and Social Change in Northwestern Tanzania under Colonial Rule. 1991.
163. *Dag Lindström:* Skrå, stad och stat. Stockholm, Malmö och Bergen ca 1350–1622. 1991.
164. *Svenbjörn Kilander:* Den nya staten och den gamla. En studie i ideologisk förändring 1991.
165. *Christer Öhman:* Den historiska romanen och sanningen. Historiesyn, värdestruktur och empiri i Georg Starbäcks historiska författarskap. 1991.
166. *Maria Ågren:* Jord och gäld. Social skiktning och rättslig konflikt i södra Dalarna ca 1650–1850. 1992.
167. *Stina Nicklasson:* Högerns kvinnor. Problem och resurs för Allmänna valmansförbundet perioden 1900–1936/1937. 1992.
168. *Lars Petterson:* Frihet, jämlikhet, egendom och Bentham. Utvecklingslinjer i svensk folkundervisning mellan feodalism och kapitalism, 1809–1860. 1992.
169. *Alberto Tiscornia:* Statens, godsens eller böndernas socknar? Den sockenkommunala självstyrelsens utveckling i Västerfärnebo, Stora Malm och Jäder 1800–1880. 1992.
170. *Iréne Artæus:* Kvinnorna som blev över. Ensamstående stadskvinnor under 1800-talets första hälft - fallet Västerås. 1992.
171. *Anders Fröjmark:* Mirakler och helgonkult. Linköpings biskopsdöme under senmedeltiden. 1992.
172. *Hernán Horna:* Transport Modernization and Entrepreneurship in Nineteenth Century Colombia. Cisneros & Friends. 1992.
173. *Janne Backlund:* Rusthållarna i Fellingsbro 1684–1748. Indelningsverket och den sociala differentieringen av det svenska agrarsamhället. 1993.
174. *Agneta Breisch:* Frid och fredlöshet. Sociala band och utanförskap på Island under äldre medeltid. 1994.
175. *Åsa Karlsson:* Den jämlike undersåten. Karl XII:s förmögenhetsbeskattning 1713. 1994.
176. *Elisabeth Elgán:* Genus och politik. En jämförelse mellan svensk och fransk abort- och preventivmedelspolitik från sekelskiftet till andra världskriget. 1994.
177. *Lennart Thorslund:* Humanism mot rationalism. Mora 1890–1970: Om två förhållningssätt och deras betydelse i småstadens planeringshistoria. 1995.
178. *Paul A. Levine:* From Indifference to Activism. Swedish Diplomacy and the Holocaust; 1938–1934. 1996.
179. *Bengt Nilsson:* Kvinnor i statens tjänst – från biträden till tjänstemän. En aktörsinriktad undersökning av kvinnliga statstjänstemäns organisering, strategier och kamp under 1900-talets första hälft. 1996.